Christian Mission in Eschatological Perspective

Lesslie Newbigin's Contribution

edition afem
mission academics 29

Jürgen Schuster

 VKW

This book ist part of the series edition afem – mission academics,
ed. by Klaus W. Müller, Bernd Brandl,
Thomas Schirrmacher and Thomas Mayer.
http://www.missiologie.org

Bibliographic information published by Die Deutsche Bibliothek
Die Deutsche Bibliothek lists this publication in the Deutsche National bibliografie; detailed bibliographic data are available on the Internet at http://dnb.ddb.de.

ISBN 978-3-941750-15-9 (VTR)
VTR Publications
Gogolstr. 33, 90475 Nürnberg, Germany, http://www.vtr-online.de

ISBN 978-3-938116-82-1 (VKW)
VKW (Culture and Science Publ.)
Friedrichstr. 38, 53111 Bonn, Germany, http://www.vkwonline.de

ISSN 0944-1077 (edition afem – mission academics)

© 2009 by Jürgen Schuster

This publication is based on a dissertation for the degree of PhD in Intercultural Studies at Trinity International University, Deerfield, Illinois, USA.

All rights reserved.
No part of this book may be reproduced in any form or by any means without permission in writing from the publisher,
VTR Publications, Gogolstr. 33, 90475 Nürnberg, Germany,
info@vtr-online.eu, http://www.vtr-online.eu

Cover Illustration: VTR

Printed in the UK by Lightning Source

Dedicated to the late
Paul G. Hiebert (1932-2007),
a mentor who modeled academic excellency
and spiritual integrity
combined with a true interest in people

Contents

Foreword 9
Abbreviations 10
Acknowledgments 11
Introduction 12

Chapter 1
Introducing the Research Topic 13
1. Research Topic 13
   1.1. Research Concern 13
   1.2. Problem Statement 14
   1.3. Research Questions 14
2. Precedent Literature 15
   2.1. Historical Framework: Mission and the Kingdom of God in the Twentieth Century 15
   2.2. Theological Framework: Theology and the Kingdom of God 29
   2.3. Works on Lesslie Newbigin 32
   2.4. Hermeneutical Considerations 37
3. Data and Analysis 43
   3.1. Primary Data 43
   3.2. Data Analysis 43
   3.3. Structure of the Dissertation 44

Chapter 2
The Kingdom of God in Newbigin's Writings
(Diachronic Analysis of His Early Writings) 46
1. Early Emphases 47
2. "The Kingdom of God and the Idea of Progress" (1941) 49
   2.1. Lecture I 50
   2.2. Lecture II 52
   2.3. Lecture III 55
   2.4. Lecture IV 58
   2.5. Summary 61

3. The Unity and Mission of the Church (1948-1953) 62
   3.1. "The Reunion of the Church" (1948) 62
   3.2. "The Duty and Authority of the Church to Preach the Gospel" (1948) 65
   3.3. "The Evangelization of Eastern Asia" (1950) 67
   3.4. "The Household of God" (1953) 70
   3.5. Summary 78
4. The Christian Hope (1951-1953) 79
   4.1. Eschatological Hope – Cosmic and Universal 79
   4.2. Death and Resurrection – Radical Discontinuity 80
   4.3. Decisive Victory and Consummation 81
   4.4. Real End of History 81
   4.5. Eschatological Hope as Motivating Force for the Present 82
5. The Unity of God's Story with His World (1954-1960) 84
   5.1. God's Story with Humankind 84
   5.2. Salvation as Historic Fact 85
   5.3. All Nations Drawn into One Story 86
   5.4. The Evaluation of Secularization 88

Chapter 3
The Kingdom of God in Newbigin's Writings
(Synchronic Analysis of His Later Writings) 92

1. The Kingdom of God 92
   1.1. God's Action – No Human Program 92
   1.2. The Presence of the Kingdom – The Announcement of a Fact 94
   1.3. The Cross as Victory over the Powers 95
   1.4. The Sign of the Cross as Mark of Authenticity 97
   1.5. Eschatological Tension between the Presence and the Future of the Kingdom 99
   1.6. The Lordship of Christ and the Kingdom 100
2. The Unity and Mission of the Church 102
   2.1. The Church as Community of Reconciliation 103
   2.2. The Unity of the Church as Ongoing Challenge 105
   2.3. The Structures and Ministries of the Church in Light of Its Missionary Calling 107
   2.4. The Unity of the Church as Missionary Witness 112

2.5.	The Church as Hermeneutic of the Gospel	112
2.6.	The Church as Servant Community	113
2.7.	The Church as Sign, Instrument, and Foretaste of the Kingdom	114

3. The Eschatological Hope – God's Story with His World 117
   3.1. History as Real Story 117
   3.2. History as God's Story 126
   3.3. History, Church, and World 136

Chapter 4
The Kingdom of God in Newbigin's Writings (Systematic Description) 155

1. Universal Story – God, the Father 155
2. Particular Salvation – Jesus Christ, the Son 158
3. Witness to the World – God, the Holy Spirit 159
4. Election for Responsibility – The Church as Bearer of the Witness 161
5. The Kingdom of God – Christ's Lordship in Eschatological Perspective .. 163
   5.1. The Future Kingdom – A New Creation 163
   5.2. The Present Kingdom – The Prolepsis of the End 167
6. A Comprehensive View of Christian Mission in Kingdom-Perspective 169

Chapter 5
Implications of Newbigin's Eschatological Framework for His Understanding of Mission 171

1. Holistic Understanding of Mission in Eschatological Tension 171
   1.1. Hidden, not Yet Manifest 172
   1.2. Mission in Word and Deed 177
   1.3. Suffering as the Primary Form of Witness to Jesus Christ 181
2. The Gospel as Public Truth 183
   2.1. Truth Claims in a Postmodern Context 184
   2.2. Presenting the Gospel as Meta-Narrative to the World 189
   2.3. Bringing All Aspects of Life Under the Lordship of Christ 191
3. The Church in Eschatological Tension 198
   3.1. A Christian Vision for Society – Avoiding the Fall into the Constantinian Trap 198
   3.2. Ministers in the Secular World – The Tension between an Anabaptist Model and a Reformed Model of the Church 206

3.3.	The Church as Provisional Body in Eschatological and Cultural Tension	210
3.4.	The Church Called to Mission in Unity	211

4. Bearing the Witness of the Spirit in a Pluralist Context 212
   - 4.1. Religious Pluralism 212
   - 4.2. Religion 214
   - 4.3. Continuity and Discontinuity 217
   - 4.4. Critical Engagement of Proposed Solutions 219
   - 4.5. Summary: The Gospel and the Religions 221
5. Epistemology in the Eschatological Context 227

Chapter 6
Conclusion 236

1. Retrospect 236
2. Summary 237
3. Outlook 238
   - 3.1. The Story Character of the Gospel 238
   - 3.2. The Gospel as Public Truth 240
   - 3.3. Mission in Tension 241
   - 3.4. Proclaiming Truth as Wisdom 242
4. Final Word 242

Reference List 244

Primary Literature 244

Secondary Literature 259

Foreword

The publication of *Christian Mission in Eschatological Perspective: Lesslie Newbigin's Contribution* is a major addition to the international literature on the life, work and thought of one of the truly great Christian thinkers of the twentieth century. Newbigin was a missionary to the East and the West, the North and the South. His missiological focus was global as he articulated the need to make the Gospel "public truth" in the West as well as in the so-called "mission fields" of the non-Western world. In this study, Jürgen Schuster investigates the missiological and theological thought of Newbigin by looking at how the eschatological tension of the Kingdom of God provides a cohesive framework for understanding his theology of mission.

In this book Schuster examines five areas in which the eschatological tension of the Kingdom of God sheds light on Newbigin's mission thought and practice: "mission as witness in word and deed", the importance of making the Gospel "public truth in contrast to private truth", the understanding of the Church as "sign, instrument, and foretaste of the Kingdom of God", the practice of interreligious dialogue as "leaving one's own religious achievements behind and meeting the other with empty hands at the foot of the cross of Christ", and the recognition that "the final verification of truth occurs at the end of time". This helpful organization of the various facets of Newbigin's theology of mission makes his thought accessible to numerous publics: mission scholars and practitioners, theological students and Christians interested in Gospel witness in today's world. Theological students, especially those not familiar with the Newbigin corpus, will benefit greatly by a careful reading of this book.

The deliberate focus on mission theology sets Schuster's book apart from other studies of Newbigin's contributions to missiological thought and practice. Valuable studies, past or present, have probed Newbigin's role in the Ecumenical movement, in the formation of the Church of South India. Others have investigated his theology of cultural plurality or his prophetic voice in missiology in the twentieth century. Few studies have undertaken the task of probing the coherence of Newbigin's theology of mission as Schuster has done. For this reason I commend my colleague Jürgen Schuster for his excellent work.

Tite Tiénou
Dean and Professor of Theology of Mission
Trinity Evangelical Divinity School
Deerfield, Illinois

Abbreviations

CICCU	Cambridge Inter-Collegiate Christian Union
CSI	Church of South India
COWE	Consultation on World Evangelization (in Pattaya 1980)
CWME	Commission on World Mission and Evangelism
DWME	Division for World Mission and Evangelism
FAO	Faith and Order
GOCN	Gospel and Our Culture Network
IMC	International Missionary Council
LCWE	Lausanne Committee for World Evangelization
LFMI	Laymen's Foreign Missions Inquiry
NT	New Testament
OT	Old Testament
SCM	Student Christian Movement
SIUC	South Indian United Church
WCC	World Council of Churches
WEA	World Evangelical Alliance

Acknowledgments

Reading "Anthropological Insights for Missionaries" for my Cultural Anthropology class during my Master's studies at BIOLA introduced me to the work of Paul Hiebert and implanted in me the wish to one day continue my studies under his lecturing desk. Another ten years of missionary service in Japan passed before the day finally came in which I sat in one of Paul Hiebert's classes, beginning my doctoral studies at Trinity International University. Studying under Paul Hiebert has always been a highlight of my semesters at Trinity. The fact that I was able to stay at his house in March 2006 during the time in which I had returned to Trinity to defend my dissertation and make final adjustments to my paper was a special gift for me.

One of my other first semester courses during my doctoral studies at Trinity was the class on Theology of Mission under the guidance of Tite Tiénou. I plunged right in writing a short paper on the importance of the biblical concept of the kingdom of God for a biblically focussed understanding of mission. The interest in this topic never waned. This was also the course in which I got introduced to the writings of Lesslie Newbigin which began to intrigue me.

It was no less a figure than George Hunsberger who in a brief conversation in Wheaton helped me focus my dual interest in the relationship between the kingdom of God and mission on the one hand and my interest in the writings of Lesslie Newbigin on the other in such a way that the intersection of these two areas of interest became the focus for my dissertation.

It was still a long way to go from that conception of the topic to the final copy of the dissertation. I am excited that all three of the above mentioned scholars agreed to be on my doctoral committee and I am deeply grateful for their input and help along the way. I am also excited that my doctoral advisor Tite Tiénou agreed to write the foreword to the publication of my thesis.

During the research and writing phase I started teaching at the Theological Seminary of the Liebenzell Mission. I am thankful to Heinzpeter Hempelmann and my colleagues at Bad Liebenzell for their understanding and encouragement along the way. Towards the end of the writing process I profited a lot from David Kramer and Christel Wood who at various stages of my writing have contributed to correcting grammatical and idiomatic errors. Both have worked very thoroughly and made valuable suggestions. However I do want to point out that I am solely responsible for any errors that one may find in this work.

Special thanks go to my wife Anette and my daughter Kimberly for their sacrifices along the way, for their patience and their support during the work on this project.

Three years have passed since the defense of my dissertation. It is now finally published in the year that marks the 100th anniversary of Lesslie Newbigin's birthday. It is my hope that this work may help to further the understanding of Newbigin's theological thought and elicit some of the implications of the relationship between eschatology and mission for us to consider.

Bad Liebenzell, June 2009
Jürgen Schuster

Introduction

Missiology as a discipline is placed at the intersection of theology and the human sciences, dealing with the understanding of God as well as with the understanding of humans and trying to help build the bridge across which the gospel is carried to reach human beings in their specific contexts. It is therefore an ongoing concern of missiology to integrate theology with human sciences and with the practice of mission. The goal is neither merely correct thinking, nor finding pragmatic strategies, but gaining a Christ-perspective in order to grow in doing mission "in Christ's way."

This dissertation intends to contribute to the theological reflection on the foundations of the church's mission by looking at one element of mission theology, namely the relationship between the eschatological tension of the kingdom of God and the mission of the church and the resulting implications for mission practice.

Chapter 1

Introducing the Research Topic

This first chapter introduces the research topic, looks at precedent literature, and delimitates the area of research.

1. Research Topic

To introduce the research topic I will outline the research concern, the problem statement, and the research questions.

1.1. Research Concern

During the 20th century the missionary movement has continued to struggle to clarify its understanding of mission. What came to be known as the conciliar-ecumenical wing of the mission movement in the latter half of the century tended to define major biblical concepts like "the kingdom of God," "salvation," and "shalom" in world-immanent terms, thus dissolving the tension of transcendence and history towards the historical side. The evangelical wing of the mission movement on the other hand has tended to dissolve the tension towards the transcendent side. For a certain period of time evangelicals have been reluctant to use the same terminology as ecumenicals, probably in order not to create more confusion. Attentive theologians have pointed out the fallacies of the above mentioned reductions. They have refocused on the comprehensive meaning of the term "kingdom of God" and its usage in the biblical texts, especially on its importance in the life and teaching of Christ.

The understanding of mission was subjected to another theological reduction on the side of evangelicals in the sense that it was often presented simply as obedience to Christ's command "Go and make disciples." However at least since the 1952 meeting of the IMC in Willingen, it has become clear that the biblical basis for mission is not only broader; mission also extends its roots deeper in that it grows out of the very heart of God. Therefore biblical motivation for mission is more than just dutiful obedience to Christ's command. It grows right out of the heart of God's concern with and love for his creation.

The NT expresses clearly that for Christ the concept of the kingdom of God was at the very core not only of his own ministry (Mark 1:14-15; Matt 12:28), but also of the ministry he entrusted to his disciples, both before and after his crucifixion and resurrection (Matt 10:7; Luke 10:9; Acts 1:3-8; Fee 1991). If the relationship between the kingdom of God and his own mission as well as the mission of the church was so central for Christ, it is a relationship we dare not neglect in our understanding of mission. The church at any time is in need of the study of the relationship between mission and the kingdom of God. This focus will help the church to (1) renew and strengthen its biblical motivation for mission, (2) throw light on the essence of the church and its mission to the world, and thus (3) shape its ministry goals and methods.

One key characteristic of Jesus' understanding of the kingdom of God is its eschatological tension, the dualism of the presence of the kingdom and of its future (see Cullmann 1962; Ladd 1974a). The mission of the church is placed right into the middle of this tension of the "already now" and the "not yet." It is this relationship between the eschatological tension of the kingdom of God on the one hand and the mission of the church on the other that I will look into. To focus my research, I chose to look at one person who held both of these foci together in his theological thinking, namely the late missionary, bishop, and ecumenical leader James Edward Lesslie Newbigin.

When I first read Newbigin's "Open secret. Towards a theology of mission." (95os)[1] I was very intrigued. It is hard to point out exactly what fascinated me. Newbigin's writing was clear and unpretentious but at the same time deep and profound. His theological perspective was clearly that of a missionary, a missionary thinking theologically. This sparked my own interest as a missionary. It corresponded to my own conviction about theology and mission, namely that it is important not only to bring theology to bear on mission practice, but rather to let theological understanding penetrate mission in both theory and practice. Newbigin, I believe, gives us a good example.

1.2. Problem Statement

Focusing the above research concern on the data of my study, I formulate the following problem statement: *What is the significance of the eschatological tension of the kingdom of God in the theology of mission of Lesslie Newbigin as found in his writings?* To answer this question, the following research questions must be answered.

1.3. Research Questions

I propose three research questions:

1.3.1. What Is Newbigin's View of the Kingdom of God?

This question touches at least three major areas, namely God's involvement in creation and in the history of humankind, the relationship between the kingdom of God and the world, and the relationship between the kingdom of God and the church. How is God involved with his creation? How does he

---

[1] For all references to primary sources I have chosen to use the code that is suggested by Hunsberger (Hunsberger 1998a), Foust (Foust et al. 2002) and the Newbigin-Net (www.newbigin.net). This code identifies each reference by year of publication followed by the initials of the title (e.g. "The open secret (rev. ed.)" from 1995 is "95os"). This quotation method has become a standard in research that deals with Newbigin. For all other literature I follow Turabian rules.

involve himself in human history? What is the meaning of history? How are salvation and the reign of God related to humankind as a whole? What is the relationship between the kingdom of God and the church? What are the implications for the relationship between the church and the world? These are the questions to raise.

1.3.2. What Is Newbigin's Understanding of Mission?

The question of mission touches on even more areas. Topics to look for are: mission and the Trinity; mission and election; mission and community (the church); mission and unity; mission and culture (cultural pluralism); mission and other religions (religious pluralism); mission in both word and deed; mission and the cross. To all of these Newbigin speaks. I suppose that in this dialogue with the many tangents Newbigin's understanding of mission was shaped. This interaction is what I have examined in his writings. Since this area is very broad, the goal has been to gain an overview and summarize Newbigin's view of mission.

1.3.3. How Do the Kingdom of God in Its Eschatological Tension and the Mission of the Church Relate to Each Other?

This will be the core question for the analysis. The focus is on the interrelation of the kingdom of God, the church, and mission, and of these three in relationship to the world and the history of humankind. *What is the significance of the eschatological character of God's involvement in human history for the mission of the church to the world?* That will be the focus of this research.

2. Precedent Literature

There is an immense amount of literature both on the historical and the theological framework for interpretations of the kingdom of God. This section tries to present a brief overview on both of these subjects as background for the research as such. I will also look at precedent works on Lesslie Newbigin. And finally, a brief outline of the hermeneutical premiss for this research project is included.

2.1. Historical Framework: Mission and the Kingdom of God in the Twentieth Century

"The Kingdom of God is a theological minefield as well as a vast theme, but I have dared to rush in where theologians fear to tread" (Cray 1988, 24). It is impossible to provide an exhaustive overview on the role the kingdom of God has played in the understanding of mission in the 20th century. I will attempt to point out key incidents and people that shaped the development of the theme during the lifetime of Lesslie Newbigin. I am aware of the danger of reductionism in this kind of summary. Nevertheless an attempt has to be made to understand the development of the theme in the wider mission movement, because Newbigin was part of this process and can only be understood in this context.

Uneasy Tensions

The key watershed in the interpretation of the kingdom of God and its consequent influence on the understanding of mission was doubtless the development in the 1960s, especially the time between the Third Assembly of the WCC in New Delhi (1961) and the Fourth Assembly in Uppsala (1968), culminating in sharp disagreement between the ecumenical and evangelical understandings of mission. The assembly of the CWME in Bangkok (1973) and the International Congress on World Evangelization in Lausanne (1974) express these different understandings.

While we can discern these two distinct periods – before New Delhi and after Uppsala – different understandings of mission existed in the IMC already before 1961. Before 1950 the split ran roughly between Continental and Anglo-American missiologists. The issue was a different understanding or at least a different emphasis regarding the tension between the present dimension and the future dimension of the kingdom of God. However up to 1961 attempts were continuously made in the IMC to reach an understanding of the kingdom of God that would be shared on both sides of the Atlantic. Regarding this period, Glasser speaks of an "uneasy orthodoxy" (Glasser and McGavran 1983, 90). The developments after New Delhi grew out of these earlier theological differences. These theological tensions are often presented and contrasted as two polar points and associated with the terms "ecumenical" and "evangelical." However we need to keep in mind that this is not a discussion about two polar understandings. The differences must rather be viewed as different points along a continuum. There are many positions that one can take and that are taken by different scholars along this continuum. As long as these convictions are based on a shared commitment to Jesus Christ as Lord and to the Scriptures as *canon*, these different convictions need to be taken seriously. Glasser points out:

> All those who are theologizing on the Christian mission confess that Jesus is Lord. As a result, we must take them seriously; they deserve to be heard. Even the most radical conceptualization of the Christian mission is worthy of serious study, provided, of course, it be evaluated in the light of the total witness of Scripture – our only infallible rule of faith and practice. (Glasser and McGavran 1983, 8)

In the spirit of this statement I attempt a summary of the developments of the 20th century regarding the understanding of mission and its relationship to the kingdom of God.

From Edinburgh (1910) to Evanston (1954)

In the time before New Delhi mainly two historical-eschatological views influenced the understanding of mission in the IMC. Wiedenmann in his overview (Wiedenmann 1965) mentions altogether five major views of eschatology and summarizes them in two categories, two historical-eschatological views and three ahistorical eschatological views. Representatives of the three ahistorical views of eschatology are Karl Barth (*transcendental eschatology*), Rudolf Bultmann (*existential eschatology*), and Paul Althaus (*actualized eschatology*). The common aspect of these three understandings is their ahistorical character. The encounter between God and the human being happens in history, but history itself remains without meaning. It is a circumstantial element. These views of eschatology have had a more indirect influence on the understanding of mission. Their primary influence has been in the area of hermeneutics.

In contrast, two other views of eschatology take history seriously in the sense that they emphasize the influence of salvation on history as such. The encounter between God and human beings does not only occur in specific historical circumstances but has a direct impact upon the historical development of humankind. The two views that had a major impact on the understanding of mission are *realized eschatology* and *salvation-historical eschatology*. Realized eschatology was stronger in the Anglo-American world, while the salvation-historical view of eschatology is rooted in the German theological tradition.

The discussions on the kingdom of God were re-initiated by Johannes Weiss and Albert Schweitzer with their concept of "consequent eschatology." Their critique of the liberal view of the kingdom of God (Ritschl), which had been seen mainly as a moral program with an evolutionary emphasis on gradual growth, called for critical reflection. In reaction to Weiss and Schweitzer, the Social Gospel movement at its height in the 1920s, with its emphasis on social involvement and the world-immanence of the kingdom, rejected any apocalyptic dimension. In stark contrast to this was the dispensationalist theology with its strict division between an earthly, political kingdom for Israel (both in the past and as apocalyptic kingdom for the future) and the spiritual blessings of salvation bestowed to the church in the present dispensation. The debate between dispensationalism and the social gospel movement has been part of the liberal-fundamentalist debate with its height in the 1920s in America (see Kraus 1958).

In the Anglo-American world it was C. H. Dodd who recaptured the apocalyptic dimension of the kingdom which Weiss and Schweitzer had pointed out, while at the same time moving beyond their one-sided apocalyptic view of the kingdom, which is also found – in a different form – in dispensationalism. Dodd interpreted the kingdom as being present; the apocalyptic expectation is fulfilled. "He argued that for Jesus the Kingdom was present, that Jesus taught the reality of the Kingdom as realized in his own ministry, the eschatology of Jesus is 'realized eschatology'" (Perrin 1966, 58).

In Germany, the development was quite different. The optimism of the evolutionary model was shattered through the experience of World War I. Karl Barth's "theology of crisis" is the landmark of that crisis of liberalism. In the German mission movement Karl Hartenstein and Walter Freytag are examples of those who emphasized a future-eschatological framework for an understanding of mission. This grew out of the influence of Pietism which is already found in Gustav Warneck's theology of mission. It was also supported by the work of Oscar Cullmann in NT scholarship (Cullmann 1962).

The understanding of the kingdom of God was an important theme at the Jerusalem Conference in 1928. Continental mission representatives emphasized the eschatological nature of the kingdom, while Anglo-Americans placed a strong emphasis on human beings "building the kingdom." Their emphasis was on social justice issues, the change of the social order, and the creation of a Christian civilization (Yates 1994, 65-70).

This "view of mission as 'building the kingdom' was to be very apparent in the LFMI" (Yates 1994, 70-71). The LFMI was a huge collection of data, describing the state of mission in India, Burma, China, and Japan in the 1920s and was summarized in Hocking's report "Re-Thinking Missions" (Hocking 1933). The report turned out to be very controversial because of its theological stance.

> He [R. E. Speer] and others, like J. A. Mackay and K. S. Latourette, discerned a shift, not simply in a greater emphasis on the social implications of Christian mission away from individualistic evangelism, but in the central issue of the person of Christ. ... Certainly, the report was critically weak on the church, which occasionally seemed an optional extra to the kingdom and community development. (Yates 1994, 91-92)

The German delegation made their concerns heard at the meeting of the IMC in Tambaram in 1938 (Schlunk 1939). They emphasized the future orientation of eschatology and its implications for mission, against what they perceived to be an "obsession with the idea of the Kingdom of God, namely the realization of the Kingdom of God in this world," an enthusiastic "immanence-eschatology" (Sautter 1985, 115). Sautter comments that this was the first time the salvation-historical view of mission was expressed on the ecumenical level (Sautter 1985, 121).

In 1946, Cullmann presented his contribution to the debate about the interpretation of the kingdom of God (Cullmann 1962). In contrast to Dodd, Cullmann emphasized the tension between the present and the future dimension of the kingdom in Jesus' teaching. For Jesus, the "decisive redemptive activity of God [is] already taking place in his own ministry; [however] for him this did not coincide with the Parousia" (Perrin 1966, 135). This tension between the "already now" and the "not yet" of the kingdom, between its present and future dimension, is today generally accepted as fundamental. Bosch points out, that "practically all contemporary schools of eschatology and of missionary thinking, in one way or another, are offshoots of the salvation-history approach – even if some of them might prefer to deny this ancestry" (Bosch 1991, 503-504). Nevertheless differences remain regarding the emphasis on either the present or the future dimension of the kingdom of God.

At the first meeting of the IMC after World War II in Whitby, Canada (1947), these differences had lost some of their divisive force. The delegates felt the need to unite across national boundaries and emphasize the common task of evangelism (Metzger 1953).

One of the most influential meetings of the IMC for a formulation of a "theology of mission" was the meeting of the IMC in Willingen, Germany (1952). The end of the colonial era, growing feelings of nationalism in Asian and African nations as well as the rise of communism presented the mission movement with new challenges. In Willingen an attempt was made to formulate a new theological basis for mission in which the mission of the church was grounded in God's mission, namely the sending of his Son and of his Spirit. This became a foundational axiom for mission in a post-Christendom era, today shared by conciliar-ecumenical, evangelical, Roman-Catholic, and Orthodox missiologists. However the discussion at Willingen showed that the former differences were not overcome. Hoekendijk's critique of ecclesiocentrism and his emphasis of a theology of the apostolate were presented at Willingen. He understood the *missio dei* as God's involvement in the world, apart from the church, and bypassing the church. This understanding came to the fore later in the 1964 report of the study group on "The missionary structure of the church" (Margull and World Council of Churches 1968).

In preparation for the Second General Assembly of the WCC in Evanston (1954) a study group had presented a report on the subject "Christ – our eternal hope" (Advisory Commission 1954). An initial draft of this report was first published in the Ecumenical Review (Advisory Commission, Newbigin, and Visser't Hooft 1951). The responses to the initial report (Horton et al. 1952) and the fact that this report was not fully accepted by the Evanston assembly (World Council of Churches 1955) underline the controversial nature of the issue.

From New Delhi (1961) to Bangkok (1973)

New Delhi then brought the integration of the IMC into the WCC. The IMC was continued as the DWME (later CWME). This move was evaluated in a variety of ways. The supporters saw it as a necessary consequence of a new realization of biblical ecclesiology (the church is mission; mission is the very nature of the church). It also was seen as a necessary corrective for the post-Christendom era, leaving the traditional distinction between sending churches and mission fields behind. Organizationally it was hoped that this move would overcome the dichotomy between the mission organizations and the now independent national churches on the mission fields. Critics on the other hand feared the loss of the missionary character of the former IMC. The evangelical critique of New Delhi was concerned mostly with a gradual change in the understanding of missions (Henry 1961a, 1961b) and with the implications which the integration of Orthodox churches into the WCC would have for missions (Henry 1961c). Evangelicals who had been involved in the IMC but had remained critical of the WCC began to see themselves as the – sole – true heirs of the movement that had begun in Edinburgh. This was a false identification, as Van Engen points out (Van Engen 1996, 134), but it contributed to the later development of an evangelical international network.

The 1960s brought the gravest changes so far for an ecumenical understanding of mission. "Barthian theology lost its hold on World Council of

Churches leadership, and the perspectives of Bultmann and his disciples gained the centre of the stage" (Glasser 1986a, 85). Symptomatic was a conference of the World Student Christian Federation in Strasbourg (1960). There students rejected lecturers like Barth, Kraemer, Newbigin, Niles, and Visser't Hooft and sympathized with Hoekendijk's revolutionary call: "We don't want high churchmanship. We want high worldmanship! The Church must turn towards the world and lose itself in it! The Christian must become 'the man for others'" (Glasser 1986a, 85-86). Secularism – which had been perceived as the archenemy of mission at the Jerusalem meeting (1928) – was now greeted as a welcome friend. Van Engen summarizes the influence of Hoekendijk's view:

> Missiologically this antichurch bias brought about a change in the mission order, from God-church-world to God-world-church. What mattered was the presence of *shalom* in the world: 'World and kingdom are correlated to each other; the world is conceived of as a unity, the scene of God's great acts; it is the *world* which has been reconciled (2Cor 5:19), the *world* which God loves (John 3:16) and which He has overcome in His love (John 16:33); the *world* is the field in which the seeds of the kingdom are sown (Matt 13:38) – the *world* is consequently the scene for the proclamation of the kingdom' (…). Thus Hoekendijk developed a series of couplets: kingdom and world, gospel and apostolate. In all this grand vision there was no mention of, and no room for, the church or the churches. 'Hoekendijk wanted the Kingdom of God, shalom, and service in the world to replace the Church as the central locus of mission and evangelization' (…). Thus there was a need for a *Church Inside Out* (…), which essentially amounted to the euthanasia of the church. (Van Engen 1996, 154-155)[2]

Two events were especially central for shaping the understanding of mission in the WCC. In the years 1964-1967 a WCC study group dealt with the subject "mission and structures." Moderate missiologists like Newbigin had hoped for new structures as a vessel for a renewed vigor in evangelism. However the study group built on Hoekendijk's view of God's involvement with the world. For the church this meant it had to find new ways of determining where God was at work in the world, and of assisting him in that work. It was the time of the birth of liberation theologies. God was perceived at work in revolutionary movements. Salvation was now seen not only in its universal scope, but – more importantly – it was seen as world-immanent salvation. Mission was reinterpreted as humanization. This was a direct result of Hoekendijk's emphasis and of the school of realized eschatology. The future dimension – the "not yet" that Cullmann had pointed out – was largely ignored. The eschatological tension was lost.

A second contributing event was a study of the FAO movement about "God in nature and history." Here too, realized eschatology with its emphasis on the present prevailed. The goal of God's work in nature and history was defined as the unity of humankind under the headship of Christ. The task of

---

[2] Emphases in quotations are always reproduced as in the original unless noted otherwise.

the church was to facilitate this unity. The focus shifted from proclamation to engagement and identification with the world (Müller-Fahrenholz 1974).

The 1963 World Mission Conference in Mexico had already emphasized the "conviction that God is somehow at work in the secular events of our time, beyond the bounds of the church" (70msc, 194). Newbigin states:

> If the Tambaram meeting had placed the Christian mission firmly in a churchly context, and if Willingen had struggled unsuccessfully to break out of this, Mexico must be regarded as especially significant for the fact that it conceived the missionary task in the context of what God is doing in the secular events of our time. (70msc, 194)

This new understanding of mission was confirmed at the Fourth General Assembly of the WCC in Uppsala in 1968 and five years later at the World Mission Conference in Bangkok (1973). Evangelicals who spoke out for a different view of evangelism (evangelism as proclamation) were dismissed (see Glasser 1973, Beyerhaus and World Council of Churches 1973). Van Engen points at the irony that a World Council of Churches adopted a missiology and an ecclesiology that "exclude[s] the church as the primary locus of the kingdom and the primary agent of God's grace in the world" (Van Engen 1996, 155).

In his essay on the developments from 1948 to 1968 Newbigin indicates that in these 20 years the ecumenical movement had faced questions concerning the form and structure of mission, but that it would now face questions about the substance of the gospel (70msc, 197). He could not have been more right. It turned out that on this question opinions would differ even more.

Evangelical Formation (1966-1974)

Meanwhile in 1966 evangelicals had met for two important congresses. Both the Wheaton congress and the Berlin congress were milestones for evangelicals to consolidate. The most influential meeting, however, was the 1974 International Congress on World Evangelization in Lausanne. Here an international group of evangelical representatives expressed their shared commitment to world mission/evangelism as both proclamation and service. The conference was clearly held in the shadow of the conflicting views of mission that had come to the fore in Uppsala and Bangkok. However it was not a conference of protest, but rather a forward looking meeting, emphasizing the cooperation and the shared vision among evangelicals for evangelism. In this sense, it was perceived as a direct continuation of the Edinburgh conference and the IMC conferences that followed after 1910. The fear that Newbigin had expressed before the integration of the IMC into the WCC in New Delhi had come true: Evangelicals had not followed the IMC integration into the WCC but had now formed another successor of the IMC.

Evangelicals were, however, not a homogeneous unit. Bosch distinguishes roughly between three groups (Bosch 1976). While all of them agree on their basic commitments and their critique of the WCC's interpretation of mission as humanization, their emphases are different. In 1970 a group of German theologians and missiologists published the Frankfurt declaration (see Beyerhaus 1971). In seven theses they declared their understanding of mission and dissociated themselves from the WCC's new paradigm of mission. Beyerhaus became the spokesman for this group. However it is interesting to note that in his first critique of Uppsala Beyerhaus still calls for a mutual openness for both evangelicals and ecumenicals and for a willingness to learn from each other in order to focus on a truly biblical understanding of mission (Beyerhaus 1971, 54-58). In his critique of the Bangkok conference (Beyerhaus and World Council of Churches 1973) the tone is different. Here the split between evangelicals and ecumenicals seems permanent. Beyerhaus sees fundamental differences arise from a different view of the Scriptures and a different hermeneutic (Beyerhaus 1996). While most evangelicals would agree with this analysis, the courses of action that are suggested vary. Rather than taking the split between ecumenicals and evangelicals as a *fait accompli* evangelicals like John Stott and Arthur Glasser explicitly call for continuing efforts in order to reach a shared understanding of mission (Glasser 1979, 99). The publications of this group of evangelicals do not lack anything in clarity, but they are written in a more conciliatory tone. And thirdly, there is the group of "radical evangelicals." In Lausanne they came mostly from Latin America. Their emphasis continues to be on the challenge that social injustice and poverty pose for mission, and how evangelicals should respond to this challenge. In Lausanne they published a separate declaration "A response to Lausanne," not as a counter-declaration but as an addendum to the Lausanne covenant. As such it was welcomed by those responsible for drafting the Lausanne covenant. This discussion on the relationship between evangelism and social ministry has continued in the evangelical movement through the years and led to declarations like the Consultation on the Relation of Evangelism and Social Responsibility (1982, Scherer and Bevans 1992), the Consultation on the Church in Response to Human Need (1983, Scherer and Bevans 1992), and the Kingdom Manifesto (Hathaway 1990).

So while evangelicals were far from being homogeneous, they were nevertheless able to focus on their shared concern and express it in this truly international forum at Lausanne. Van Engen comments: "Out of the 2,473 participants at Lausanne, nearly one half were from non-Western countries. These Third World theologians who had not inherited the fundamentalist reduction would call Lausanne to a more wholistic reaffirmation of historic evangelical mission theology" (Van Engen 1996, 136).

Beyond Dichotomies

The following year, 1975, the Fifth General Assembly of the WCC was held in Nairobi. Compared to Uppsala and Bangkok, the tone was much more subdued. "The euphoria of Uppsala made way for more sober realism" (Bosch 1976, 76). Mortimer Arias in his paper called

> the WCC back to this 'essential priority', and to the fact that evangelism is the Church's *primary* task, and remains its *permanent* task. ... Arias reject[ed] all dichotomy between 'vertical' and 'horizontal', between 'evangelism' and 'so-

cial action', between 'soul' and 'body'. He therefore advocate[d] a 'holistic' approach to evangelism. (Bosch 1976, 76-77)

Reflecting back on the developments in the 1960s and early 70s Bosch summarizes: "Reviewing the past decade and a half we could – admittedly in an over-simplified manner – say that the sixties and the beginning of the seventies revealed a growing polarization between 'ecumenicals' and 'evangelicals' but that there has been a significant – if not easily perceptible – shift since about 1973" (Bosch 1976, 77). He continues:

> [T]here are indications of a shift in thinking in recent years. In ecumenical circles we increasingly discern a rediscovery of the importance of evangelism, in evangelical circles we note a new emphasis on the Christian's social responsibility. In both groups this is coupled with a preparedness to exercise self-criticism. (Bosch 1976, 79)

Melbourne (1980) and Pattaya (1980)

Bosch's optimism seemed justified in light of the more conciliatory tone of the director's address at the 1980 WCC conference on World Mission and Evangelism in Melbourne. Castro spoke of evangelism, proclamation, and announcing the kingdom. "We are here in a conference on evangelism. This Kingdom of God for which we pray must be announced, and announced as Good News" (Castro 1980, 261). He emphasized the importance of Jesus of Nazareth as the King of God's kingdom. However he also said: "The proclamation of the Gospel of the kingdom includes an invitation to join the kingdom, to participate in its struggles. Evangelism, then, becomes revolutionary engagement ..." (Castro 1980, 262). In the words of one observer, Melbourne

> specifically referred at times to the fullness of the Kingdom beyond time and in spiritual dimensions. Yet Melbourne did have a heavy focus on a this-worldly kingdom, or at least on signs of the Kingdom in this world construed not in terms of the totality of human experience and culture in this world but predominantly in socioeconomic terms. ... The liberation envisaged was primarily from economic and political distress, from the evils wrought by wrong social structures and abuses of authority. (Stowe 1981, 32-33)

While Stowe acknowledges the validity of such liberation efforts, he states:

> But to concentrate the attention of a rare Conference on World Mission and Evangelism on that task, and to do so under the theme of 'Your Kingdom Come' is to create the impression that achieving a decent livelihood and at least minimal civil liberties for all the world's people is to draw closer to the Kingdom of God. And to me that seems unbalanced. (Stowe 1981, 33)

Another evangelical observer, Clark Pinnock, expresses similar concerns, but calls for a stronger evangelical participation in the WCC:

> Did the Melbourne assembly do anything to bridge the gaps between ... Bangkok ... and Lausanne? Yes, I think it did, in a measure. The emphasis at Bang-

kok on human liberation was certainly present at Melbourne – but then again it had to be. It is a scriptural concern. But also present was a strong concern to reach all peoples with the good news about Jesus. (Stockwell 1981, 54-55)

Pinnock adds:

> The WCC needs, if I may say so, the evangelical witness. Certain biblical themes tend to get left out if evangelicals are not present. The tendency to interpret the gospel solely on the horizontal level and mission in terms only of social reconstruction has to be confronted and corrected. The WCC does tend to forget, without necessarily denying it, our Lord's command to spread the gospel among all nations, and we need to remind them of that. (Stockwell 1981, 55)

In June 1980, only a few weeks after Melbourne, evangelical representatives met in Pattaya (Thailand) for a Consultation on World Evangelization (COWE). As the title suggests this consultation was focusing explicitly on evangelism. The center of this conference were the 17 study groups which dealt with evangelism among different religious groups. Their reports were consequently published as Lausanne Occasional Papers. While Melbourne tried to adopt a more conciliatory tone regarding the relationship of the WCC to the evangelical wing of the mission movement, this was not univocally reciprocated at Pattaya. Scott comments: "[W]hile mutual appreciation at leadership levels between the CWME and LCWE exists, many rank and file COWE participants remain suspicious of, and even hostile to, ecumenical understandings and practices of mission" (Scott 1981, 66-67).

However at Pattaya again a group of evangelicals drafted a "statement of concerns" that was eventually signed by one-third of the consultations' participants. In it they called attention to the "social, economic and political institutions that determine their [i.e. people groups'] lives and the structures behind them that hinder evangelism." They suggested a "World Congress on Evangelical Social Responsibility" (Scott 1981, 71-72). Generally speaking however, Pattaya was more conservative on the issue of evangelism. Even while affirming the Lausanne covenant, "Pattaya did in fact retreat from the position advanced at Lausanne" with regard to the holistic integration of evangelism and social engagement (Scott 1981, 73). The evangelical discussion was no doubt overshadowed by the concern to distinguish the evangelical position from the WCC's strong emphasis on involvement in social and political struggles.

Evangelism as Proclamation and Social Involvement

The relationship between evangelism as proclamation (word) and evangelism as liberation (deed) continued to dominate the debate in the 1980s. In 1982 the WCC Central Committee published the "Ecumenical Affirmation: Mission and Evangelism." Scherer and Bevans remark, that this

> may be the single most important ecumenical statement on mission in this period ... containing the basic convictions of the ecumenical movement on mis-

sion and evangelism. ... The document has been warmly acclaimed in both conciliar and non-conciliar circles as a statement of convergence. (Scherer and Bevans 1992, 36)

On the evangelical side there were two meetings which need to be mentioned. In 1982 a group of fifty missiologists, mission leaders, and theologians met in Grand Rapids and published a statement "Evangelism and Social Responsibility: An Evangelical Commitment" (Scherer and Bevans 1992). In 1983 World Evangelical Fellowship held a "Consultation on the Church in Response to Human Need" in Wheaton. Again the introductory comment of Scherer and Bevans:

> [T]he Wheaton 1983 statement on 'Transformation: The Church in Response to Human Need' remains the landmark evangelical document on the biblical relationship between gospel ministry and the kingdom of God. ... In the wider context of both divine creation and eschatology, Wheaton 1983 relates the goal of transformation to the biblical vision of the kingdom of God. The statement has ramifications for a whole range of Christian activities, not merely evangelization. (Scherer and Bevans 1992, 281)

These documents show the two camps moving closer to each other. In line with this is the Stuttgart Consultation (1987). The WCC CWME had invited church representatives – both evangelicals and others – to discuss the issue of evangelism, taking the 1982 Ecumenical Affirmation as a starting point. Scherer and Bevans comment that the consultation "served as a bridge between conciliar Christians and evangelicals in the period before San Antonio and Lausanne II. The statement is noteworthy for its emphasis on 'wholistic' or 'integral' evangelism" (Scherer and Bevans 1992, 65; Samuel and Hauser 1989).

San Antonio (1989) and Manila (1989)

The year 1989 again brought two conferences on world mission and evangelism: the World Conference on Mission and Evangelism in San Antonio sponsored by the WCC CWME (Wilson 1990), and the International Congress on World Evangelization in Manila sponsored by the LCWE, also known as "Lausanne II" (Stott 1996). At San Antonio the focus of the social-political involvement in the struggle for liberation was extended to include the ecological concern for preserving creation (Wilson 1990). With regard to the conciliar-evangelical relationship, a "letter from those with evangelical concerns" at San Antonio addressed to the Lausanne II Conference in Manila is important (Wilson 1990, 190-194). Bailyes summarizes: "This letter was deeply appreciative of the many good things that were enriching in the experience of those who had taken part. The letter welcomed 'the importance given to the cross,' and for the 'ample opportunity' there was 'for evangelical concerns to be voiced' and expressed in conference documents" (Bailyes 1996, 495-496). Part of the letter reads:

> We feel that the expression of concern for the rights of the poor must not be misunderstood as showing that the World Council of Churches has relin-

> quished the central concern of devotion and faithful witness to Jesus. For he is the very basis for the compassion and justice that requires that the voice of the poor be heard. But care is needed lest this emphasis be misused to redefine the central Christian affirmations in terms of the most strident cries against oppression. Jesus was indeed a prophet and exercised a prophetic ministry. But unless Jesus is also acknowledged as the Saviour crucified for the sin of the world and the Lord risen as the victor over all evil, we are without hope and without God in the world.
>
> We have been encouraged by the way in which Christians from many traditions have joined here in confessing Jesus Christ as Lord and Saviour of the world and in affirming that they cannot point to any other way of salvation but Jesus Christ. We ask that you join us in refusing to identify the WCC declarations about the cries of the oppressed for justice as a retreat from an affirmation of the centrality and finality of Jesus Christ. (Wilson 1990, 191-192)

The Manila Manifesto responded and took up the issue of the relationship between evangelicals and those who are not part of the evangelical movement in Part II, Section 9. I continue to quote in length:

> Our reference to 'the whole church' is not a presumptuous claim that the universal church and the evangelical community are synonymous. For we recognize that there are many churches which are not part of the evangelical movement. Evangelical attitudes to the Roman Catholic and Orthodox Churches differ widely. Some evangelicals are praying, talking, studying Scripture and working with these churches. Others are strongly opposed to any form of dialogue or cooperation with them. All evangelicals are aware that serious theological differences between us remain. Where appropriate, and so long as biblical truth is not compromised, cooperation may be possible in such areas as Bible translation, the study of contemporary theological and ethical issues, social work and political action. We wish to make it clear, however, that common evangelism demands a common commitment to the biblical Gospel.
>
> Some of us are members of churches which belong to the World Council of Churches and believe that a positive yet critical participation in its work is our Christian duty. Others among us have no link with the World Council. All of us urge the World Council of Churches to adopt a consistent biblical understanding of evangelism.
>
> We confess our own share of responsibility for the brokenness of the body of Christ, which is a major stumbling-block to world evangelization. We determine to go on seeking that unity in truth for which Christ prayed. We are persuaded that the right way forward towards closer cooperation is frank and patient dialogue on the basis of the Bible, with all who share our concerns. To this we gladly commit ourselves. (Stott 1996, 242-243).

Lausanne II thus confirms a commitment to both a holistic view of mission and the unity of the church on the basis of "a common commitment to the biblical Gospel." In this last short reference the issue of hermeneutics is implicitly raised, but not expanded.

After San Antonio and Manila

As part of the evangelical movement, a group of missiologists has continued to work on an integrated view of evangelism and social involvement, building on the 1983 paper "Transformation: Consultation on the Church in Response to Human Need" (Scherer and Bevans 1992). Their papers deal with theological foundations (theology of the kingdom) as well as with practical issues (Samuel and Sugden 1999).

Chris Sugden, one of the spokespeople of this group, wrote the introductory comments for the publication of a letter that was written by a group of evangelicals who participated in the Eight Assembly of the WCC in Harare, Zimbabwe (Samuel 1999). Sugden summarizes: "They wished to expose the liberal control of the WCC, to challenge it to begin to reflect its evangelical constituency more faithfully, and to clarify the role that Evangelicals will play in coming years, both in monitoring the WCC and in promoting mission and evangelism" (Samuel 1999, 13). He also points out, that

> [t]he letter reflects a difference of opinion among Evangelicals on the most appropriate way to relate to the World Council. It affirms that Evangelicals will continue to devote energy to local, regional and national expressions of the ecumenical vision. But those Evangelicals who are members of churches that are members of the WCC and have worked in its structures for some time are more hesitant about the future than those from independent and smaller evangelical groups who look to the WCC as a possible partner in future activities. (Samuel 1999, 14)

This observation of a spectrum of opinions restates the variety of viewpoints that was expressed at Manila (Stott 1996, 242-243).

Summary: Two Voices

In conclusion of this historical summary, two voices may summarize the challenges for both evangelicals and ecumenicals. Arthur Glasser addresses the evangelicals and their tendency to focus explicitly on evangelism as proclamation:

> If God's tomorrow means the end of exploitation, injustice, inequality, war, racism, nationalism, suffering, death, and the ignorance of God, Christians must be 'signs' today of God's conquest of all these 'burdens and evils' through the cross and resurrection of Jesus Christ. No longer can evangelicals confine themselves to the single priority of proclaiming the knowledge of God among the nations and settle for the status quo of everything else. Of course, Christians shall not establish the kingdom, much less bring it to fullness. Any Trinitarian theology of mission worth its salt will show that God alone will accomplish this. The consummation of human history and the manifestation of the kingdom in power and glory will be the work of God alone. But this does not mean that Christians today dare indulge the luxury of indifference to the moral and social issues of today. Only those are 'blessed' who are the merciful, the peacemakers, the persecuted for righteousness sake: 'Theirs is the kingdom of heaven' (Matt 5:7-12). (Glasser 1987, 63)

Speaking for and to the ecumenical movement, Lesslie Newbigin closes his comments on the 1996 Conference on World Mission and Evangelism in Salvador:

> The WCC has given courageous leadership in the struggle for peace and justice in the fight against racism and in concern for the integrity of creation. It has been the prime mover in the search for closer Christian unity. But in so powerfully challenging the churches on these issues it does seem to have lost the missionary passion that was the vital force that created the ecumenical movement in the closing years of the nineteenth and the opening years of the twentieth centuries. The demand for unity among the churches and the demand for justice and peace among the nations, if they are not rooted in what God has done for all the world in Jesus Christ, can themselves become new forms of domination. There cannot be any greater task, or any deeper joy, than to tell the world what God has done for us in Jesus Christ and to enable others to know, love, and serve him as Lord and Savior.
>
> The World Council of Churches can only be what its member churches make it. As one who is a member of a member church, I cannot speak as a critic from outside. I can only pray and work and hope that God, who has so marvelously created and sustained the World Council of Churches throughout half a century, may grant it a deep renewal of joy in the Gospel, which may enable it to fulfill in a greater measure the desire of our Lord that those who believe in him may be one, that the world may believe. (97dgc, 52)

Epilogue: Roman Catholic Missiology

So far in this historical summary I have completely ignored the Roman Catholic contribution to mission theology. Many evangelicals joyfully identified themselves with the publications of Vatican II (1963-1965), namely *Ad Gentes* and *Lumen Gentium*, especially in their clear emphasis on evangelism and the necessity to announce the good news to those who have never heard it yet (Glasser and McGavran 1983; Glasser 1985). Also the papal encyclopedia *Evangelii Nuntiandi* (1975) was greeted with great appreciation. However the picture of Roman Catholic mission theology is far less homogenous than a reading of these papers may suggest. The decline of the number of Catholic missionaries from the West, the debates on liberation theology with its implicit universalism and its repudiation of classical evangelism, the reevaluation of other religions in their salvific value and the emphasis on inter-religious dialogue as substance of evangelism all point out that the Roman Catholic mission theology is struggling with the same issues as the conciliar-ecumenical and evangelical mission theologies.

Evangelical studies of mission theology need to continue to take these developments in the Roman Catholic church into consideration as well as developments in the Orthodox churches. Here I have chosen to limit myself to the developments in the conciliar-ecumenical and evangelical camps, because the focus of this overview is to outline the backdrop for exploring the mission theology of Lesslie Newbigin.

2.2. Theological Framework: Theology and the Kingdom of God

The amount of literature on the kingdom of God is vast. Perrin and Fuellenbach – to name just two scholars – provide an overview over the theological developments and a summary of the exegetical issues (Perrin 1966, Fuellenbach 1995). In his discourse on the kingdom of God Snyder has summarized present understandings of the kingdom with eight different models. These are:

> (1) The kingdom as future hope: the *future* kingdom; (2) the kingdom as inner spiritual experience: the *interior* kingdom; (3) the kingdom as mystical communion: the *heavenly* kingdom; (4) the kingdom as institutional church: the *ecclesiastical* kingdom; (5) the kingdom as counter-system: the *subversive* kingdom; (6) the kingdom as political state: the *theocratic* kingdom; (7) the kingdom as Christianized culture: the *transforming* kingdom; and (8) the kingdom as earthly utopia: the *utopian* kingdom. (Snyder 1991, 18)

These models present different facets of the kingdom of God. Snyder argues that they must be seen together, supplementing each other. For an evaluation of the different models, Snyder points out six different polarities that are held in tension in the biblical texts. The better a model integrates all of these polarities the better it is an expression of the biblical view of the kingdom (Snyder 1991, 17). Snyder names the polarities as: (1) present versus future, (2) individual versus social, (3) spirit versus matter, (4) gradual versus climactic, (5) divine action versus human action, and (6) identification of church and kingdom versus differentiation between church and kingdom; "the tension between seeing the church and the kingdom as essentially the same or as clearly different" (Snyder 1991, 16-17).

Snyder also provides a series of questions to check the correspondence of any model of the kingdom to Jesus' message on God's reign (Snyder 1991, 128-129). Referring to Snyder, Fuellenbach summarizes these questions:

> (1) Does Jesus Christ remain the ultimate reference point in a given model? Since he emerges more clearly from scripture than the profile of the Kingdom, the Kingdom must be interpreted in the light of Jesus Christ. Jesus embodies in his person all the six polarities.
>
> (2) Does the model help generate and maintain a vital Christian community of worship, witness, and mutual interdependence, or does it undermine it? The Kingdom is a social reality and not merely a private hope or a mental theory.
>
> (3) Does the model inspire and nurture redemptive Christian living in the world? The most faithful and useful models are those that undergird the church's mission in the world, promoting both an immediacy of witness and action and a certain patience based on the confidence that the Kingdom is fundamentally God's work, not ours. (Fuellenbach 1995, 63)

Snyder has tried to systematically summarize different aspects and understandings of the kingdom and has given us several checkpoints for testing the various views for their correspondence to the overall biblical view. Fact is that while the kingdom of God was the main theme of Jesus' proclamation in his earthly ministry, he did not leave his disciples with a systematic definition. We must assume that Jesus began by building on the current Jewish understanding of the kingdom. However the NT makes clear that Jesus did in fact reshape the disciples' understanding of the kingdom by introducing them to the "mysteries of the kingdom," those aspects of the kingdom of God that had not yet been made known through OT prophecy (Matt 13:11; Ladd 1974a, 218-242). Rather than providing a comprehensive discourse on the kingdom of God, Jesus pointed out a number of important characteristics of the kingdom in his teaching. Snyder's use of models as a hermeneutical tool tries to bring into focus the characteristics of the kingdom which the NT presents.

To give a brief digest of my understanding of the kingdom of God I refer to Wilbert R. Shenk and George E. Ladd. Shenk summarizes:

> The reign of God, thrust to the center of history in the Christ-event, is the horizon within which God's redemptive mission is being fulfilled. The reign of God (*basileia*) originates with God and expresses God's saving will and purpose. The redemptive power of God is now being guided by a strategy that is being made explicit before the world in the ministry and life of Jesus the Messiah. It is God's will to deliver the creation from the powers of decay and death.
>
> Something extraordinary has been set in motion instead of *futurum*, ordinary time, a prolongation of the old, the world is introduced to *adventus*, a new beginning. The reign of God is to be realized through the inauguration of a new order – characterized by life, peace, and justice/righteousness – which assuredly will supplant the old order, the reign of death. God wills that life, not death, have the last word. (Shenk 1999, 9-10)

About the establishment of God's reign in the present, Shenk says:

> The coming of God's reign disturbs the status quo by triggering two reactions. First, because it exposes the egocentric structure of human nature and behavior, it is perceived to be a *skandalon*. This gives rise to *krisis*, the moment of truth that calls for decision in light of the new possibility: "Repent! Turn toward God and be incorporated into the new order." This is both invitation and warning. Those who refuse God's gracious offer will remain in the grips of the old order and its destiny. God's reign challenges human motivation and character at the deepest levels by unmasking the nature of power that is unsubmitted to the will of God. (Shenk 1999, 10)

Ladd gives a definition of the kingdom that expresses well the tension between its present and future dimensions:

> [T]he Kingdom of God is the redemptive reign of God dynamically active to establish his rule among men, and that this Kingdom, which will appear as an apocalyptic act at the end of the age, has already come into human history in the person and mission of Jesus to overcome evil, to deliver men from its

power, and to bring them into the blessings of God's reign. The Kingdom of God involves two great moments: fulfillment within history, and consummation at the end of history. (Ladd 1974a, 218)

These brief summaries show the comprehensive character of God's kingdom (it is the biblical meta-narrative, God's story with his world and his answer to the problem of evil and the human dilemma), its thrust (it is God's goal to re-establish his shalom), its decision-character (the message of Christ's lordship calls every person to a decision), and the temporal tension between its present fulfillment and its future consummation. In this context the calling of the church has to be understood as participation in the *missio dei*.

Glasser has given us an example on how to develop a theology of mission from the overarching story of God's kingdom (Glasser et al. 2003). Shenk in his own way defines the relationship between kingdom, mission, and church.

> Three things must be kept in focus. First, the rule of God is prior to mission. Indeed, mission is the means by which God's reign is being realized in the world. In the second place, as a corollary, we note that mission is prior to church. The church can only be called into being by the preaching of the gospel of the kingdom. Jesus began by proclaiming this gospel and gathering together those who responded. These he taught and then commissioned to continue doing what he was doing. In this age the task of proclaiming the gospel is never finished, for each generation must hear it for themselves. The church becomes something other than a living witness to the gospel when it seeks to preserve the faith through an institution or sacerdotal system. Rather, the church lives out of the gospel by proclaiming the gospel. Third, at Pentecost the Holy Spirit endowed and equipped the disciple community to continue the mission of Jesus Christ in the world (…).
>
> The calling of the church is to glorify the Triune God (1) by faithfully witnessing to the reign of God, and (2) by living as a sign of that reign. To state it differently, the church has a single purpose, which consists of two aspects. These two dimensions cannot be sustained in isolation from one another. They must be held together and allowed to interpenetrate if this purpose is to be realized. (Shenk 1999, 15)

Here we come across Newbigin's terminology (the church as a sign of the kingdom). Shenk depicts the role of the church for the world and for humanity as a whole by expanding on the church's calling to be both a witness to and a sign of the kingdom.

> The missionary church witnesses by being a "contrast society" (Lohfink 1984, 157-163) or "microsociety" (Miller 1993, 137-145) in which the life-defining features of the larger society are transformed so their destructive power is redeemed. For example, conventional peoplehood based on blood, soil, and culture is transmuted through the regenerating work of the Suffering Servant of God, wherein the meaning of blood, soil, and culture is restored to what God the Creator intended. Indeed, mission combines two fundamental thrusts – the universal and the particular – in one action and one relationship. The universal

moves to bring all under the sovereignty of God, thereby relativizing all other loyalties and claims. The thrust of particularity moves toward every people and each person for each bears the image of God. None is excluded from the reach of God's love; all are invited to be reconciled to God. (Shenk 1999, 16)

Van Engen in his definition of mission expresses a similar relation between kingdom, mission and church (Van Engen 1996, 26-27). Hiebert, in his essay on "Evangelism, Church, and Kingdom," makes us aware of the danger of reductionism in our mission paradigms. A truly integrated view of evangelism, church, and kingdom needs the focus on Christ, the king. Hiebert quotes E. Stanley Jones:

> [A] rediscovery of the Kingdom without the rediscovery of the King would ... be a half-discovery, for it would be a kingdom without a king. ... Jesus shows us what God is like and also what the kingdom of God is like in operation. The kingdom of God is Christlikeness universalized. (Hiebert 1993, 159)

This focus on Christ as the king keeps us from reducing the kingdom of God to a concept which then becomes open to be defined by human ideologies. While these references here simply serve to sketch the pre-understanding with which I approach the study, the research itself will show that we are already treading on Newbigin's territory.

To round up this section on the theological framework a brief definition of the term "theology of mission" should be added. Van Engen defines "*theology of mission*" as "[a] discipline that reflects on the presuppositions, assumptions, and concepts undergirding mission theory" (Van Engen 2000, 949). In a similar way, Anderson defines: "Theology of mission is concerned with the basic presuppositions and underlying principles which determine, from the standpoint of Christian faith, the motives, message, methods, strategy and goals of the Christian world mission" (Anderson 1971, 594). Both of these definitions point out the comprehensive character of the discipline and its foundational character as partner for mission practice. Theology of mission is thus the theological reflection on God's salvific work and on the sending of his church into the world. It critically engages the worldview, culture, and socio-economic-political structures in which the mission of the church takes place. It takes God's self-revelation in his word as a point of reference for its reflection. Its goal is twofold: (1) to grow in the understanding of the mission of the church, laying the foundation, and (2) to draw out the implications for mission practice, aiding the church in its task.

These are the pre-understandings with which I approach this project. The research and analysis itself will have to bring to light Newbigin's understanding of these issues.

2.3. Works on Lesslie Newbigin

This research project is meant to be a contribution to a growing circle of scholarship which focuses on interpreting Newbigin and building on his legacy. Here I review briefly a few key works on Newbigin which are part of this circle of scholarship. I am aware that there are more works that deal with Newbigin. However my access to dissertations and research papers on Newbigin's life's work was limited. Therefore I had to limit myself to a few works which, however, contribute substantially to a thorough understanding of Newbigin. I did include "A scandalous prophet" (Foust et al. 2002) for its proximity to the present debate and for the variety of understandings which in one way or another draw on Newbigin's work.

2.3.1. "Lesslie Newbigin: A Theological Life" (Wainwright 2000)

I begin with a recent "theological biography" on Newbigin. Wainwright's book is both a biography of Newbigin's life as well as an introduction to his many writings. Wainwright's work shows the embeddedness of Newbigin's writings in his ministry. He introduces the reader to both published and unpublished works of Newbigin. For example, he cites Newbigin's student papers from Oxford and his lectures on the kingdom of God in India in 1941 – which were later published by Wainwright in 2003 (see 41kgip) – as well as other materials from the archive at the Orchard Learning Resources Centre of the University of Birmingham at Selly Oaks (U.K.). Wainwright introduces the variety of subjects Newbigin dealt with, like evangelism, mission, the church in the world, the ecumenical unity of the church, the gospel and social responsibility, the critical encounter of the gospel with culture, and religious pluralism, both in India and in the West.

Wainwright presents Newbigin's writings basically in a chronological framework. However he expands this framework and puts the chronology aside when he introduces later writings that refer to the same subject at an earlier point in the biography. This breaks the chronological order, but it enhances the clarity of thought and allows the reader to see Newbigin's thinking on a specific subject as it developed over time. His work is a good introduction to the life and works of Newbigin.

The following works on specific aspects of Newbigin's writings are presented in chronological order.

2.3.2. "Bearing the Witness of the Spirit" (Hunsberger 1998a)

Hunsberger in 1987 wrote on the significance of election for Newbigin's theology of cultural plurality. He rewrote his work for publication in 1998. The central question that the fact of cultural plurality poses is: How can it be that one event in history should be so central as to be determinative for all humankind? Newbigin answers this question by referring to the doctrine of election. Election brings the universal scope of salvation together with the particularity of the Christ event. Hunsberger here speaks of the "missionary character" of the doctrine of election. It is in this framework that Newbigin deals with cultural plurality and the universality of the gospel. Hunsberger points out that Newbigin depicts the relationship between gospel, church and culture not as a linear polarity, but rather as a triangular relationship. He sees the interaction of three cultural spheres in the missionary encounter: the gospel in its cultural form, the missionary and his or her culture, and the local culture of the people to whom the gospel is communicated. Hunsberger pictures these relationships in a triangle of gospel, church, and culture with three axes: the gospel-culture axis, the gospel-church axis, and the church-culture axis (Hunsberger 1998a, 238). The gospel-culture axis focuses on conversion and deals with (a) the question of the relevancy of the gospel for a specific culture (continuity) as well as (b) the call to transformation of that culture (discontinuity). The church-culture axis depicts the missionary dialogue and deals with the question of (a) adherence to the global church tradition (continuity) as well as (b) the freedom of the local church for finding culturally appropriate expressions for the gospel and the local church's response to it (discontinuity). The gospel-church axis depicts "the 'reciprocal relation' between the church and the Bible by which the church represents the Bible in the encounter with cultures and the Bible critiques and reforms the church while it is doing so" (Hunsberger 1998a, 238). Here too we find a dialectic of continuity ("the church represents the Bible in the encounter with cultures") and discontinuity ("the Bible critiques and reforms the church while it is doing so"). Speaking about the relevance of Newbigin's work for today, Hunsberger points out that this disentangling of the issues of gospel, church, and culture allows the churches of the West to take a step back and critically "engage their 'own' culture in a missionary way" (Hunsberger 1998a, 278). As Newbigin's life was characterized by the double focus of being a missionary to India and being a missionary to the West, so his "theology of cultural plurality" (Hunsberger) impacts both missionary encounters.

2.3.3. "As the Father Has Sent Me, I Am Sending You" (Goheen 2000)

Goheen looks at the missionary character of the church in Newbigin's writings. He structures his work in two parts. In the historical section (approx. 100 pages) he looks at two paradigm shifts in Newbigin's thinking: (1) "From Christendom to a missionary ecclesiology," which roughly covers the time from 1909-1959, namely Newbigin's upbringing, his theological studies, and the early years in India. And (2) "From a Christocentric to a Trinitarian ecclesiology," which occurs in the years from 1959-1998 when Newbigin was involved in the IMC and the WCC; he returned to India as bishop for Madras; and he engaged the post-Christendom culture of the West during his retirement in England. The historical section provides an overview of how Newbigin's thinking has been shaped over time through his engagement of new challenges. However the analysis of Newbigin's work later will show that the principle outline of his thinking did not change during his lifetime.

Part two of Goheen's book is a systematic summary and analysis of Newbigin's view of the church in mission. This is much more extensive than part one (approx. 300 pages), and it is an important contribution, since Newbigin never attempted a systematic summary of his ecclesiology. Goheen focuses on three main issues: "the relation of the church to God, to its own mission, and to its religio-cultural context" (Goheen 2000, 115). He divides each of these into two separate chapters: The mission of God as the context for the church's missionary identity (chap. 4); the missionary character of the church (chap. 5); the missionary church as institution (chap. 6); the task of the missionary church in the world (chap. 7); the missionary church in the cultural context (chap. 8); and the missionary church in the Western culture (chap. 9).

In his summary, Goheen points out two areas of continuing relevance for Newbigin's work. First he mentions the understanding of mission in the WCC. Here he refers to the debate between Newbigin and Raiser on Christocentrism and cosmic Trinitarianism. As a second area of relevance, Goheen points to the work of the GOCN. He argues that the GOCN presents a more negative view of both culture and Christendom than Newbigin does. And he sees a stronger tendency towards an "alternative community" model for the church than in Newbigin's writings. Goheen argues, the GOCN needs a more balanced view on these issues.

In critique of Newbigin, Goheen points out areas of weakness in Newbigin's writings: his exposition on the role of the Father and the Spirit and their work in creation and history, his definition of culture, and his integration of Anabaptist and Reformed views of the church. However, for Goheen these are not so much areas of criticism. They are rather areas which call for further reflection. He is well aware that Newbigin wrote out of involvement with pressing issues in his ministry. "Newbigin was a highly contextual thinker. His discussion of each of these aspects of the church's mission was forged in the heat of pressing problems and issues. The need remains today to bring his insights to bear on different problems and new contexts" (Goheen 2000, 330).

2.3.4. "A Scandalous Prophet" (Foust et al. 2002)

This book is a collection of very diverse papers, read at an international conference in Birmingham in November 1998, titled: "The way of mission after Newbigin." All authors try to point out areas of relevance in which we have to move beyond Newbigin. Some do so by building on Newbigin's work. Others apparently see little or no relevance in Newbigin's thought for the present new challenges. Some viewpoints clearly contradict Newbigin's. For example, Aleaz in his call for pluralistic "community of communities" emphasizes the importance of contextual theology, which for him means a move away from and beyond the "particular Jesus" to "the universal Jesus, avoiding christocentric universalism. ... People from diverse religio-cultural backgrounds will, in terms of their contexts, decide the content of the gospel" (Aleaz 2002, 170). In another essay Schmidt-Leukel single-handedly dismisses the Trinitarian model for understanding mission (Schmidt-Leukel 2002, 57). It is hard to see, how these authors attempt to build on Newbigin. Their emphasis is rather on pointing out the limitation of Newbigin's theological framework for the current debate. Instead they propose religious pluralism as a paradigm to embrace. They do call our attention to an important question, however, in the context of current globalization trends. The challenge is for mission to be distinct from globalization and not to become a movement for globalizing the Christian religion. This is a concern they share with Newbigin (see Taber 2002, 186). However the issues are more complex than authors like Aleaz (2002) and Aydin (2002) indicate in their papers.

Mission as globalization of the Christian religion vs. religious pluralism is not a valid dichotomy. This polarization of arguments is a simplistic reduction of the complexity of alternatives.

Other authors demonstrate a thorough familiarity with Newbigin and build on his work constructively with a focus on present challenges. Foust in his essay points out a dualism in Newbigin's epistemology. Newbigin applies Polanyi's epistemology of "tacit knowledge" and argues, that each participant in the dialogue can only speak from his or her own position. There is "no privileged position for knowing that is above all others. We must therefore pursue truth from that perspective (epistemology from below)" (Foust 2002, 161). On the other hand, Newbigin – like Polanyi himself – rejects a pluralistic, relativistic view of knowledge which one might conclude from the above position. "Newbigin also held that Christians had been given the ultimate meaning to the universe in the person Jesus Christ and that Scripture was testimony to that fact (thinking from above)" (Foust 2002, 161). Foust asserts that Newbigin moves from one position ("epistemology from below") to another position ("thinking from above") as the need arises. "Consequently when the position of thinking from below brings difficulties to Newbigin's position, he can (and does) simply move to the thinking-from-above perspective to solve the historical dilemma he faces without necessarily noting he has done so" (Foust 2002, 161). However this does not mean that Newbigin retreats to a position that can no longer be challenged. Quite to the contrary, he turns with his contribution to the hermeneutical community and presents it for further deliberation.

> [I]t was in and through the public debate that ideas and knowledge would gain strength and authority through the verification of others or would be diminished when sufficiently challenged in the arena of public debate. This was, of course, a Polanyian concept. The end result was that Newbigin was less concerned with producing a systematic theology than with making his thoughts accessible to a wide audience for the purpose of determining their merit and for adding to the authority of the tradition in which he saw himself. (Foust 2002, 161)

This epistemological dualism is an expression of Newbigin's commitment to and conviction of the truth of God's revelation on the one hand, and the realization of the contextuality of all knowledge on the other hand. However Newbigin does not refer to revelation in order to claim a superior position for himself. He recognizes the partiality of all human knowing and therefore commits himself and what he has to say to the hermeneutical community. Newbigin is convinced of an "eschatological verification." The "verification of the truth as found in Jesus Christ will not be revealed fully until the end of human history" (Foust 2002, 161). Using a term coined by George Hunsberger, Foust speaks here of an "eschatological epistemology" (Foust 2002, 162). However, he says, "Newbigin has left those of us who follow some epistemological work to do" (Foust 2002, 162).

Hunsberger and Goheen also have papers published in this collection. Hunsberger looks at the role of the Christian community for evangelism in a post-modern transition. He emphasizes the necessity for being (1) a true community, (2) a community that is committed to truth, and (3) a community that knows it is sent. In his section on commitment to truth he characterizes truth as being personal truth, perspectival truth, and practiced truth. He addresses the objections raised by the post-modern hermeneutics of suspicion and sees the church in the present challenged to present truth to the world as practiced truth, demonstrating the authenticity of truth in everyday life.

Goheen picks up the theme of his dissertation and calls for critical reflection on the alternative community model of the church. He cautions that the church must not become a "parallel community." The way to avoid this pitfall is to integrate an alternative community model with the understanding of the church as the firstfruits of renewed humankind.

> In other words, alternative community must be an image not only for the church gathered as community but also for the church dispersed in the world. It is this kind of ecclesiology that will lead to a ministerial leadership and ecclesial structures that will equip believers for their callings. In this, I believe, Lesslie Newbigin has left us with a challenge and some direction. (Goheen 2002b, 54)

Taber argues from the NT for the "Gospel as authentic meta-narrative" (Taber 2002). His concern is to point out a way for understanding the gospel as universal meta-narrative without on the one hand remaining stuck in a modern globalization paradigm nor on the other hand in a postmodern spirit giving up the idea of a unified view of humankind altogether. This concern of Taber for the "gospel as authentic meta-narrative" is one that he shares with Newbigin as the various references in Taber's paper illustrate.

Forrester writes about "Lesslie Newbigin as public theologian," pointing out the influence of the ecumenical biblical theology on Newbigin and Newbigin's contribution to the social and political issues of his time (Forrester 2002). This topic will be part of chapter five.

This collection of essays entails a great range of viewpoints, all looking at the question: Where do we go from here – "The way of mission after Newbigin"? The challenge remains to try to understand Newbigin and draw out the implications of his contribution for present and future challenges.

2.4. Hermeneutical Considerations

The spectrum of hermeneutical approaches is as broad as the spectrum of the interpretation of the kingdom of God. Thiselton presents an overview (Thiselton 1992, 556-619). Here I will limit myself to a brief summary of the critical realist paradigm.

2.4.1. Beyond the Deconstruction of Objectivity

Kirk in his introductory article in "To stake a claim. Mission and the Western crisis of knowledge" (Kirk and Vanhoozer 1999) provides a summary of the current tendencies in philosophy and epistemology. He identifies six trends that have resulted from the shattering of the assumption of objectivity: asserting a priority of ethics over epistemology, a preoccupation with language and its role in the process of knowing, the role of social construction in the process of knowing, a growing emphasis on anthropology (namely a reflection on the knowing subject), the challenge of the many and the one (pluralism and universality), and a higher degree of skepticism than before (Kirk 1999, 15-17). To the "Cartesian anxiety" (the loss of rationality as basis for all knowledge) another anxiety is added, namely the "Kantian anxiety." It is no longer possible to simply equate the real with what we know, or to equate it with the language that signifies what we know. "The 'Kantian' challenge is how to make sense of the notion of truth and the relation of language to the real world" (Kirk 1999, 20). As a result, "[t]he mind is not a mirror but a filter of nature. For post-Kantians, then, the predicament is that we construct the world with historically variable and culturally conditioned conceptual schemes" (Kirk 1999, 21).

In light of this deconstruction of "objectivity" the relationship between knowledge and reality needs to be redefined. Hiebert distinguishes between the positivist hermeneutics of modernity, the instrumentalist hermeneutics of post-modernity, and critical-realist hermeneutics that seeks to overcome the relativism of post-modernity (Hiebert 1994; Hiebert 1999).

A *positivistic hermeneutics* equates reality with signs. This approach neglects the subjective dimension of knowledge. It's limitations become especially obvious in a cross-cultural context, where the same reality is related to different signs and different mental images. Polanyi has shown that even the so-called objective knowledge of science rests on the subjective commitment of the researcher to the hermeneutical community and its traditions and methods. This recognition shatters the myth of purely objective knowledge.

Instrumentalist hermeneutics holds that the correlation between reality and sign is present only in the mind of the person. Meaning is defined not by a link between sign and signified, but simply by the differentiation between the different signs. The reference to the signified object is therefore arbitrary and not inherently linked to the sign. Meaning is no longer found in a text but only in the mind of the reader. Knowledge becomes purely subjective. Carried through consistently, this hermeneutical approach makes communication in fact impossible, because correspondence between meanings that are held by different people cannot be verified at all. This kind of verification is in fact not even wanted. Instrumentalism promotes a pluralism of meanings.

> So not only must the notion of univocal meaning in texts be abandoned, but because meaning finally resides in the interpreter, there are as many meanings as there are interpreters, even if interpreters are multiplied indefinitely. That means no one meaning can ever be thought to be superior to any other meaning; there is no objective basis on which to evaluate them. (Carson 1996, 74)

Critical realist hermeneutics overcomes the sharp contrast of the above approaches. It holds on to the correlation between sign and reality while at the same time recognizing the limitation of knowledge that the instrumentalist view has brought to our awareness. It deals with three, rather than two variables, namely: reality, sign, and mental image. Critical realism holds that mental images are not accurate photographs of reality, but rather maps that guide our understanding and help us gain a comprehensive view of reality. Maps are selective and in this sense reductionist in their representation of reality. However they reflect reality and can be tested against this reality. While their presentation of reality is only partial, they allow for a structured overview. Also, maps are compatible with other maps that portray the same reality. In other words, even though we know only partially, we can in fact know reality. And where we compare our maps of reality with the maps of others and test both of our maps for their correspondence to reality, we gain a more adequate and more comprehensive view of reality. Carson uses the mathematical example of the asymptote and summarizes:

> A curved line may approach a straight line asymptotically, never quite touching it but always getting closer, so close, in fact, that all of differential and integral calculus – that branch of mathematics without which it would have been impossible to put human beings on the moon – depends upon such models of closeness. The model is useful precisely because it never touches the axis. In exactly the same way, we may not aspire to absolute knowledge of the sort only Omniscience may possess, but the 'approximation' may be so good that it is adequate for placing human beings on the moon. The point of all such models is that although none of us ever knows any complicated thing exhaustively, we can know some things truly. Our confidence in what we know may not enjoy the certainty of Omniscience, but it is not condemned to futility. (Carson 1996, 121)

The characteristics of critical realism are threefold: (1) a commitment to a true correspondence between knowledge and reality; (2) a humble recognition that our knowledge is only partial; and (3) a commitment to a community approach to hermeneutics. The limitations of knowing only partially are best substituted and corrected by a community approach to understanding (see Hiebert 1994; Hiebert 1999).

Newbigin in one of his last writings makes a similar hermeneutical distinction between three approaches when he talks about different interpretations of the unity of the church. He says:

> Everything now depends on how we interpret this situation. One way is to settle for mutual recognition and coexistence, for a relationship of conviviality but not of total mutual commitment. This is the easy way, which evades the pain of mutual criticism and mutual correction. It calls for no reformation. It is cheap, and (one is bound to say) it almost inevitably tends to reduce the value of what it deals with. It risks making the question of truth less serious than it is.
>
> Another way, the opposite of this, is to insist that Christian doctrine is an integral whole, no part of which can be surrendered without corrupting the whole, or at least that there are "essential" elements that can never be compromised.
>
> But there is a third possibility, and it depends absolutely on the centrality of Christ and his atoning deed. It is to see the entire Christian church as a company that lives only by the grace of God to sinners, a company that does *not* possess in any of its divided parts the fullness of what is "essential" but that

God nevertheless in his mercy sustains as witness to and foretaste of his blessed reign.

> This third way of understanding creates the possibility and the necessity *both* of radical mutual criticism in light of what we believe to be God's intention for his church *and* of mutual acceptance as those who have been accepted by God in his mercy to those who fall short of his purpose. (93reit, 4)

Newbigin's first paragraph illustrates the understanding of the unity of the church according to the instrumentalist paradigm; his second paragraph illustrates the positivist paradigm; and his third paragraph corresponds to critical realist hermeneutics. In the text that follows Newbigin leaves no doubt that he sees the third option as the only valid approach to church unity. Without pushing the point too far, this paragraph may be seen as an expression of Newbigin's hermeneutical approach in general.

2.4.2. Critical Realist Hermeneutics and Theology

How does the critical realist paradigm apply to biblical hermeneutics and theology?

2.4.2.1. Critical Realist Hermeneutics Confirms That There Is "a Meaning in the Text."

Vanhoozer argues:

> It is possible to believe in a single correct interpretation without believing that one has full possession of it. There is conflict in interpretation because literary knowledge, like all knowledge, is provisional and open to correction. Yet it is only open to correction because there is an independent standard: determinate textual meaning. (Vanhoozer 1998, 300)

He adds: "Just how confident can we be as interpreters that we have discovered the meaning of the text rather than ourselves and our own projections? The short response is to say both that *our knowledge ... must be tempered by humility ..., and that our skepticism ... must be countered by conviction*" (Vanhoozer 1998, 462). Hunsberger states in a similar way:

> That is, much as we must come to agree with the postmodern critique of modernity's confidence in reason, and the postmodern assertion that there is no one rationally defensible version of the truth and that all our claims to know it and efforts to state it are particular and provisional, nevertheless it is inherent to Christian faith that something is believed with "universal intent" and believed to have correspondence to some truth that actually is so. (Hunsberger 2002, 101)

So critical realism starts with the premise that there is truth to be known. Regarding the process of how textual meaning can be determined, Vanhoozer draws on insights of speech-act theory. Speech-act theory sees three elements in the process of communication. Communication consists of a locutionary, illocutionary, and perlocutionary act. The locution of the text refers to its propositional content; the illocution of the text refers to its energy and direction; the perlocution of the text refers to its momentum (Vanhoozer 1998, 301). While the locution and illocution of a text are determined once and for all in the past ("meaning accomplished"), the perlocutionary force of the text requires the reader's response in order to be fulfilled ("meaning applied"). "When authors successfully enact their intentions, we can say *meaning accomplished*; when these meanings are brought to bear on other texts and contexts and so achieve perlocutionary effects, we should say *meaning applied*" (Vanhoozer 1998, 262). Vanhoozer refers to this as the distinction between "meaning" and "significance." He thus argues for the singularity of determinable meaning – with the recognition that the knowledge of this meaning is partial and correctible – and accepts a plurality of significance.

Through the distinction between the locutionary, illocutionary, and perlocutionary acts of speaking, speech-act theory allows a closer look at the different aspects of the hermeneutics of texts: the author's intention, the structure and genre of the text, and the reaction of the prospective reader, which the author intended.

Ricoeur in fact divides these into separate entities by stressing the decontextualization of the text from the author and the recontextualization of the text into the world of the reader. He distinguishes between meaning behind the text (presumed authorial intent) and meaning in front of the text (recontextualization to the horizon of the reader). For Ricoeur the text – through decontextualization – becomes independent of its author. "To begin with, writing renders the text autonomous with respect to the intention of the author. What the text signifies no longer coincides with what the author meant; henceforth, textual meaning and psychological meaning have different destinies" (Ricoeur and Thompson 1981, 139). While Ricoeur tries to overcome Schleiermacher's focus on the psyche of the author, he ends up with an autonomous text, disengaged from its author. The focus of hermeneutics then is the recontextualization of the text into the context of the reader. This is what Gadamer calls the "fusion of horizons" (Ricoeur and Thompson 1981, 62). Speech-act-theory – different from Ricoeur – allows the interpreter to hold the author, the text, and the reader together. It identifies meaning by looking at both content and genre of the text and thus determines its perlocutionary force. This allows for an understanding of what the author meant, without referring the interpreter to psychological divination. At the same time, it recognizes the role of the reader who needs to respond to the text in order for the perlocutionary dimension to be enacted. Speech-act-theory allows the interpreter to take into account the post-modern critique of positivist hermeneutics, as well as the post-modern emphasis on the importance of the reader, without renouncing the meaning in the text. It upholds the critical realist claim that there is meaning – truth – to be known.

2.4.2.2. Critical Realist Hermeneutics Is Aware of Contexts.

Critical realist hermeneutics calls for a study of all historical and cultural contexts involved, that is of the context of the author, the context of the original reader, the context of the current reader, and – in the situation of a missionary encounter – the context of the person to whom the missionary wishes to communicate. Hunsberger speaks of this when he says that truth is perspectival:

> [T]ruth is perspectival. This is different from acknowledging that our knowing is always partial, or tainted. It surely is both. But to say that truth is perspectival is to affirm that it is inherent in the circumstances of life, created as they are by the one who is the truth, that human existence is by nature particular, contextual, and relational, and all knowing is relative to the language and culture creations that human societies establish, adapt, and transmit. (Hunsberger 2002, 102)

This, however, does not result in a relativistic plurality of knowledge and meaning. It is here that the hermeneutical community plays a central role.

2.4.2.3. Critical Realist Hermeneutics Emphasizes the Hermeneutical Community.

Hunsberger, in his discussion of perspectival truth, continues that there is no "necessary absolute relativity (which would be a contradiction in terms, at any rate). Rather the relativity of knowing forces a communal and dialogical approach to all truth seeking" (Hunsberger 2002, 102). The hermeneutical community includes both the global church and the church in its historical dimension. This emphasis on the global and the historical community of the church is also found in Newbigin's writings. He was strongly committed to the tradition of the church, and strongly committed to the ecumenical unity of the church. It was to this community that he submitted his contribution for further debate.

2.4.2.4. Critical Realist Hermeneutics Thinks Cross-disciplinarily.

In the critical-realist paradigm different disciplines of study are neither opposed to one another, nor unrelated. If they look at the same reality, their findings – as far as they correspond to reality – necessarily complement each other. This is true for different theological approaches (e.g. systematic theology with a synchronic focus and biblical theology with a diachronic focus). It is also true for the relationship between theology and social sciences or natural sciences. Again, Newbigin demonstrates this cross-disciplinary thinking in the way he draws on the writings of for instance Polanyi and makes his findings an integral part of his own argument.

In summary, a critical realist approach to theological studies affirms that there is truth to be known. At the same time it is aware of the limitations of human knowledge and therefore humbly follows the lead of God's Spirit and seeks the community of sisters and brothers who are committed to the same Lord, in order to grow together towards a better understanding of truth. In the words of Frances Young:

> We may have proper confidence in what is revealed in Christ only as long as we recognize that inevitably God's truth is but dimly and inadequately grasped. We need to recognize with humility that we do not have a God's-eye view.

That must mean admitting a kind of practical relativism. Yet we affirm one God who created one universe. Ultimately truth is not relative but universal. It's our knowledge of what is universal which is relatively limited. That balanced perspective is essential. (Young 2002, 91)

Final verification and full knowledge of truth is eschatological in the sense that it can be fully known only when God's story with the world is coming to its end (Foust 2002, 162).

A careful study of Newbigin's writings will confirm a similar hermeneutical approach. At this point the hermeneutical concern is, however, simply introduced to clarify my own position as a researcher, not to make any conclusive statement on Newbigin's hermeneutical position.

3. Data and Analysis

This section gives a brief outline of the data I have analyzed and the structure of the dissertation.

3.1. Primary Data

The primary data for my research are articles, books, and manuscripts written by Lesslie Newbigin. Detailed bibliographies of Newbigin's writings are available at Hunsberger 1998a, 280-304, Goheen 2000, 443-462, and Foust et al. 2002, 252-287. "Newbigin Net" continues to publish electronic copies of Newbigin's materials for research purposes in the Internet at *http://www.newbigin.net*. The best source for unpublished materials is the Orchard Learning Resources Centre of the University of Birmingham (U.K). It has an archive collection of Newbigin's correspondence and manuscripts (see *http://www.olrc.bham.ac.uk/*).

I have delimited my research to Newbigin's writings. Most of Newbigin's published materials I have been able to access. Access to unpublished materials, however, was limited. With regard to the research topic I do not think that this is of any real significance. It will become clear that Newbigin's thinking is consistent throughout his publishing career. I therefore do not expect any changes in his thinking as expressed in his unpublished materials.

3.2. Data Analysis

This dissertation is a qualitative analysis of theological literature in its historical context. The method of data analysis builds on the hermeneutical principles outlined above. For the analysis this has the following consequences:

First, my goal is to reach as close an understanding of Newbigin's thought as possible. I will pay close attention to Newbigin's terminology and concepts in order to try to understand him on his own terms rather than through a grid which is imposed from outside.

Second, I will pay attention to the historical and theological contexts in which Newbigin wrote. Since his writings grew out of specific circumstances, the influence of the context can be assumed to be significant.

Third, I will try to further clarify Newbigin's position and its implications by relating and comparing his ideas to the work of other scholars. This corresponds to Newbigin's own practice, who understood himself and his contribution as one voice in the community of scholars.

The goal of this research project is a descriptive analysis of the topic in Newbigin's writings with the hope that Newbigin's understanding can then inform our own understanding of the relationship between the kingdom of God and mission.

3.3. Structure of the Dissertation

The main body of this dissertation consists of four chapters. In chapters two to four I look at Newbigin's writings with a special focus on those topics that relate to this study. In chapter five I will point out how the eschatological framework serves as a central point of reference for Newbigin's theology of mission, his theology of religions, as well as his epistemology in general.

Chapter two is structured diachronically. Here I look in detail at Newbigin's early writings. It is interesting to observe that the main themes of his early writings all deal with subjects related to this research project. Newbigin gave lectures on the kingdom of God and contrasted it with the "idea of progress" in 1941. He wrote on the character of the church in light of the formation of the CSI, a process in the 1940s in which he played a central role and which strengthened his ecumenical convictions deeply. He then was a member of the committee that prepared the second assembly of the WCC in Evanston 1954 on the topic "the Christian hope," a focus on the eschatological dimension of the Christian faith. And as associate general secretary of the WCC he carefully observed the developments that followed the collapse of the colonial empires in the 1960s and tried to interpret these in light of a biblical view of the history of humankind.

On each of these occasions we find him speaking and writing on such topics as the kingdom of God, the unity and mission of the church, the eschatological hope of the Christian faith, and trying to see the footsteps of God's dealing in secular history. Newbigin was led to all of these topics in the course of his ministry assignments. Interestingly enough they all contribute directly to this study. Since we are dealing with early writings here, it is advisable to take a close look in order to see if and how some fundamental themes are expressed at this point and how these lines are drawn out in later writings.

To cut off chapter two at the time around the mid 1960s is in a sense arbitrary. I chose to do so for two reasons. First, after I had read his early writings I was surprised to find that they focused on themes that are directly related to my study. The diachronic reading led me to discover a series of topical foci that not only laid out the framework for my study but also supported the preliminary assumption about the importance of an eschatological understanding of the kingdom for Newbigin's understanding of mission. Discovering the basic markers of the thematic framework in Newbigin's early publications was the reason to cut off chapter two at a point at which those themes were thoroughly introduced. There was a second reason. It became obvious that at some point it was necessary to switch from a diachronic study to a synchronic study. Otherwise the details would be overwhelming and the study would lose clarity. Based on these considerations I chose to switch from a diachronic to a synchronic study of Newbigin's writings around the mid 1960s, at a time when the major subjects for this research project (kingdom, church, eschatological hope, history) were introduced. So with chapter three I continue my analysis in a synchronic mode, keeping the historic background of the various writings in mind but summarizing them in a synchronic view. Here I concentrate on the four major subjects outlined in chapter two and follow up on how Newbigin solidifies his thinking. While I continue to look at four issues (kingdom of God, church, eschatological hope, and God's involvement in history) I choose to summarize the third and fourth subject under one heading ("The eschatological hope – God's story with his world"). This allows for greater clarity in the presentation and avoids duplication.

Chapter four gives a summary of Newbigin's theology of mission with a special focus on the eschatological tension of the kingdom. Finally, chapter five looks at the implications of the eschatological framework for Newbigin's understanding and practice of mission. I will show that for Newbigin's theology the eschatological orientation towards the future fulfillment of the kingdom and the focus on the present king are foundational and provide the framework for his understanding of mission.

I have deliberately chosen to quote Newbigin extensively, because I find it important to listen to his specific way of expressing things. This is important because Newbigin always refused to be described by common categories. By focusing on his way of expression I hope to further an understanding of his work that is true to his own intention.

I have not included a biographical sketch of Newbigin's life. For that I refer the reader to a brief article by West in the *Biographical Dictionary of Christian Missions* (West 1998) as well as to articles by Conway (Conway 1994) and Hunsberger (Hunsberger 1999), and, of course, to Newbigin's autobiography (85ua, 93ua).

Chapter 2

The Kingdom of God in Newbigin's Writings (Diachronic Analysis of His Early Writings)

As a student Lesslie Newbigin came into contact with the SCM in Cambridge. In this context he made a commitment to Christ. From the beginning his faith was shaped in a truly ecumenical, even cosmic perspective. Newbigin recalls:

> As I lay awake a vision came to my mind, perhaps arising from something I had read a few weeks before by William Temple. It was a vision of the cross, but it was the cross spanning the space between heaven and earth, between ideals and present realities, and with arms that embraced the whole world. I saw it as something which reached down to the most hopeless and sordid of human misery and yet promised life and victory. I was sure that night, in a way I had never been before, that this was the clue that I must follow if I were to make any kind of sense of the world. ...
>
> I was beginning to have a thrilling sense of sharing in a worldwide Christian enterprise which was commanding the devotion of men and women whose sheer intellectual and spiritual power was unmistakable. I became, even as a second-year undergraduate, a reader of the *International Review of Missions*, and the Christian faith into which I was growing was ecumenical from the beginning. (85ua, 12-13)

This ecumenical perspective shaped his ministry as missionary and bishop in India (1936-1958 and 1965-1974), his involvement in the IMC and the WCC (1958-1965) as well as his active engagement with the culture of the West during his retirement years (1974-1998).

Newbigin always considered himself a missionary. It is from this position that his writings need to be understood. They grew out of bible studies and lectures prepared in the course of his ministry. This gives his writings a special flavor, but does in no way diminish their academic quality. (Newbigin was granted honorary doctoral degrees from 6 universities.)

Newbigin appeals to a wide spectrum of readers from evangelicals to liberals. He consistently refused to be categorized himself. Out of his truly ecumenical view of the church as being one in essence Newbigin refused to take sides in this division. This is not to say that he compromised his position or evaded questions. He simply could not perceive the church of Christ divided into factions (see 94awis, 104). Even more so because he saw the categories "liberal" and "fundamentalist," as he calls them, derived from a specific Western epistemology which needs to be challenged by the gospel.

Newbigin reflected critically not only on the intellectual, cultural and theological questions of his time, but also on the foundations of the debates themselves. He consistently refused to answer those questions which – according to his understanding – the bible itself does not answer clearly. And he called attention to the fact that the questions we ask are instrumental in shaping the development of the debate as a whole.

> As always, everything depends upon how we formulate the question. If we insist that the Bible must answer our questions in the way we formulate them (whether about the destiny of the soul or about the future of our society), we shall find ourselves faced either with silence or with contradiction. If, on the other hand, we suspend our questions and try to listen to the way in which the Bible puts the issue, I think we may find that we are not shut up to what seem like impossibilities. We must suspend the argument for a moment and try to attend to the way the Bible portrays the human situation. (88cfwr, 331)

So Newbigin walked a narrow line, careful not be caught in the paradigm of the present age, instead concentrating on the perspective with which the bible itself frames the issues.

In light of this it becomes clear that it will not be an easy task to depict Newbigin's view adequately. Newbigin refuses neat categories and the researcher has to be aware of the danger of interpreting Newbigin's writings from his or her own perspective, imposing one's own categories on his work. With this danger in mind, I attempt to walk through and summarize the major elements of Newbigin's view of the eschatological tension of God's kingdom and its relevance to his understanding of mission.

1. Early Emphases

In 1938 when Newbigin had returned to England for two years because of injuries from a bus accident in India, he wrote a short essay for the Spectator, the last in a series of articles entitled "Can I be a Christian?" This short article already reveals a number of themes that would become central in Newbigin's later writings. For one, he refuses to domesticate the gospel as a mere answer to human problems. He insists that the gospel "is a fresh and original word addressed to [man] from beyond the range of his problems by God, his maker. It is therefore bound to appear, in the first place, irrelevant" (38cibc). This emphasis to let the gospel itself set the agenda and to refuse to make the human question the starting point of theology is characteristic for all of Newbigin's work. Second, Newbigin insists that the question of truth and falsehood is not a matter of taste. "No one, whatever his protestations, really believes that the difference between truth and falsehood is of the same kind as the difference between black and white coffee. No one is without some awareness of the authoritative claim of goodness and truth to be obeyed" (38cibc). This fundamental conviction about the nature of truth has shaped Newbigin's engagement with Hinduism in India and with religious pluralism in general. Related to this conviction is Newbigin's emphasis on the character of the gospel as historical fact, the "one unique saving act of God, by which history is cut in two." That is the third fundamental theme which appears here and runs through Newbigin's work. The cross of Christ is "this unique act of God in history whereby forgiveness is freely offered to me and to all men." Newbigin acknowledges that this view is "regarded as intolerable by the majority of my contemporaries" for different reasons, one being that "such unique significance" cannot be attached to "any single historical event" (38cibc). It is this actual involvement of God in human history, however, which represents the uniqueness of the gospel. This thought is developed later by Newbigin in his booklet "What is the gospel?" written for students in India:

> Hindu thought for the most part conceives God as the timeless Absolute, for whom history can have no real meaning. For such thought, revelation is given in mystical experiences, when the soul sinks between time and circumstance and finds unity with the unchanging One. Particular events cannot reveal God: they belong to the world of variety and change which hides God from our eyes. To identify God's revelation with a particular person or event is simply to misunderstand what revelation is.
>
> In the sharpest possible contrast to this, the Bible conceives God as personal will, actively engaged in forwarding His purpose in human history. Thus revelation is through concrete historical events and there is no revelation apart from such events. It is through what He does that He shows what He is. The Biblical view of God is thus precisely contradictory to the Hindu view of God at its central point. (42wig, 5; cited in Wainwright 2000, 61)

The involvement of God in human history is only possible because God is personal. This emphasis on the personal character of God is something Newbigin shares with his teacher John Oman (see e.g. Oman 1960, 75ff). The fundamental conviction that God is personal, that he has acted and is involved in human history, is foundational for what Newbigin has to say on the kingdom of God later on.

In another early essay (37cfmw) Newbigin deals with Macmurray's book "Freedom in the modern world." Newbigin looks at the role and the understanding of duty in Christian ethics. He sees duty as belonging

> to the road which Christians must travel, but not to the goal to which they go. Since it concerns what ought to be, but is not yet, it belongs to the world of imperfection, but this does not mean that it can be forthwith discarded by those who have breathed the air of the Kingdom of Heaven in which all Creation shall obey God's will as a long response in which duty need have no place. (37cfmw, 91-92)

The basis for Christian obligation and duty is not an impersonal law, but the will of a personal God. It is this will of God, not a utopian vision of what we may hope someday will be, which forms the counterpart to the imperfection of the present. It is this personal will which will bring about the future state that it wills. This future state of "perfect communion with a personal God known to us in Christ as infinitely loving" is "the day of the revealing of the sons of God for which the earnest expectation of the Creation waits, and of whose liberty we have now the foretaste" (37cfmw, 92).

Newbigin in his brief reference to the "Kingdom of Heaven" uses the term in a future sense. But he places it in the tension between what "ought to be but is not yet" and speaks of a "foretaste" of what is to come, of "breathing the air of the Kingdom of Heaven." From his earliest writings on we find this tension between the present as foretaste amidst imperfection on the one hand, and a final fulfillment in the future on the other. The key to the understanding of this tension is the will of a personal God, who will lead to fulfillment that which he has set forth to do. It is this presence of a personal will which distinguishes the kingdom of God from all ideologies, and which forbids its reduction to a mere mechanical law of progress.

Newbigin at that time could still speak of a "Christian understanding of progress."

> This picture of the world in terms of an upwelling, blind process or urge is very much in the ascendant in our time. It underlies the Nazi philosophy of race and blood, and the Marxist materialist interpretation of history. It is profoundly different from the Christian understanding of progress, which is based on the awareness that God can speak to us even in the sinful present, summoning us forward through the unconditional claims of duty to a better future. For such a faith, human progress is seen as from start to finish a response to the divine summons. (37cfmw, 66)

Wainwright observes a difference here to Newbigin's later writings, in which Newbigin "insisted on a much more radical break between human capacity and achievement and 'the kingdom of God'" (Wainwright 2003, ix). That is well observed. However we need to recognize that even here Newbigin clearly distinguishes a Christian understanding of progress from the secular idea of progress. The key distinction is the centrality of a personal God who is not just a "God of personal religion" but is "the sovereign Lord of the world" (37cfmw, 67). Already we see Newbigin's strong concern that God must not be domesticated into a private area of personal salvation but that he is seen for what he is, Lord of the universe and as such Lord of human history. "Human progress" in this context is not the result of a natural evolution or of human achievements but is the result of the response to the divine summons.

2. "The Kingdom of God and the Idea of Progress" (1941)

This theme of "progress" is revisited by Newbigin critically in his Bangalore lectures in 1941. When Newbigin was invited to give these lectures at the United Theological College, he took the opportunity to work further on the ideas that had occupied him during his time as a student at Westminster. In his autobiography, after describing what he calls "a turning point" in his theological journey as a student at Cambridge, Newbigin says:

> At the end of the exercise I was much more of an evangelical than a liberal. ... But this shift in no way implied a lessening of commitment to political and social issues. I was in fairly frequent touch with Joseph Oldham and his work in preparation for the Oxford Conference on 'Church, Community and State', and in my last year led a study on 'The Kingdom of God and History' in which I tried to get leaders of the University political societies involved. This became the focus of my most passionate theological interest towards the end of the course. (85ua, 31)

The Bangalore lectures play an important role in understanding Newbigin's view of the kingdom of God. Wainwright who edited and published the material in 2003 says in his introduction: "Lesslie himself pressed on me the significance of these Bangalore lectures as his first full treatment of themes that would continue to occupy him throughout his life" (Wainwright 2003, viii). In line with his understanding of God's real and personal involvement in the history of humankind Newbigin holds to "the fully real character of biblical eschatology." Wainwright summarizes Newbigin's position: "Newbigin asserted both the fully real character of biblical eschatology, versus the reductively symbolic, and the constitutive value given by God to the present stage of salvation history as the prolepsis, but only the prolepsis, of the End" (Wainwright 2003, ix).

2.1. Lecture I

In the first lecture Newbigin defines the idea of progress as

> the idea that human society has become better and will go on becoming better. It is the idea that ignorance and sin can be and will be gradually eliminated from human life, until a time shall come when men shall live together in perfect brotherly love, equipped with perfect knowledge. (41kgip, 5)

He emphasizes:

> Note that the idea of *man's* moral growth, and *man's* mastery over the world, are here central. Man is to become god-like; earth is to become paradise. And note also that this consummation is presented not as a hope only, or an aspiration, but as something which *shall* be – a destiny. (41kgip, 5)

This view of progress can only develop where history is understood as real and linear. The emphasis on the real character of history corresponds to the biblical understanding of history. "The biblical interpretation of history as a real process in which real events happen, events that is to say which have significance for God Himself" (41kgip, 8). With regard to the linear character of history, Newbigin will later qualify that. For the moment he speaks of the sense of direction in human history and how this is rooted in Hebrew thinking.

> Among the ancient peoples whose thought has come down to us, so far as I know, only the Hebrews and the Persians held a view of history from which the idea of progress could conceivably have emerged. For both of these, history was a real process, with a real goal. But that goal was 'The Day of the Lord,'

not a natural consummation brought about by forces within human history, but a final victory of God over the powers of evil, and a final establishment of His Kingdom, His effective rule. Unlike the Greeks, therefore, the Hebrews and the Persians looked for their golden age to the future rather than to the past. (41kgip, 9)

Over time, however, the understanding of the kingdom changed into a completely other-worldly view, which continued throughout the Medieval church, where the kingdom of heaven was understood as the realization of the final hope beyond death. "There was no expectation, and no place for any expectation, that the world would become a better place" (41kgip, 10).

The modern idea of progress then grew out of the rationalism of the 18th and the romanticism of the 19th century. Its basic idea is "the belief that history is a story of development from the crude to the refined, from the less to the more perfect" (41kgip, 11). The development is seen as automatic and inevitable. It becomes a law of life. Darwinism is one expression of this belief. The success of the capitalist system with its rapid increase of wealth simply added momentum to this optimistic view of history.

Newbigin challenges this "dogma of progress" by asking the question by which criteria development is evaluated.

> If man is essentially good, then growth in man's knowledge and in man's lordship of earth and sky and sea and air is progress. But if man is not good, but essentially sinful, this growth of power will lead him into deeper disaster. Thus unless this very large question is settled, the dogma of progress derives no clear support from the fact that knowledge is cumulative. (41kgip, 13)

Not all proponents of progress argue from a natural law. Others simply place their expectation of future progress on the observation of progress in the past. "[P]rogress has in fact taken place and may therefore reasonably be expected to go on taking place" (41kgip, 14). Again Newbigin argues with a reference to the paradoxical character of the human being. While he does not deny the possibility of nobility and change for the better, he also does not close his eyes to the possibility of changes for the worse.

> The true reading of history seems to be this, that every new increase of man's mastery over earth and sea and sky opens up possibilities not only of nobler good, but also of baser and more horrible evil, and that even those movements of social progress which can point to real achievement in the bettering of society have to be put side by side with these equally real movements of degeneration which have sometimes actually arisen out of the same social improvements. (41kgip, 16)

Again others hold on to the idea of progress "as a *faith* in the possibility of a better world in the future" (41kgip, 16). The betterment of the human situation here becomes the utopian goal for which humanity strives. Newbigin's critique focuses on the devaluation of human beings as mere tools in the process of building a perfect society. If people suffer and work for the betterment of society which lies in the distant future, "we are making them means to an end which does not include their own personal fruition – in which they can have no part at all" (41kgpi, 17). As we will see later, this becomes an important argument for Newbigin against dissolving the eschatological tension towards a utopian world-immanent view of God's kingdom.

2.2. Lecture II

In his second lecture Newbigin looks at two different views of Christian eschatology.

> One is the belief that this world is going to be gradually subdued by the Spirit of Christ, working through His servants, until at last God's rule is complete and perfect, His will is done in [sic] earth as it is in heaven. This belief is often expressed in terms of the phrase 'the Kingdom of God,' and the prayer 'thy Kingdom come' is understood as a prayer that this gradual process may be hastened. ...
>
> On the other hand there is the view that the true object of hope for a Christian is a state of being beyond death, in which he will share with the whole communion of saints in the eternal bliss of the vision of God. (41kgip, 19)

These two different views of eschatology exemplify the controversy between the "social gospel" and what Newbigin calls the "individual gospel." And Newbigin argues,

> there can be no doubt, historically speaking, that the popular Christian doctrine of the Kingdom of God, interpreted as meaning the progressive realization of good in the life of the world, is simply a Christianized version of the secular idea of progress. ... We must, I think, candidly admit that the idea of earthly progress towards a Kingdom of God on earth cannot possibly be derived from the Gospels by themselves, but is the interpretation of the gospel teaching by men who came to it with minds molded as to their whole preconceptions by the secular idea of progress. I think that is simply an historically true statement. (41kgip, 21)

This is an example how Newbigin critically examines the hermeneutical key by which a specific interpretation is formed. The modern idea of progress becomes the lens through which the biblical concept of the kingdom is interpreted.

Newbigin criticizes both views of the kingdom as they stand independent from each other. The view of the kingdom of God as the establishment of a perfect society on earth brings with it a split in the future hope. Public eschatology and private eschatology are split in two. The kingdom is understood as the "perfect society on earth from which all but the last generations are shut out, and where they enjoy the perfection which they have not striven for but simply walked into," while on the other hand "all the preceding generations who are balked of that earthly kingdom which they strove for enjoy, as a kind of reward for their labors and as a substitute for their disappointed hopes, the bliss of heaven" (41kgip, 22). That amounts to an instrumentalization of these former generations. Apart from that, Newbigin argues, there simply is no "perfect human society under the biological and spiritual conditions of human life as we know them. As long as man is a biological organism subject to the

Chapter 2: The Kingdom of God in Newbigin's Early Writings

usual law of decay and death, then perfection as our spirits thirst for is unattainable" (41kgip, 22). That is Newbigin's critique of the idea of a gradual establishment of the kingdom of God in this world.

On the other hand, the idea of the "individual gospel" is not true to the Christian concept of salvation either. It narrows the focus on individual redemption; and it sees the characteristic of redemption as being saved *from* the world. However the biblical understanding of salvation is corporate in nature, not individualistic. And its focus is on the redemption *of* the world (41kgip, 23-24). Also, the individualistic view robs human history of its meaning.

> According to this view, the significance of life in this world is exhaustively defined as the training of individual souls for heaven. Thus there can be no connected purpose running through history as a whole, but only a series of disconnected purposes for each individual life. History, on this view, would have no goal, no *telos:* it could only have, so to speak, a full stop when the last individual soul had left it for the heavenly world and its business as a training ground for souls was done. (41kgip, 24)

This individualization of hope renders the gospel meaningless to the challenges of the human situation in modern society. Today the majority of relationships are no longer direct and personal but require complex social and political control. Newbigin concludes: "Somehow or other we have to find a view which does justice to both aspects of the problem – individual and social – and which resolves the apparent contradictions between them" (41kgip, 26).

Newbigin closes his second lecture by summarizing a few central aspects of NT eschatology. He begins by outlining the Jewish background for understanding the kingdom of God which believes in God's present rule in heaven and awaits his rule on earth for the future. This eschatological coming of God's rule on earth will replace the current earthly order, abolish corruption and death, and establish the sovereignty of God on earth (41kgip, 27). Here the tension between the presence of the kingdom and its future is still understood as the dualism of heaven and earth. God's rule is present now in the transcendent kingdom. It will become reality on earth only in the future. But the hope that is associated with this eschatological awaiting of God's rule is corporate in nature.

> Note that this is essentially a corporate hope. ... It is not universalist, for the prelude to it is the destruction of the organized forces of wickedness, but neither is it individualist. It is social and cosmic, concerning men as a whole, and not only men but the whole created world also. (41kgip, 27)

What is new in the NT view of God's kingdom is that the eschatological future has become present in the person of Jesus Christ.

> [T]he central proclamation of the New Testament is that in Christ the new age has already dawned. In the words of the very first proclamation of the gospel, "The Kingdom of God has come near." In Christ the powers of the new age are at work. The domain of Heaven has touched that of earth and God's rule is actually being exercised in the world through Jesus. Those who accept Him come within the sphere of operations of the powers of the Kingdom: they may in fact

> be said to have been translated out of the present age into the new age which is to come. The new age is no longer something in the distant future. It is already present proleptically. Christians have already, as it is said, tasted the powers of the age to come.
>
> Or, using the metaphor of space instead of that of time – they are said to be a colony of heaven, an outpost of the transcendent Kingdom of Heaven within the ordinary world of men. (41kgip, 27)

So in the coming of Jesus Christ we experience the coming of the future, the fulfillment of the eschatological expectation. Eschatology becomes reality. Here Newbigin necessarily has to concern himself with Dodd's realized eschatology. Realized eschatology emphasizes that the last things are no longer matters of a distant future; they are realized facts. Newbigin, however, sees both a present realization and a future realization of eschatology in the NT. He therefore balances Dodd's realized eschatology with a futurist eschatology. "The phrase 'realized eschatology' can only be used properly if the word 'eschatology' is, so to speak, put in inverted commas. For obviously, in the strict sense, the last things have not yet come to pass: the world still goes on" (41kgip, 28). Based on this synopsis of realized eschatology and futurist eschatology Newbigin critiques Dodd:

> This point is worth making because Dodd seems to deplore futurist eschatology as a declension from the genuine eschatology of the Gospels and of Jesus, which was realized eschatology. Some kind of futurist eschatology there had to be and must always be. Its character was necessarily governed by what they had already tasted of the powers of the age to come, but it is unquestionable that the first Christians did look forward as well as back. (41kgip, 28)

Thus Newbigin from the beginning sees the tension in the NT between a present realization of the eschaton and a future realization. He closes his second presentation by pointing out three characteristics of NT eschatology:

> Firstly, it carries on the Old Testament belief in a cosmic renewal or restoration. It is neither to an otherworldly heaven, nor to a gradual improvement of earth that the New Testament looks forward, but to a divine act by which all created things are to be renewed. (41kgip, 28)

Newbigin speaks here of a new "human commonwealth with all its appurtenances newly created according to the divine will" (41kgip, 28). The OT belief is only modified insofar as in Jesus Christ "the character of God's rule has been revealed," and that in Jesus "the powers of the new Kingdom are already at work."

"The second main point to be noted about the New Testament eschatology is that the full establishment of the Kingdom is first of all a day of judgment" (41kgip, 29). All men will be judged according to their deeds and the final decision will be made about the admission to or exclusion from the kingdom. And thirdly, Newbigin points to the role which death and resurrection play.

> In the third place, according to the New Testament eschatology the relation between our present life in this world and our life in the new world of the King-

dom is understood in terms of death and resurrection. The resurrection of Christ from the dead is itself the proof of God's purpose for those who believe in Christ. (41kgip, 29)

Life in the kingdom is not simply an extension of this life.

> This life is under sentence of death. No conceivable extension of it could fit it for participation in the new kingdom. It is doomed to die – to see corruption complete its work. The physical frame, the personality as we understand the term, all achievements in personal character and in social effort – all is doomed to be lost in the dust of history. But yet, by a miracle of which the sprouting of corn from the buried seed is a faint analogy, a new life is given by God – a resurrected life fit for the new age. (41kgip, 30)

These characteristics of biblical eschatology remain important for Newbigin throughout his life. Biblical eschatology is looking forward to cosmic renewal – neither to an otherworldly heaven nor to a gradual improvement of earth. The establishment of the kingdom requires the judgment on all human beings and all their deeds. And this renewal will take place only through death and resurrection.

2.3. Lecture III

Newbigin in his third lecture deals with a number of objections to the idea of a literal last day. In a first section he criticizes Dodd's view of realized eschatology. He agrees with Dodd on the eschatological nature of the kingdom of God as well as on the fact that the eschaton always bears on our present action. His point of criticism is that Dodd makes the eschaton merely symbolic by denying a literal future fulfillment.

> Dodd brings out with the utmost clarity the fact that eschatology is fundamental to biblical thought and for the thought of Jesus. But in interpreting eschatology exhaustively as realized eschatology, he makes it formal and symbolic rather than factual. In Jesus, he says, the eschaton entered into actual human history. And the eschaton is always present as judgment, death, and resurrection for each moment of history. It is a new, vertical dimension by which history is constantly being judged and re-created. Thus the Christian's duty is not to rest hope on the unrealized future: the future can give us nothing that we have not already got. Our duty is to seek perfection now at every moment in concrete obedience to the will of God. By so doing one is living in the eschatological order. …
>
> In all this it is quite clear that the eschaton has ceased to be, literally, the end of history – that is to say, an unrealized future event – and has become exclusively a symbol for certain spiritual experiences of the Christian life. (41kgip, 32-33)

Newbigin does not reject the idea that the eschaton bears upon our present life. But he argues that it can do so only because there is a real future that casts its shadow backwards across time into the present.

> Now it is of course plain that the only significance of eschatology, as of any other doctrine, is its bearing upon actual life and thought now. The eschaton, the end, enters into our present experience by qualifying all present action; that is its significance. But the point is whether it does not lose that significance unless it be also a fact which is really going to happen. ... Only if there be real belief that an end is coming, will that end qualify what goes before it with the peculiar beliefs and feelings which we call eschatological. The eschatological in Christian experience is the shadow of the eschaton cast backwards across time, but if the eschaton is itself non-existent, then the shadow must disappear. (41kgip, 33-34)

Newbigin uses as a comparison the certainty of death as a future event that brings with it an awareness of our mortality, which bears significance for our every day lives. "Mortality is a present fact because death is a future certainty in the same way, it seems to me, that all talk about eschatology as an element in Christian thinking is a mere beating of the air, unless it be really the case that some day there is really going to be an eschaton" (41kgip, 34).

Newbigin follows up on the question of why the idea of a real end of history is rejected. He sees the influence of Greek philosophy in "the belief that time cannot be a reality for God" (41kgip, 34). God is seen as supra-temporal being, transcending time. Any talk of temporality in relation to God must therefore be symbolic. From this it follows that eschatology as the goal of God's involvement with the world must also be understood symbolically, not as an expression of real time.

Newbigin counters this symbolic understanding of time with two arguments. First, he says, "[w]e all believe that God can alter the future. ... We do not believe that God can alter the past (Aquinas). It involves self-contradiction. Therefore past and future are radically different for God Himself" (41kgip, 36). Newbigin's second argument is that time is essential for understanding spiritual life to a degree that space is not.

> You cannot conceive spiritual life except in temporal terms. For example, repentance. After doing some wrong, you mentally turn away from it and try to set it right. After is not symbolic but literal. ... If you reverse the temporal order – apologize first and do the evil deed afterwards – then the spiritual fact is different, not repentance but hypocrisy. (41kgip, 36)

Newbigin therefore concludes that time must be understood literally. Not that it would make time absolute, to set it above God. He sees time as part of God's creation which is as real for him as the rest of his creation.

> For God it [time] is real, but it is ultimately subject to Him. We may conceive eternity as the completion of His work, when His purpose is accomplished and succession is no more, and God rests. ... When His work is done, He rests. His working is time – real for Him, but subject to Him; real for us and not subject to us. His rest is eternity. (41kgip, 37)

Newbigin does not allow the Greek philosophical understanding of time to determine the biblical understanding of time and eschatology. From this perspective Newbigin holds on to both the literal fulfillment of a future eschaton and its significance for the present.

> The oft repeated phrase that in the Christian life the Kingdom of God is already proleptically at work means just this: the prolepsis is not a metaphysical marvel like some recent so-called experiments with time. It is the self-communication of God's will, grasped by faith here and now, which enables us already to live in the light of its final goal. (41kgip, 37-38)

The view of a personal God acting in real history is foundational for Newbigin's interpretation of biblical eschatology. Where time and the eschaton are understood as real and not merely symbolic, eschatology also includes a literal understanding of the final judgment.

> Now what does this mean? It is a statement about present spiritual fact; thus far we can agree with Dodd. It is a fact relevant now at every moment. But is it only that? Look at the phrase 'the final judgment': 'final' is a temporal phrase; it means last of a series in time. To say that the final judgment is that of God is to say that at the end of the temporal process God will judge and that after that there will be no appeal. (41kgip, 41)

The idea of a future final judgment is also necessary in order to make sense of the moral dilemma of the present. If there were no future final judgment, the present experience that evil succeeds and good fails remains unresolved and is ultimately unbearable. "I do not think the conflict between what is and what ought to be is spiritually bearable unless we believe that somehow, sometime, it is going to be resolved. And I think that the word 'ought to be' has in it also, as an undertone of meaning, 'ultimately shall be'" (41kgip, 40). Newbigin thus rejects the understanding that in Christ the idea of divine punishment is superseded. With Tillich he sees the death of Christ not as the eschaton, but as the "center of history" (41kgip, 43). That means the future dimension of the eschatological hope is not dissolved into the present. Instead, denying the literal future fulfillment of NT eschatology would mean "to write off hope ... as a misunderstanding" (41kgip, 39).

We have already seen that Newbigin does not understand history as the gradual growth of goodness over the powers of evil. Instead he understands the historical developments as real growth of both goodness and evil. The end of history is therefore neither the arrival at a perfect state of humanity nor an arbitrary cutoff by God which arrests the growth of goodness. It must be understood in light of the conflict between good and evil which calls for a final vindication of goodness against all evil, where evil is finally eradicated.

> We have accepted rather the view that history is a growth of good and evil side by side, a real growth of good – a real attainment of progressively higher goods, but along with this an equally real growth of evil – a growth in the power and range of evil forces. If this be the true view of history, then a catastrophic eschaton might not be arbitrary but necessary. ... If this be the true reading of history, then the consummation of God's purpose, as it has been grasped and served by faithful men in all ages, can only come by the destruction of evil and cosmic renewal such as the New Testament envisages. That

would be not an arbitrary interruption of the slow and painful growth of goodness, but its only true fruition. (41kgip, 44)

The vision of a real end of history and a literal day of judgment raises the question of universal salvation and – as its counterpart – the question whether the possibility that some of God's children may be lost is a failure of God's purpose with humankind. Newbigin has to acknowledge the possibility and the fact that sometimes a person shuts himself off from God's love.

> That seems to be part of the implications of human freedom, and we do not know of any means by which God can certainly prevent it. I do not see how, once we have granted the fact that this is so, we can theoretically deny the possibility that it may continue to be so. The settled direction of some human souls does seem to be downwards, and even the revelation of God's love on the cross only seems to accelerate that movement. There is no more awful fact in the universe, but it is a fact. And I do not find anything in the Gospels to contradict it. (41kgip, 45)

Newbigin adds two words of caution however. First, the judgment of God will not be arbitrary but just. And second, "the only right way to think about this matter is to think about it in relation to oneself. This is because the final judgment is a wholly inward judgment, and we do not wholly know the inner heart of any other" (41kgip, 45). This exercise of restraint regarding the judgment of others is typical for Newbigin. It is found throughout his writings. Here he captures the biblical emphasis that the gospel always reaches us as a personal call from God directed to ourselves. The gospel is not a providing of information with which to cognitively order my view of the world but a calling that brings my life under the claim of God.

2.4. Lecture IV

In his final lecture Newbigin draws the lines together "to suggest a picture of what seems to me the right kind of eschatological hope. In the center of the picture is the hope of a new world, a re-created universe in which the travail of history shall find its completion and its rest" (41kgip, 46). This new world will not be the result of human activity but of a divine re-creation. Human efforts and institutions – even at their best – are still characterized by egotism, pride and impure ambition. Therefore, they cannot lead in a straight line of gradual development to the establishment of the kingdom of God. "There is no straight line of development from here to the Kingdom" (47kgip, 47). Even the best of human contributions are overshadowed by the reality of death and will be "buried in the dust of failure and death" (41kgip, 47). Christian eschatology has to take death seriously. But it can do so from the perspective of the fact of Christ's resurrection. "[D]eath and resurrection are the connective terms between the present life and the re-created life of the new age" (41kgip, 46).

> Our faith as Christians is that just as God raised up Jesus from the dead, so will He raise up us from the dead. And that just as all that Jesus had done in the

days of His flesh seemed on Easter Saturday to be buried in final failure and oblivion, yet was by God's power raised to new life and power again, so all the faithful labor of God's servants which time seems to bury in the dust of failure, will be raised up, will be found to be there, transfigured, in the new Kingdom. Every faithful act of service, every honest labor to make the world a better place, which seemed to have been forever lost and forgotten in the rubble of history, will be seen on that day to have contributed to the perfect fellowship of God's Kingdom. ... [A]ll who have committed their work in faithfulness to God will be by Him raised up to share in the new age, and will find that their labor was not lost, but that it has found its place in the completed Kingdom. (41kgip, 47)

How this happens we do not know. Paul uses the analogy of grain and wheat (1Cor 15:35ff). There is a sense of discontinuity as well as a sense of continuity. Nevertheless, death remains a mystery. It cannot be explained. All we have is the fact of the resurrection of Christ which is the foundation for our hope.

This hope of the resurrection and re-creation is both personal and cosmic. "Resurrection is to a new life in a perfected society" (41kgip, 48; see also 56ss, 122-125). Resurrection is not merely the creation of a new body for the individual soul. It is the re-creation of the cosmos. This double focus of the Christian hope – personal and cosmic – is the answer to the question of God's purpose for the individual soul on the one hand and his purpose for the history of humankind on the other. Both of these purposes must be seen together.

> Now these two are perfectly reconcilable if the aim of history is the creation of a perfect fellowship. For the only full fruition for the individual soul is in fellowship, and a perfect fellowship itself implies perfect souls who form it. Man is, we know, made for true community, and without it there is no fullness of spiritual stature for him. (41kgip, 49)

Here Newbigin finds the answer to the apparent contradiction between the individual and social dimension of biblical hope (see page 53; 41kgip, 26). The eschatological hope is the fulfillment of both. The hope that every single act of service here on earth which is committed to Christ will be found again in the re-creation of the cosmos is the answer to overcoming the split in the human mind between hoping for one's "own perfection in an otherworldly heaven" on the one hand, and "the desire to labor for that perfect fellowship on earth which he knows he cannot see" (41kgip, 49) on the other.

> That perfect society, the fully accepted and accomplished rule of God in men's hearts, therefore is the object of a Christian's hope and longing. And he knows that even though he himself must go out into the darkness of death, and that even though all his efforts for the creation of a better society on earth must in the end be buried and forgotten, yet none of this is lost. In that day it will all be found to be there raised up, transfigured. ... Whoever is faithfully seeking – whether as an engineer, an economist, a politician, a craftsman, a teacher, or a friend – to overcome that which militates against true human fellowship and to create such fellowship in great ways or in small, may be assured that even

though all the visible results of his labor perish before his eyes, it is no more lost than is he himself if he dies in faith. (41kgip, 50)

This view of the resurrection – personal and cosmic – and the hope that all human action committed to Christ is not in vain but will be transfigured and found again in the fulfillment of the kingdom of God sets the stage for Newbigin's perspective on Christian action in the world.

Christian action is not "to be conceived of as 'building the Kingdom of God.' Flesh and blood cannot inherit the Kingdom of God" (41kgip, 51). It would be false, however, to conclude that all we have to do is to passively await the realization of the kingdom by God himself. Newbigin refers to Albert Schweitzer's phrase, "that Christian action is a prayer for the coming of the Kingdom ... such action is a kind of prayer offered to God that He may hasten His Kingdom" (41kgip, 51).

> It invites a man to long for and pray for the goal, and to make his prayer articulate in work. And it offers him the certainty that in the end the goal will be realized. But at the same time it makes it quite clear to him that when that blessed hour comes, he will have to say not "*I* have succeeded," but "God's will has been fulfilled. Thanks be to God." (41kgip, 52)

The motives of Christian action are therefore obedience to the rule of God in gratitude to Christ, and hope for the completion of God's kingdom. "His gratitude impels him to acts of love towards men, but he also acts in hope – hope of the final completion of God's Kingdom in a perfected fellowship" (41kgip, 52-53).

Keeping this characteristic in mind, Christian action has to also concern itself with politics. The complexity of modern life limits the possibilities of the individual to change his or her situation. "To foreswear politics means surrendering control of 75 percent of life to forces over which neither the Christian, nor anyone else, has any control. That cannot be called a serious attempt to implement the requirements of God's rule" (41kgip, 53). However Newbigin calls for realism. He sees the task of Christians in politics not in developing fantastic plans of a future world order, but rather in "efforts of a humbler kind to deal concretely with existing evils and put them right" (41kgip, 54). He calls for political and social action when the opportunity presents itself to the Christian. Here Newbigin refers to men like Shaftesbury and Wilberforce. However Newbigin also points out that

> while political action is obligatory, it is not the only means, and probably not the most fundamental means, by which society will be changed. I think it is historically true that the biggest social consequences of Christianity have originated in movements which did not begin by aiming at social reform at all. (41kgip, 54)

Newbigin applies his thinking to the work of the church in India among the poor and powerless. The church must neither be hopeless in sight of the immense problems, nor must it set the transformation of the Indian society as its goal.

> [T]he point is that that [i.e. the transformation of India] is not our goal, great as that is. If transformation of Britain had been Wesley's goal, he would never have achieved it. Our goal is the holy city, the New Jerusalem, a perfect fellowship in which God reigns in every heart, and His children rejoice together in His love and joy. To that we look forward with sure hope, and for its sake we offer up to God all that we do in response to His invitation to love our neighbor as we ourselves have been loved. And though we know that we must grow old and die, that our labors, even if they succeed for a time, will in the end be buried in the dust of time, and that along with the painfully won achievements of goodness, there are mounting seemingly irresistible forces of evil, yet we are not dismayed. We do not need to take refuge in any comfortable illusions. We know that these things must be. But we know that as surely as Christ was raised from the dead, so surely shall there be a new heaven and a new earth wherein dwells righteousness.
>
> And having this knowledge we ought as Christians to be the strength of every good movement of political and social effort, because we have no need either of blind optimism or of despair. (41kgip, 55)

This final passage of Newbigin's lecture summarizes the application of his theological thinking to the practice of Christian action. It is action motivated by gratitude and hope, which is able to address the issues of the world without blind optimism or despair, but with a realism that takes into account not only the human situation but also the fact of Christ's resurrection and the inherent promise of the fulfillment of God's kingdom. It is here that the hope of a real future fulfillment of the kingdom of God works itself out in the present.

2.5. Summary

The essential elements of Newbigin's early exposition on the kingdom of God are:

(1) Biblical eschatological hope has a corporate and a cosmic dimension. As corporate hope it must neither be interpreted universalistically nor individualistically. As cosmic hope it looks forward to a cosmic restoration, not to an otherworldly heaven or to a gradual improvement of the earth.

(2) NT eschatology is characterized by the tension between the present and the future realization of the eschaton. A realized eschatology must be balanced by a futurist eschatology. NT eschatology is looking forward to a real end of history.

(3) The present history must be understood not as a gradual growth of the kingdom but as growth of both, good and evil. History and its end are only rightly understood in light of this conflict. The final day of judgment will bring the eradication of all evil and the final establishment of God's reign.

(4) The only way to the establishment of God's kingdom is the way through death and resurrection. There is no direct line from the present to the establishment of God's reign. Even the best of human contributions have to pass through the judgment of death. But whatever has been offered to Christ in this world will be found in the new creation as a contribution to God's kingdom.

(5) This eschatological perspective provides both realism and hope for Christian involvement in the issues of the world. Christian actions are not understood as the establishment of God's reign but as prayers directed to God to bring about his kingdom. The kingdom is not established by human action but by an act of God himself.

3. The Unity and Mission of the Church (1948-1953)

In his autobiography Newbigin tells about the numerous facets of his work as a district missionary. In his ministry he placed great emphasis on developing and keeping relationships to the various churches in the Kanchipuram district and to the local leaders, assisting them in visitation and street preaching as well as strengthening their engagement for the good of the community. Developing local leadership that was independent from outside finances and enabling local leaders to lead their churches and evangelize their surrounding villages was one of Newbigin's main emphases. Even though Newbigin's assignment later did not allow him to continue this intensive fellowship in working together with the local village leaders, these early contacts and the grass-root experience at the level of the local churches did flow into his theological reflection on the church as did his experience as bishop at Madurai. The church became the subject that Newbigin reflected on and wrote about during these years (1939-1948), culminating in the booklet "The household of God" (53hg). For the purpose of this study I will only highlight a few aspects of Newbigin's understanding of the church as it relates to Newbigin's view of the kingdom of God.

3.1. "The Reunion of the Church" (1948)

Newbigin's view of the church focuses on the organic aspect, the church being the body of Christ. The traditional hierarchical structure between missionaries and national pastors with the missionary being the leader of the organization creates a false assumption "that the work of preaching the Gospel, ministering the sacraments and building up the Body of Christ, is a relatively unimportant occupation compared to the work of administering a large organization" (85ua, 70). Newbigin calls for the missionaries to rethink their roles in ministry and their relationship to national leaders. The challenge is to come as a servant, humble, ready to be partner and colleague, and at the same time to empower the local ministers and churches. The missionary

> must be able to recognize both that it is right that he should be in the background and should leave to his Indian brethren the responsibility which they claim; and also at the same time to recognize that there is a longing for the support and strength that he can give, and to have grace to give it in ways that strengthen and do not weaken the independence and sense of responsibility of the Indian Church. (45ofmi, 94)

When Newbigin was elected convener of the committee on union of the SIUC in 1942 it became his challenge to motivate the SIUC to accept the agreement that had been formed after more than 20 years of deliberations with the goal of uniting three churches to the CSI. In this position Newbigin had to reflect and write on the question of the unity of the church. He critiques the Ceylon Scheme of Union, which makes the unity of the churches dependent on the re-ordination of those ministers who have not received the episcopal laying-on of hands (48csu, 162). Newbigin asks the churches to reconsider and make their unity dependent simply on a mutual recognition of the churches and their ministries. He votes against any form of re-ordination and proposes instead the CSI as a model for church unity. This model is explained and defended in "The Reunion of the Church: A Defence of the South India scheme" (48rc), and later republished with a revised introduction (60rc). Wainwright summarizes the main argument of the book as application of the doctrine of justification to the life and structures of the church; the role of the episcopate for the unity of the church; and the proposal of the CSI model in preference over the Anglican model of supplemental ordination (Wainwright 2000, 86).

There is one section in the book in which Newbigin deals with the tension "that the Church exists both in eternity and in time" (48rc, 70-83). Here Newbigin summarizes part of his Bangalore lectures. He critiques an understanding of eschatology that makes the eschaton a symbol for the present and does not hold on to a real future end of the world accompanied by the judgment of God.

> No one now needs to be reminded that the whole New Testament message is set firmly in the framework of this eschatological faith and cannot be understood apart from it. ... "The Eschaton has entered into history." But I have the impression that the recent re-emphasis upon the eschatological character of the whole New Testament has been achieved at the cost of removing the whole group of ideas which we call eschatological from the realm of reality to that of symbol. (48rc, 73)

Parallel to his argumentation at Bangalore Newbigin asserts:

> The eschatological element in the Gospel is there because the eschaton is a future certainty. Belief in eschatology without belief in a real end is like belief in religion without belief in God. ... The eschaton only enters into our experience because it qualifies our present existence. But it can only qualify our present existence if it be a future certainty. ... I venture to express the opinion, therefore, which is impossible adequately to support in a few short paragraphs, that the message of the New Testament cannot be interpreted *exclusively* in terms of "realized eschatology." There is a real end to history, and that end is not yet. (48rc, 74-76)

It is in this framework that Newbigin understands the place of the church both in history and in eternity.

> I do not think one can help feeling, as one reads the New Testament, that this intense sense of being already members in a kingdom that is beyond history is part of the very stuff of its message. ... That sense of belonging already to God's kingdom, and that eager hope for the manifestation of the Kingdom in glory, belong to the very essence of Christianity. ... The New Testament, and all authentic Christianity, lives between the accomplished redemption on the Cross and the longed-for victory when Christ shall come in glory, between thankfulness and hope. The Church takes its bearings afresh, so to say, on these two landmarks of its faith, every time it meets to show forth the Lord's death till He come. ... The Church lives with its eyes on these points because it lives in history the life of God who is beyond history. (48rc, 76-77)

This positioning of the church in between the two landmarks of the kingdom of God – its past revelation and its future consummation – has implications for Newbigin's understanding of church unity. Newbigin rejects two extreme positions, on the one hand the Catholic position on the unity of the church which insists solely on outward and institutional continuity (48rc, 39), and on the other hand the Protestant position which "affirms that the unity of the Church is a spiritual unity, that outward unity of organization is not of the essence of the Church, and that true Christians are in fact united already" (48rc, 24). While the Catholic position arises from a focus on the presence of God's reign (the church as an expression of the kingdom now), the Protestant position too easily relegates the question of church unity into the future and is satisfied with a spiritual unity. For Newbigin the unity of the church is of its essence, because the church is the firstfruits of "humanity re-made in Christ" (48rc, 48). There has to be one body in order to present to the world one Lord and one gospel. How can a church which is divided along cultural, economic or social lines be the community in which humanity is to be united (48rc, 182)?

> The unity of the Church is of its Essence: ... [A]s there is but one Lord Jesus Christ so there can be only one Church. Christ cannot be divided. ... There is one Spirit, and it follows that there is one Body. If the Body is divided it is because Christians are not spiritual but carnal, not walking after the Spirit, but after the flesh. (48rc, 52-54)

Newbigin looks at the question of church unity from the perspective of "spirit," "body," and "flesh." Just as we as individuals live as earthly bodies in the world and yet are called to live according to the Spirit, not according to the flesh, so the church too is called to live as one body in the world, but to live according to the Spirit, not according to the flesh. Whenever the church places its emphasis on some type of practice or tradition instead of the cross of Christ, there will be disunity of the church and carnal behavior (see 1 Corinthians 2-3). Here too the eschatological tension comes to bear on the church. As the church lives in the present it must not give in to the temptation to live according to the paradigm of the present, but to live according to the Spirit. Only thus the church is true to its calling to be an eschatological community, a regenerate humanity.

Newbigin worked hard to bring this theological conviction to bear on the reality of the church – both in India and beyond. His concern for church unity is not grounded in an idealist view of the church but in his eschatological understanding – living in this world but living according to the Spirit. One can understand why and how he was moved at the unification service in Madras on September 27, 1947 (see 85ua, 94-97).

This emphasis on the unity of the church in no way diverts Newbigin's attention from the mission of the church. Quite to the contrary, the mission of the church requires its unity.

> That which makes the Church the Church is at the same time the thing which gives it its mission. That which reduces the Church to a series of associations is at the same time that which destroys the possibility of evangelism in its true sense and transforms it into the proselytizing effort of some human enthusiasm. ... That same divine grace which reconciled them in one body also sends them out as ministers of reconciliation, beseeching men on behalf of Christ to be reconciled to God. ... The connection between the movement for Christian reunion and the movement for world evangelization is of the deepest possible character. The two things are the two outward signs of a return to the heart of the Gospel itself. (48rc, 18-19)

Both the concern for mission and the concern for unity grow out of the central message of the gospel which is a message of reconciliation. It is impossible for the church to be a community of reconciliation and yet at the same time to be divided. Therefore "[t]here is the closest possible connection between the acceptance of the missionary obligation and the acceptance of the obligation of unity. That which makes the Church one is what makes it a mission to the world" (48rc, 11). At the time when the IMC was preparing to join the WCC in New Delhi Newbigin wrote the introduction to the revised edition of "The Reunion of the Church:"

> [W]hat is now becoming plainer is that mission and unity cannot rightly be separated from each other, and that the task of drawing all God's people into one fellowship, so that there may be one flock as there is one Shepherd, is something that belongs to the intrinsic nature of the Church until the End. (60rc, xxx-xxxi)

3.2. "The Duty and Authority of the Church to Preach the Gospel" (1948)

Newbigin deals with the missionary obligation of the church in an essay for the upcoming Amsterdam assembly written en route to India in 1947 (48dacp). He points out that the authority of the church is rooted in Christ's authority. And he points out the quality of the gospel as proclamation of a story, as "news of God."

> The earliest and simplest statement of the Gospel is "The time is fulfilled and the Kingdom of God is at hand." ... [T]he Gospel is the proclamation of a se-

ries of events in history which have been – from their first dawning – proclaimed to be decisive for human history and for every individual. (48dacp, 23)

Newbigin summarizes the gospel-story in five major themes: creation, fall, election, redemption, and consummation. In these themes Newbigin follows God's involvement with "His human family." Already at this early stage Newbigin speaks about the necessity of election for the passing on of God's salvation. The personal character of love demands that the message of salvation is passed on through interpersonal relationships and that it leads to participation in a new community. "It is thus not chance but inner necessity of love's nature, that the Gospel of God's love should reach us in the form of an invitation to join a particular human fellowship. God's purpose of love must be worked out through election" (48dacp, 29-30). Again Newbigin points out the role of the church in light of the eschatological dimension of history.

> [T]he clue to all God's dealings with His human family is to be found in the Church, the particular, visible, historical society in which men and women are bound together in the communion of the Holy Spirit, and which grows through history by holding up Christ before men in Word and Sacraments, and by ministering His love to them in its common life. ...
>
> His purpose is to sum up all things in Christ (...). Of this purpose the Church is the first fruit and the agent. (48dacp, 30-34)

Newbigin at that time already speaks about the indivisibility of preaching and service, a theme which we find throughout his writings and which is also rooted in his eschatological view of salvation, as his reference to "false hopes" shows.

> Preaching divorced from concern for all men's needs will be words set against deeds, for men will not believe the message of God's grace if they do not see signs of that grace in the messengers. Service of men divorced from preaching will be but mocking men with false hopes, for there is no place other than the Cross where men may be reconciled to God, and every man must go there himself. (48dacp, 32)

It becomes clear here that Newbigin understands the gospel not as some kind of religious teaching but as the story of God who acts in history. He has revealed himself in the sending of his son. In the person of Christ he has also revealed the final outcome of history. And it is this message which confronts every person and calls for a final decision.

> History is not a meaningless repetition of cycles; it is real and moves to a real climax. ... [T]he Gospel is the message that the eternal Lord of history has revealed Himself in history in order to confront man with the final issue of his life on earth.
>
> God's revelation of Himself in Christ is the revelation of the meaning of history as it is in the counsel of God, and those who by faith apprehend the revelation look for the end of history when the secret of God's purpose shall be ap-

> parent to sight ... [when] the Kingdom of God shall be revealed in glory. (48dacp, 33-34)

The eschatological tension is expressed in the terms "something which has happened and which at the same time points to something about to happen" (48dacp, 33). Already the church "truly shares in the divine life and tastes the powers of the age to come" (48dacp, 32).

The soberness of the historical situation after WWII on the one hand and the unity of the world-wide church which was beginning to form itself in 1948 on the other hand amplify the outlook towards the eschatological consummation of history and underscore the task of the church in the present with a vision for the whole of humanity.

> [F]aith eagerly awaits the day heralded in Christ's first preaching when faith shall be lost in sight and the Kingdom of God shall be revealed in glory. Until that day the Church must confess before the world the faith by which she lives, and so play her part in hastening that day's dawning. History moves to a real climax, away from the social equilibrium which belongs to man's natural inheritance, and towards the final crisis where heaven shall stand nakedly revealed and men must enter on their heavenly inheritance or perish. The Church is bound by her own faith to take history seriously, and in this hour of history when on the one hand the sin of man threatens the utter destruction of human life, and on the other the Church has been granted a new vision of her world-wide unity, Christians will look up in hope knowing that their redemption draws near. This is an hour when the Lord is forcing us to see the whole destiny of the human race in the light of His eternal purpose, and when there is laid upon the Church, through which He has willed to make his purpose known, the duty and authority to proclaim to all men His saving acts. "Behold, now is the day of salvation." (48dacp, 34-35)

Here we have a comprehensive statement of Newbigin's position regarding the topic of this study, namely the relationship between his view of the kingdom of God and his view of the mission of the church. God is directing history towards its goal, which is the revelation of the kingdom of God in glory. The church is eagerly expecting this final day of both judgment and heavenly inheritance, the day when God will reach his goal with humankind. Yet the church is set into the middle of the historical developments to witness God's purpose to the world. It is given "the duty and the authority to proclaim to all men His saving acts." The participation in this mission is in itself a contribution to the dawning of the final day.

3.3. "The Evangelization of Eastern Asia" (1950)

In 1949 Newbigin reads a paper at a conference in Bangkok dealing with the above topic. In six theses he tries to summarize briefly the situation in which the church in Asia is placed, pointing out some of the tensions between the traditional cultures and the invasion by western culture and technology on the one hand and the crisis of the western culture on the other which has now shaken the modernist idea of inexorable progress. In this context, Newbigin asserts, the church must "confront this world, which has all but lost the sense of any ultimate standard of judgment, with the truth that it has a Judge, a Judge and a Saviour, who has come and will come again" (50eea, 140). The church has to place a new emphasis on that part of its message "which was most neglected during the period of the unhindered expansion of western culture – the eschatological" (50eea, 140). Newbigin rejects the "perversions" of the interest in the eschatological, "a morbid curiosity about signs and dates … and a contempt for the great tasks of political and social and economic justice" (50eea, 141). Instead his concern is to bring the eschatological hope of the church to bear on its task of the evangelization of this world, in word and deed.

> I submit to your prayerful consideration this conviction that the Gospel which we preach must be filled, as the New Testament is filled, with a vivid awareness of its eschatological setting, with a vivid consciousness of the fact that we speak as those whose citizenship is in heaven, from whence also we wait for a Saviour who shall fashion anew the body of our humiliation, that it may be conformed to the body of His glory; as those who hope ardently for His coming again and in whom that hope, which no threat can take away, begets a life of loving service to all men. Unless the church has a message from beyond the world, it will not move the world by one hair's breadth. (50eea, 141)

Only a perverted view of eschatology leads to a withdrawal from the world. For the church and its involvement in the world it is instead essential that its love be fed by a hope that comes from beyond this world. The church will not be able to live out its mission without being rooted in this eschatological hope. In the same context Newbigin exhorts: "The very character of the Church's deeds of love and service is surely determined by this reference to the eternal Kingdom. The citizens of heaven are to carry out the laws of heaven here on earth" (50eea, 141). The awareness of its eschatological hope and the outworking of this hope in the present is what Newbigin sees as essential for the church in its mission.

> The Church has always two simultaneous duties. It has firstly to strengthen and make more real the citizenship of all its members in heaven. In word and sacrament, in prayer and communion, it must be leading its members to an ever deeper rooting in the eternal order … until they know more and more certainly that heaven is indeed their home, and the love and joy and peace of heaven become their very life. In this task the Church will often have to leave the world behind. …
>
> Secondly, and all the time, the Church has to involve itself and all its members more and more deeply in all the affairs of the world, to be engaged up to the hilt in all its temptations and sorrows, its shame and despair, its strife and labour, its struggle with disease, injustice and every manifestation of evil; and in all this to bear about in the body the dying of the Lord Jesus, that the life also of Jesus may be manifest in it. It is always relatively easy for the Church to do one of these things and neglect the other. Its task is to live in the tension of loy-

alty to both tasks, and in that place, in that tension, to bear witness to the Gospel. (50eea, 142-143)

Newbigin here captures well the accent of biblical prophecy. Prophecy is never simply a word about the future. It always bears on the present. Newbigin shows how the mission of the church lives out of its eschatological hope, and how this hope so shapes the church that it engages itself in the issues of the world, never loosing its eschatological perspective. Newbigin not only points out *that* the eschatological hope of the church works itself out in its involvement with the world, but also *how* it works itself out, namely in bearing the marks of Christ's suffering. The cross as the mark of the authenticity of the church's mission will be part of the later discussion.

Newbigin expresses his conviction that the church only is truly church as church in mission.

> The truth is that the Church is not the Church in any New Testament sense unless it *is* a mission. ... I very much like the phrase of Professor Emil Brunner, 'The Church exists by mission as fire exists by burning'. To change the metaphor, the Church is not a pool into which we can put the fish which the evangelist has caught; it is the outflowing stream of Christ's love, drawing all men to itself. By detaching mission from the Church, and thinking of it as a separate activity, we have grievously corrupted in practice our whole conception of what the Church is. (50eea, 142)

The church must be understood from the perspective of its sending into the world. It is not primarily an organization but an organism of believers, in which every member takes part in that mission directed towards the world. In this context Newbigin picks up the growing awareness in the WCC of the ministry of laypeople (see Congar 1985, orig. ed. 1957, Kraemer 1958). Newbigin calls for the training of Christian laymen "to be effective Christians within their own special vocations" (50eea, 144). The ministry of laypeople must be seen not as service to the *church*, but as part of the mission of the church to the *world*.

> 'The layman is the minister, the ambassador of Christ, in his office, his classroom, his farm. His mission is not simply to make known Jesus Christ to all those with whom he comes in contact, but still more *to show how a servant of Jesus Christ understands and exercises the job of which he has charge. That is his chief job in the Church.*' In other words, it is on the Christian layman in his job, from Monday to Saturday, that the responsibility rests for seeing that – so far as in him lies – the will of Christ is done here on earth. That is his first task as a member of the Church. ...
>
> [T]he Church's *work in the world* is work which professional ministers cannot do; it is the work of countless Christian laymen in all their varied daily tasks serving Christ in their daily work. (52clwc, 186-187)

We will see how these early accents continue to appear in Newbigin's later writings.

3.4. "The Household of God" (1953)

In his preparations for the 1952 Kerr lectures on the nature of the church Newbigin took the opportunity to expand his ecclesiology beyond the context of South India. The result was the book "The household of God" (53hg; 98hg) which "has achieved the status of a classic" (Wainwright 2000, 98). Not only was it translated into French, German, Chinese, Japanese and Russian. It also "influenced the writing of 'Lumen Gentium,' the [Vatican II] Council's dogmatic constitution of the Church" (Wainwright 2000, 98).

In this book Newbigin looks at the question of church-unity in light of the eschatological tension and in light of the missionary obligation of the church (98hg, 190). For Newbigin these are essential marks without which an understanding of the church is simply impossible. He identifies three different theological emphases in defining the central characteristic of the church. He calls them the Protestant, the Catholic, and the Pentecostal view.

3.4.1. Protestant, Catholic and Pentecostal Views of the Church

The Protestant view of the church concentrates on the proclamation of the word, the administration of the sacraments and the response of faith. These three elements constitute the church. The shortcoming of this view, Newbigin points out, is "that it gives no real place to the continuing life of the Church as one fellowship binding the generations together in Christ" (98hg, 57). The proclamation of the word does not take place in a vacuum but always as "an event in the life of an actually existing Christian Church or fellowship of some kind, [it] presupposes such a fellowship, and cannot be severed from it." As such it is both "word of Christ" and word "of that particular Christian body" (98hg, 58-59). The result of the strong Protestant emphasis on word, sacraments and faith is a weakened view of the unity of the church. Newbigin critiques:

> The Church cannot be defined *simply* as that which is constituted by the event of the preaching of the Gospel and the administering of the sacraments. It belongs to its true nature that it is a continuing historical society, that society which was constituted and sent forth once for all by Jesus Christ. (98hg, 71)

The continuation of the church as historical society is precisely what the Catholic view emphasizes. And Newbigin finds support for this view of the church in the NT.

> The Church, as the sphere wherein the first-fruits of the age to come are experienced within this present age, will not be a merely spiritual reality whose outward forms and signs will be a sort of dead husk enclosing the living seed. On the contrary, it is in accordance with the whole biblical standpoint that the sphere of salvation should be a visible fellowship marked by visible signs wherein God uses material means to convey His saving power, and wherein, therefore, there is an earnest and foretaste of the restoration of creation to its true harmony in and for God's glory, and of man to his true relation to the created world. (98hg, 79)

The tension between the Protestant and the Catholic viewpoint is related to a false dichotomy between spirit and body. Newbigin points out, however, that for Paul "the terms body and spirit are not contraries. More often they are correlates. The true, basic, and constantly repeated contradiction is between spirit and flesh. Body is a term which can be used in close connection with either of them" (98hg, 85). Newbigin takes the fact seriously that not only do individual creatures live both spiritually and bodily but so does the church. It is the church in a particular place and time, connected to the global church through a particular tradition through which the gospel came to the people. In a sense Newbigin expresses here the foundations of contextual thinking and contextual theology. This is interesting precisely because for Newbigin the fact that the church is always rooted in a specific context does not lead to a fragmentation of churches and theologies. On the contrary, he emphasizes the oneness of God's story with his people and his world. Newbigin underscores the fact "that being in Christ means being incorporated in a visible society which is – in principle – undivided and continuous, binding all men and all generations in the one body of Christ, from His coming until His coming again" (98hg, 92). From this understanding Newbigin argues for a comprehensive view of the Protestant and Catholic positions:

> We conclude that, just as it belongs to the heart of the biblical doctrine of the Church that our incorporation in Christ is by faith, so it is no less central to this doctrine that our incorporation is by baptism into a visible fellowship which is the body of Christ in Corinth, in Rome, in the world; and that our participation in the life of the body is maintained by our sharing in the one loaf and the one cup in one undivided fellowship. The Church ... is the continuing life of Christ among men in a body which grows by the addition of new members but is itself essentially continuous and indivisible. There is but one Christ and therefore but one body of Christ ... Its unity is not merely ideal or spiritual: it is visible, social, organic; effected, revealed, and sealed in the fellowship of the one table. (98hg, 97-98)

However Newbigin's criticism of the Catholic viewpoint is that it does not adequately deal with the question of sin in the church.

> From its very beginnings the Church faces us with the dark mystery of sin by which she lives and acts in a manner that contradicts her essential nature. She who is essentially one is divided; she who is essentially holy is unclean; she who is essentially apostolic forgets her missionary task. No doctrine of the Church can be true which does not match this dark mystery of sin in the Church with a doctrine of the divine grace profound enough to deal with it without evasion, and which does not in some measure explain how a body which by sin denies its own nature is yet accepted by God and used as the means of His grace. (98hg, 108)

Newbigin's critique of the Catholic position is that it makes the mark of apostolic succession the only criterion for the evaluation of the church while generously looking past the fact that the church may deny its very own nature by its sinfulness. The fact that the church too only lives by the grace of God seems forgotten when it comes to the formation of the criterion for the evaluation of the church.

Newbigin argues that neither position – the Protestant nor the Catholic – in itself is enough to fully characterize the church.

> [T]he Church is not *merely* the witness to Christ; it is also the body of Christ. It is not merely the reporter of the divine acts of redemption; it is also itself the bearer of God's redeeming grace, itself a part of the story of redemption which is the burden of its message.
>
> We have already looked at the distortions which occur when either of these two elements is given absolute priority over the other. On the one hand the Church is defined simply as that which bears the apostolic witness: where the true witness is, there is the Church. The final result of this is that the Church comes to be defined, as in orthodox Lutheranism, exclusively in terms of assent to precisely formulated doctrinal statements. On the other hand the Church is defined simply as the continuation of the apostolate: where the apostolic succession is, there is the Church. ... In both cases the Church becomes something which can be identified by purely natural standards and categories. ... The question: Where is the Church? can thus – on these premises – be answered without any reference to the presence or absence of the Holy Spirit. (98hg, 122)

Here Newbigin argues that we need a third element to qualify the understanding of the church; he calls it the Pentecostal position. Its central focus is that the church is the community of the Holy Spirit (98hg, 111), that it lives by the power of God's Spirit (98hg, 124). As such the church is the firstfruits of salvation.

The danger of a one-sided Pentecostal view of the church is to divide the Spirit from the body, "forgetting that as there is one Spirit so there is one body" (98hg, 142). Newbigin sees a true understanding of the church only in a comprehensive view that incorporates the elements of the three positions.

> I have tried to show that all the three answers which we looked at are true; we are made members in Him by hearing and believing the Gospel, by being received sacramentally into the visible fellowship of His people, and both of these only through the living presence of the Holy Spirit. At the same time I tried to show that when any one of them was taken as alone decisive, error and distortion followed. (98hg, 174-175)

3.4.2. The Essence of the Church in Eschatological Tension

However the three aspects do not simply add up to a static view of the church. The church can only be understood in an eschatological dimension. It cannot truly be defined in terms of what it now is, but only in terms of the final revelation of what it will be. The understanding of the church from the viewpoint of its eschatological consummation must be brought to bear on the understanding of the church in the present. Both the question of the church's unity and the question of its mission must be understood in light of the eschatological end.

Chapter 2: The Kingdom of God in Newbigin's Early Writings

> The Church is the pilgrim people of God. It is on the move – hastening to the ends of the earth to beseech all men to be reconciled to God, and hastening to the end of time to meet its Lord who will gather all into one. Therefore the nature of the Church is never to be finally defined in static terms, but only in terms of that to which it is going. It cannot be understood rightly except in a perspective which is at once missionary and eschatological, and only in that perspective can the deadlock of our present ecumenical debate be resolved. ... The whole meaning of this present age between Christ's coming and His coming again is that in it the powers of the age to come are at work now to draw all men into one in Christ. When the Church ceases to be one, or ceases to be missionary, it contradicts its own nature. Yet the Church is not to be defined by what it is, but by that End to which it moves ... It is a perspective inseparable from action, and that action must be both in the direction of mission and in that of unity, for these are but two aspects of the one work of the Spirit. (98hg, 22-23)

At the core of the eschatological tension is the clash and the overlap of two ages, the "present age" and the "age to come." While the age to come has already begun in the present, the present age is still present and the age to come is still to come. The two ages "so to speak, overlap, lie alongside one another, and fight with one another in the world and in the soul of every Christian" (98hg, 157-158). The tension of living in this overlap of ages is so much part of the Christian experience (98hg, 151-152; 76bsr8) that the Christian life is inconceivable apart from this tension. "Once this tension of longing and hope, this pressing forward to the goal which is still beyond our sight, goes out of the Christian life, we cease to be – in the apostolic sense – partakers of Christ (Heb. 3. 14)" (98hg, 167). What is true for the life of individual believers applies also to the church.

> The true mark of the man in Christ will be that the more he grows in holiness the more will he know that he is a sinner, and the more will he long for and press on towards the fullness of sanctification 'with all the saints'. That paradox, familiar to every Christian, is perhaps the simplest way of expressing the paradox of the Church's being. The moment the Church begins to think that it possesses the fullness of divine grace, it has fallen from that grace. This means that Luther was surely right in saying that justification by faith is an article by which the Church stands or falls. The Church is both holy and sinful, because for man 'in the flesh' the only true holiness is that which renounces every claim to a righteousness of its own and casts itself only upon the grace of God in Jesus Christ. (98hg, 168-169)

As this tension cannot be relieved in the life of the individual believer so it can and must not be dissolved in the life of the church. Newbigin carefully observes the character of the eschatological tension in the life of the church and qualifies it with Luther's term *"simul justus et peccator"* (being justified and yet being a sinner at the same time). The character of this tension changes completely when it is understood as a tension between an (imperfect) visible church and a (perfect) invisible church. Here Newbigin sees the Greek dichotomy of matter versus spirit creep in which essentially destroys the eschatological tension. This is Newbigin's critique of Luther.

> But if this is true, then Luther abandoned his deepest insight when he substituted for the true, biblical picture of a Church both holy and sinful, a false and unbiblical distinction between the spiritual Church and the material Church or between the invisible Church and the visible Church. Both of these related pairs of terms have the effect of relaxing the true eschatological tension which is involved in recognising that in Christ we, along with all our brethren, are accepted as His while we are yet sinners. ... Every attempt to slacken that eschatological tension by supposing now some sort of true Church within the Church, involves a concealed – and sometimes open – pharisaism. ... When this attempt is allied with a distinction between the so-called spiritual Church and the so-called material or institutional Church, a distinction which violates the whole biblical doctrine of the unity of creation, then the way is opened wide for a profoundly unevangelical and un-Catholic sectarianism. (98hg, 169-170)

This is a very astute criticism. Newbigin shows that the use of the Greek dichotomy of spirit versus matter as hermeneutical key for the understanding of the eschatological tension not only stands in contrast to a biblical view of creation, but also results in relaxing the eschatological tension. I will refer to another example of that in chapter five. Newbigin therefore argues for a view of the church which derives its understanding of the essence of the church from the eschaton and brings this understanding to bear on the present character of the church. The church – even in its present form – is the firstfruits of salvation, the beginning of the new humankind in Christ, a real new creation. Yet at the same time it is aware of its unholy character and its struggle with sin and is all the more longing for the fullness of salvation to be revealed. As the church is pressing forward to the end of time in its longing, it is also pressing forward to the ends of the earth in the proclamation of the witness to salvation.

> It is here, in this visible community, that God is savingly at work reconciling the world to Himself, precisely because the salvation which He purposes is not merely private and spiritual but corporate and cosmic.

> This being so, the very essence of the Church's life is that she is pressing forward to the fulfilment of God's purpose and the final revelation of His glory, pressing forward both to the ends of the earth and to the end of the world, rejoicing in the hope of the glory of God. The treasure entrusted to her is not for herself, but for the doing of the Lord's will, not for hoarding but for trading. Her life is to be forever spent, to be cast into the ground like a corn of wheat, in the ever-new faith and hope of the resurrection harvest. Her life is precisely life under the sign of the Cross, which means that she desires to possess no life, no security, no righteousness of her own, but to live solely by His grace. When she becomes settled, when she becomes so much at home in this world that she is no longer content to be forever striking her tents and moving forward, above all when she forgets that she lives simply by God's mercy and begins to think that she has some claim on God's grace which the rest of the world has not, when in other words she thinks of her election in terms of spiritual privilege rather than missionary responsibility, then she comes under His merciful judgment as Israel did.

> In relation to our present argument I think this means that we must abandon the attempt to define the Church's *esse* in terms of something that it has and is. (98hg, 175-176)

In contrast, the church needs to be defined in terms of that which has been given to it by the Spirit through the death of Christ and in terms of the completion Christ will bring about at the end of time. In this tension the church exists only by God's mercy. In this awareness and humility it is called to live in the world as a community that not only proclaims but also lives reconciliation. The church is God's new order, the realization of peace and holiness despite its own entanglement in sin and blindness. That is part of the eschatological tension which defines the character of the church.

> It [the Church] is an eschatological reality in which the peace and holiness and truth of God's kingdom truly exist here and now in men and women who are at the same time involved in the sin and self-seeking and blindness of this age.

> ... God has established his new order in Christ. That order is the inner meaning of all human, and indeed of cosmic history. It is that in which all history is to be consummated and by which it is to be judged. (54rgo, 546-547)

3.4.3. The Mission of the Church in Eschatological Tension

Since the eschatological tension in the church reveals itself as the tension of *simul justus et peccator* the church cannot but live in humility by God's grace and at the same time in expectation of the consummation of salvation. In this tension it is given the task of extending to the world the witness of God's salvific acts and the invitation to his kingdom. That precisely is the meaning of the present age, the reason why the end is delayed.

> The meaning of this 'overlap of the ages' in which we live, the time between the coming of Christ and His coming again, is that it is the time given for the witness of the apostolic Church to the ends of the earth. The end of all things, which has been revealed in Christ, is – so to say – held back until witness has been borne to the whole world concerning the judgment and salvation revealed in Christ. The implication of a true eschatological perspective will be missionary obedience, and the eschatology which does not issue in such obedience is a false eschatology. (98hg, 181-182; see also 98hg, 186-187)

Thus the mission of the church can only be understood in this eschatological tension. It is characterized by the NT understanding that salvation is both universal in scope and corporate in nature. Salvation is the "restoration to the whole creation of the perfect unity whose creative source and pattern is the unity of perfect love within the being of the triune God. It is in its very essence, universal and cosmic" (98hg, 188). This universal character of salvation is rooted in the scope of God's love, "a love that reaches out after all men, goes to all lengths to recover one lost sheep, and cares and must ever care for the rebel and the traitor with all the passion of Calvary" (98hg, 189). The fact that salvation is corporate in nature qualifies it as reconciliation and restoration of a new community, in communion with God and with each other.

> It belongs to the very heart of salvation that we cannot have it in fullness until all for whom it is intended have it together.
>
> It is because this is the nature of salvation, that our experience of it now must have the character of a foretaste, an earnest; that we who have the first fruits must yet groan waiting for our adoption; ... We cannot enjoy the fullness of salvation until we have it together in the fullness of His body the Church. The new man into which we would fain grow up is a corporate humanity, wherein all the redeemed from every tribe and tongue are made one harmonious whole. ... The eschatological tension cannot be understood apart from the tension of missionary obligation. (98hg, 189-190)

Again Newbigin points out that the character of salvation necessarily requires that it can only be communicated and passed on by a community in which reconciliation and the restoration of community are the essential marks.

> [A] salvation whose very essence is that it is corporate and cosmic, the restoration of the broken harmony between all men and between man and God and man and nature ... must be communicated in and by the actual development of a community which embodies – if only in foretaste – the restored harmony of which it speaks. A gospel of reconciliation can only be communicated by a reconciled fellowship. ... In other words it will be communicated by the way of election, beginning from one visible center and spreading always according to the law that each one is chosen in order to be the means of bringing the message of salvation to the next. (98hg, 190-191)

Regarding the interrelatedness of the eschatological tension with the missionary obligation of the church Newbigin summarizes:

> Thus from whichever angle we look at the salvation which Christ has won for us, we see that its implicate is the world mission. The final consummation of God's purpose awaits the fulfilment of the world mission, and this not because of any defect in God's power or grace, but because this belongs to the character of the salvation He has purposed for us. 'The same Lord is Lord of all, and is rich unto all that call upon him: for, Whosoever shall call upon the name of the Lord shall be saved. How then shall they call on him in whom they have not believed? and how shall they believe in him whom they have not heard? and how shall they hear without a preacher? and how shall they preach except they be sent? (Rom. 10, 12-15). The consummation depends upon sending, upon mission. And the mission is itself the sign of the coming consummation. 'This gospel of the kingdom shall be preached in the whole world for a testimony unto all the nations; and then shall the end come.' (98hg, 191-192)

Underscoring this relationship between the eschatological tension and the missionary obligation of the church, Newbigin can say:

> Between the Church militant here on earth, longing for the full possession of that which she has in foretaste, and the consummation for which she longs, the marriage supper of the Lamb, there lies the unfinished missionary task. The first answer to her prayer, 'Come, Lord Jesus,' is His commission – 'Go ye into all the world – and lo, I am with you.' (98hg, 193)

3.4.4. Implications for the Understanding of "Mission" and "Church"

Having established this theological foundation, Newbigin points out how the thinking about mission needs to change. First he criticizes the distinction between church and mission which has led to the fact that

> in the thinking of the vast majority of Christians, the words 'Church' and 'Mission' connote two different kinds of society. The one is conceived to be a society devoted to worship, and the spiritual care and nurture of its members. ... The other is conceived to be a society devoted to the propagation of the Gospel, passing on its converts to the safe keeping of 'the Church'. (98hg, 194)

This dichotomized view of church and mission destroys the eschatological tension. It removes mission from the core of the church and thus leads to an institutionalized view of the church. It narrows the perspective of the church to the challenges of its immediate surroundings instead of allowing it to understand itself as part of God's global story. And it is in danger of making the church a religious institution for individual salvation. The role of the community as foretaste of the kingdom is here no longer in view.

> When the eschatological and missionary perspective has been lost from the thinking of the Church, its task comes to be conceived in terms of the rescue of individuals one by one out of this present evil age and their preservation unharmed for the world to come. (98hg, 197)

For Newbigin it is the eschatological tension in his understanding of the church which provides the right balance against an institutionalized view of the church and a church-centered understanding of mission. Here Newbigin deals with Hoekendijk's critique of the church which was expressed in the 1950s and early 1960s. For Hoekendijk the church is at best instrumental in God's dealings with the world. In contrast Newbigin emphasizes that the church is more than an instrument of God's mission. It is a foretaste of salvation.

> The church is both a means and an end, because it is a foretaste. It is the community of the Holy Spirit ... The Church can be instrumental to the divine purpose of salvation only because she is much more than instrumental – because she is in fact herself the body of Christ.

> In other words, just as we must insist that a Church which has ceased to be a mission has lost the essential character of a Church, so we must also say that a mission which is not at the same time truly a Church is not a true expression of the divine apostolate. An unchurchly mission is as much a monstrosity as an unmissionary Church. (98hg, 199-201; see also Goheen 2004, 105)

The church cannot be understood apart from its participation in God's mission. At the same time, mission cannot be understood without a view for the church as community in which the salvation of humankind takes its beginning. By drawing the two together Newbigin critiques the radical developments that in the 1960s lead to a split between the salvific work of God in the world on the one hand and the role of the church on the other.

At the same time this interwovenness of mission and church makes the question of the unity of the church a matter of the church's essence.

> The Church's unity is the sign and the instrument of the salvation which Christ has wrought and whose final fruition is the summing-up of all things in Christ. In so far as the Church is disunited her life is a direct and public contradiction of the Gospel, and she is convicted of substituting some partial or sectional message for the good news of the one final and sufficient atoning act wrought in Christ for the whole human race. ... We cannot be Christ's ambassadors, beseeching all men to be reconciled to God, except we ourselves be willing to be reconciled one to another in Him. (98hg, 202-204)

Based on this deep theological conviction Newbigin expresses the hope that a new vision for mission will also lead to a new effort to work towards the unity of the church as a whole.

> I do not think that a resolute dealing with our divisions will come except in the context of a quite new acceptance on the part of all the Churches of the obligation to bring the Gospel to every creature; nor do I think that the world will believe that Gospel until it sees more evidence of its power to make us one. These two tasks – mission and unity – must be prosecuted together and in indissoluble relation one with another. ... Our task is, firstly, to call upon the whole Church to a new acceptance of the missionary obligation to bring the whole world to obedience to Christ; secondly, to do everything in our power to extend the area of co-operation between all Christians in the fulfilment of that task, by seeking to draw into the fellowship of the ecumenical movement those who at present stand outside of it to the right and to the left; and thirdly, to press forward unwearyingly with the task of reunion in every place, until all who in every place call upon the name of Jesus are visibly united in one fellowship, the sign and the instrument of God's purpose to sum up all things in Christ, to whom with the Father and the Holy Spirit be all the glory. (98hg, 206)

At a time when the international mission movement was rethinking the missionary task in light of the phrase "mission as *missio dei*" Newbigin put forward a view of the church which placed it in the overall context of the unfolding of the kingdom of God – the church participating in the *missio dei* – and which held together the issues of church, mission, and unity. While Newbigin's emphasis was unique – here I am referring to his comprehensive view of what he calls the Protestant, Catholic and Pentecostal viewpoints – he developed the very theme that had been central in the IMC from the beginning of the 20th century, namely the church in mission, with "a focus on the end" (see Schwarz 1994).

3.5. Summary

The breaking in of the age to come into the present age has led to an overlap of the two ages. This is the eschatological tension of the "already now" of God's reign and the "not yet" of its consummation. The church takes its essence from the age to come (being the firstfruits of salvation, the provisional incorporation of humanity into Christ), yet it lives in the present age.

The overlapping of the two ages is brought about by the postponing of the end. This has is evidenced in the mission of the church. The church is called to carry the witness of Christ's victory to the ends of the earth till the end of time and thus extend the invitation to all people to become part of the eschatological community of salvation.

The universal character of salvation which is expressed in the mission of the church is rooted in the universal character of God's love. The corporate character of salvation implies that the church is not an instrument for the mediation of private salvation. It is rather the foretaste and firstfruits of salvation which the consummation of Christ's reign will finally and fully reveal, the beginning of the restoration of humankind.

Therefore both the unity of the church and its mission cannot be understood apart from the eschatological tension. Unity is God's gift to the church (reconciliation as foretaste and firstfruits of salvation). At the same time it is an ongoing challenge for the church which is characterized by the tension of *simul justus et peccator*. The mission of the church is the participation in God's mission, extending the message of salvation to the ends of the earth and looking forward to the consummation of God's reign at the end of time.

4. The Christian Hope (1951-1953)

Newbigin's active participation in the worldwide ecumenical movement began – one may say – with his attendance of the inaugural assembly of the WCC 1948 in Amsterdam, his involvement as chairman and drafter in a group of 25 theologians preparing the theme of the second assembly of the WCC in Evanston, and his contribution to the World Mission Conference in Willingen 1952. The theme that occupied Newbigin's thinking at that time was "the Christian hope."[3] Reporting on the work of the study group which met at Rolle, Switzerland in 1951, Newbigin outlines his understanding of Christian eschatology the characteristics of which we have already seen in his Bangalore lectures in 1941.

4.1. Eschatological Hope – Cosmic and Universal

For Newbigin it is important that the Christian hope is not broken up in two fragments: hope for humankind, on the one hand, in the form of hope for human progress or the establishment of the kingdom of God; and hope for the individual, on the other hand, in the form of hope for individual personal salvation.

> I have suggested that, in fact, we have broken up this Christian hope into two fragments neither of which can stand alone – the hope of a personal future be-

---

[3] The basic facets of Newbigin's understanding of the Christian hope are also found in the Report of the Advisory Commission on the main theme of the Second Assembly (Advisory Commission 1954). Newbigin was involved in the drafting of this document.

yond death, and the hope of a perfect society on earth. The one secures some sort of meaning for personal life at the cost of making the whole cosmic process meaningless. The other gives a meaning to the drama of world history at the cost of destroying the meaning of each individual life. (53ch, 112)

The hope we see in the NT is "the hope of Christ's final victory by which history is consummated and brought to its end, a consummation in which both the meaning of the whole cosmic process and the meaning of my individual life is achieved and revealed" (51wich, 464).

4.2. Death and Resurrection – Radical Discontinuity

New Testament hope is resurrection hope. But resurrection also means death and judgment. In this context Newbigin introduces the term "radical discontinuity," a term which he later uses in his theology of religions to describe the relationship between the religions and the gospel.

> There is a radical discontinuity – not a complete discontinuity, that would be meaningless, but a radical discontinuity – between that final consummation and this on-going history, whether personal or corporate; a discontinuity indicated by the words 'death' and 'resurrection'. (51wich, 464)

As Newbigin has stated earlier, there is no direct line between human efforts and the establishment of the kingdom of God. We cannot establish the kingdom of God (53ch, 114). All things have to meet Christ's judgment. On the other hand Newbigin emphasizes the element of continuity through death and judgment: "That is the Christian hope: that every act of obedience to God, however apparently insignificant and historically ineffective, can be committed to Him now, immediately, in the present, with the sure confidence that it is kept until the day of the final victory" (51wich, 465). This hope and expectation gives meaning to what we do and at the same time exhorts us to contribute what we can, knowing that we, too, must appear before the judgment seat of Christ.

> It means that we are to commit all our obedience to Christ, knowing Him, that He is able to keep that which we have committed to Him against that day, knowing that even though all our works may seem to fail and to be lost in the rubble of history, and though we ourselves must at the last return to the dust, nothing committed to Him is lost, and He is able to complete that which He has begun in us and in the world. He is the judge before whom we have to answer for every indifference to the needs of His brethren, for every failure to act when action was needed, whether that action was giving a cup of cold water to a thirsty man at our door, or throwing ourselves into the long and perhaps bitter political struggle that will be needed if the wealthy nations of the West are to bear and share the burden of the hungry millions of Asia. And He is the Saviour to whom we can commit all our labour and all our witness, as a sort of visible prayer for the hastening of the coming of His Kingdom. (53ch, 114-115; see also Advisory Commission 1951, 74-75)

4.3. Decisive Victory and Consummation

Newbigin uses as an illustration the distinction between D-Day and V-Day to clarify the relationship between the decisive victory of Christ on the cross and the consummation of his victory at his second coming, an illustration which we also find in Cullmann (Cullmann 1962).

> Christian hope, therefore, is something which is solidly based upon both the past and the present. It is based upon the accomplished victory of Christ and upon His continuing reign at the right hand of the Father. I know no better way of illustrating the atmosphere, so to say, of the New Testament, no better way of illustrating the particular quality of hope as it seems to me that the New Testament presents it, than from the experience of countless people on the Continent – in the occupied parts of Europe during the days between D-Day and V-Day. ... With Christ, we have the beginning of the end, we are living between D-Day and V-Day, between the decisive breakthrough, as it were, and the final victory. There is a fight, but we live in a certain and sure hope of victory, based upon what He has done. (51wich, 465)

Christian hope is aware of both events and builds on both. The decisive victory has already been won. But the consummation of Christ's victory has not yet come. The fight that Newbigin refers to here is the conflict between Christ and the powers, the conflict between God's love and evil. In his death on the cross Christ took it upon himself to absorb the ultimate thrust of the powers of evil by directing the deadly thrust upon himself. What looks like a defeat of God's love by the powers of evil, is in fact the decisive victory of love over the evil one. "He who won thereby the only victory by which evil can be defeated, the victory of love which bears all evil and remains itself. That victory is necessarily a hidden victory. That is the necessary character of love's victory" (53ch, 112-113). This hidden victory of Christ against evil is, however, the beginning of a new humankind and it needs to be proclaimed to all.

> Because He is the new Adam, because He died for all, because He is the maker of all and the lover of all, this Gospel is to be preached to all nations and to every creature. Witness is to be borne to all. All are to be reconciled. All are to be knit together in one Body. (53ch, 113)

4.4. Real End of History

The Christian hope of the consummation of Christ's victory is directed towards a real end of history. Again Newbigin rejects any interpretation that relegates the eschatological hope into the realm of the symbolic.

> [A]ll this is directed to and bounded by a real end, a real consummation, a real fulfilling of all and more than all our longings, a brimming over of the cup, a real journey's end. The Spirit and the Bride say, 'Come!' And He saith, 'Yea, I come quickly'. ... He will visibly terminate and consummate the world history in which He is now at work hiddenly. There will be a real end. (53ch, 114-115)

Any symbolic interpretation of the end which denies an actual future coming of Christ Newbigin refutes as the "dangling of a carrot before the nose of the donkey." It would in fact be the denial of the eschatological hope.

> [S]urely this is to make the Christian hope into something like the proverbial carrot dangled before the nose of the donkey – something which is always just ahead, but never reached. If Christians really believed that that was the truth, there would be an end of hope. (54pccc, 122)

While we expect a real end of history, we do not know the time of the end. This is something God has not revealed to us. All we know is that death is the boundary of human life, that there will be a real end to history, and that we all will appear before Christ as judge and savior (53ch, 115). However the church knows its task and it can go forth in hope and expectation, looking backward on the fact of Christ's victory on the cross and his resurrection as well as looking forward to the outworking of this victory that God has promised for the future.

> The Gospel is to be preached to all the nations and then shall the end come. ... In the knowledge that He has promised it we are to be patient in hope, hope that can never be disappointed and that sends us full of hope into every situation, however seemingly hopeless. And constrained by His love we are to press on to every nation and into every human situation as the witnesses and ambassadors of the King who has come and is to come, and who is yet with us now, even to the end of the world. (53ch, 115-116)

Anticipating the consummation of history, the church is called to engage in the task it has been given. Here Newbigin can speak – in reference to Matt 24:14 – of the church "hastening" the final day by its involvement in mission (48dacp, 34), or in another context: "he has allowed the consummation of His purpose to wait upon our obedience, and entrusted to us the task of making His victory known and effective in every nation and in every sphere of life" (54pccc, 123). Thus the eschatological hope for a real end of history becomes the motivating force for the church in its mission.

4.5. Eschatological Hope as Motivating Force for the Present

It is important to note how central for Newbigin the role of hope is for the church in the eschatological tension and in its sending. The Christian hope is stronger than everything that may disappoint it. It is this hope which sends the members of the church into the world as witnesses and ambassadors and keeps them going in the face of all frustration. This can only be so because Christian hope is not an expression of what we wish for. It is instead founded upon what God has done in the past and is doing in the present. And it is founded upon his promise.

> When we speak of the Christian Hope we must first of all make it clear that the hope of which we speak is something quite certain, more certain than tomor-

row's dawn. ... The Christian hope of which the Bible speaks, and of which we here speak, concerns something which is utterly certain, something that we wait for with eager expectation and yet with infinite patience because we know that it will never deceive us. And it is so because it is rooted in what God has done and in what He is doing. ... It is based upon solid ground in the past and in the present. It is based upon things that have been done and things that have been given, things which are in themselves the most glorious that we can know in this world, and yet things which point beyond themselves to something yet more glorious to come. The New Testament uses such words as "first-fruits" and "earnest" to describe this forward-pointing character of what has been done and given. (54pccc, 118)

Newbigin summarizes the foundation of the Christian hope in the phrases: "Christ who has come," and "Christ who is with us." Based on these facts is the expectation "Christ who is to come" (54pccc). Thus Christian hope is thoroughly Christocentric, building on what Christ has done and awaiting what he will do.

Newbigin points out that the central message of the church to the world is concentrated in a christological confession. "It is summed up in the single sentence with which the Church first faced the world – 'Jesus Christ is Lord.'" (53ccgc, 515). Newbigin explicates: That means

> firstly, the abandonment of the belief that man can ultimately plan his own history. ... It means, secondly, that there is a radical discontinuity between all human manifestations of power and the ultimate power by which history is shaped toward its end. ... It means, thirdly, therefore, that our hope is fixed on that which is beyond history. ... There is no evading the radical otherworldliness of Christianity. That is precisely the secret of its power to change the world. ... Fourthly, to say that Jesus Christ is Lord is to acknowledge that he alone is to be obeyed here and now. ... What the Christian can do and must do in this world, can only be done because he serves a Kingdom not of this world. He can truly serve his day and generation on earth because he loves and longs for Heaven. (53ccgc, 515-517)

The distinctive feature of Christian hope is that it is anchored beyond history and looking forward to a real end of history. Yet at the same time it is directed towards the world. Eschatological hope does not lead to a retreat from the world but provides the church with strength to face the challenges of the world. Hope thus leads each member of the church

> to see and do God's will in his own place, his own job, his own nation, and to offer that obedience in every place, whether in success or in failure, whether in the light of fame or in the shadow of obscurity, to the Lord who is at the right hand of the Father, who shall come again to judge, and whose kingdom shall have no end. (53ccgc, 518)

Precisely because the Christian hope is anchored beyond history the church can make a difference in the world. It provides both the motivating force as well as the realism for the church's engagement in the issues of the world. The power for change is "from beyond."

> The Church is a pilgrim people, with its hope fixed on that which eye hath not seen nor ear heard. ... The Church is uncrushable and undefeatable precisely because and in so far as its hope is fixed not upon the success of its own programme but upon His appearing, upon the manifestation of His victory in the sight of all nations. ... The Church only has power to move the world because it has its centre of gravity, its fulcrum, outside of the world. A message which has its centre within this world may re-arrange some of the constituents of this world, but cannot move the world. The Gospel, which comes to us from the other side of death, has its power to move the world precisely because it does not belong to the world. (54lwlc, 8-9)

5. The Unity of God's Story with His World (1954-1960)

Closely related to the eschatological hope of the Christian church is the biblical understanding of the history of humankind as *one* story, God's story with his world.

5.1. God's Story with Humankind

In a short essay from 1954 Newbigin points out the unity of the bible as one book, telling this story of which God is the main actor.

> [W]e are making the tremendously bold claim that God really has a purpose for the world and for all men ... [W]e ask them to read the Bible. There they will find a sort of outline of world history, beginning with the creation and ending with the glory of God's perfect kingdom; but the central thread of the history is the story of God's people. And the centre point of the story is the birth, life, death, resurrection and ascension of Jesus and the coming of His Spirit to His disciples. It is from that centre point that we understand the whole Bible, both the Old Testament and the New. Everything in the Bible points towards Him, and then points outward from Him to the end of the world and the ends of the earth. (54wsot, 75-76)

Newbigin sketches with a few strokes the characteristics of God's story with this world. The framework of this story is captured with the words "creation" and "glory of God's perfect kingdom," the beginning and the end point of the story respectively. The thread which runs through the story is God's dealing with his people. Newbigin does not understand the way God deals with his people exclusively in the sense that God would deal with Israel and the church but not with the world. On the contrary, God's dealing with his people always has the whole of humanity in mind. This is where the doctrine of election plays such an important role. The center and turning point of history is found in the events of Christ's life and the coming of the Spirit. It is the center point in the sense that the OT looks forward to this day and the NT looks backward to it and tells and interprets this center of the story. The events of Jesus' life are the center point of history because he stands in the middle between creation and fall on the one hand and the consummation in the new creation on the other. But Christ is also the turning point of history because in his death and resurrection he has given a new direction to the history of the world. In his coming he has brought the powers of the new age into the present. Therefore human existence is no longer a being unto death but a being unto life. In the person of Christ the destiny and direction of world history have been revealed.

> Everything in the Bible is to be understood by its reference to Him; He is the turning point of the story. The purpose of everything in it is to lead us to Him. We do not understand any of it rightly if it does not lead us to Him; but equally we do not understand Him rightly except by seeing Him where He is, at the centre and turning point of actual history. That is why we need the whole Bible. (54wsot,76)

The bible tells this story and interprets the events of world history from God's perspective. Only through this interpretation can the whole of the story be understood. The revelation of the story to the church is not a matter of exclusive privilege but a matter of responsibility for the whole. It is through the community of the elect that the purpose of the story is to be revealed to the world, and in this process humankind is recreated as God's family.

> God works by this method of election, of choosing one to be the means of bringing in the next, because His purpose is not to pick out an individual here and there for His kingdom, but to re-create for Himself that one family which He purposed in the first creation. (54wsot, 72-73)

So both the centrality of Christ in the history of humankind and the calling of the church form an essential part of God's story. Election becomes the key which brings together the particularities of God's acting and the universal scope of his purpose. It is the characteristic of God's overarching story with its eschatological focus.

> God is in control of history. ... History is in his grip, and he continues to propel it to the end for which all things were created – namely that they might be consummated in Christ. The centre point of all history is the invasion of the End into the midst of the story, in the man Jesus in whom the word was made flesh. By that invasion, the crisis of history is precipitated. Slowly but inexorably all men and all nations are brought within the range of that event and are faced with issues for which natural religion has no place – the issue of the ultimate consummation of all things. (63jsmc, 29)

5.2. Salvation as Historic Fact

The fact that the bible is a record and an interpretation of God's dealings in world history and that in the process of God's story people of all nations are drawn into his story, distinguishes the bible from other religions and their religious instruction. Salvation in the biblical understanding is thus intrinsically bound to particular historic events, events which happened once for all, which will not be repeated, and which extend in their meaning to all of humankind. The biblical story thus binds salvation to the particular events in the life of Christ, culminating in his death. "[T]hat atoning act is directed to the whole human race, and not to anything less. Christ died for all men" (55qutr, 28). The mark and the goal of this salvation is not the retreat from the world but reconciliation and the creation of a new community. Salvation can therefore not be an individualistic matter because it is in essence the renewal of community. This clearly distinguishes the biblical understanding of salvation from for example the Hindu view of salvation which Newbigin encountered during his years in India.

In his critique of Hinduism Newbigin argues that each participant in the interreligious dialogue has to start out with his or her own faith commitment. A neutral outside viewpoint from which to evaluate the different religions and their truth claims is simply not available to us. Newbigin critiques the implied superiority of Hinduism when it relegates the Christian idea of revelation to a lower level of religious consciousness. The principal assumption in Hinduism that the diversity of the phenomena is part of the illusional world of *maya* is no logical and compelling conclusion from the observation of the plurality of phenomena, however intriguing it may be. It is simply a faith-commitment from which the Hindu starts out in his understanding of the world (61ftow, 39). That places the Hindu with his interpretation of the world on the same level as the Christian. In his dialogue Newbigin then presents his own starting point – namely the historical character of salvation – and argues for the coherence and the unity of the Christian view of salvation and history.

This shows how for Newbigin the understanding of world history as God's story with an eschatological goal is essential not only for understanding the church and its mission but also for understanding the character of the gospel and its relationship to other religions. This will be part of the later discussion (see chapter five).

5.3. All Nations Drawn into One Story

Newbigin interprets the emergence of "a single world civilization" into which all nations are drawn in an eschatological perspective (58lmc, 59scmt). One world civilization also means a single world history.

> That is the meaning of the period of history in which we live. All men and all nations are being gradually but inexorably brought to face the ultimate issues which Jesus raises for man. Gradually but inexorably the nations and races are being brought out of their separation, out of their isolated histories, into one universal world-history of which Christ is the centre. (58lmc, 5)

For Newbigin such a coherent view of history also requires a belief about the direction of history as such. Without a sense of purpose and direction there is no sense of history, because individual historical facts and events cannot be evaluated for their significance if there is no overarching story.

> [T]here can only be a world history if there is some belief as to the direction in which mankind as a whole is moving, in the light of which events can be judged significant or otherwise. There cannot be a world history without some belief as to the course of the story as a whole – that is to say, as to the origin and destiny of man. (59scmt, 182)

While the Western understanding of history originally grew out of a biblical eschatological view of the history of humankind as a whole, that faith has now been secularized and transformed into the idea of progress. With this transformation important changes have taken place. God has been moved out of the center. The human being has become the main actor. God's eschatological purpose for the world has been transformed into a world-immanent goal of a better human society which can and will be reached by human efforts. The fact of human sinfulness is ignored in this optimistic vision of history.

> The secularized and distorted form of this Christian faith has transmuted the hope of God's kingdom transcending history into the hope of a new order within history to be achieved by man's progressive mastery of nature and of his own affairs. ...
>
> The tragic element in our human situation today is that the secularized and distorted Christian eschatology, the faith, that is to say, which finds the significance of human life in the achievement of a new order of human society on earth – is achieving global extension and penetration just at the time when – by the outworking of its own inner falsity – it stands self-condemned in the lands of its origin. (59scmt, 182-183)

So while it is true that the nations are drawn into one story, Newbigin does not share the optimism that underlies the Western idea of progress. He sees it rather as a tragical development that the secularized version of the eschatological hope is gaining ground worldwide, a vision which does not include a realistic understanding of the human being as a sinner nor an allowance for God's involvement in world history.

For Newbigin the developments towards a unified view of humankind are not mere historical coincidences. Rather he sees the history of humankind moving towards a final clash of Christ and Antichrist, "the true Saviour of the world, or the bogus saviours who purport to offer mankind final security and well-being in terms which belong to this world, that is to say, which belong to this side of death" (59scmt, 185).

> We face an increasingly unified world whose central driving conception is a secularized and distorted form of the Christian eschatology – a faith in the ultimate power of man to establish on earth the order that he wants. To that we have to oppose simply the word of the Gospel – not an ideology, not a programme, not a religion, but simply Jesus Christ, crucified, risen and ascended, the lowly Servant of all men and the exalted King and Head of the whole hu-

man race. We have only one message, and only one authority for delivering it; our message and our authority is Jesus Christ. That is the one Name given under heaven for the salvation of mankind. It is enough that we stand under that Name. (59scmt, 189)

Into this broad cosmic picture the church is placed with its mission to bring the gospel to the world. The gospel here is not understood as one religious voice among others. Newbigin does not place the gospel into the category "religion" at all. It is rather the proclamation of the lordship of Christ over all areas of human existence which challenges human beings not only and not even primarily in the religious sphere of their lives. The challenge of the gospel extends to all spheres of human existence and calls for all aspects of life to be brought under the rule of Christ.

We see already how for Newbigin the characteristic of the gospel is intrinsically bound to the fact that it is a story, God's story, which encompasses all of humankind. The gospel must therefore not be turned into a religious teaching. It is – as he later calls it – "public truth." The task of the church is to present to the world the true nature of this gospel. It is this mission which becomes the key for understanding world history as a whole.

> For the missionary work of the Church is not one of the strands of which world history is composed: it is the clue to world history. The gospel is the announcement of the end of world history. It concerns the whole human race and it is of such a character that there is an obligation in it to bring it to the whole human race without delay. (60lmc, 61)

5.4. The Evaluation of Secularization

Newbigin recalls a key experience in 1957 which set his mind on a new topic and influenced his thinking during the 1960s.

> I had been asked to give a lecture for which I was quite unprepared. I therefore spent the entire night hours on the plane from Bombay to Rome reading right through the New Testament and noting every reference to 'the world'. The result of this was to set my mind moving in a new direction in which it was to travel for the next ten years. My thoughts for the past decade had been centred in the Church. This fresh exposure to the word of God set me thinking about the work of God in the world outside the Church. The result was a lecture in which I advanced the thesis that 'what we are witnessing is the process by which more and more of the human race is being gathered up into that history whose centre is the cross, and whose end is the final judgement and mercy of God.' I was talking not just about missions but about the total shift from a cyclical to a linear way of understanding history, brought about by the impact of 'development'. (85ua, 152-153)

Newbigin initially interprets the results of the Western idea of development rather positively, since this idea leads to an experience of liberation among the people of Asia who have so far lived in structures that did not allow them to accept a biblical view of the world. "The effect of this is to destroy beyond the possibility of repair the ancient sacral types of society, in which the whole human community was held together by religious sanctions" (63jsmc, 27). Newbigin envisions the possibilities for people to be liberated from religious and social traditions which have held them captive for centuries. It is this process of liberation in which Newbigin sees the "operation of forces originating in the Gospel itself" (63jsmc, 28). What missionaries have attempted for 150 years is furthered now by the process of secularization.

> The process of secularization in India is accomplishing the kind of changes in patterns of human living for which Christian missionaries have fought with such stubborn perseverance a century and a half ago – the abolition of untouchability, of the dowry system, of temple prostitution, the spread of education and medical service, and so on. (66hrsm, 17)

Looking back on the historical developments in world mission Newbigin sees that "[m]issionaries in Asia and Africa have been agents of secularization even if they did not realize it. ... [T]heir teaching and practice has the effect of disintegrating the sacral bonds that have traditionally held society together" (66hrsm, 18). People are becoming critical of accepting the identification of cosmic powers with the existing socio-political order (66hrsm, 29). The growth of this kind of critical awareness diminishes the influence of established religious traditions and opens people to a new view of the world. Newbigin thus interprets secularization as a positive development as it contributes to the dismantling of traditional structures which have held people captive. He is optimistic about the opportunities for the gospel to fill the emerging vacuum.

The new view of the world brings with it a linear view of history which incorporates all nations into one history and leaves behind traditional circular views. Here Newbigin endorses van Leeuwen's understanding "that the process of secularization is the present form in which the non-western world is meeting biblical history" (66hrsm, 27; see Leeuwen 1964). Leeuwen actually got the impetus for his book from Newbigin's lecture which I mentioned at the beginning of this section (see 85ua, 153).

This process of secularization, however, applies not only to Non-Western cultures but also to Christendom itself.

> There are no more Christian societies. ... Christians are in a radically new situation, which is neither the Constantinian situation of a Christian sacral society, nor the pre-Constantinian situation of a pagan sacral society, but something new and different: a society which has been secularized irreversibly by the operation of forces originating in the Gospel itself. (63jsmc, 28)

Secularization of the Christian society, however, is an ambiguous enterprise since it also enforces the secularization of the Christian eschatological hope. Already in 1959, before he positively evaluated the developments of secularization, Newbigin had expressed the recognition that it was not the gospel which was filling the vacuum of the dismantled structures but rather the secularized form of the Christian eschatological hope, namely the idea of progress (see 59scmt, 183). That of course leads to new distortions in the view of the world.

Despite his optimism for the opportunities of the gospel in the wake of the secularization of traditional structures and worldviews Newbigin is aware of the danger associated with the process of secularization. He sees the central danger in the fact that men and women lose their sense of responsibility before God and thus head towards disaster and self-destruction. For Newbigin the process of secularization is only positive insofar as it supports the liberation from traditional, oppressing structures and ideas which have hindered people from accepting a biblical view of the world. Wherever this movement of liberation does not lead to a true recognition of the human being before God it will finally lead to self-destruction.

> [T]his movement of worldwide secularization is a genuine continuation of that liberation-history which is the central theme of the Bible. Just for that reason I am driven also to believe that this movement is misunderstood if it is seen out of that context; that it will recoil in self-destruction. Specifically I suggest ... that if the mastery which is given to man through the process of secularization is not held within the context of man's responsibility to God, the result will be a new slavery; ... that if the dynamism of 'development', the drive to a new kind of human society, is not informed by the biblical faith concerning the nature of the Kingdom of God it will end in totalitarianism; and ... that if the secular critique of all established orders is not informed and directed by the knowledge of God it will end in a self-destructive nihilism. (66hrsm, 38-39)

Newbigin critiques the idea of development and progress with an eschatological view of God's kingdom. Only when all things are centered around the person of Jesus Christ the goal of a new humankind will be reached. All attempts to establish a just and perfect society apart from Christ must lead to new slavery, totalitarianism, and in the end self-destruction. So Newbigin does not endorse secularism as a basis for a secular state, but he still welcomes the process of secularization and interprets it as part of God's story with humankind. He can therefore say that a secular society can only work

> if religion continues to be a living reality. Secularity is not by itself enough to sustain a human society in being. ... Secondly, and more fundamentally, I want to express the conviction that the idea of a secular society can only be rightly understood in the context of a biblical understanding of history. (66hrsm, 134-135)

Here Newbigin's use of the term "religion" is not very precise. The context shows that it needs to be understood in contrast to "secularity" or "secularism," a worldview which takes God out of the center. This is what Newbigin resists despite his endorsement of the process of secularization. The processes of secularization and the establishment of a secular society can only succeed when God remains the central figure for human life and history. The question of course arises: In what sense is this kind of society a "secular" society? We will return to the tension between a secular society and a Christian state later.

Based on this conviction Newbigin emphasizes the missionary task of the church in light of the process of secularization.

> [T]he proper Christian response to the process of secularization must include commitment to the world missionary task. ... The Christian church in every land is called to the task of being witness to what God is doing in this worldwide process, so that those who are being drawn out of their traditional securities into this new and perplexing freedom may be helped to understand this experience as what it truly is, a calling to new responsibility before the Lord of history. (66hrsm, 136-137)

That is the true reason behind Newbigin's optimism regarding secularization: It sets the stage for the church to call people of all nations to understand and order their lives – both private and public – in light of the lordship of Christ, whose reign extends over all.

Newbigin in his later years is more critical in his use of the word "secular." Reflecting back on the early 1960s he says about himself: "It meant that I began the 'secular decade' of the 1960s with some enthusiasm for the 'secular interpretation of the Gospel,' and was more ready to see its weaknesses before that decade ended" (85ua, 153). In his later essay "The myth of the secular society" Newbigin explicitly questions the assumption that a secular society can provide a neutral framework for understanding the world. Since any society has to define the basis for its structure and community it necessarily endorses a specific view of humanity and the world, which means it is not and it cannot be neutral. Therefore a secular society, in the sense of a society which is neutral with regard to its religious views and its worldview, is simply an impossibility (89gps, 211-221). In one of his final publications Newbigin also deals with the relationship of a biblical worldview and a secular society (98fp). This will be part of a later discussion.

However, one has to recognize that even in the 1960s Newbigin never lost sight of the fact, that the "triumph of secularization is certainly not the triumph of the Kingdom of God" (66hrsm, 29). While he sees God actively at work in history and while he is looking to find the traces of God's working, Newbigin does not lose sight of the eschatological dimension of world history. Newbigin's awareness of the secularization of the biblical concept of the kingdom of God in Western society exemplified in the idea of "progress," which goes as far back as 1941, saved him from falling into that very trap in his own understanding of mission and history.

This overview of Newbigin's early writings out of India points out the key elements in Newbigin's thinking as it relates to the subject of this study. These are: his view of the kingdom of God, his view of the church, his view of eschatology, and his view of the history of humankind. The question now is: Have these fundamental lines of thinking changed in his later writings, and if so, how? Or can we detect the same foundations in his later writings? To these questions we now turn.

Chapter 3

The Kingdom of God in Newbigin's Writings (Synchronic Analysis of His Later Writings)

In this chapter I will pick up the themes of chapter two and follow Newbigin's portrayal of these topics in his later writings, beginning approximately 1960.

1. The Kingdom of God

In his Bangalore lectures on the Kingdom of God Newbigin critiqued the idea of progress as a secularized form of Christian eschatology. There is no direct line from this present world to a world characterized by God's shalom. There has to be death and resurrection, a new creation. Only that which corresponds to God's character will be brought into this new world. Newbigin criticized the dualism of social and individual salvation and spoke of the need to view these two aspects together. Salvation is corporate by nature. It is social and cosmic without being universalist. Salvation concerns humankind and the whole created world, not just any number of nomadic souls. Also, Newbigin critiqued a one-sided realized eschatology which denies a real future consummation. The kingdom of God is both present and future and is concerned with a real world. That is the framework from which Newbigin developed his understanding of the role of the church in this world. In this section I will develop how Newbigin in his later years depicts the kingdom of God and where he places his emphases.

1.1. God's Action – No Human Program

Newbigin consistently argues that the decisive event for the history of this world did not grow out of human history as a natural event. It is not a matter of development and progress but an act brought about by God.

> God's purpose for the world is accomplished by the sending of His Son. ... The figure of Jesus does not simply rise out of human history; if that were so, we could look forward to yet greater developments. Jesus was sent once for all by the Father to reveal and establish His reign. Jesus is 'not of this world'; He is sent by the Father into this world. This sending is a dateable event in history – secular history. (58lmc, 6)

The decisive action is taken by God, not by us as human agents. The church's actions are derived from the fact that the kingdom of God has already come among humankind in the person of Jesus Christ. That means the kingdom is not a program for human development. This kind of interpretation would fall into the utopian trap and bring with it the instrumentalization and devaluation of individual human beings.

> We must frankly accept the fact that the New Testament teaching about the kingdom of God cannot be converted into a programme for a perfect society at some date in the remote future, whether to be achieved by evolutionary "development" or by revolution. If it were to be so, then all of us now living and all who now suffer under evil powers are for ever excluded from the blessing, for all of us will be dead long before it appears. The kingship of God is not a kingship that treats the men and women now living as mere instruments for a purpose in the fruition of which they will have no share. (87mcw, 28)

Instead Newbigin reminds us that biblical eschatology takes both, human individuals and the history of humankind, seriously. Taking human individuals seriously means to see them not merely as a means for reaching a better world. Taking human history seriously means to view the world not merely as a training ground for individual souls to reach a future state of bliss.

> One alternative is a view of the future shaped by an evolutionary, progress-oriented vision. Hope is then pinned to the vision of a perfect human society at some future date in history. We have become familiar with various forms of this intra-mundane eschatology in the past 200 years. It evokes little belief today except among Marxists living under non-Marxist governments. Its defects are obvious. It tends inevitably to marginalise the human persons now living, treating them as expendable in view of the glory to be revealed to their descendants. It distorts the relations between old and young in society. It tends to lead in the end to a widespread denial or diminution of the rights of individual human persons. (93kogh, 9)

The counterpart to this understanding is the devaluation of history which goes hand in hand with the individualization of the Christian hope and a retreat from any involvement in the struggles of the world, a subject to which we will later turn when we look at the challenge of Christian involvement in the world.

Newbigin points out the tension which results from on the one hand a refusal to treat the kingdom as a human task and on the other hand a refusal to retreat from the world in inactivity. In the middle of this tension is the fact that it is God who is the decisive agent. How strongly Newbigin views God as the decisive actor of his kingdom is seen in his evaluation of the end of Christian mission work in China:

> Can you contemplate the destruction of our most magnificent efforts for the Kingdom of God and take it as a sign of the coming of the Kingdom? Can you face the end of the great work of Christian missions in China and take it as a sign of the coming of the Kingdom? Or are you thinking of the Church's mission as the work that we do, building for God through the decades till His Kingdom comes? (60lmc, 62)

If God is the decisive agent, how then is the action of the church related to God's kingdom? It is not to sit still and merely wait for the consummation of the kingdom to come. The church, too, is called to act. But its actions are to be derived from the fact that the kingdom is already present in the person of Jesus Christ and in the gift of the Holy Spirit. And its actions are to be understood as signs pointing towards the kingdom, rather than as acts establishing the kingdom.

> I know that some will denounce this language as escapist, but in fact it is simply realist. The best of our programmes are still full of the seeds of their own corruption. We do not establish God's kingdom. That kingdom, that kingly rule, has been given to us in the form of the suffering servant, the wounded healer, the crucified liberator. God's kingdom is a given fact, and our actions for justice and compassion are at the very best only signs, pointers to help men and women to turn round so that it becomes possible for them also to believe in the reality of that kingdom, to have a foretaste of its liberating power, to follow in the way of the cross and to find in it life – a life that death cannot threaten. (87mcw, 11-12)

The actions of the church are put in perspective by focusing on God as the decisive actor of the kingdom. The nature of the kingdom is that it is built on God's action.

1.2. The Presence of the Kingdom – The Announcement of a Fact

In the person of Jesus Christ God has acted in such a way that the kingdom of God is no longer simply the expectation of a future day of salvation. The kingdom of God has appeared in history. The presence of the kingdom is announced as a historical fact.

> It is not the launching of a programme. It is not the promulgation of a new doctrine. It is not a call to moral or religious reformation. It is, strictly speaking, a news-flash. Something has happened. There is a new fact to be reckoned with. The kingdom, the reign of God, has come near. (87mcw, 1)

The appearance of the kingdom is a historical fact which brings a new reality into the present, a foretaste of the final consummation. The gospel is the announcement of this fact. At the same time it is an invitation to become part of this new reality. We are not merely looking at a statement about a fact. We are confronted with a new reality which requires us to make a decision about it. The new reality is the reestablishment of God's shalom, the restoration of humanity to its true calling.

> 'Peace be unto you'. Peace, the peace of God, is His ultimate gift. It is the sign of the presence of God's kingdom. It is the condition in which men are restored to their true humanity, because they are reconciled with their Maker. It includes all the benefits which Christ was sent to bring – deliverance from evil, forgive-

ness of sins, wholeness of body and mind, sonship of God and brotherhood with men. That peace is Christ's gift. (58lmc, 7)

This new reality is present today as the foretaste of God's final shalom. It is the sign which accompanies the witness of the church to the world. The church is called as witness to this new fact of the presence of God's kingdom, confronting people with the good news and its implications. Again the emphasis is not on the church to be the agent of change but – in both its words and its actions – to be the witness to the reality of salvation today and to its future fulfillment. That qualifies the church's involvement in movements that promote change.

> The Church is not required (as speakers sometimes suggest) to try to control or overcome the revolutionary movements of our time. These movements are themselves inexplicable apart from the impact of ideas and ways of life derived from the Bible upon the peoples of the world. The Church is rather called to be present everywhere within these movements as the witnessing, suffering servant of God, believing in his sovereign rule and becoming the place where that rule is made manifest, the place, therefore, where men are called upon to decide for or against God. (63rtdt, 43-44)

Newbigin says this at a time when the general mood of the mission movement was swinging towards the paradigm called for by Hoekendijk that God was involved in the world apart from the church. Newbigin rejects this dichotomy and, while not denying God's involvement in the world, continues to see the role of the church as witness in both word and deed to the presence and to the future of God's kingdom. The church must neither be devalued as irrelevant to God's salvific work in the world, nor must it be overestimated as if it were the agent to bring about God's reign.

1.3. The Cross as Victory over the Powers

While the presence of the kingdom is a new fact in history, established by God, it is nevertheless still a hidden fact. "[T]his presence is veiled. It is not obvious to the naked eye of unconverted men and women" (89gps, 105). It has come in a way that was completely unexpected. To perceive the presence of God's kingdom in the person of Jesus Christ people have to look in a different direction. They have to be converted. In this context Newbigin speaks of a literal "U-turn" in the sense of "turning around to look in a different direction." He refers to one of his experiences while visiting an Indian village to illustrate the point that conversion is more than a moral turn-around. It is rather a reorientation which leads to a completely new perspective on the world (89gps, 105; 87mcw, 2). It is in this U-turn that people's eyes are opened, so that they can begin to see the presence of God's reign today. Precisely because the kingdom is still hidden, the church is called to witness to it and invite people to this U-turn in order for them to perceive this new reality.

The reality of the presence of the kingdom is seen on the other hand in the conflict that the coming of Christ has brought to the fore.

> It follows from this that this hidden presence creates crisis and conflict. The powers that be, both in their outward form as the established religious and cultural and political structures, and in their inward reality as the principalities and powers of this age, are challenged and fight back. The presence of Jesus precipitates the hour of the power of darkness (Luke 22:53). ... The presence of Jesus strips the masks of righteousness and piety from the face of the powers. It does so precisely because in him the kingship of God is veiled, hidden in a humble and powerless man. The power of God is not of the same kind as the powers of this dark age. (89gps, 105)

While the presence of God's king is still hidden to human eyes it is nevertheless clear to the powers who are being challenged and whose masks are torn off in the presence of this king. The presence of Christ throws a new light on the powers which control human lives. They are unmasked, revealed for what they truly are.

Newbigin here basically follows Berkhof's understanding of "powers," who interprets the NT references to powers as referring to structures and institutions, rather than to personal spiritual beings (Berkhof 1977, 23-26). Newbigin points out the ambivalent character of these powers.

> It is important for practical Christian discipleship to maintain the tension and balance which is implied in the word 'provisional'. On the one hand, structures are necessary for the maintenance of human life as it is. Christ has not destroyed the powers. Even our personal and family life would be impossible without a framework of custom within which we normally behave. If we had to act every moment in a vacuum, with no structure of custom to guide us, we would soon go crazy. So also political structures are necessary. I think it is necessary to stress this at the moment. In a good deal of the literature that I read about 'power to the people' I detect more than a whiff of unreality. In no circumstances do 'the people' exercise power except through some kind of structure – which can itself become demonic. Anarchism has a respectable history, but Christians are not anarchists, for Christ has not destroyed the powers. But, on the other hand, it is equally necessary to insist that the authority of the structures is provisional and not final or absolute. Christ has disarmed the powers. Christians, therefore, are revolutionaries. They believe that structures can be and have to be changed, and that no structure, even the most venerable (such as the Law of the Old Testament), has absolute authority. Only Christ has absolute authority, and in Christ we are called to keep all structures under review and to change them when necessary. (76bsr8)

So while Newbigin agrees that the structures are necessary for the ordering of human life – as they were created by Christ and for Christ (Col 1:16) – he also sees the necessity for a constant critical reflection of them. Wherever the powers assume a state of autonomy they place themselves in contrast to the lordship of Christ; they turn demonic.

The coming of Christ means the unmasking of the powers and the confrontation with them. They are seen in contrast to and in conflict with Christ. The central message of the NT is the story of how the victory was won in this conflict. At first sight the death of Christ appears to be the defeat of God's king by the powers of evil. However, the NT throughout presents a different interpretation of the event. As the lordship of Christ was hidden to the eyes of the disciples' contemporaries and was revealed only to the elect, so the victory of Christ over the principalities and powers, too, is a hidden victory. It is revealed only to those who are called to be its witnesses to the world.

> And so he goes to the cross, the cross that is both the final parable and the final "mighty work", the place where the kingdom of God, his power and wisdom, is hidden and revealed. To those who are called to be its witnesses it will be revealed by the resurrection; to the rest it is nonsense and a scandal, a blasphemous caricature of God's kingdom. How can a man crucified as a rebel and a heretic be the embodiment of the wisdom and the power of God?
>
> But it is there, on Calvary, that the kingdom, the kingly rule of God, won its decisive victory over all the powers that contradict it. There, as Jesus said, the ruler of this world was cast out (John 12:32). For the cross is not a defeat reversed by the resurrection; it is a victory proclaimed (to chosen witnesses) by the resurrection. And so the risen Lord gathers together his defeated and despairing disciples and sends them out to be the witnesses of the victory of the kingdom, to embody and to proclaim the rule of God. (87mcw, 5-6)

That the church always saw in the death of Christ the victory over the powers of evil is illustrated by the fact that the early paintings of the crucified Christ portrayed him as a victorious warrior with his head held high, "the victorious challenger of all the powers of evil. This is the true understanding of the cross as the New Testament teaches us. The cross is not abject submission to the power of evil; it is the price paid for a victorious challenge to the powers of evil" (87mcw, 25). Newbigin summarizes:

> The new age is defined by the threefold affirmation in which we declare the mystery of faith:
>
> - Christ has died, once for all disarming the principalities and powers.
> - Christ has risen, and now reigns at the Father's side until all his enemies submit.
> - Christ will come again, and the glory of his reign will be manifest to all. (89gps, 111)

1.4. The Sign of the Cross as Mark of Authenticity

The disciples and the church are part of this conflict. In the same way as the confrontation and unmasking of the powers has led to suffering in the life of Jesus Christ, it will also lead to suffering in the life and mission of the church. In the same way that suffering was the mark of Jesus' ministry, it also becomes the mark of the church's ministry. Newbigin even sees the suffering of the church as *the* mark of authenticity that distinguishes its witness as true witness. In his exposition of John 20:21 Newbigin says:

> We have to remind ourselves again of the significance of the little word "as". It is the manner in which the Father sent the Son that determines the manner in which the church is sent by Jesus. Its mission is governed by the manner of his. We are reminded again of the pattern of his mission as it is outlined for us in the four gospels. And lest the full meaning of that word "as" should be missed, he shows them his hands and his side. It was the scars of the passion in his risen body that assured the frightened disciples that it was really Jesus who stood among them. It will be those same scars in the corporate life of the church that will authenticate it as indeed the body of Christ, the bearer of his mission, the presence of the kingdom. It will not be enough for the church to place a cross on the top of its buildings or in the centre of its altars or on the robes of its clergy. The marks of the cross will have to be recognizable also in the lives of its members if the church is to be the authentic presence of the kingdom. …
>
> Jesus stood in their midst and said "peace be with you", showed them the scars of that atoning passion by which alone peace is made between sinful men and women and their holy Creator; and then sent them out to be the bearers of that peace into the life of the world – but always in conformity with the way by which peace was made, the way of the cross. (87mcw, 23, 30)

The conflict arises from the confrontation of the powers and principalities with the claim of the lordship of Christ. The church, too, is called to unmask and confront the powers in the name of Christ.

> [T]here will be the need for courage. Our wrestling is not against flesh and blood but against the principalities and powers – realities to the existence of which our privatized culture has been blind. To ask, Can the West be converted? is to align ourselves with the apostle when he speaks of taking every thought captive to Christ, and for that – as he tells us – we need more than the weapons of the world. (85cwbc, 7)

It is essential that the church in its mission remain true to the way in which Christ confronted the powers. This is what Newbigin calls "the way of the cross." In its mission the church has not always followed the way of the cross. Acting from a position of dominance and control has provoked distrust and resistance. Newbigin argues that the church in its attempt to present the gospel as public truth – a new fact in history which extends its claim not only on the private sphere of individual religious experiences but also on the public sphere of social and communal life – can only expect to meet with a positive response if it approaches the world in the way of the cross.

> The world will rightly distrust any claim by the church to a voice in public affairs, remembering that the freedom of thought and of conscience which the Enlightenment won was won against the resistance of the church. But the freedom which the Enlightenment won rests upon an illusion – the illusion of autonomy – and it therefore ends in new forms of bondage. Yet we have no right to say this until we can show that we have learned our lesson: that we understand the difference between bearing witness to the truth and pretending to

possess the truth; that we understand that witness (*marturia*) means not dominance and control but suffering. (85cwbc, 7)

Thus the cross of Christ is more than the content of the church's message. It is also the mark of its mission as it was the mark of the mission of its Lord.

1.5. Eschatological Tension between the Presence and the Future of the Kingdom

The emphasis on suffering instead of control is rooted in the tension between the presence of the kingdom and its future. Newbigin continues to point out this tension and does not dissolve it in either direction.

> The tensions in the teaching of the New Testament about the kingdom are not, therefore, to be rationalised away. The kingdom is both present and future. It is present in that, through the total work of Jesus, we are given here and now the foretaste, the first-fruit, the arrabon of its grace and peace. It is future in that the story of which our lives are a part, the story of creation and of the human family, is not a meaningless and mindless pantomime but a movement directed towards a real goal, a real event in which it becomes clear that something has been accomplished which makes all the agony and conflict worthy of our participation as rational and moral beings. That goal, that accomplishment, which forms the proper horizon for purposeful action, is in one sense known and in another sense not known. It is known in that in Jesus we have seen the one in whom all human and cosmic history is in the end to find its coherence. Therefore where he is present, the end is at hand. Our true horizon beckons here and now. It is here, at the very door. But in another sense the goal is not known. It is, according to a saying which surely cannot have been invented by the Church, unknown even to Jesus. In all this tangled web of good and evil which makes up the human story, only the Father knows what possibilities for good remain, what further frontiers remain for the human family to cross, what further opportunities for new good remain. Only he knows when and how to bring the story of his creation to its completion. For the practical business of discipleship the implications of this knowing and not knowing are clear. We know the one who is to come, but we do not know when and how he will come. Therefore 'you must be ready, for the Son of Man is coming at an hour you do not expect' (Luke 12, 40). (93kogh, 12)

Newbigin argues that the tension between the presence and the future of the kingdom is not to be understood as a distinction between "incomplete" and "complete." Christ's present reign is in no sense incomplete; it is rather hidden and not yet manifest. "Jesus does now reign at God's right hand, but this reign is hidden in heaven. It will become manifest. What is now hidden will be revealed: this is the exact meaning of apocalypse" (89gps, 105-106). So the consummation is not the completion but the revelation of Christ's reign. This is an important qualification on how to understand the tension between the presence and the future of God's kingdom. It has consequences for a truly holistic understanding of mission as we will see later.

1.6. The Lordship of Christ and the Kingdom

One of the challenges of the church in this tension of the presence and the future of God's kingdom is to unmask the powers in their assumed autonomy as usurpers who attempt to take Christ's place. Newbigin himself does so in his ministry. He challenges the assumed autonomy of economic structures (see his critique of Marxism and capitalism) as well as the presumed objectivity of – what Polanyi calls – the Western "plausibility structure" (see 83os84, 86fg, 89gps, 91tt, 95pc). He questions the uncritical acceptance of dominant cultural influences or the uncritical application of sociological principles on the character and ministry of the church (see e.g. his critique of denominationalism – 80ykc, 60; 85cwbc, 7 – or his critique of the principles of the church-growth school – 95os, 121ff). The central question always is: What does it mean to bring this aspect of human existence, this part of the life of the church under the lordship of Christ? To cite but one example:

> Let me try now to come a little closer to contemporary realities and to spell out what might be the implications of this answer for our churches in this western world. I think that the first implication must be a radical break with the ideology of capitalism. Our timid compromise with this ideology has persisted too long. The ideology of the free market can only be accepted by a church which has retreated into the private sector. The free market system works by means of the unremitting stimulation of consumer demand among those who have the purchasing power to make that demand effective. Translated into biblical language, this is to say that it works by the unremitting stimulation of gluttony among those who already have enough. It necessarily channels resources into the production of goods according to the demand of the relatively prosperous and not according to the need of the poor. In every democratic society which has adopted the principle of the free market, it has been found necessary almost at once to use the powers of Government to prevent the limitless exploitation of the weak and defenseless. It can be reasonably argued that in certain circumstances a 'mixed economy' in which there is a balance between the power of the free market and the power of the State, is the best available system. But acceptance of the ideology of the free market is, I think, forbidden for a Christian. It is important to say this just because its power is so all-pervasive. On the other hand, this break with the ideology of capitalism should not lead the Church to a new alliance with the ideology of Marxism. It is necessary to say this in the present context. (80ykc, 51-52; see also 83os84, 40)

Newbigin continues to point out the need for challenging an unrestrained capitalism also – even more so, one might say – after the collapse of the Marxist system.

> Marxism and capitalism, twin children of the Enlightenment, have fought a long battle, and one has been defeated. But that is not the end of history. It creates a new situation in which there is a more urgent need than ever before for the Church to unmask the illusions and deflate the hubris of modernity and to affirm the true end of history which is offered to us now in the person of the one who is both Alpha and Omega and is Lord of all. (92eh, 2)

Chapter 3: The Kingdom of God in Newbigin's Later Writings

For Newbigin exposing the powers is never an end in itself. It is only the necessary concomitant to the proclamation of the lordship of Christ. To this the church has to witness. And Newbigin expresses clearly that there can be and must be no separation between the kingdom and the king. Wherever the name of Jesus is separated from the proclamation of the kingdom the message is distorted. One cannot talk about Jesus apart from the kingdom of God; and one cannot talk about the kingdom of God apart from the name of Jesus.

> When the message of the kingdom of God is separated from the name of Jesus two distortions follow, and these are in fact the source of deep divisions in the life of the church today. On the one hand, there is the preaching of the name of Jesus simply as the one who brings a religious experience of personal salvation without involving one in costly actions at the points in public life where the power of Satan is contradicting the rule of God and bringing men and women under the power of evil. Such preaching of cheap grace, of a supposed personal salvation that does not go the way of the cross, of an inward comfort without commitment to costly action for the doing of God's will in the world – this kind of evangelistic preaching is a distortion of the gospel. It is seductive, and we must be on our guard against it. A preaching of personal salvation that does not lead the hearers to challenge the monstrous injustices of our society is not mission in Christ's way. It is peddling cheap grace. On the other hand, when the message of the kingdom is separated from the name of Jesus, then the action of the church in respect of the evils in society becomes a mere ideological crusade, inviting men and women to put their trust in that which cannot satisfy. It is to betray people with false expectations. Worse than that, it is to deliver people into the hands of demonic powers, for whenever a particular political or social programme is identified with the kingdom of God, those who follow become the victims of forces that they cannot control. We have seen that in every revolution from the French Revolution twohundred years ago to Ayatollah Khomeni's revolution today. To separate Jesus from the kingdom, to preach Jesus without the kingdom, or to preach the kingdom without Jesus, is to betray our generation and it is to divide and destroy the church. The gospel is this: that in the man Jesus the kingdom has actually come among us in judgment and blessing. It is now the reality with which we have to deal – whether in our most private devotions or in our most public actions in the life of society. (87mcw, 9-10)

Newbigin's view of the kingdom is therefore strictly Christocentric. Any talk of the kingdom that does not focus on Christ as the king is distorting the picture. That is the fundamental critique of any secularized form of an eschatological hope. It is also the principal critique against a church-centric view of the kingdom, because it is not the church but Christ who is at the center. He is the central agent in establishing the kingdom. And it is at the same time the principal critique against a view of religious pluralism that sees the establishment of a peaceful human society primarily as a human challenge that needs to be addressed simultaneously from various religious centers. For Newbigin there is no unity for humankind if Christ is not at the center. God's kingdom is irreversibly connected to the name of Jesus.

This close connection between Jesus and the kingdom also becomes the guideline that protects the church from swerving in the other direction, namely to reduce the eschatological hope to a hope of eternal bliss for individual souls. Newbigin carries through his earlier critique of a dualistic understanding of salvation either as individualistic salvation or as social engagement. For him only a synopsis of both aspects is true to the gospel. And the key to keep that balance is for Newbigin to remain focused on the person of Jesus as the king of God's kingdom. The salvation of the cosmos is bound to the person of Jesus Christ, the Lord over all. Out of this cosmic vision of salvation flows the realistic but hopeful engagement of the church in the world.

> This faith enables us to be at the same time realistic and hopeful. We can be realistic, knowing that no human project can eliminate the powers of darkness as they operate in human life. This realism delivers us from the utopian fanaticisms which have condemned millions of people to misery and death in the cause of an imagined future. But at the same time we can be hopeful, acting hopefully in apparently hopeless situations, not dreaming of an absolute perfection on this side of death, but doing resolutely that relative good which is possible now, doing it as an offering to the Lord who is able to take it and keep it for the perfect kingdom which is promised. In this sense, to use a phrase of Schweitzer, our actions in the public life of the world are acted prayers for the kingdom. They do not themselves lead directly to the kingdom. They are acted prayers for its coming and as such they act as signs of its reality and so enable others to act in hope. (89gps, 114-115)

This attitude of service based on realism and hope derives from a view of the lordship of Christ which is at the center of the biblical understanding of the kingdom of God. Its eschatological future is but the manifestation of this rule of Christ. We will discuss this in section three of this chapter.

2. The Unity and Mission of the Church

In his early writings Newbigin emphasized that the unity and mission of the church are inseparable. Only a reconciled community is able to bring the message of reconciliation to the world. The church is the eschatological community, the firstfruits of the new humankind, or in Newbigin's famous triad, the "foretaste, instrument and sign of the kingdom." Following these keywords I will try to outline Newbigin's treatment of the church in his later writings.

At the time when the IMC was integrated into the WCC in New Delhi Newbigin was one of the people involved in drafting the New Delhi statement "The Church's Unity" (see Wainwright 2000, 113ff). In the second paragraph of this statement Newbigin expressed what he deeply believed:

> We believe that the unity which is both God's will and his gift to his Church is being made visible as all in each place who are baptized into Jesus Christ and confess him as Lord and Saviour are brought by the Holy Spirit into one fully

> committed fellowship, holding the one apostolic faith, preaching the one Gospel, breaking the one bread, joining in common prayer, and having a corporate life reaching out in witness and service to all and who at the same time are united with the whole Christian fellowship in all places and all ages in such wise that ministry and members are accepted by all, and that all can act and speak together as occasion requires for the tasks to which God calls his people. (quoted in Wainwright 2000, 114)

These few lines reveal with great fervor Newbigin's theological convictions and the vision he continued to work for. As we have seen Newbigin derives his understanding of the character of the church from its eschatological goal. However he is well aware of the tension between this goal and the real state of the church at his time. So the statement continues:

> This brief description of our objective leaves many questions unanswered. We are not yet of a common mind on the interpretation and the means of achieving the goal we have described. We are clear that unity does not imply simple uniformity of organization, rite, or expression. We all confess that sinful selfwill operates to keep us separated and that in our human ignorance we cannot discern clearly the lines of God's design for the future. But it is our firm hope that through the Holy Spirit God's will as it is witnessed to in Holy Scripture will be more and more disclosed to us and in us. The achievement of unity will involve nothing less than a death and rebirth of many forms of church life as we have known them. We believe that nothing less costly can finally suffice. (quoted in Wainwright 2000, 114)

2.1. The Church as Community of Reconciliation

With reference to Paul's criticism of the fractions in Corinth Newbigin repeatedly calls the state of separation between the churches and denominations "carnal."

> He [Paul] used the word that must have stung more than any other he could have chosen; he said "You are carnal". Can we doubt that we are under the same condemnation? That when we put the names of men, the human traditions of piety and teaching in which we have been nourished, in the place of the One raised up on earth that all men might be drawn to it, we are in fact carnal – putting our trust in the traditions of men rather than in the Lord. (60muc, 18; see also 61icd, 14)

For Newbigin the unity of the church is a question of its essence not a secondary matter of its form. This is rooted in his understanding of the church in its eschatological dimension as stated in a paper in 1973: "the Church is the provisional incorporation of mankind into Jesus Christ" (73fsvu, 4), a recurring expression in Newbigin's writings (e.g. 83ckac, 7-8; 94es, 53). In the church God is proleptically reaching his goal with humankind; he is giving to this community what he intends as his eschatological gift to all of humankind. This places the church in a temporal tension between the present gift of God's salvation and the future consummation of this salvation. And it defines the church's relationship with humankind in general. The church is on its way towards the consummation of history, when it will reflect "the full richness and variety of mankind" (73fsvu, 5).

> This Church then, this one new family created by God in Christ out of all tribes and nations and peoples, is set by God in the midst of the world as the sign of that to which all creation, and all world history moves. It is the body of Christ, the new man, the second Adam, the new human race, growing up into its full stature and drawing into itself men of every kind. (60muc, 16-17)

In this perspective the church cannot understand itself as a community which exists for itself or for only a part of humankind. The church as the firstfruits of the new creation is a church with a perspective for all of humankind and for the sake of the world.

> [T]he Church is a body that contains all sorts and conditions of men. It is not a segregation but a congregation. It is not for men of a particular sort, or race, or temperament, or culture; it is for man as man – or rather for man reborn as child of God. It is simply the home for the whole human race, wherein all men of every kind will be able to say, "This is my Father's house." Nothing human ought to be alien to the Church except sin. It is the one place where every human distinction is transcended and where mankind is restored to its proper character as one family. (61icd, 11-12)

When the church is understood "as the provisional incorporation of humankind into Jesus Christ" it follows that its present task is to extend that invitation of God to people of all times and places.

> But I would continue to insist that we cannot rest content with any other model of Church order than that it must be such as to offer effectively to every human being in each place, and to mankind as a whole in all times and places the invitation of God to be reconciled to him and to one another through that atoning work which Jesus Christ has accomplished once for all by his incarnation, death and resurrection from the dead. (83ckac, 14)

The foundation for the existence of the church is the fact that reconciliation has been achieved. Atonement was accomplished by Christ. The church as the anticipation of the new humankind is a work of God himself. In the church the reality of this reconciliation – with God and with each other – is realized. The reconciliation of men and women with God in Christ creates a new fellowship among those reconciled. Therefore the unity of the church belongs to its essence as God's community of reconciliation.

> It is the place where the fruit of Christ's mission is already present in foretaste and as an earnest of that which is to come. It is the place where the forgiveness of sins, peace with God through Jesus Christ, and eternal life in Him, are already enjoyed in foretaste. It is the place where God's people on earth are already permitted to have a share in the worship of the Church in heaven. It is, as St. Paul says, a colony of heaven, a place where the divine life is actually available to men in foretaste, in a life of fellowship with God and His redeemed children through common participation in the Holy Spirit. (58obog, 19)

Thus the unity of the church is fundamentally a theological issue. It is a new reality created by God. Attempts to work towards a unity of churches in the WCC are an expression of an ontological unity which is prior to the human realization of it.

> The *koinonia* in the opening phrase of our [WCC] Basis is a common participation in the reality of the triune God through the incarnation and the atonement wrought in Christ and through the continuing work of the Holy Spirit. This is the reality which is ontologically prior to the decision of various church leaders to form a council; it is the reality which makes that decision necessary. The WCC exists because of this pre-existing reality. (85fc, 175)

From the theological and ontological character of unity as God's act it is inconceivable that the church could live in disunity. That would be a denial of the eschatological promise and a contradiction of the purpose and mission of the church (61icd, 9). One cannot adequately understand Newbigin's emphasis on church unity if one does not grasp the theological underpinnings that compel him to deal with the subject. The unity of the church is of its essence because it is a community of reconciliation. And only as a community of reconciled people can it be a convincing witness to the world. On the basis of this understanding Newbigin addresses the question of what to do about the state of separation that characterizes the landscape of Christian churches today.

2.2. The Unity of the Church as Ongoing Challenge

Newbigin is well aware of the many different answers that are given to the challenge of the practical implications of church unity.

> What kind of unity are we talking about? Is it that we all return to the bosom of 'Mother Church' – in Rome, Jerusalem or wherever? Is it a sort of federation of globally organised denominations? Is it one standard-type congregation in every place? Or is it a 'spiritual unity' in which we are polite to each other but go our separate ways? (75bwku, 487)

One of the questions of the newly founded WCC has been how to deal with different ecclesiologies of its member churches. The Toronto statement of the Central Committee from 1950 affirmed that "no church is obliged to change its ecclesiology as a consequence of membership in the World Council" (see 85fc, 177). Newbigin is concerned that this statement may be misunderstood. In retrospect he says

> But it would have been better if the word "consequence" could have been replaced by the word "condition", for surely the WCC is in no position to assure its member churches that the process of "mutual correction" which the Amsterdam Message looked forward to will leave our ecclesiologies permanently unaffected. That would be to absolutize relativism, to accept pluralism as a permanent principle and to abandon the hope that we can be led to the place where we can agree in the truth of the gospel. (85fc, 177)

So while Newbigin does not see a shared ecclesiology as a precondition for unity in the WCC, he nevertheless advocates that the WCC needs to clarify what kind of unity it wants to pursue. Newbigin for his part is not satisfied with a state of peaceful coexistence or cooperation on the basis of the "interdenominational principle," as important as this has been for the birth of the ecumenical movement (85fc, 176). Newbigin refers to the original description of the goal for church unity in the WCC:

> At the Third Assembly in New Delhi (1961) a first effort was made to give a rather precise picture of the goal: it spoke of all who bear the Name of Christ living in a fully committed fellowship in each place, yet in such a way that this fellowship was recognizable as one throughout the world and throughout the centuries. (75bwku, 487)

This is what Newbigin proposes: A "'fully committed fellowship' in each place, in which these separate [denominational] identities are surrendered and a new identity is given" (75bwku, 491). In this context he can speak of the necessity that our denominations must die in order to make way for a new kind of unity (76aopa, 306). On his way towards this position Newbigin himself has had to refine his understanding of the church by gaining an appreciation for the historic episcopate. For Newbigin this meant a new view for the unity of the church as a society continuing through the centuries. He did not accept the Anglican insistence on the unbroken continuity of the historic episcopate. Viewing the historic episcopate as a doctrine or a touchstone to distinguish between the "true Church and its counterfeit" was not an option. But his own view of the church was certainly widened through this examination that was entailed in the process of the unification of the CSI (see 82buc). A similar process on a larger scale is what he presents as a challenge to the member-churches of the WCC. The agreements of Amsterdam (1948) and Toronto (1950) were only a first step on the way.

> This declaration of neutrality – necessary at the time – could not be more than provisional. It could not take the place of a serious effort to define the goal. The World Council of Churches cannot be permanently uncommitted about the form of unity which God wills for the Church, because it is itself a form of unity. Obviously it is not and does not claim to be more than a transitional form – a camp-site on the road towards the real goal. But if those in charge of a camp-site do not agree about the road, the camp-site becomes a shantytown, and eventually a slum. The question of the nature of the unity we seek is not a timeless question which can be taken up or postponed at our pleasure. There is a time limit after which the options do not remain open. To remain permanently uncommitted about the goal of unity would have meant to accept the present conciliar form of collaboration as the permanent force of Christian unity. And it does not need to be repeated that – by the standard of any reputable ecclesiology – this is the wrong form. (76aopa, 289)

The necessity is to move ahead to a shared understanding of unity considering first of all the theological foundations.

What is certain is that we cannot stand still. The WCC has taken as its starting point the "churches" as they now are. It has, in the classical Toronto Statement of 1950, eschewed any claim to have one required definition of the nature of the unity which God wills, though it has sought at various times to sketch a vision of it. It is a fellowship of churches in which competing and conflicting visions can confront one another in dialogue. But dialogue is not an end in itself. Its purpose is to come to a fuller grasp of the truth. For that we have to be continually pressing forward, ready to face honestly the painful process of mutual correction "until we all attain to the unity of the faith and of the knowledge of the Son of God." (85fc, 180-181)

Newbigin's call for ongoing critical reflection extends not only to the theological foundations of the church but also to its structures in order for the church to remain true to its mission and not become concerned about its own aggrandizement (71rsh, 75).

2.3. The Structures and Ministries of the Church in Light of Its Missionary Calling

This causes Newbigin to take a second look at the churches and denominations, at their structures and ministries. For one, Newbigin is well aware that no one denomination in its present form can become the church home for all of the human race.

> As a missionary in India I have often been asked: "Are you really so narrow-minded as to think that you are going to enroll the whole human race in your little group? Are you like the frog that thinks its little pond is the whole ocean?" With all my heart I can answer that I long for every human being to be a Christian. But – in all loyalty to the church of my fathers – I have to confess that I cannot wish for every human being to be a Presbyterian. ... None of our churches is a big enough fellowship to be a home for the human race. Only a universal fellowship can be the adequate bearer of a universal Gospel. (61icd, 12)

Secondly, Newbigin distinguishes between the NT usage of the term "church" for a local congregation and the current usage of the term.

> I am more and more impressed by the fact that the language which the New Testament uses about the Church presupposes a multiplicity of small groups in which all the members can have a personal knowledge of and care for one another; it is almost impossible to transfer it directly to the institutions we call denominations, or even to the typical urban congregation. (70cu, 73-74)

This focus on the term "church" as small-scale local community implies a critique of the present form of the WCC. The WCC is called to be more than a committee of representatives of various denominations that each span the world. In the strict NT sense of the word *ekklesia* a denomination cannot be called a church. Newbigin in his critique points to the analysis of sociologists of religion. They have made us aware that a denomination is the visible form taken by bodies of Christians who have accepted the privatization of their religion. In other words, it is a form of syncretism: it allows the expression of Christian faith to be determined by factors deriving from another, and alien, system of belief – in this case, the beliefs which have controlled the public life of the West since the Enlightenment. Denominationalism is essentially the product of the North American experience in the late eighteenth and nineteenth centuries, but it has increasingly become a global phenomenon, imposing its assumptions even on churches whose base beliefs are incompatible with it. (85fc, 179)

While Newbigin affirms the validity of different strands and traditions that have brought people to faith in Christ and nourished them in the faith, he nevertheless is convinced of the necessity to leave denominational divisions behind.

> I would affirm the need for a radical break with that form of Christianity which is called the denomination. ... The denomination is the outward and visible form of an inward and spiritual surrender to the ideology of our culture. Neither separately nor together can the denominations become the base for a genuinely missionary encounter with our culture. (85cwbc, 7)

Newbigin is convinced of the necessity to overcome denominational divisions out of his theological understanding of the church as one community, united in one Lord; therefore no other names must be allowed to separate what is to be one in Christ. This one-ness must be visible and must be experienced.

> The crucial question is this: can there be a manifestation of the life of the Church in each place which is – on the one hand – so open, so free, so welcoming of variety and even contradiction, that men and women of every kind can be at home in it; and – on the other hand – so deeply rooted in the saving work of Christ crucified and risen that its members can accept one another, forgive one another, love one another, belong to one another? Can there be a visible and recognizable and therefore local expression of the fact that what God has done in Jesus Christ is nothing less than the destruction of all the powers that separate men from God and from one another, or must this be only a truth that remains in the mind, above involvement in space and time? Can there be a Eucharist in everyplace on every Lord's Day where all who confess Christ as Lord and Saviour can meet – with all the vast diversities and contradictions that belong to our human condition, and share the same loaf and the same cup, give thanks to the same God, and go out to continue his mission in the world? Such a unity implies the death of all our denominations as we know them. It implies the surrender of every name, every claim to identity, so that the name of Jesus alone may be on our lips, and so that we may find our identity only in the fact that we belong to him. It is nothing abstract or theoretical. It is immensely costly. It involves long and patient work to reach the mutual understanding without which there cannot be such a mutual commitment. (76aopa, 306)

Newbigin argues for the difficult twofold task of working out a shared understanding of unity on the one hand and working out accompanying structures that express the shared conviction on the other. With regard to structures Newbigin argues for cultural awareness but not for cultural captivity.

Chapter 3: The Kingdom of God in Newbigin's Later Writings

The structures of the church must be patterned according to the structures of any given society without becoming absorbed into the patterns of this society. It is a call for "critical contextualization" (see Hiebert 1994).

> As the Church is for all mankind, it follows that – in relation to each segment of mankind – the Church will be the Church *for* that segment – be it nation or province or local community. The Church does not try to demolish the forms of society (except in so far as they contradict the purpose of God for mankind as revealed in Jesus Christ), but rather accepts them as the provisional form in which the new humanity is to be made manifest. (73fsvu, 6-7)

This accommodation or contextualization of the church's structures is kept in creative tension by the claim of the gospel as it exemplifies essential characteristics of the church. "In one sense the Church is having to adjust itself to the changes in society; in another, it is having to adjust itself to the demands of its own Gospel" (73fsvu, 8). As criteria for discernment in this process Newbigin suggests two fundamental principles: (1) That leadership needs to be patterned according to Christ's leadership, namely "leadership in the way of the Cross." "It is leadership in self-negation, in bearing the sin of others, in washing the feet of the disciples. It is going before on the way of the Cross, that others may follow after" (73fsvu, 11). And, (2) the church needs to care for the marginal. These are two aspects which are to be found in any church if it is true to the gospel. In this way Newbigin takes seriously both the cultural issues with regard to the form and structure of the church and the theological issues which determine the essence of the church.

With this framework Newbigin is free to address the question of new church structures for a changed world. He is convinced that we need new flexible structures with smaller groups where new initiatives can freely find expression (70cu, 74). In his attempt to explore ways for new church structures he is quite radical in his critique of the status quo. The sole focus on the territorial parish is an obvious relic of the Christendom era. The denominational "gathered congregation" on the other hand is a result of the privatization of religion in Western society. The system of a salaried professional ministry has been carried over from the parish system to the "gathered congregation." All of these are basically paradigms of the past. While Newbigin sees a continuing relevance of the parish church model as one unified church for a given community, he stresses the fact that the church needs to look for new structures to apply this model to the present situation. Understanding the church as community in a specific place can no longer be limited to a geographical sense. The character of social networks in an urban environment which transcend geographical boundaries calls for local communities in different sectors of society – "be it factory, university, city council, professional association or whatever" (80ykc, 67). Here the church needs to look for new kinds of ministries that answer to these challenges (80ykc, 58).

> It seems to me clear that the development of this kind of congregational life will call for congregations which are related to the different sectors of the secular world as well as those which are related to the geographical areas of resi-

dence. It is characteristic of an urbanised and highly differentiated society that the normal person belongs to several different 'places' at the same time – the place of his residence, the place of his work, and perhaps the place of his other cultural interests. In this sense one has to say that everyone belongs at the same time to several neighbourhoods. The 'neighbour' is not just the one so defined by geographical propinquity of residence. There is therefore need that the forms of the church should include congregations which are based on these other neighbourhoods. I do not think that the geographical parish can ever become irrelevant or marginal. There is a sense in which the primary sense of neighbourhood must remain primary, because it is here that men and women relate to each other simply as human beings and not in respect of their functions in society. But it is clear, I think, that alongside these geographically defined units of the Church's corporate life, there is need for other basic Christian congregations shaped by the other kinds of neighbourhood. The corollary of this will be that it is essential for the Church also to have strongly developed units of a larger kind in which these smaller units can join from time to time in forms of celebration, worship and fellowship which transcend these narrower divisions. (80ykc, 64-65)

In these communities the gospel can only be carried forward through the ministry of lay people, specialists in their respective fields. This calls for a new view of ministry, a stronger involvement of lay people.

> I refer to the very deep-seated and persistent failure of the churches to recognize that the primary witness to the sovereignty of Christ must be given, and can only be given, in the ordinary secular work of lay men and women in business, in politics, in professional work, as farmers, factory workers and so on. Much stress has already been laid on this during our Assembly, and yet it can hardly be repeated too often. Christian witness is primarily not something which happens under the official auspices of the Church and in the presence of its ordained ministers or officers. It is given in the acts and words of countless Christian men and women from Monday to Saturday, in field and factory, in office and classroom. (60whal, 28)

What Newbigin suggests here is a fundamental rethinking of the structures of the church which orients itself on the task of the church's mission to the world, where the encounter of the gospel with the world takes place in and through the lives of the members of the church in their everyday social relationships. The structures of the church must be geared towards that encounter.

> What is also clear is that the development of these more flexible patterns of congregational life will call for much more flexible and varied styles of ministry. The assumption that the ministry must normally be a full-time salaried profession is a survival from the Constantinian settlement which cannot rule our present thinking. It is an obviously and often-noted fact that the most rapidly growing churches in the world today are – in general – those which make full use of a nonstipendiary ministry developed by the methods of apprenticeship from within the membership of the whole church. My own experience as a missionary in India has convinced me that the rapid expansion of the Church into unevangelised areas can best be achieved by analogous methods – trusting the

> Holy Spirit both to find His own way of bringing men and women to Christian faith and to equip those so converted with the gifts needed to lead others into that faith. I have seen the Church grow through the multiplication of new congregations which were led from the beginning by the new converts themselves. Here the traditionally trained and salaried ministers of the Church served to encourage, support and train the local leaders – who were ordinary farmers, shopkeepers or labourers. The leadership remained in the hands of these local people and the Churches grew and multiplied by a process of spontaneous communication along the natural lines of human relationships. (80ykc, 65-66)

The penetration of secular society with the gospel can only be reached with this decentralized approach that takes the social setting of each Christian seriously as the place for the witness of the gospel.

> I do not believe that the role of the Church in a secular society is primarily exercised in the corporate actions of the churches as organized bodies in the political or cultural fields – even when these actions are cleansed of ontocratic pretensions and bear the genuine marks of suffering and witness. On the contrary, I believe that it is exercised through the action of Christians as lay people, playing their roles as citizens, workers, managers, legislators, etc., not wearing the label "Christian" but deeply involved in the secular world, in the faith that God is at work there in a way which is not that of the "Christendom" pattern. (74sh, 224)

This is what Newbigin describes with the term "the church as hermeneutic of the gospel." One result of this openness for new structures of the church is that the focus of its definition needs to shift from its borders to its center.

> The more we stress the need that the Church should develop a new open-ness to the world, a new flexibility in its structures and new styles of ministerial leadership to meet the changing patterns of secular life, the more necessary it is to stress the centrality, and finality of Jesus Christ for everything in the life of the Church, the fundamental reality of personal conversion to him and of confession of his name. With the kind of openness and flexibility which I have advocated, it may be difficult to say exactly where the boundaries of the Church lie; this does not matter provided we are clear and make clear to others where the centre lies. An entity can be defined either in terms of its boundaries or in terms of its centre. The Church is an entity which is properly described by its centre. It is impossible to define exactly the boundaries of the Church, and the attempt to do so always ends in an unevangelical legalism. But it is always possible and necessary to define the centre. The Church is its proper self, and is a sign of the Kingdom, only insofar as it continually points men and women beyond itself to Jesus and invites them to personal conversion and commitment to him. (80ykc, 68)

Newbigin cannot provide definite answers in his attempt to point towards future structures and ministries of the church. But he makes the effort to show where he sees the challenges. He makes suggestions for creating new structures that realize unity on the local, regional, national and global level (73fsvu, 14-16). In his analysis he is aware of the sociological changes that affect the networks of human beings in the growingly urban societies of today. Writing in 1973, he is alerting the reader to the role supranational business firms might play in the future, diminishing the role of the nation state. In these observations he demonstrates a keen awareness of changes which were still lying in the future at that time, but the consequences of which we are experiencing today and which continue to challenge the church.

The reflection on the structures and ministries of the church must take the understanding of the church's essence and its mission as its starting point. From there the church needs to develop structures and ministries which are culturally appropriate and adequate to the tasks the church faces. But the one sign that will provide credibility to the mission of the church is its unity.

2.4. The Unity of the Church as Missionary Witness

Newbigin's emphasis on the unity of the church culminates in the interrelatedness of its unity and its mission.

> The unity of Christ's people, for which He prays, is a unity "that the world may know that thou hast sent me and hast loved them even as thou lovest me." It is a unity for the sake of the world, the world which God made and loves and for which He sent His Son. (61icd, 22)

It was Newbigin's experience of the mission fields which led to his conviction that "disunity among the churches is not merely unfortunate but intolerable" (76aopa, 288). Thus of the mission movement in the early 20th century the ecumenical movement was born. The concern for unity grew out of the missionary context and passion (76aopa, 288). But it would be a mistake to interpret the movement towards unity merely as a pragmatic appeal for a convincing mission strategy. The church is understood as "the provisional incorporation of mankind into Jesus Christ" (73fsvu, 4). It is called to be the foretaste of the new creation, the firstfruits of a new humankind. As such, the oneness of humankind in the new creation must be reflected in the church today. Jesus' prayer refers to this proleptic character of the eschatological community, the taste of a community in which reconciliation is experienced. Unity means reconciliation and communion. In the context of mission the unity of the church becomes much more than an inner-church issue. The different pieces – unity and mission – fall into place as interlocking pieces. The church in unity thus becomes the hermeneutic of the gospel for the world.

2.5. The Church as Hermeneutic of the Gospel

In his ministry as bishop in India when Newbigin was visiting the village congregations that were part of his diocese he was often asked to speak not only in the churches but to also speak to the Non-Christians before entering the church.

> I have often stood at the door of a little church, with the Christian congregation seated on the ground in the middle and a great circle of Hindus and Muslims standing around. As I have opened the Scripture and tried to preach the Word of God to them, I have always known that my words would only carry weight,

would only be believed, if those standing around could recognize in those sitting in the middle that the promises of God were being fulfilled; if they could see that this new community in the village represented a new kind of body in which the old divisions of caste and education and temperament were being transcended in a new form of brotherhood. If they could not see anything of the kind, they would not be likely to believe. ...

In the middle of this world God has set His Church as His witness. He expects His Church to be recognizable as His family. He expects that the glory which He gave to His Son, and which has been given to us, will be visible to the world in the common life of a redeemed brotherhood. (61icd, 24-25)

This places the verbal witness of the church in a much wider context. People outside of the church need to see how the gospel relates to the issues of life, how it shapes the church as a community, and how it can contribute to the society as a whole.

It is the Church as a whole which has to be the hermeneutic of the Gospel, and the question which has to be asked about these and other movements of fresh outreach into the world is whether they contribute to the renewal and reshaping of the life of the ordinary local congregation in every place. And the question which has to be put to every local congregation is the question whether it is a credible sign of God's reign in justice and mercy over the whole of life; whether it is an open fellowship whose concerns are as wide as the concerns of humanity, whether it cares for its neighbours in a way which reflects and springs out of God's care for them, whether its common life is recognisable as a foretaste of the blessing which God intends for the whole human family. (80ykc, 63-64)

The visible community of believers becomes the key for the world to see the meaning and relevance of the gospel, to understand God's goal for human life and to enter into the truth.

The gospel is so strange that no kind of arguments can bring a person to accept its truth. The only real hermeneutic of the Gospel is a community of people who believe it, celebrate it and live by it. All the statistics about how people are brought to faith confirm this. And it corresponds to the nature of the Gospel itself. The words 'repent and believe' are followed by the summons: 'Come with me'. It was only by being in the company of Jesus that the disciples could begin to learn what it means that the Kingdom of God is at hand, that God reigns. (90ea, 339)

Thus the community of believers is the hermeneutic of the gospel which translates God's story of salvation into the life of people and invites them to become part of this story.

2.6. The Church as Servant Community

To speak of the church as the hermeneutic of the gospel includes both its verbal and non-verbal witness. For Newbigin the split between the two is rooted in the Greek dualism of matter versus spirit rather than in a biblical paradigm.

What I am trying to stress is that we are dealing here with something which is not, as it were, one of the possible activities of the Church. We cannot say: 'A church may or may not be active in social service'. A congregation cannot say: 'This Church is not interested in social service: it is interested in something else.' It is not this kind of question that we are dealing with. We are dealing with a question which concerns the integrity of the Church itself, its fundamental character as a Church. (71csc, 260)

But Newbigin is not satisfied with the mere fact that a church is socially involved in the life of the people. He self-critically asks the question whether the social involvement of the church is really a matter of identification with the marginal. Whenever the church operates from a position of power, unjust structures may remain unchallenged and unchanged. Newbigin critiques:

It seems to me that we must recognise that, with few exceptions which I shall speak of in a moment, our social work has not had the effect of putting us decisively on the side of the oppressed. I don't think that the Church creates in the mind of anybody the impression of a society which is basically on the side of the oppressed, on the side of the exploited. It creates the impression of being a society which accepts, and is content to benefit from the established order, and at the same time to reach out the hand of charity as far as possible to those who are the victims of that order. (71csc, 263)

This was written at a time when the WCC financially supported organizations which fought racism with military force. Newbigin looks back at the main Christian tradition which has accepted as a last resort the idea of a "just war," and here Newbigin raises the question if on that basis the idea of "just revolution" can be ruled out categorically. Newbigin is not proposing the use of force. He is trying to unmask any identification of the church with the position of the powerful, which is conceived by the marginal as hypocrisy and as will to power. Newbigin instead challenges the church to truly identify with the oppressed in a way that they themselves will perceive as true identification. He closes his argument by emphasizing the need to combine the demand for justice with the demand for compassion and reconciliation. This corresponds to his other writings, where he puts a second quality next to this identification with the marginal. It is ministry in the sign of the cross, ministry that aims for reconciliation in an attitude of service (see 80ykc, 56; 95os, 108). The church can only approach its task of witnessing in word and deed, of identifying with the marginal in an attitude that is characterized by the willingness to suffer rather than by an attitude of domination and control which will always lead to reservation and doubt on the side of the world (see 87mcw; 85cwbc).

2.7. The Church as Sign, Instrument, and Foretaste of the Kingdom

The triad – "sign, instrument, and foretaste of the kingdom" – has become the central phrase with which Newbigin describes the role of the church in this world (see 87mcw, 12). It places the church in the eschatological tension between the presence and the future of the kingdom. With this phrase Newbigin argues against a mere functional understanding of the church which took hold in the IMC and WCC in the 1950s and 1960s.

> Newbigin's threefold description of the church was forged in the crucible of an encounter with the ecclesiology of Johannes Hoekendijk (…). Hoekendijk believed that the church could be sufficiently defined by its function, i.e. its participation in God's work in liberation, seeking justice, and peacemaking in the world. Newbigin protests this interpretation of the church. The church cannot be understood solely in terms of its instrumental role within society. The church is also a place where the life and salvation of the kingdom is experienced in foretaste. (Goheen 2004, 105)

Newbigin holds the different aspects together. He continues to see the church as the "agent of God's mission" (63rtdt, 24). However the placement of the church in the middle of the eschatological tension qualifies this statement and guards it against a triumphalistic misunderstanding. "The Church is not promised success; it is promised the peace of Christ in the midst of tribulation, and the witness of the Spirit given out of the Church's weakness and ignorance" (63rtdt, 78). It is the Spirit who is the arrabon of the kingdom, the foretaste and down payment, the promise of the fulfillment.

> The Holy Spirit is the arrabon of the kingdom. It is not just a verbal promise. It is a real gift now, a real foretaste of the joy, the freedom, the righteousness, the holiness of God's kingdom. It is real now. But its special character is that it carries the promise of something much greater to come and makes us look forward and press forward with eager hope towards that greater reality that lies ahead. And it is this that makes the church a witness to the kingdom. The witness is not essentially a task laid upon the church; it is a gift given to the church. It is an overflow of Pentecost. (87mcw, 17; see also 80ykc, 37-38)

Newbigin's description of the church as the foretaste of the kingdom can only be adequately understood when we think of the church as the new community created by the Spirit, who is himself the foretaste of the kingdom. It is the Spirit who creates the community of reconciliation, which is then the foretaste of God's kingdom to the world.

> It [the spoken word] is only significant if it is represented by a visible community in which the unity of mankind is being realized in foretaste through the actual reconciliation of rivals and enemies in one visible body. In other words, the relation between the unity of the Church and the unity of mankind can be properly stated by saying that the Church in every time and place is called to be such that it is a credible sign, instrument and first-fruit of God's purpose to establish his reign of righteousness and peace for the whole of mankind, for the calling of the Church is to be the incorporation of all mankind into Jesus Christ. (83ckac, 2)

The church is also the instrument of God's kingdom. Newbigin qualifies this in order to keep the church from falling into the trap of overestimating its contribution or becoming triumphalistic by emphasizing that the kingdom of God is not a program for the church: it is God's work. The contribution of the church as instrument of the kingdom is to establish in this world signs of God's kingdom, actions which are prayers directed to God to bring about the fulfillment of his promise (41kgip, 51).

> The kingdom is, quite simply, the reign of God. This is so fundamental that it is constantly forgotten. We are not dealing here with a programme, a campaign, a promotional 'drive' for which the techniques of high-pressure salesmanship or military planning would be appropriate. Nor are we engaged in the support of a 'good cause' about which it is possible for us to be optimistic or pessimistic. (80ykc, 34)

The church derives the understanding of its ministry from the person and ministry of Christ and thus becomes a sign of the kingdom. Newbigin picks up the phrase "church for others" and qualifies it Christologically. The church is church "for" the world in the same sense that Christ has been and is "for" the world. This is not an uncritical identification with the world nor an instrumental dissolving into the world. It means being a sign of God's reign for the world to see.

> It will be a church which is in the world but not of the world. That over-used phrase has been replaced in recent talk by the phrase 'a church for others', and we can accept that description provided that the preposition 'for' is rightly understood. It has to be understood Christologically. The Church is to be 'for' others in the same sense in which Christ was and is 'for' the world. In the light of the previous discussion we may be more precise and say 'a church which is a sign' of the Kingdom in the same sense in which Jesus was a sign of the Kingdom.' Clearly this means a church which does not exist for itself or for what it can offer to its members; a church which is not offering personal salvation to its members apart from the salvation which God offers to the whole world, apart from the destiny of the nations and the cosmos. It means a church which is a credible sign of the *malkuth yahweh*, the just and loving rule of God over his whole creation and his whole family. (80ykc, 45)

This is a costly enterprise. The church is placed in this very conflict which was characteristic for the ministry of Christ. To challenge the powers und to identify with the marginal will mean for the church that it too has to bear the marks of suffering which characterized the ministry of Christ. Precisely in this way it is instrument and sign of the kingdom.

> How can the Church become a credible sign to all peoples of every kind, a sign of the kingship of God as it is set forth in the Bible – a kingship which offers the fulness of life, peace, justice and holiness; and at the same time requires the total obedience of every creature? The only possible answer to this question is that the Church can become such a sign insofar as, and only insofar as, her life is assimilated to the life of Jesus who was himself the only sign given of the Kingdom, Jesus himself the crucified King who bears in his risen body the marks of his passion (John 20:19-23). Only the Church which bears those marks can be recognisable as the body of Christ and recognisable therefore as a

> sign of the Kingdom. To spell this out more explicitly the Church can be a sign of the Kingdom insofar as it follows Jesus in steadfastly challenging the powers of evil in the life of the world by accepting total solidarity with those who are the victims of those powers; insofar as, by accepting in its own life the weight of the world's wrong it exposes and judges the wrongdoers in the act of saving both them and their victims. (80ykc, 50-51)

With this threefold characterization of the church – sign, instrument, and foretaste of the kingdom – Newbigin places the church in the middle of the eschatological tension that characterizes God's story. The fact that the eschatological consummation is "not yet" forbids any triumphalistic understanding of the church. It rather underscores the servant character of the church as being Christ's church for the world. It is not the church which is at the center of this story. It is Christ who is the center, his incarnation and ministry, his death and resurrection. In his view of the church Newbigin keeps the eschatological focus with the person of Christ at its center.

> In the New Testament it is clear that the only sign of the Kingdom is Jesus himself. The central task of the Church, as it prays 'Your Kingdom Come!' is to bear witness to him in whom the kingdom has come, to call all men to that U-turn in the mind which we call conversion so that they may acknowledge him as King and join his whole Church in the prayer: 'Come, Lord Jesus!' (80ykc, 69-70)

3. The Eschatological Hope – God's Story with His World

The question of God's involvement in history is the place where biblical eschatological hope meets the realities of human existence. The church is involved right at the center of this encounter. However in order to understand its involvement better it is necessary to look in detail at the biblical perception of history and God's involvement in it. Newbigin was challenged to do just that through his ministry in India where he met a view of history that was diametrically opposed to the Western view and to the biblical view.

3.1. History as Real Story

Newbigin understands history as a real story. This is in contrast to the Hindu concept of *maya* which understands historical events as a kind of magical play which arises out of *Brahman*, the only true reality there is.

3.1.1. Circular and Linear Understandings of History

India's view of history is characterized as a cyclical one. The law of *karma* and the doctrine of *samsara* determine the nature of individual human lives as well as the nature of history and cosmic development in terms of a cyclical pattern.

> A missionary in India learns to realize that there are certain ways of understanding the world that are so fundamental that they have never been questioned in all the revolutions of Indian thought from the Buddha to the Mahatma, from Gautama to Gandhi. I mean, for example, the doctrines of karma and samsara which see human life in terms of the wheel of nature, the endless cycles of birth, growth, maturity, decay, death, and then a new birth. That is, strictly speaking, the "natural" way to understand human life – the life of the individual and the life of nations. (89gps, 96)

In contrast to this circular view of life which is characteristic for Asia stands the Western view of history, based on a linear meta-narrative which sees history moving progressively in a specific direction. The conviction that humans are able to master nature and history has led to a self-confidence in the West which is convinced of the superiority of the linear meta-narrative over the circular one and attempts to lead history to its perceived goal.

> The most powerful and pervasive of all the narratives has been the cyclical one. Human life, like the rest of the natural world, moves in an endlessly repeated cycle of birth, growth, maturity, decay and death. Religion is then a matter of release from this wheel continuously kept in motion by our karma – the deeds (good or bad) which must have their fruit in the next rotation of the wheel. The 'meta-narrative' of modernity has been linear, the onward march of human mastery over nature. With this master-story it is easy to understand how those who see themselves as the vanguard of the human march can claim to embody the goal of history. The rival narratives have been eliminated. (92eh, 1)

Newbigin, however, does not identify the linear Western view of history with the biblical one. Instead he chooses a third geometrical figure in order to characterize the biblical view of history.

> The Christian narrative has a shape which is neither cyclical nor linear. It is U-shaped. The creed is U-shaped, from the source of all being, down into the depths of hell, and back to the glory of the new creation. Every human life must follow this pattern from the sheer gift of being, a gift from the hand of God, down through manifold trial and struggle to death itself, and, even in death, the assurance and the foretaste of the new being. Christ, and Christ alone, is the end of history, because in Him, the crucified and risen Lord, the new creation is already present. Christians, of all people, have been warned to recognize bogus messiahs. (92eh, 1)

This differentiation between the biblical view and the Western view is important. However it is also important to recognize how the Western view of history grew out of an encounter with the biblical view. Newbigin traces the major steps of this encounter. At the time of the collapse of Rome it was Augustine who laid the foundation for the Western view of history for more than 1000 years to come. This view of history saw God as the decisive actor, leading and guiding the history of the cosmos to its God-determined end. In the 18th century this view was fundamentally challenged by a human-centered view of history. It is almost ironic to see that while cosmology had changed from an earth-centered, human-centered universe to a helio-centered universe, thus revealing the micro-character of the human being, the meta-narrative regarding nature and history began to shift its focus away from a theo-centric understanding towards an anthropo-centric understanding, being fascinated by the human mastery of nature in science and technology. This led to a fundamental shift in Western thinking regarding the understanding of history. The human being became the central actor of history, the master of human destiny. Christian eschatological hope was relegated to the area of private beliefs. In the sphere of public life a secularized version of the Christian eschatological hope took root, the idea of progress.

> The change can be illustrated most vividly by looking at what happened to the teaching of history in schools and universities. From the time of Augustine and Orosius up to the eighteenth century, world history was taught on the basis of that vision of history which is embodied in the Bible. The Bible is in the form of a universal history and its vision of the meaning and end of universal history derives from the events which are associated with the names of Abraham, Isaac and Jacob, Moses, Jesus. The new vision of universal history was quite different. It derived from the new experience of mastery over nature through science and technology. It saw man as the bearer of the meaning of his own history. From this point of view the names and events of which the Bible speaks can have only a very marginal significance. Consequently the teaching of history now takes two different forms. In the secular classroom 'world history' is taught in terms of the new vision; in the 'religious instruction' classes the biblical history is still taught, but it is taught rather as a series of parables illuminating the problems of personal life. (80ykc, 49)

A closer look at the changes that took place during the 18th century in Europe reveals two different sources or stages in this development, namely the age of reason and the romantic age.

> But what exactly was the change which took place at that point in the way the Western European tribes understood their history? There seem to have been two stages. There was first the eighteenth-century concept of 'progress'. This was a typical product of the Age of Reason. It saw the new ways of knowledge developed in the seventeenth and eighteenth centuries as the key to unlimited future mastery over nature. It was not interested in the past; that was a period of darkness which had little to contribute to real knowledge. Interest was centred on the future when the last king would have been strangled with the guts of the last priest and all the irrational tyrannies of the past abolished. The second stage came with the Romantic Movement. Its characteristic product was the idea of development. In contrast to the idea of progress, this was interested in the past. It saw history as the unfolding of that which had been present from the beginning. Whereas the Age of Reason had seen the world in terms of timeless truths, valid equally for the Greek and Roman and for the Frenchman of today, the romantic age saw things as continually developing. It therefore became passionately interested in the past, and out of that interest the vast labours of the nineteenth century historians were born: The fact that the ideas of progress and of development were later fused into a single general consciousness of move-

ment towards an ever brighter future should not obscure the distinction between the two ideas in their beginnings. (79cjh, 198-199)

The alleged superiority of the linear Western view of history seemed to demonstrate itself up until the middle of the 20th century. Newbigin too in the 1960s initially interpreted the process of secularization as a positive development through which all nations were drawn into one single history, and circular understandings of human life were dethroned from their long held positions of influence, thus freeing people for a new view of the world.

> The revolutionary character of our time arises from the fact that whole peoples who have lived for millenia without the expectation that human life would ever be radically different from what it has been are now persuaded of the possibility of a wholly new order of existence. The content given to this vision of a new order varies; but the form of the hope is recognizably the same everywhere. It has not arisen from any of the ancient non-Christian systems of thought. It has arisen from the contact of these systems with the impulses that have come from a culture shaped by the biblical understanding of the meaning of history. (63rtdt, 39-40)

Newbigin did not, however, identify this development with the establishment of the kingdom of God. As early as in the late 1950s he was aware that the Western view of a unified world history, into which the nations were drawn, was but a secularized form of Christian eschatology.

> The origin of this conception of a single human destiny is in the so-called Christian West. It is a secularized form of the Christian eschatology. Whether in its Marxist, or in its liberal forms, it is a product of the history of the Christian West, and ultimately of the biblical conception of history and of the Kingdom of God. (60whal, 22)

However it was only later that Newbigin expressed himself more critically about this development. In 1983 he points out that the embrace of the world's cultures by the West and its view of modernity and progress has to be understood as domination rather than inclusion of the peoples and cultures of the world. He calls for critical reflection on how the Western view came to be what it has become.

> Yet during the past three centuries the descendants of these same tribes have extended their culture into every part of the world, dominating and often destroying more ancient cultures, and creating for the first time a common civilization which embraces the whole earth – not in the sense that it includes everyone, but in the sense that it has a dominating role, at least in nearly all the great cities of the world. To most of the world's people it has appeared as the bearer of "modernity" – with all its implications of technical mastery and unlimited powers of discovery, innovation and control. W.E. Hocking, writing in 1956, could still speak with unshaken confidence of the almost timeless and universal validity of this culture:

> "Today we seem to be standing on the threshold of a new thing, civilization in the singular. ... For the first time our entire world-space is permeated with

> ideas which, as Locke said about truth and the keeping of faith, 'belong to man as man and not as a member of a society'. Here and there in the Orient there is still revulsion from the clinging localisms of western thought and practice, but none towards what we may call the Clean Universals, the sciences, the mathematics, the technics – these it claims not as borrowings from the west, but as its own. In giving birth to the universal, the west has begotten something which can never again be private property." [reference to Hocking 1956, 51]
>
> Hocking's words express the assurance of a culture which was still confident of the universal validity of its way of seeing things. Today we are required to look afresh at this "way of seeing" which is in fact being questioned, and to enquire about its origins and credentials. (83os84, 5-6)

So we find at the beginning of the 20th century two lines which have developed from Christian eschatology – the meta-narrative of human mastery of nature and history ("the idea of progress"), and the individualization of the eschatological hope. Both find their continuation in developments in the 20th century. The experience of two world wars followed by a collapse of the colonial empires meant a major crisis for the idea of progress which underlies the linear, optimistic view of human mastery of history. It appeared that this collapse left a vacuum in the West. So Newbigin comments in 1963:

> The idea of general universal progress has broken down, leaving behind either some sort of Utopian fanaticism – Marxist or other – or else scepticism and despair. For those who have not given way to despair and who have not accepted the Marxist interpretation of history, there does not seem to be any generally accepted alternative framework for the understanding of events. (63rtdt, 21)

This loss of hope becomes increasingly apparent in the closing years of the 20th century.

> In the closing decades of this century it is difficult to find Europeans who have any belief in a significant future which is worth working for and investing in. A society which believes in a worthwhile future saves in the present so as to invest in the future. Contemporary Western society spends in the present and piles up debts for the future, ravages the environment, and leaves its grandchildren to cope with the results as best they can. One searches contemporary European literature in vain for evidence of hope for the future; rather, in Jürgen Moltmann's words, it is characterized by cold despair, loss of vision, resignation, and cynicism. (89gps, 90-91)

The loss of an overarching meta-narrative that gives meaning to history as a whole is accompanied by a shift in the understanding of rights of man which have moved center stage during the time of the Enlightenment. The original shift in emphasis during the Enlightenment had been from the duties of each person to his or her rights. This led to the explicit formulation in the founding charter of the New World of the right of each person "to pursue happiness." But while this was originally tied to the pursuit of what Hannah Arendt called "public happiness," the emphasis gradually shifted to an individualized understanding of happiness. The loss of an overarching meta-narrative must necessarily lead to the loss of a shared understanding of public happiness. The nation-state thus is forced into the role of becoming the guarantor for each individual to be able to pursue his or her own happiness. This individualization of interests is part of the current crisis of the Western welfare states. The collapse of a shared meta-narrative and the individualization of interests result in an irresponsible behavior of a society with regard to its future generations. "Spend now and someone else will pay later" (89gps, 112).

> Mediaeval society had emphasized the idea of the duties involved for each person by his or her position in society. From the Enlightenment onwards, it was the "rights of man" which seemed axiomatic. To the founding fathers of the new republic created in the New World to embody the principles of this new philosophy, it seemed necessary and natural to begin with the famous words: "We hold these truths to be self-evident, that all men are created equal, that they are endowed by their Creator with certain inalienable rights; that among these are life, liberty and the pursuit of happiness; that to secure these rights governments are instituted among men, deriving their just powers from the consent of the governed." The rights of the human person are the unquestioned starting point from which all else follows. These rights include the right to the pursuit of "happiness". Happiness (bonheur) was hailed by the eighteenth century philosophers as "a new word in Europe". In place of the joys of heaven to which the mediaeval person was encouraged to look forward, Enlightenment people looked forward to "happiness" here on earth. This would come within the reach of all through the cumulative work of science, liberating societies from bondage to dogma and superstition, unlocking the secrets of nature and opening them for all. ...
>
> The nation state has taken the place of God. Responsibilities for education, healing and public welfare which had formerly rested with the Church devolved more and more upon the nation state. In the present century this movement has been vastly accelerated by the advent of the "welfare state". National governments are widely assumed to be responsible for and capable of providing those things which former generations thought only God could provide – freedom from fear, hunger, disease and want – in a word: "happiness". (83os84, 13-15)

This individualization of interests and the overwhelming expectation from the institution of the state to provide what only God can give must necessarily lead to a collapse. While some do indeed sense the collapse of the idea of progress others continue to interpret political developments at the end of the 20th century according to the linear optimistic pattern of modernity. They see in the overcoming of the cold war, with its polarization of First and Second World, the achievement of a unity that will serve as basis for the common work of the betterment of the human race. In a Hegelian way this is even announced as the "end of history."

> A former official in the US State Department, Francis Fukuyama, has written a book entitled 'The End of History and the Last Man'. Its thesis is that, with the collapse of Marxism as a world-power, history as we have known it has come

to an end. Of course the human race will go on, but the age-long battle between civilizations and ideologies is over. There is now only one civilization: liberal democratic capitalism. The only future is the onward march of this form of human life. Of course there will be pockets of resistance to be dealt with in due course – Islam, and old style dictatorships for example. But from now on the whole human race has only one goal: the progressive enlargement and perfection of this form of society, equipped with ever more sophisticated technologies to ensure its smooth working. This is, of course, not the first announcement of the end of history. Hegel, who is in the background of this new form of realized eschatology, saw the end of history in the rise of the Prussian state. What is interesting is not this nonsense in itself, but the question why it is taken so seriously. A conference of 1000 intellectuals in London has gathered to hear the guru in person. Why should anyone take this seriously? (92eh, 1)

Newbigin does not share in this optimism. He takes the crisis of the linear and optimistic Western model more serious and sees it challenged by the biblical paradigm as well. The collapse of the idea of progress is a challenge to the linear understanding of history which was characteristic of modernity. At the same time this crisis of the idea of progress has reinforced the split between the public and private sphere that was introduced in the West through humanism. The loss of a singular meta-narrative for the public sphere of life in the West has opened the doors for a new influx of the Asian understanding of human existence which focuses on the interiority of human beings (see 79cjh, 202), where meaning is found not in the directedness of the human story but rather in the inner experiences of human beings. That loss has led to a plurality of individual narratives in which the particular events themselves play only a subordinate role, namely insofar as they contribute to individual growth and enrichment. The relegation of the Christian eschatological hope into the private sphere seems to fit seamlessly into this general development.

> With the collapse of the belief in progress, Christians in the affluent societies have tended to lapse into a purely privatized eschatology, which pins any hope that it has to the vision of personal blessedness for the soul after death. This naturally diminishes the sense of responsibility for public affairs. (89gps, 113)

We will have to come back later to this individualization of the eschatological hope when we look at the role the church plays in the encounter of God with human history.

3.1.2. History as Selection and Interpretation of Facts

History as a subject of human reflection does not consist simply of the sum total of all events that ever happened. It is not merely a collection of facts. History is the selection and interpretation of facts. It is the specific arrangement of historical events which then gives order and meaning to the whole.

> All history involves selection among the vast mass of possible material. This selection has to be on the basis of what is significant from the point of view of the story which the historian has to tell. His data, of course, are not the happen-

ings themselves, but the evidence for these happenings available in documents, archaeological finds, and oral traditions. These data are themselves the products of some decision about what was significant enough to be remembered or recorded. At every stage decisions have been made and are being made about what is significant. Historians debate endlessly the question of meaning in history, but it seems clear that no history could be written at all without some presuppositions about what is significant and therefore about the meaning of the story. (89gps, 71)

Every writing of history requires some sense of the meaning of the story as a whole. Without some presuppositions about the meaning of the story the historian does not have any guidance whatsoever about what is significant, what contributes to the story. In other words, without any understanding of the meaning of the story, there is no history at all. There is merely a vast array of events that cannot be brought together as a whole. It is here that Newbigin sees the bible play an important role.

> It is impossible to write history without some vision of its meaning from which judgments of significance can be made. And if there is no meaning, why be a historian?
>
> The Christian tradition affirms that God has made his mind and purpose known to some (not to all) people through events in history – not all events but some, the memory of which is treasured in the Christian tradition. ...
>
> The biblical record as we have it comes from a community which (with wide diversities of interpretation at many points) understood history in terms of a purpose of God to bring salvation to the world through a particular people among all the peoples of the world. (89gps, 72, 76)

The bible distinguishes itself from other religious literature by providing a comprehensive understanding of history as a whole. It is not primarily concerned with religious doctrine or with devotional writings. Its uniqueness is found in the fact that it provides an overarching view of human and cosmic history, and that the meaning of individual life stories can only be grasped in the context of this bigger picture.

> The Bible is unique among the sacred scriptures of the religions in that it offers an interpretation of history as a whole, human history and cosmic history, and not just of the life of man apart from this history. Its centre of attention is not, if one may put it so, the possibility of man's escaping out of this world into another; it is the promise of God coming to this world to redeem it and to complete what he has begun. (76bsr8)

The biblical overall view of history is not merely the backdrop for individual life stories. They do find their meaning only in reference to and in the embeddedness in the story as a whole. "The way we understand human life depends on what conception we have of the human story. What is the real story of which my life story is a part?" (89gps, 15).

This characteristic of the bible has not always been clearly in view. The developments in the West, with the relegation of religion into the private sphere of beliefs and values, have also changed the way the bible is viewed there. The church has not been immune to the danger of interpreting the bible as its specific "book of religion."

> A learned Hindu friend has several times complained to me that we Christians have misrepresented the Bible. He has said to me something like this: "As I read the Bible I find in it a quite unique interpretation of universal history and, therefore, a unique understanding of the human person as a responsible actor in history. You Christian missionaries have talked of the Bible as it were simply another book of religion. We have plenty of these already in India and we do not need another to add to our supply."
>
> Surely this complaint has some justice. Certainly the Bible is sharply differentiated from the sacred books of the East at exactly this point. Unlike them, it sets out to speak of human life in the context of a vision of universal, cosmic history. Although, of course, it contains a great variety of material – legal codes, prayers, wise sayings, and moral instruction – it is, in its overall plan and in a great part of its content, history. It sets before us a vision of cosmic history from the creation of the world to its consummation, of the nations which make up the one human family, and – of course – of one nation chosen to be the bearer of the meaning of history for the sake of all, and of one man called to be the bearer of that meaning for that nation. The Bible is universal history. (89gps, 89)

The loss of a unifying meta-narrative in the West which has accompanied the collapse of the idea of progress has led to a plurality of stories. The difference between this plurality of stories and the biblical story is that the bible is not satisfied with providing one more religious story among other interpretations. The bible claims to tell the overarching story. At the same time it locates and roots individual life stories in the overarching story. It is thus concerned with the same historical facts that any historian is dealing with. The gospel is – to use Newbigin's famous phrase – not part of a private sphere of values and beliefs but of the public sphere of facts. That distinguishes it from other religious stories or personal interpretations.

> In this sense, the church shares the postmodernists' replacement of eternal truths with a story. But there is a profound difference between the two. For the postmodernists, there are many stories, but no overarching truth by which they can be assessed. They are simply stories. The church's affirmation is that the story it tells, embodies, and enacts is the true story and that others are to be evaluated by reference to it. The world, so far as recorded history enables us to know, has always been full of stories, myths which expressed in story form the way of understanding the human situation. Such myths do not claim factual truth, in the sense that their veracity can be checked against the record of contemporary witnesses or accessible artifacts. They express eternal truths in story form. By contrast, the story that the church tells is a competitor in the field where secular historians tell the story of a society, a nation, a civilization, or the story of the world. The church's story is not a different kind of story from the one these histories tell; its difference is with respect to the interpretation of

the records which are the raw material common to them all. It is not a special kind of history isolated from the work of secular historians. It is, if you like, a counterhistory, interpreting the same evidence in a different way. (95pc, 76-77)

It is this rootedness in history which gives the gospel its special character. The gospel not only interprets historical events, presenting an overarching story. Its central message is that God is indeed not only involved in history, but is its main agent. History is God's story.

3.2. History as God's Story

The biblical view of history centers on a number of convictions which need to be looked at in more detail. It sees God as the central actor in history. It holds that the meaning of the story has been revealed in the middle of the story, while the story is still going on and the end has not yet happened. And it claims that God has revealed the meaning of the story to some human beings and has entrusted to them the task of carrying the revelation of the meaning of history to all other human beings.

3.2.1. God as Agent

According to the biblical view of history God is the central agent of history. Human agency is responsive agency. Men and women as created beings are given responsibility to act. It is responsive, responsible action – answering to the call that the creator has given to his creatures. Human agency does not diminish God's ability or his freedom to act. God in fact revealed himself as the central agent of history from the beginning when he called creation into being. His actions run through cosmic history from the time of creation to the final vision of a new heaven and new earth. It would not make sense to speak of God acting at all, if his acts did not concern the world in which we live.

> If God does not act in history, what meaning can there be in saying that God acts at all? And if there is no category in which we can speak of God acting, what meaning can we attach to the word "God"? Many of our contemporaries would, of course, answer "Exactly! The word 'God' stands for nothing real at all." The presupposition of most historical scholarship since the Enlightenment has been that God is not a factor in history. (89gps, 69)

The anthropocentric view of the world that is characteristic for the time of modernity focuses on the questions of cause and effect in the cosmos. The universe is seen as a closed system which can be explained in these categories. The biblical vision extends beyond that. The request "Your kingdom come" is based on the conviction that the fate of the universe is not determined by the laws of cause and effect but by the will of a personal God who acts.

> We do not believe in a closed universe. The prayer [Your kingdom come] implies that this universe is not a closed system. And therefore we believe not in the mighty power of nature, but in the mighty power of the one by whom all things exist and from whom they have their being from moment to moment.

> And we call upon the Holy Spirit who is given to us as the first fruit, the foretaste, the first instalment, the pledge of the new covenant, of the creation for which we long, to renew us so that we become witnesses and agents of the new creation within the womb of the old, sharing in the suffering, the travail of birth, but full of hope because we know we have already received the pledge of the new creation. (90chs, 9)

A God who acts in relationship to his creation must necessarily act in the particularities of space and time. The idea of a universal revelation of supracultural truths, not related to the specifics of history and geography, is a philosophical construct that does not take into account the particularities of the acts of a God who is a personal being with a personal will. God's deeds are accompanied by his words, which interpret what is happening. The gospel is the story of God's deeds, interpreted to the community which he has called out of the world. It is passed on in this community as the story, the metanarrative, that gives meaning to the whole. The gospel is therefore in essence a story, a narrative, not a dogma or an edifying teaching.

> The gospel, the account of these actions, is always in narrative form: "The Word became flesh," "God so loved the world that he gave his one and only Son …," and so forth. The ecumenical creeds are also in narrative form. Above all, the Bible, taken as a whole and in its canonical form, is a unique interpretation of cosmic and human history in which the human person is seen as a responsible actor in human history, always being called to respond to the initiatives of the one who is both Creator and Savior. This book is unique. None of the other sacred scriptures of the world's great religions have a character anything like this. (95pc, 52-53)

Biblical truth is in essence historical truth. It extends beyond the dichotomy of modernity and postmodernity. For modern thinking, truth is fundamentally propositional truth, factual truth, stating what is true apart from historical and cultural particularities. For postmodern thinking, truth is fundamentally relational truth, personal story. Statements about truth are not true per se; they can only be true in the sense of being true for me or true for you, true in specific particularities. This is the epistemological dilemma on the borderline between modernity and postmodernity. The biblical understanding of truth transcends this dichotomy. Historical truth is in essence both factual and relational. It is concerned with both the factuality of events and their interpretation in relation to other human beings, including the self. It is concerned with both facts and people. It not only shows the overarching story, but places each individual story in this bigger context and thus gives meaning to both, the whole and the parts.

3.2.2. The Rehabilitation of Purpose

The modern scientific approach to the world has limited itself to looking at the categories of cause and effect in its explanation of the world. Excluding purpose as a category for scientific explanation has been an intentional, deliberate decision, "on purpose." The exclusion of a personal God, a personal will as possible explanation for the understanding of the world has resulted in the relegation of purpose out of the public sphere of facts into the private sphere of beliefs and values.

> Now the figure of God has disappeared into the shadows. He may exist or he may not; the question is not vital. We have learned to understand things in a different way. The way to "explain" things is to analyze them into their smallest parts and show how everything that happens is ultimately governed by the laws of physics. If a thing or a happening can be understood as the mathematically calculable interaction of its parts, then it is "explained." Things are not to be explained in terms of purpose, because purpose is a function of the beliefs and values of the person whose purpose it is. Things are to be explained in terms of their causes, of what makes them happen. All happenings have causes, and all causes are adequate to the effects they produce. The ultimate goal is to understand everything in terms of the physics and chemistry of its constituent parts. Human life is ultimately to be understood as the product of an endless series of random happenings in the physical world. Chance and causality are the sufficient "explanation" of all that is and all that happens. ... The world so understood is the world of what are called "facts," the facts which we "know" and which everyone needs to learn. It is a closed world of cause and effect, a world from which purpose has been excluded as a category of explanation, and in which – therefore – there can be no judgment of "good" or "bad." It is a world, as we say, of value-free facts. (89gps, 36-37)

This self-limitation of scientific research on cause and effect has been borne out of a specific concern for certainty through objectivity – the exclusion of everything subjective and personal – and has led to a public worldview that does not take purpose into account for the explanation of the world. Newbigin points out the limitations of this kind of explanation. While it is possible to know the intricate details of a machine (how it works), this does not mean that one knows what this machine was built for in the first place. As long as one does not know the purpose, it is impossible to pass any moral judgment.

> To take one of MacIntyre's examples: from the factual statement, "This watch has not lost five seconds in two years," you may immediately conclude, "This is a good watch" – provided that "watch" is already understood as an instrument for keeping time. If "watch" means only a collection of bits of metal which can be used according to the personal preference of its owner for decorating the sitting room or for throwing at the cat, then no such conclusion follows. If "watch" is understood only in terms of the physics and chemistry of its parts, no such conclusion follows and everyone is free to have his or her own opinion as to whether it is a good watch or not. (85cwbc, 5)

So understanding purpose is really essential for gaining a more complete understanding of the whole. But since purpose is a subjective category, rooted in a personal will, it requires personal communication in order to be understood.

> Purpose is a personal word. It implies a mind which has a purpose real in the mind though not yet realized in the world of objects; it can be known only by listening to the person whose purpose it is. But for understanding cause we

> have to examine what is already there in the world of objects. This is a different kind of enterprise, as different as dissecting a brain to find out how it works is from listening to a person to find out what he means. Both are proper activities in their proper place. But clearly the elimination of the question of purpose can only be a methodological strategy; if there were no such thing as purpose then the scientist could have no purpose in adopting this strategy. The scientist acts purposefully when, as a decision on method, he investigates cause and ignores purpose. Plainly it is an error to move from this section on method to the conclusion that there are no purposes at work in nature other than the investigative purpose of the scientist. (85cwbc, 6)

Newbigin here points out the fallacy of the supposed conclusion that purpose does not constitute a category for understanding. The fact that purpose is not part of our Western understanding of public truth does not mean that there is no such category as purpose. It only means that it has been – on purpose – excluded as category of explanation in the public sphere. With his argument Newbigin rehabilitates purpose as a category for understanding meaning.

3.2.3. Knowing the Purpose of History

To know the purpose of something requires personal communication. Observation in itself may prove insufficient for understanding purpose. Only if prior experience allows me to interpret what I observe, will I be able to conclude from my observations what the purpose of a thing is.

> Suppose that going along a street, we observe men at work with piles of bricks and bags of cement, and we guess that a building is being erected. What is it to be? An office? A house? A chapel? There are only two ways to discover the answer: we can wait around until the work is complete and inspection enables us to discover what it is. If we cannot wait until then, we must ask the architect, and we will have to take his word for it. (95pc, 57)

Newbigin applies this example to the understanding of the cosmos.

> If the work in question is not the building of a house but the creation and consummation of the cosmos, the first alternative is not available to us. We shall not be present to examine the end product of cosmic history. If the whole thing has any purpose (and of course we may decide, as postmoderns do, that it has no purpose), the only way we can know that purpose is by a disclosure from the one whose purpose it is, a disclosure which we would have to take on trust. There is no escape from this necessity. ... The question whether the cosmos and human life within it have any purpose other than the individual purposes we seek to impose on things is one that cannot be decided by observation. If we live with a prior assumption that human life has no purpose, then we shall act accordingly, and there will be no possibility whatsoever of discovering its purpose. As I have argued, only by an act of disclosure of the purpose of human life can we learn that it indeed has a purpose, and such an act of disclosure can only be personal, a revelation. (95pc, 57-58)

Knowing the purpose of the cosmos requires the self-communication of the creator to his creation. That is the role of biblical revelation. Underscoring the importance of revelation as personal disclosure for understanding purpose, Newbigin at the same time points out the limitations of what theologians call "general revelation." Newbigin does not at all deny all knowledge of God among those who do not yet know him through his word. He knows from his own missionary experience about the necessity of some kind of continuity in order to be able to talk about God at all. But he points out that in order to know God's purpose for his creation, personal communication is needed which goes beyond general revelation.

> If we may use the term "general revelation" for that awareness of God which seems to be part of human nature wherever it appears (even when it is suppressed), we have to add that this general revelation, valid as it is, cannot communicate the purpose of God for his creation. ... The use in the early books of the Pentateuch of ancient names for God, such as El Shaddai and El Elyon, and the identification of these as names for the God whom Israel knows as Yahweh, shows clearly that there is a continuity between the story which the Bible tells and the religious life of the peoples of the ancient world. Every missionary who seeks to proclaim the gospel in a new language has to rely on this continuity. He has to use one of the words which that language already had for God and which the people who speak that language used before they ever heard of the Bible. Without using that word the missionary cannot begin to communicate. In other words, what I have called general revelation is, in some way, presupposed. But it does not follow from this that the biblical story can be properly told simply as part of the history of religions in what Europeans call the Middle East. If there is a real continuity, as there is, there is also a discontinuity. God has done a new thing, but that does not mean that God was previously absent from the scene. The new thing is radically new and gives a new revelation of who God is and what his purposes are. (89gps, 73-75)

While the observation of the cosmos and of history reveal traces of God, these observations do not suffice in order to understand God's purpose with his creation. This is underscored by the fact that God has self-restricted his freedom to act by granting his creatures a measure of independence. Because of this self-restriction it is true on the one hand that God does reveal himself in history; but it is at the same time true that not all of history does reveal God.

> Everything that I do is an expression of my mind except insofar as I am compelled by outside forces to act against my will. If, by definition, God is not under compulsion by outside forces, it would seem that everything that happens in the world is an expression of God's mind. Plainly the Christian tradition affirms that some things which have happened express God's mind, but not all. God reveals himself in history, we would say, but not all history reveals God. How can these two things be affirmed? In part the answer lies in the subject of our next chapter, the logic of election. In part it lies in our belief about the relation of the world to God. In contrast to the monistic, pantheistic, and panentheistic thinking which is always present as an attractive option, we believe that in his creation of the world God gave it a measure of independence and to that ex-

tent limited his own freedom. Things therefore happen in history which are not in accordance with the will of God but represent a contradiction of his will. (89gps, 71)

This ambivalence underscores the necessity of a clear revelation of who God is and what his purposes are with this world. God has revealed himself most clearly in the incarnation of his son.

3.2.4. Christ as Center and Turning Point of History

In both Eastern and Western philosophy it is assumed impossible that a particular historical event could bear universal significance in such a way that it provides access to truth which transcends history. But this is precisely the way the creator as personal God has chosen to reveal himself and to give human beings access to himself. The incarnation of Jesus Christ together with his ministry, his death and resurrection have brought the presence of God's reign into the midst of history. Jesus did not come like the Zealots of his time, trying to establish the rule of God by force. Nor did he retreat from public life into a monastery to simply pray and wait for God's kingdom like the Essenes. "What he did was to challenge the public life of the nation, at the place and time of its most passionate sensitivity, with a claim to kingship which was at the same time quite uncompromising and completely vulnerable" (83os84, 36). In the person of Jesus Christ the rule of God has become present in human history. His presence and his death mean a fundamental change in the relationship between God and humankind. In Christ – centering in his death and resurrection – a new reality is created and presented. The powers that have resisted God have been challenged to face their maker and have been defeated. In this sense Jesus Christ is the center and turning point of history. "The Christian faith ... implies that events took place which changed fundamentally the relations between God and man and instituted a new era in human life. History now possesses a centre. From this centre it derives its ultimate meaning" (J. H. Oldham, quoted in 79cjh, 201).

> The public history of mankind will be seen as a coherent reality which has a real centre and a real end. The centre (in the Christian understanding) is the life and death and resurrection of Jesus. The end is not, of course, the end-product of historical development as conceived in the eighteenth century doctrine of progress; to think that would be to deny the judgment upon history which is embodied in the cross. The end is the new creation of which the resurrection of Jesus is the first-fruit. But this new creation is the true consummation of the shared history of mankind and of nature. It is symbolized not in the idea of disembodied survival for the individual, but in the vision of a city which is at the same time the gift of God and the true goal of the story of civilization. The meaning of the story as a whole will have been grasped in the only way which is possible, not by induction from the generality of experience but by a revelation in the form of happenings which are grasped by faith as the selfcommunication of the one whose purpose the story embodies. The 'happenedness' of these events which form the clue to the whole will be essential to the faith. And the faith will be expressed in a life of discipleship in the shared life of human-

ity, seen not just as illustrations of the faith or as exercises in personal spiritual growth, but as participation in the story whose centre has been discerned in the events. (79cjh, 204-205; see also 89gps, 86)

There is a strong focus on the reality and particularity of historical events. In the particularities of the person of Jesus of Nazareth God revealed himself and turned around the course of history. This has universal consequences, even in the present. Like Newbigin says, the life of the Christian community is the participation in and the embodiment of the story whose center is Jesus Christ. Christ will lead the story to the fulfillment of the final vision of the unity of humankind in the presence of God – not as a world-immanent development but in the final advent of his second coming. Again the focus is on the historical factuality of this outcome.

> Christians of all persuasions pray, "Your kingdom come." What are we, as Christians, asking for when we so pray? We already believe that God is the Supreme Ruler. If, nevertheless, we pray for Gods kingly rule to come, then we are asking for something different from the present state of affairs. ... We are looking for something new, radically new. If, however, there can never be within history something radically new, what is the point of this prayer? In truth, of course, we are emboldened to pray this prayer, to make this unreasonable petition, because we believe that in Jesus this kingly rule has in fact broken into our history in an event which is without analogy except the analogy of creation and the analogy of the final consummation of all things. Apart from these unique events, for which there are no other analogies, the petition would surely be a mere aspiration without justification in the experience of human history. (95pc, 82)

Newbigin names three events in history which are without analogy to anything else in history. They can only be compared to each other. Each one of these events is a direct and decisive act of God. These three events in time are creation, the advent of God's reign into history in the person of Jesus Christ, and the final consummation of all things. These events are the beginning, the center, and end of history respectively. What is true for all three of them is that they are real historical events. None of them must be interpreted as merely symbolic. Newbigin here continues his critique of a realized eschatology that does not expect a real future consummation of history.

> The New Testament writers all seem to think in terms of a real goal, a real end to history, a consummation to which we look forward and which is 'nearer to us now than when we first believed' (Rom. 13.11). This is true even of the Johannine texts which, in spite of their strong evidence of commitment to a 'realised eschatology', nevertheless speak emphatically of a future consummation (e.g. John 6.39f.; 12.48; 1 John 3.2). It is this which provides the horizon for purposeful action. (93kogh, 8)

The way to this fulfillment of history is not one of gradual progress. It is instead the continuation and intensification of the conflict that was initially provoked by the rebellion of the powers against God. Christ in his ministry and death has unmasked the powers and deprived them of their authority.

This conflict has been part of history ever since and it is going to intensify towards the end as the message of Christ's decisive act challenges men and women in all nations and cultures with the ultimate question. "Jesus is the determinative center of all history, as He is its beginning and its end. The ultimate question is, 'Faith in Jesus, or unbelief?'" (60mcan).

The problem with the secularized interpretation of the biblical eschatological hope in modern Western society has been its failure to recognize the destructive power that is at work against God's purposes and therefore also against humankind. As a result of that failure the idea of progress served to fuel optimism instead of realistic hope. The attempt was made "to reproduce in history the power of the resurrection without the marks of the cross" (89gps, 112). The conflict with the powers of rebellion that was brought to the surface through the coming of Christ and that found its first culmination in his cross was not recognized. This crisis ultimately concerns every human being. It calls all of us to face the ultimate decision.

> The coming of the Messiah precipitates the crisis of human history. In him God presents every man, and the whole of mankind, with the possibility of receiving or rejecting the end for which he created all things. The whole of human history, after the coming of Christ until his coming again, is the pressing of this choice to the final issue. And the Church is the body which understands this, which is called to bear witness among the nations to the real meaning of the events amid which we live, and thereby to present to all men and nations the concrete alternatives of acceptance or rejection. (63rtdt, 25)

Jesus himself foretold this intensification of the conflict and the role the church would have to play therein.

> Finally, the whole thirteenth chapter of St Mark is dominated by the assurance that God is leading all things to a final consummation in which the powers of antichrist will muster all their strength against the Kingdom of God and will be finally vanquished. The process of polarization goes on to the end. The conflict grows more acute, the decisions become more urgent. There is no gradual ascent to a perfect world. World history does not contain in itself the secret of its own redemption. The Church, which is embedded in world history, belongs to it, and bears witness to its true beginning and end, is nevertheless apart from world history, in the sense that its witness is to an end which is not merely implicit in the story itself. The relation of the Church to man in his history is, therefore, not merely one of solidarity, but also one of separation. Here also the Church, when it is faithful, follows the Lord who by his very solidarity with men pronounced the divine judgment on them, whose Cross was both the ultimate sign of his complete identification with sinful men and also the point at which God's total rejection of man's sin was manifested. (63rtdt, 46)

But the intensification of the resistance of the powers against Christ is not the end. It will lead to the consummation of the victory over the powers of rebellion. Jesus Christ, the Lord, will bring about what is promised to us in the Spirit who is a foretaste and pledge of that which is to come.

The horizon of all our action in the world, therefore, is not an earthly utopia but the heavenly city which is God's new creation. The key to a right answering of our question lies in a true eschatology. The Bible closes with a vision of the holy city coming down from heaven to earth. It is the vision of a consummation which embraces both the public and the private life of men and women. There is no dichotomy between these two. Those who die before that day are laid to rest in a "dormitory" around the church where the living continue to worship. When the Day comes, all together will share the same end – judgment and, for the blessed, the heavenly city. (83os84, 34-35)

The main markers of the biblical interpretation of history are clear. In the person of Jesus Christ a new reality was brought forward, namely the reconciliation of the cosmos with God. This event has become the center of history. The powers of rebellion have been defeated in Christ's death on the cross. Even though they continue till today in their resistance and are thus intensifying the crisis, the decisive victory has already been won. And in the end Christ will bring to fulfillment that vision that is promised and experienced as foretaste and downpayment in the person of the Holy Spirit.

This real end of history will be something completely new. But at the same time it will be merely the revelation and consummation of what has been true since the death and resurrection of Christ. For the establishment of God's kingdom is not something that is incomplete in the present. It is already complete, but it is hidden. And it will be revealed at the apocalypse, the end of history.

3.2.5. Christocentrism and the Trinity

Newbigin's understanding of the role of Christ has remained the same despite the development of his thought towards a stronger trinitarian view. Goheen emphasizes the change in Newbigin's thinking, speaking of a "paradigm shift" from "a Christocentric to a trinitarian ecclesiology" (Goheen 2000). Newbigin himself is aware of the widening of his thinking in light of new challenges that presented themselves to him in the course of his ministry. However he refuses to let the trinitarian emphasis lead to a relativization of the person and role of Christ. A trinitarian view is no substitute for Christocentrism. The two can only be viewed together. In light of this recognition, it may be debatable whether this widening of Newbigin's thinking really qualifies as a paradigm shift. The refusal to relativize the role of Christ is explicitly expressed in Newbigin's debate with Raiser.

Raiser in the early 1990s calls for a paradigm shift in the WCC. He describes the old paradigm of the WCC, referring to Visser't Hooft as its representative, as "christocentric universalism." The main characteristics of this paradigm were its clear Christocentric focus (salvation is only in Christ), its emphasis on the church, and its universal perspective (history as the central category for understanding God's salvific work in this world).

The emerging new paradigm of the ecumenical movement challenges the old understanding of missions in all three areas. In light of the increasing awareness of religious pluralism, the Christocentric focus is called into question. Christian theologians have called for a shift away from Christocentrism towards Theocentrism. Also, the role of the church has been challenged. God is seen at work in the social and political movements of this world, apart from the church. And the new focus is on diversity. It challenges the former universal perspective. Universalism is too much tied to the image of an oppressive "ecumenical domination." The new paradigm calls for "ecumenical solidarity" (Raiser 1991, 63). In summary, the new paradigm is characterized by a general shift away from the global/universal towards the particular, a postmodern emphasis, one might say. This is demonstrated in the call to focus on the historic Jesus rather than on the cosmic Christ.

As characteristics of the new emerging paradigm Raiser mentions three key issues: First, there is a new focus on the Trinity, especially the social, relational aspects of the Trinity. The triune God is seen as "being-in-relationship of those who remain distinct and different" (Raiser 1991, 96). As such the Trinity brings together diversity and unity, and thus provides not only the origin but also the model for the unity of the "household of life." The traditional "kingdom"-terminology with its focus on the father and the father-son relationship is part of the old paradigm. Second, the focus shifts away from history as the main category for understanding God at work towards "life as a web of relationships." This shift tries to embrace all of creation in its understanding of salvation. Yet it de facto amounts to the dissolving of the eschatological direction of world history. The focus is on the current state of the cosmos as household of life, not on the direction and the eschatological goal of God's story with the world. And third, the substitution of the unity of the church with the unity of the *oikumene* as "one household of life" which "embraces all of God's creation" (Raiser 1993, 19) relativizes the role of the church.

Newbigin engages Raiser's proposal. While he agrees on the necessity of a trinitarian model for mission, he qualifies:

> [A] Trinitarian perspective can be only an enlargement and development of a Christo-centric one and not an alternative set over against it, for the doctrine of the Trinity is the theological articulation of what it means to say that Jesus is the unique Word of God incarnate in world history. (93reit, 2)

Newbigin criticizes Raiser's "almost total neglect of the missionary factor in the ecumenical movement," and the obscurity in the distinction between church and world. "For Raiser the task of the church is not to Christianize the world but to change it (...), and it is the *oikumene* (not the *ecclesia*) that comes down as a city from heaven" (93reit, 4). The fact, that Raiser never mentions the Ecumenical Affirmation on Mission and Evangelism is of great concern to Newbigin. "Indeed this total amnesia in respect of the missionary and evangelistic work of the churches is (for me) the most remarkable feature of the book." And: "To allow the worldwide missionary and evangelistic calling of the church to disappear from the agenda of the WCC (as this book effectively does) is much more than a 'paradigm shift'" (93reit, 5).

Newbigin's critique of Raiser shows his concern that a trinitarian view must not be interpreted as a substitute for a Christocentric view. A trinitarian theology that remains true to the NT cannot mean the relativization of the Christological center, because all that is included in salvation, is and will be given to us in the unique and particular person of Jesus Christ. In this sense Goheen can summarize the Raiser-Newbigin debate by saying:

> At each point, the parting of ways between Raiser and Newbigin finds its ultimate source in their differing assessments of Jesus Christ. A future paradigm of mission depends on the answer given to the question that Jesus posed to Simon Peter: 'Who do you say that I am?' (Goheen 2004, 109)

Intrinsically bound to this Christocentric view is Newbigin's understanding of history with its direction towards a real end. Here too Newbigin's position is distinctively different from Raiser's. A focus on the "one household of life" which "embraces all of God's creation" must never be allowed to displace the focus on the eschatological direction of history. Rom 8:19ff instead points out how not only the church but the whole cosmos is longing for and looking forward to the day in which the one who is the center of history will bring about the consummation of God's redemptive reign. The salvation of the "one household of life" is thus intrinsically bound to the historical event of the consummation of Christ's reign.

3.3. History, Church, and World

The question which arises from this Christocentric view of history is of course: What is the role of the church in history? What is the relationship between church and world?

3.3.1. Neither Dichotomy between nor Identification of "World History" and "Salvation History"

Cullmann in his study (Cullmann 1962) did distinguish between world history and salvation history. The two were separated with the fall and will be united again with the *parousia*. World history will then be drawn into salvation history. On the other hand we have the concept of the "cosmic Christ" which was presented by Joseph Sittler in New Delhi in 1961. Sittler argued for the necessity of viewing the two biblical themes of creation and redemption closer together. That of course has implications for the understanding of history. God is then seen at work not primarily in the church or through the church but in the world. Sittler's emphasis has strengthened Hoekendijk's idea of God being at work in the history of the world apart from the church.

Newbigin's view differs from both of these understandings. He does not identify the work of God with the developments of human and cosmic history (see Bosch 1976, 60). One may think here of those references that conclude that there is no direct line from our present efforts to the establishment and consummation of the kingdom of God. On the other hand Newbigin also says that there are not two different kinds of history. The bible does not distinguish between a sacred history and a secular history. World history is not merely a backdrop for God's story. This would in fact render world history meaningless with regard to God's true purposes. Newbigin's understanding grows out of his truly cosmic view of salvation.

> The Church is indeed the agent of God's mission and a clue to his dealing with mankind, but this does not mean that the work of God in the world is to be simply identified with the progress of the Church in mission and unity. It does not mean that the events of secular history are mere background for the story of the Church, or merely scenery for the drama of salvation.
>
> Plainly the Bible does not permit us to look at the matter in this way. The Gospel of God, with which both Testaments are concerned, does not refer merely to one of the strands of man's cultural history. It refers to the beginning and end of all things and therefore to the real meaning of all that happens. It follows that there cannot be an absolute separation between the history of our redemption, and the sacred story of the Old and New Testaments, the story of the Church and the whole story of mankind. The Bible does not make such a separation. The point here is not merely the obvious one that the story of Israel is intertwined with that of the pagan nations round about. It is that the whole history of these pagan nations is in the hands of God and is propelled by him towards the end which he has revealed to his own people. (63rtdt, 24)

The reign of God extends over all of creation. God does not want to save us from the world in the sense of "out of the world," "away from the world." God aims to save the world. Without falling into the universalist trap Newbigin insists on viewing the universal reign of God and the cosmic scope of salvation together. God is not merely intervening in history from the outside as if world history in general were something outside of his concern.

> It is common to hear theologians speak of the Gospel as God's 'intervention' in human history. But is God absent from human history apart from this intervention? Is the world outside the Church 'an atheistical patch in the universe'? Is God not at work in the affairs of the world outside the bounds of the body that confesses Christ as Saviour? The Bible does not allow us to doubt that he is. (63rtdt, 27)

It is important to recognize the tension in Newbigin's understanding. He neither distinguishes between a secular and a sacred history, nor does he simply identify the two. Both secular and sacred history deal with the same facts. However the interpretation is quite different.

> The church's story is not a different kind of story from the one these histories tell; its difference is with respect to the interpretation of the records which are the raw material common to them all. It is not a special kind of history isolated from the work of secular historians. It is, if you like, a counterhistory, interpreting the same evidence in a different way. (95pc, 77)

Nowhere can this difference be better perceived than in the interpretation of Christ's death. To any historian the death of Jesus of Nazareth must look like a failure and public shame. However the contrast between this view and Paul's interpretation in Col 2:15 could not be sharper: "Having disarmed the powers and authorities, he (Christ) made a public spectacle of them, triumphing over them by the cross." It is not Christ who is made a public spectacle, but it is the powers of rebellion who are being put to shame by Christ. Both interpretations are looking at the same event, but they are diametrically opposed to each other.

Why is it so important for Newbigin to avoid the dualism of a sacred and a secular story? We find here an underlying motif that recurs regularly in Newbigin's thinking. He is opposed to the split in Western thinking between what he calls the public and private sphere. And he challenges the assumption that religion is part of the private sphere and not of the public sphere. Accordingly Newbigin argues against any split between a secular and a sacred story. This dualism would only underscore the split that was caused in the West by humanism. Newbigin, therefore, rejects the claim of some theologians that while the crucifixion of Jesus is a historical event the resurrection of Jesus is not to be interpreted as such. It is precisely this kind of dichotomy that Newbigin challenges.

> Perhaps the point that I am making can be highlighted by observing that some theologians have affirmed that, while the crucifixion of Jesus is an event in history, the resurrection is not. Of course this drives a wedge right through the heart of the Christian creed. If, in fact, the tomb was not empty on that Sunday morning, then the crucifixion of Jesus has to be understood quite differently from the way it is to be understood if the tomb was empty. The church's affirmation is that the story it tells is the true interpretation of all human and cosmic history and that to understand history otherwise is to misunderstand it, therefore misunderstanding the human situation here and now. (95pc, 77)

So the story which the gospel tells does not deal with different historical facts than the stories other world histories tell. But it gives a different interpretation of what is going on (see Bosch 1991, 508). And it is the task of the church – as it was the task of Israel – to communicate that interpretation which could not otherwise be gained.

> When Israel is told 'You are my witnesses' (e.g. Is 44: 8), it is plain that Israel is not being summoned to help God to cope with the otherwise unmanageable powers of the pagan empires, or to organize a movement which will carry out God's purposes in contradistinction to the godless purposes of these empires. They are but a little thing in God's hands. He raises them up and casts them down as he will. Israel's role is to be – precisely – witness of his purpose to these pagan nations to whom it would be otherwise unintelligible. Israel knows what God is doing – or ought to know; the others do not. The revelation of his nature and will which God has given to Israel equips her to understand the meaning of what he is doing. (63rtdt, 24-25)

Israel – the church – knows what God is doing through God's revelation. That must be our next concern.

3.3.2. Knowing the Outcome in the Middle of the Story

The gospel is in essence a story. For Newbigin that is the central characteristic of biblical truth. And we as human beings are part of the story. We are still in the middle of things. The problem of course is that in order to act in a meaningful way, one must have some sense of where the story is going, what its outcome is going to be. As actors who are still in the middle of the story we don't know its end. We have only two options: We must either form our own hypothesis about the outcome of history, or we can listen to the one who is in charge of the story, trust his word regarding its outcome, and act accordingly. Either way we have to act on the basis of a personal choice and commitment.

3.3.2.1. The Role of Revelation

We have looked at the necessity of revelation in order to understand the purpose of the creator for his creation (see 3.2.3). Newbigin approaches the subject again from the perspective of the human being as actor in world history who is still in the middle of the story, who cannot know the outcome of the story, but needs to have some sense of its meaning and goal in order to act meaningfully.

> Normally you cannot be sure what is the point of the story until you have reached the end. There can always be surprises at the end, and in the best stories there are. How then can we, who are still in the middle of the cosmic story, know what the point of the story is, or whether it has any point at all? Only if the author of the story has let us into the secret while we are still in the middle. There can be no other possibility. And here of course, when we speak of "the author letting us into the secret," we are talking the language of revelation. (89gps, 91)

Thus to understand the gospel as historical truth has consequences for Newbigin's epistemology. Our knowing the end of the story and our interpretation of it depends upon our initial choice and commitment. The fundamental question is: Who do I trust? Whose interpretation of the story is most reliable? "Indubitable knowledge of the meaning and goal of history will only be available when history has reached its terminus" (89gps, 93). Here we are at the heart of Newbigin's "eschatological epistemology" (Foust 2002, 162) which we will look at in more detail in chapter five. Newbigin challenges the church to present its interpretation of history to the world, based on God's revelation with regard to its outcome and its meaning. He sets Augustine before us as an example.

> What Augustine offered was a "post-critical philosophy" in the sense that it began with the revelation of God in Jesus Christ and claimed that the acceptance by faith of this revelation provided the starting point for the endless enterprise of understanding. The revelation furnished a new framework for grasping and coping with experience. It overcame the old dichotomies from which classical thought could not escape – the unbridgeable division through all reality between the "sensible" and the "intelligible" (corresponding to the modern division between "material" and "spiritual"), and the irrationality that turned all human history into a conflict between "virtue" and "fortune" – between human courage and skill on the one hand and the blind power of fate on the other. The

revelation of God in Jesus Christ, articulated in the doctrine of the Trinity, provided a way of understanding which overcame these dichotomies. To accept the trinitarian model means to believe that the power which rules all events in the visible world and the power that can illuminate and fortify the inner person is one with the man who went his humble way from Bethlehem to Calvary in the days of Pontius Pilate. The starting point for this new understanding was faith. Augustine quotes Isaiah "Unless you believe you will not understand" (7:9). Faith is not a terminus but a starting point from which understanding can begin. This model is offered for acceptance by faith as the way to understanding. Its motto is *Credo ut intelligam*, I believe in order that I may understand. (83os84, 24)

In one short sentence Newbigin summarizes the involvement of the trinitarian God in history: The Father as "the power which rules all events in the visible world," the Spirit as "the power that can illuminate and fortify the inner person," and the Son as "the man who went his humble way from Bethlehem to Calvary in the days of Pontius Pilate." This is the understanding of the universal rule of the Father and its relation to the particularities of specific historical events in the life of the Son, relating this rule of God to the individual life stories through the work of the Spirit, thus bringing the universal story and the individual stories together to one meaningful whole.

It is the call of the church as bearer of the revelation to communicate God's view of history and trust the Spirit to invite people to make this the foundation of their view of history.

3.3.2.2. The Role of Election

The doctrine of election may be regarded as a centerpiece of Newbigin's theology (see Hunsberger 1998a). Apart from the doctrine of election one cannot understand Newbigin's theology. However it is important to realize that his understanding of election is embedded in the eschatological tension. It is an integral part of the eschatological orientation of God's story as a whole with its universal focus throughout.

What are the characteristics of Newbigin's understanding of election? First, he points out that election is the basic principle by which God works throughout the bible. God is not only the initiator of the beginning of the cosmos as its creator. He is also the initiator of the call that lays a claim on a person's life, a call for trust and obedience to God. And wherever a person follows this calling, their life story is integrated into the overarching story in which God works out his salvation for the cosmos. This can be seen throughout the bible, from the calling of Abraham to the calling of the disciples.

> And yet it is plain that the doctrine of election is central to any true exposition of the Bible. From the very beginning God chooses, calls, and sends particular people. God is always the initiator. The words of Jesus to his disciples, "You did not choose me; I chose you," are in line with everything in the Bible from beginning to end. (89gps, 80)

The focus of this calling is clearly on the inclusive side, not on the exclusive side. In the election of the few God is concerned with the inclusion of all in God's story of salvation, not with the exclusion of the non-elect. This is obvious right from the beginning in God's call of Abraham (Gen 12:1-3). His calling does not mean the exclusion of the nations from God's blessing; quite to the contrary, the calling of the one means the participation of the many in the blessing of God.

> It is the universality of God's saving love which is the ground of his choosing and calling a community to be the messengers of his truth and bearers of his love for all peoples. Once again we have to remember that neither truth nor love can be communicated except as they are embodied in a community which reasons and loves. (89gps, 85)

This inclusive focus of God's election has not always been an emphasis in the history of theology. And it has therefore obscured the view that election is rooted in God's love for all, not merely for some. For Newbigin this inclusive focus and the rootedness of election in God's love for all is central for gaining the right perspective. The doctrine of election therefore must not be understood as election for privilege but as election for responsibility. It is not only the elected person himself who is in focus but the universal scope of God's love.

> They are chosen not for themselves, not to be the exclusive beneficiaries of God's saving work, but to be the bearers of the secret of his saving work for the sake of all. They are chosen to go and bear fruit. To be chosen, to be elect, therefore does not mean that the elect are the saved and the rest are the lost. To be elect in Christ Jesus, and there is no other election, means to be incorporated into his mission to the world, to be the bearer of God's saving purpose for his whole world, to be the sign and the agent and the firstfruit of his blessed kingdom which is for all. ... It means that this particular body of people who bear the name of Jesus through history, this strange and often absurd company of people so feeble, so foolish, so often fatally compromised with the world, this body with all its contingency and particularity, is the body which has the responsibility of bearing the secret of God's reign through world history. The logic of election is all of one piece with the logic of the gospel. God's purpose of salvation is not that we should be taken out of history and related to him in some way which bypasses the specificities and particularities of history. His purpose is that in and through history there should be brought into being that which is symbolized in the vision with which the Bible ends – the Holy City into which all the glory of the nations will finally be gathered. But – and of course this is the crux of the matter – that consummation can only lie on the other side of death and resurrection. It is the calling of the Church to bear through history to its end the secret of the lordship of the crucified. (89gps, 86-87)

Election as call to responsibility is the call to participation in Christ's mission. It is the call to be part of that community which bears witness through history that the crucified is the Lord of all. The mission of Christ gives this calling of the church its special characteristic. It is a calling that leads to glory only through participation in the cross. It is the call to participate in the love of God for his world, including the suffering (e.g. Mark 8:34) and the joy (e.g. Luke 15:10) and the glory (e.g. Rom 8:18) that comes with it. This focus on responsibility includes the privilege of being an integral part of God's story. It is not foremost concerned with the privilege but with God's own concern (see Acts 20:24).

God's decision to work out the salvation of the cosmos and to establish the shalom in the world by the way of election is not arbitrary. Newbigin sees this choice of method rooted in the relational character of human beings and in the character of salvation itself. The fact that we as human beings depend on each other is not merely a marginal note of our existence. It is a central part of how we were made. We are created to live in relationship. This takes us back to Gen 1:26-27, the creation of man and woman in the image and likeness of God. The relational character of human existence is a reflection of the relational character of God himself, who out of his love extends the circle of his inner-trinitarian fellowship to include his creatures in this fellowship of love. Even creation itself grows out of this desire of God to extend and share his love beyond himself. The historical self-revelation of God is in essence the extension of the inner-trinitarian fellowship into human history (see Sorc, quoted in Neuer 1999, 201). The wholeness and richness of this fellowship is expressed in the biblical term shalom. Salvation is the restoration of the shalom that was lost in the fall. Therefore salvation in its essence is reconciliation and restoration of relationship. This understanding of salvation challenges the individualization of the Christian hope. And it challenges a view of Christian fellowship which sees the relationship among believers primarily in an instrumental way. Salvation is the creation of a new community. It is reconciliation with God and with each other (2Cor 5:18; Rom 5:1; Eph 2:14-22). Mission therefore is not only the task of bringing the message of salvation to another human being via the bridge of human contact. What happens in the missionary encounter is that wherever a person responds to this message, the new community is extended. A new relationship is built. Reconciliation is taking place.

> We can only understand the biblical teaching about election if we see it as part of the whole way of understanding the human situation which is characteristic of the Bible. Here, in contrast to both the Indian and the modern Western views, there is no attempt to see the human person as an autonomous individual, and the human relation with God as the relation of the alone to the alone. From its very beginning the Bible sees human life in terms of relationships. There is no attempt to strip away the accidents of history in order to find the real essence of what it is to be human. Human life is seen in terms of mutual relationships: first, the most fundamental relation, between man and woman, then between parents and children, then between families and clans and nations. The Bible does not speak about "humanity" but about "all the families of the earth" or "all the nations." It follows that this mutual relatedness, this dependence of one on another, is not merely part of the journey toward the goal of salvation, but is intrinsic to the goal itself. For knowing God, for being in communion with him, we are dependent on the one whom he gives us to be the bearer of

this relation, not just as a teacher and guide on the way but as the partner in the end. There is, there can be, no private salvation, no salvation which does not involve us with one another. Therefore, if I may venture to use a metaphor which I have used elsewhere, God's saving revelation of himself does not come to us straight down from above – through the skylight, as we might say. In order to receive God's saving revelation we have to open the door to the neighbor whom he sends as his appointed messenger, and – moreover – to receive that messenger not as a temporary teacher or guide whom we can dispense with when we ourselves have learned what is needed, but as one who will permanently share our home. There is no salvation except one in which we are saved together through the one whom God sends to be the bearer of his salvation. (89gps, 82-83)

The characteristic of biblical salvation as restoration of community requires that the message be carried forward from one person to another and that in this process the firstfruits of the new creation is in fact revealed in history today. Here we are at the eschatological roots of the doctrine of election. The call of God to individuals in the present is the call for the incorporation into the new community which has as its eschatological goal the incorporation of all the families of the earth. In this sense the church is the provisional incorporation of humankind in Christ. This calling of the church is what gives meaning to the present time between the first and second coming of Christ.

3.3.3. The Meaning of the Present Time

We have seen earlier that the church's participation in the history of this world requires a faith commitment with regard to the goal and purpose of history as such. Since all human beings still live in the middle of the story nobody has access to an outside view of history's goal. The call of God in the present is nothing less than his challenge to human beings to make the revelation of God's view of history the foundation for their acting in the world. This call extends to all aspects of human living. The challenge is not merely to cognitively accept a certain perspective of history, but to act on this understanding. We are called into the community that is characterized by the renewal of relationships and reconciliation. As a community the church is called to "indwell" God's story and live this story in this world.

> If we follow these suggestions we get a picture of the Christian life as one in which we live in the biblical story as part of the community whose story it is, find in the story the clues to knowing God as his character becomes manifest in the story, and from within that indwelling try to understand and cope with the events of our time and the world about us and so carry the story forward. At the heart of the story, as the key to the whole, is the incarnation of the Word, the life, ministry, death, and resurrection of Jesus. In the Fourth Gospel Jesus defines for his disciples what is to be their relation to him. They are to "dwell in" him. He is not to be the object of their observation, but the body of which they are a part. As they "indwell" him in his body, they will both be led into fuller and fuller apprehension of the truth and also become the means through which God's will is done in the life of the world. (89gps, 99)

Indwelling the story means to live in the tradition of the community which has received God's revelation of the meaning of history and which continues to pass this revelation on. It is not merely a passing on of the tradition, but also a call to interpret the present in light of this tradition, in order to act out the call of God today.

> The biblical record as we have it comes from a community which (with wide diversities of interpretation at many points) understood history in terms of a purpose of God to bring salvation to the world through a particular people among all the peoples of the world. This understanding is expressed in the words through which the events have been made known to us. We have access to the knowledge of these events only through the words which embodied the understanding of those who witnessed them or participated in them, and which have been treasured and handed on by those who shared this understanding. As Christians we are part of that community and have the responsibility to seek to interpret contemporary history, the history which is now in the making, in terms of the same belief. (89gps, 76-77)

The Holy Spirit is the guide who leads the church in the interpretation of the present and leads it into a deeper understanding of the purpose of history and of its own mission. The Spirit does so especially where the church encounters new challenges while carrying out its mission. In the crossing of barriers and in facing the challenges to communicate the gospel in new contexts, the Spirit deepens the understanding of truth not only on the side of the unbeliever but also in the life of the believer. Newbigin summarizes:

> According to the Fourth Gospel, when Jesus was preparing his disciples both for his departure from them and for their mission to the world, he expounded to them the relation between that which had been revealed in his earthly ministry among them and that which they would still have to learn in the course of their mission among the nations. The essential elements in this Johannine passage can be expressed in seven points:
>
> 1. There has been a decisive and complete revelation of God in the particular event of Jesus' earthly ministry. "He who has seen me has seen the Father" (14:9).
>
> 2. Nevertheless there is much that they have still to learn. The Spirit of the Father himself will be their teacher, interpreting to them his revelation of the Father (14:16). This promise is to the Church and not for the world, for the world cannot receive the Spirit (14:17).
>
> 3. Nevertheless this gift is not for the private possession of the Church; the presence of the Spirit will constitute Christ's witness to the world (15:27).
>
> 4. This witness, however, will be in the form of a contradiction of the world's most fundamental beliefs (16:8-11). The work of the Spirit will thus continue through the witness of the Church that contradiction of the world's fundamental beliefs which was historically enacted in the cross.

> 5. To the Church, however, the work of the Spirit will be "to declare the things that are to come," to interpret coming events, to be the hermeneutic of the world's continuing history (16:13).
>
> 6. In doing so the Spirit will "glorify" Jesus. It will become clear through this teaching and guiding of the Spirit that the crucified Jesus is truly Lord of history (16:14).
>
> 7. The scope of this work of the Spirit is as wide as the universe itself, for "all that the Father has" belongs in truth to Jesus (16:15).
>
> What is affirmed here is that a particular community in history, that community which bears the name of Jesus, will be given, through the active work of the Spirit of God, a true understanding of history – the ongoing history that continues through the centuries after Jesus, an understanding which is based on the particular events of whose memory they are the custodians. But this privileged position is not for their sake but for the sake of the world into which they are sent as the witnesses to Jesus in whom God's purpose for his entire creation has been disclosed. (89gps, 78)

The Spirit is thus doing a twofold work: Through the witness of the church he is witnessing to the world the revelation of God's purpose and his salvific acts; and at the same time he is leading the community of the elect towards a deeper understanding of God's truth as its members entrust themselves to the service and guidance of the Spirit. "We are invited to make a personal commitment to a personal Lord and to entrust our lives to his service. We are promised that as we so commit ourselves we shall be led step-by-step into a fuller understanding of the truth" (95pc, 66).

It is the mission of the church which gives meaning to the present age, this age which is characterized by the tension between the presence and the future of God's reign. God has set this time aside so that the kingship of Christ will be made known to all nations and all are called and invited to join in this community that is the firstfruits of the new creation (see Matt 24:14). In this sense the mission of the church is the meaning of the present age, ringing in the end of history.

> [T]he movement of which the gospel speaks is that within which world history is enclosed; that Jesus Christ is not one of the figures of world history: He is Alpha and Omega; He from whom world history begins and in whom it is to be summed up and brought to its conclusion. ... He is the sovereign Lord in whose hands are all the issues of life and death, all the complex strands of destiny for nations and civilizations as for every human soul. The Church's missionary task is not one of the good causes we have to support. It is the clue that leads to the consummation of the whole story of mankind. (60lmc, 61)

3.3.4. The Contribution of the Church to World History

What does the discussion so far mean for the church's involvement in world history? In this section I will summarize a number of key issues that Newbigin addresses in the context of God, church, and world history.

3.3.4.1. Challenging the Secularized Forms of Christian Eschatology

First of all, the church is called to recognize the secularized versions of Christian eschatology that have become part of modernity and to expose and challenge them with the gospel. This is the continuation of Christ's ministry of exposing and confronting the powers (see p. 98). Both the idea of progress and the ideology of Marxism are derived from a Christian eschatology. They have shaped Western culture extensively. After the collapse of Marxism as a political system, some see the continuation of the optimism of the idea of progress as the final stage in human history (see 92eh, 1). Postmodernists challenge this optimistic view. Newbigin, too, is critical.

> Marxism and capitalism, twin children of the Enlightenment, have fought a long battle, and one has been defeated. But that is not the end of history. It creates a new situation in which there is a more urgent need than ever before for the Church to unmask the illusions and deflate the hubris of modernity and to affirm the true end of history which is offered to us now in the person of the one who is both Alpha and Omega and is Lord of all. (92eh, 2)

The fundamental problem with both of these distortions of the Christian eschatological hope is that they present their promises of wellbeing apart from the cross of Christ. They focus on human possibilities and contributions (83os84, 35) and thus displace both the person of Christ and the fact of his cross. This is their anti-Christian character.

> The conflict is precipitated by the appearing of "false messiahs" – those, in other words, who pretend to offer total welfare on terms other than those which are offered to those who follow Jesus on the way of the cross. "Total welfare", freedom from all earthly ills as a this worldly possibility, is an idea which could only arise within a culture which was familiar with the gospel announcement that the day of salvation has dawned. The coming of the true Messiah precipitates the appearing of the false ones. The secular promise of total welfare apart from discipleship in the way of the cross has been made and could only have been made from within a society shaped by the gospel. The promise is false and can only lead to disaster. (83os84, 59-60)

Part of the disaster may be seen in the collapse of the idea of progress and the turning away from a shared vision for the future of society (89gps, 90-91). The increased focus on individual happiness and success is symptomatic of this development. It is the task of the church to raise the awareness of false interpretations of history of two types: interpretations that do not take into account the reality of the powers of rebellion and – in Newbigin's terms – try to establish a new world order by the power of the resurrection without the cross, and interpretations that are characterized by a loss of hope and perspective for the community as a whole. The exposing of the powers and false Messianic claims is an integral part of the proclamation of the lordship of Christ.

3.3.4.2. Challenging the Privatized Forms of Christian Eschatology

On the other hand the church is called to challenge the privatized version of Christian eschatology. The relegation of religion to the private sphere of beliefs and values has led to a loss of vision for responsible Christian engagement in the public sphere. That tendency was reinforced by the collapse of the idea of progress.

> With the collapse of the belief in progress, Christians in the affluent societies have tended to lapse into a purely privatized eschatology, which pins any hope that it has to the vision of personal blessedness for the soul after death. This naturally diminishes the sense of responsibility for public affairs. (89gps, 113)

The root of the problem is an underlying dichotomy which holds that the spiritual life of the Christian is separate from his involvement in the world. The two don't seem to have any connection. Newbigin challenges this dichotomy head on. Any kind of spirituality which does not include a concern for and an involvement in the issues of family, neighborhood and nation does not take into account God's involvement in the world and his purpose. Again it is Newbigin's concern to communicate a view of the story, in which each individual life is part of the overarching meta-narrative. The two cannot and must not be separated.

> What, then, are the real issues involved in this debate? I suggest that they can be understood by looking at the phrase I have just put into the mouth of a Hindu or Pietist friend: "your living relationship with God now." The issue is this: Is this relationship with God something separate from your involvement in the ongoing life of the world, your family, your neighborhood, your nation in the family of nations? Do you have, or do you seek a relationship with God in which you can really turn your back on these other involvements? Or is your relationship with God necessarily bound up with your acceptance of the part God assigns for you in his purpose for his world? If the latter is the case, then your relationship with God cannot be separated from those acts in which God has revealed and effected his purpose for the world. Your life of devotion to God will be expressed in and through your involvement with history as you are now part of it. You will understand your own life as part of a story which is not a story made up by you, not just the story of your decisions and actions, but the story which is being enacted under God's creative and providential control in the events of contemporary history. (89gps, 67-68)

Newbigin carefully distinguishes his position from two extremes. He does not propose a world-immanent eschatology that tries to establish the vision of God's kingdom in the here and now. This linear, optimistic understanding does not take into account that the kingdom comes only by passing through death and resurrection. There is a "proper otherworldliness." But that must not be confused with an "improper privatisation of hope."

> The pattern of cross and resurrection precludes any purely this-worldly eschatology. But this does not authorise or excuse what has been common in contemporary Christian thinking, namely the alliance of a (proper) otherworldli-

> ness with an (improper) privatisation of hope. The Christian hope is not merely hope for the soul, but hope for the world. If we say, as we must, that the horizon for purposeful action cannot be a putative earthly utopia at some date in the future, we have also to say that the horizon cannot be the death of the individual. The true horizon – if we follow the New Testament – is expressed in the words: 'He shall come again in glory to judge the living and the dead.' With that as the horizon, as the future to which I direct my energies, purposeful action becomes possible and hopeful. I know the one who will finally assess what I do. And this 'doing' is of course in the public field of politics, economics and culture as much as in the more private world of intimate personal relations. The sundering of these two, and the suggestion that action in one sphere is to be directed by the revelation in Christ but not in the other, is simply one of the illusions of contemporary western culture. The human being is one person whether at home or at work, and there is one judge of all his deeds. Whether at home or at work, I am part of one human family and of one world of nature. My story is part of the wider story and cannot be understood apart from it. The true horizon to which I must direct my energies can only be that which is the horizon for the story as a whole. It cannot be a private horizon. (93kogh, 11)

Throughout his life Newbigin has argued for this integrated vision. The dichotomy between the private and the public is part of a distorted Western view of the world. It does not correspond to the character of the human being as one being in both his private and public life. The modern sociological and cultural differentiation of roles may provide support for the false dichotomy. But it does not make it any more true. Furthermore, biblical ethics clearly does not allow for such a separation between the public and the private self (see e.g. Deut 4:5-8; Matt 5:16; Col 3:23). God's concern is with the world. He is not saving people out of the world. Rather he himself is coming into the world in order to fulfill his purpose.

> But, we have to ask, in what sense, is the Gospel hope for the world? What do we have the right to look forward to? We face here a deep dichotomy: we may fix our hope on the future of humanity and its institutions, or we may fix it on the future of the human person. If we do the former, the human person is marginalised. He becomes instrumental to history, for the individual does not live to participate in the realisation of history's meaning. The logical end of that road is familiar to us in such fearful experiences as those of Russia under Stalin. If we take the other road and place our hope in the eternal destiny of the human soul, history is marginalised. At best this world is only a vale of soul-making. The achievements of art, science and technology, the struggles to create a just and free society, are only – so to say – school exercises. They have no final significance in themselves. The end of that road is the cultivation of an individual piety which withdraws from the conflicts of public history. (76bsr8)

The question is: How then is this tension to be kept so that neither the individual nor history is marginalized? How is the Christian to be involved in the world, if his involvement is not to be misunderstood as the establishment of God's kingdom? What are the characteristics of the Christian's actions? Theologically, the answer has to be developed from the fact that the Christian hope lies beyond death and resurrection. Christ himself has gone this path ahead of us. We too, as well as all that we do – in public and in private – will have to pass through this gate of death and resurrection.

> [D]eath – in the biblical perspective – is the fruit of sin. It is the outward sign of the fact that none of our achievements is fit for God's glory. There is no straight road from here to there. We do not build the city of God. Our work is full of ambiguity. Wood, hay and stubble is mixed with gold and silver. Not only ourselves as human persons, but our works in history perish. Even our greatest achievements are eventually buried in the rubble of history. The road which we travel goes down below our horizon, out of our sight. The Gospel gives us a hope which heals this dichotomy because Jesus has dealt with sin and death. Because of what he has said at the beginning of this chapter [i.e. Romans 8], Paul can go on now to speak of hope for the whole creation. Christ has gone before us on that road, down into the grave which is the grave of all our hopes. And he has been raised from that grave. The resurrection of Jesus is the pledge of God's will and power to complete his purpose not only for the personal lives of those who trust him, but for the public life of mankind and for the whole of his creation. But this hope is necessarily bound up with the way that it has been made possible. Only as we share the suffering of Jesus can we also share the hope which he has made possible. The corn must fall into the ground and die if there is to be a harvest. The work of the builder must pass the test of fire. There must be travail and pain if there is to be a new birth. It is the third of these metaphors that Paul will use in the present chapter. A new creation is struggling to be born, and as we share in the travail, we share in the hope. (76bsr8)

By directing our attention to the road of death and resurrection before us, Newbigin challenges us with a realism about ourselves and the ambivalent character of our contributions to the kingdom. The fact that on this side of death nothing will ever be perfect, makes us realistic with regard to the limitations of our contributions. But the fact that nothing that is done in the name of Christ on this side of death will ever be lost in the rubble of history makes us hopeful with regard to the possibilities of our contributions to the kingdom. It is in this realism that Newbigin sketches the road ahead of us.

> Christian discipleship is a following of Jesus in the power of his risen life on the way which he went. That way is neither the way of purely interior spiritual pilgrimage, nor is it the way of *realpolitik* for the creation of a new social order. It goes the way that Jesus went, right into the heart of the world's business and politics, with a claim which is both uncompromising and vulnerable. It looks for a world of justice and peace, not as the product of its own action but as the gift of God who raises the dead and "calls into existence the things that do not exist" (Rom 4:17). It looks for the holy city not as the product of its policies but as the gift of God. Yet it knows that to seek escape from politics into a private spirituality would be to turn one's back on the true city. It looks for the city "whose builder and maker is God", but it knows that the road to the city goes down out of sight, the way Jesus went, into that dark valley where both our selves and all our works must disappear and be buried under the rub-

ble of history. It therefore does not invest in any political programme (whether conceived in the style of a restored "Christendom" or in the style of a classless society where all coercive government will have withered away) the hopes and expectations which belong properly only to the city which God has promised. There can be no repetitions of Constantine, either on the left or on the right. What is required is a faithful discipleship, following Jesus on the road he went, and living by the hope of which his resurrection is the outward pledge and the gift of the Spirit the inward foretaste. Such discipleship will be concerned equally in the private and in the public spheres to make visible that understanding and ordering of life which takes as its "fiduciary framework" the revelation of himself which God has given in Jesus. It will provide occasions for the creation of visible signs of the invisible kingship of God. (83os84, 37)

The aim of Christian involvement in the history of the world is therefore not the establishment of God's kingdom, but the creation of visible signs of that kingdom.

3.3.4.3. Signs of the Kingdom

For a biblically based understanding of the role of the church in world history a "right eschatology" is central. Only with a perspective from the end can the church determine its role for the present.

> The secular order is precisely this created order in which God has set us to do his will. A false under-valuation of the secular order, and a false over-valuation of it –spiritualism and secularism – both arise from false eschatology; the one from over-attention to the future of the individual soul, and the other from overestimation of the possibilities of human history. The clue to a right understanding of the secular order is a right eschatology. (60whal, 23)

This is a key statement for this study in which Newbigin explicitly expresses the importance that he attaches to eschatology for understanding history and the church's involvement in history, namely its participation in the mission of the triune God. What are the characteristics of the church's involvement that grow out of a "right eschatology"?

First of all, the eschatological perspective causes the church to live in expectation of the advent, not the future.

> It is advent rather than future. He is coming to meet us, and whatever we do – whether it is our most private prayers or our most public political action – is simply offered to him for whatever place it may have in his blessed kingdom. Here is the clue to meaningful action in a meaningful history: it is the translation into action of the prayer: "Your kingdom come, your will be done, as in heaven so on earth." (89gps, 102)

What is the important distinction between "advent" and "future"? Future is that which grows out of the past and the present. It is already inherent in the present and develops out of it.

> Future in the sense of *futurum* develops out of the past and present, inasmuch as these hold within themselves the potentiality of becoming and are 'pregnant

with future' (Leibniz's phrase). Only that can become which is already implicit or dormant in being, and is heralded in the trends and latencies of the historical process. (Moltmann 1996, 25)

Advent on the other hand is that which comes from outside into the present. This is what is expressed with the Greek word *parousia*. "Christ is coming to meet us." This is what the church looks forward to. It is not the expectation of the development of a better future but the expectation of the arrival (*advent*) of the Lord of history into the present.

Living in hope is the second characteristic that grows out of right eschatology. Newbigin identifies the biblical characteristic of hope in contrast to a colloquial use that might be described as 'wishful thinking.' Hope in the biblical understanding means to have a clear vision of the goal, having a certainty about the outcome of history, and being "anchored" at a place which transcends history.

> Within the community whose plausibility structure is shaped by the biblical story there is a clear vision of the goal of history – namely the reconciliation of all things with Christ as Head and the assurance that this goal will be reached. This is what gives its distinctive character to the Christian hope. In most ordinary speech "hope" means little more than desire for a better future. When I was learning to read and speak the Tamil language I slowly came to realize that it had no word for "hope." When I questioned my Hindu teacher about this, he asked me in turn what I meant by hope. Does hope mean anything? Things will be what they will be. I may wish that they turn out better than likely, but why should I wish to be deceived by my desires? This conversation helped me to realize that in English also the word "hope" often stands for nothing more than a desire for what may or may not be. In contrast to this, the New Testament speaks of hope among the great enduring realities – an anchor of the soul entering in beyond the curtain which hides the future from us, something utterly reliable. I suggested earlier that the absence of any sense of a worthwhile future was one of the marks of our present culture. By contrast one of the marks of the biblical counterculture will be a confident hope that makes hopeful action possible even in situations which are, humanly speaking, hopeless. That hope is reliable, because the crucified Lord of history has risen from the dead and will come in glory. Hopeful action means having something to which one can confidently look forward. It means having a horizon. (89gps, 101)

This certainty is rooted in the decisive victory of Christ on the cross. Because Christ won the victory on Calvary he will return (*advent*) as Lord of the cosmos into human history. In the words of Cullmann: "The fact that the *decisive turn of events* has already occurred in Christ, the mid-point, and that now the future expectation is founded in faith in the 'already', shows that the 'already' *outweighs* the 'not yet'" (Cullmann 1967, 183). Because biblical eschatological hope is rooted in the event of Christ's victory on Calvary, which has already happened, it stands in stark contrast to any idea of merely wishing for a better future.

The third characteristic that flows out of a right eschatology is that the church lives and ministers with a realistic perspective.

> This faith enables us to be at the same time realistic and hopeful. We can be realistic, knowing that no human project can eliminate the powers of darkness as they operate in human life. This realism delivers us from the utopian fanaticisms which have condemned millions of people to misery and death in the cause of an imagined future. But at the same time we can be hopeful, acting hopefully in apparently hopeless situations, not dreaming of an absolute perfection on this side of death, but doing resolutely that relative good which is possible now, doing it as an offering to the Lord who is able to take it and keep it for the perfect kingdom which is promised. In this sense, to use a phrase of Schweitzer, our actions in the public life of the world are acted prayers for the kingdom. They do not themselves lead directly to the kingdom. They are acted prayers for its coming and as such they act as signs of its reality and so enable others to act in hope. (89gps, 114-115)

The theological motif here that keeps hope and realism together is the death and resurrection of Christ (see p. 149). The death of Christ reminds us of the fact that on this side of death there can be no elimination of the powers of evil. The resurrection of Christ gives us the assurance and the clear vision of the goal of history. Thus the two elements of realism and hope are kept together. Only together do they provide the framework in which the church engages with the world. Because the church views the present situation with realism, its actions are not so much solutions to actual problems but signs which point towards the coming of the kingdom.

> In themselves, as a contribution to solving the problems of the nation and the world, our programmes are a mere drop in the ocean. Quantitatively they are insignificant. But as signs pointing beyond themselves they can be powerful indeed, leading men and women to him who is the power of God and the wisdom of God. (87mcw, 12)

At the same time they are prayers for the coming of the kingdom, awaiting and requesting the *parousia* of Christ in the factuality of history.

This tension between hope and realism shows itself in both the eagerness and the patience of the church's involvement in the world. Again, only the synopsis of the two is true to a biblical eschatology. Eagerness without patience stands in danger of losing the realistic perspective and burning itself out. Patience without eagerness stands in danger of transforming the biblical hope for the world into a vision of escape out of the world.

> The vision of the shape of things to come which the New Testament gives should enable Christians to be both realistic and hopeful, both eager and patient. The final victory of Jesus is assured, but it lies beyond the death and dissolution of both our persons and our societies. The actions that we take, therefore, will not be those which fear dictates; rather they will have the character of signs – like the action of the imprisoned Jeremiah buying a plot of land in enemy-held territory. They will be signs of hope. (83os84, 60)

Newbigin characterizes the acts of the church as signs of hope or signs of the kingdom. The acts of the church not only carry weight in themselves as acts of compassion or social change. They also point beyond themselves to the future *advent* of Christ. They point people towards Christ. That is their important contribution. The church thus takes part in the Spirit's ministry of witnessing to the lordship of Christ before the world. This witness is a synthesis of speaking, acting, and suffering. For Newbigin the suffering of the church is an integral part of the church's mission as it is derived from Christ's mission. The suffering is due to the fact that the church is placed in the middle of the conflict of the powers which are exposed in light of Christ's lordship and his victory on the cross. Suffering even becomes the mark of true witnessing.

> The task of the Church in relation to the events of world history is not to be the governor and controller of them, but to be the suffering servant and witness of the Lord, manifesting in its witness the true meaning of these events. The Church is not the instrument of God's governance of the world, but the witness of his governance both by speaking and by suffering. The closeness of our missionary thinking to the New Testament may perhaps be in part judged by the place which we accord to suffering in our understanding of the calling of the Church. ... The idea that we ought to be able to expect some kind of neutral secular political order, which presupposes no religious or ideological beliefs, and which holds the ring impartially for a plurality of religions to compete with one another, has no adequate foundation. The New Testament makes it plain that Christ's followers must expect suffering as the normal badge of their discipleship, and also as one of the characteristic forms of their witness. (63rtdt, 41-42)

A true eschatology thus frees the church for a truly meaningful involvement in the history of humankind. It takes away the pressure and burden that comes with identifying the missionary task of the church with the struggle for humanization (see 71rsh, 79). At the same time it provides the hope that even the smallest act of obedience and compassion is not forever lost but will again be found in eternity (63rtdt, 50-51; see e.g. Mark 9:41). It provides freedom for responsible action beyond the alterations of optimism and pessimism.

It is in this context that one has to understand Newbigin's references to a "Christian society" or as he can also phrase it a "Christian vision for society" (98cmsc; 98fp). The fact that the church is placed in the midst of history, and the fact that the characteristic of the gospel is "public truth" as against "private faith," both require that the church get involved in the public life of the society in which the church exists. The question is not if, but how the church should be involved in the world. This involvement of the church in the world can only be properly understood when we keep the provisional sign character of the church's involvement in mind. As Goheen points out, "[t]he church may function as salt in society, but the fullness of God's kingdom is at the end" (Goheen 2002b, 49). Living in right eschatological anticipation therefore means living by the promises of Christ – for the present and for the future.

> The Church is not promised success; it is promised the peace of Christ in the midst of tribulation, and the witness of the Spirit given out of the Church's weakness and ignorance. For the future it has Christ's promise: '... it is your

Father's good pleasure to give you the kingdom.' And for the present it has his assurance: 'Be of good cheer, I have overcome the world.' (63rtdt, 78)

The implications of this focus on a "right eschatology" for Newbigin's understanding of mission will be discussed in chapter five.

Chapter 4

The Kingdom of God in Newbigin's Writings (Systematic Description)

After looking at the data in detail I will now try to summarize Newbigin's view of the kingdom of God in the greater context of his theology of mission. Summarizing Newbigin's view of the kingdom of God requires that we look at five topics.

1. Universal Story – God, the Father

Newbigin places great emphasis on the unity of the story of humankind and on the fact that this story is God's story with humankind. This story is presented to us by the bible, which essentially is an outline of world history from creation to the new creation, the establishment of God's kingdom. That distinguishes the bible from other religious literature. "The Bible is unique among the sacred books of the world's religions in that it is in structure a history of the cosmos. It claims to show us the shape, the structure, the origin, and the goal not merely of human history, but of cosmic history" (95os, 30-31).

The story begins at creation. God's acting in history for the salvation of the cosmos cannot be understood without a view for God the creator. God is the creator of the world as a living place for humankind. Man and woman are created in God's image to be in fellowship with him and to act as his representatives in keeping and caring for creation. Being created in God's image means "that man's essential nature is to be found in a reflecting of God's love" (56ss, 18). This love of God, his shalom (peace, wholeness, well-being) in the beginning characterizes all human relationships. But human sin eventually destroys the relationship between God and man and woman, resulting in the loss of God's shalom. The essence of sin is the deification of the self. "Sin means that each man wants to be the centre of the world, that he regards his own good as more important than anything else; in other words, sin means that each man wants to be God" (56ss, 20). The loss of shalom brings disharmony and alienation to all relationships that are part of human existence. Newbigin mentions four: "Sin produces an alienation between man and God, between man and himself, between man and the natural world, and between man and his neighbour" (56ss, 33).

But God never turns his back on his creation, even when the consequences of human sin begin to destroy the living space of humankind. God remains involved in the history of his creation, protecting the world and pursuing his plan of redemption. This is the perspective of the first chapters of Genesis.

In this perspective the narrowing of the viewpoint with which the story is told, beginning in Genesis 12, is not a narrowing of God's salvific purposes. It is rather like looking through a magnifying glass to see God working out his universal purpose in the particularities of the life of one man, one family, one nation – always with a view for the whole. It is a "particular election-history with a universal goal" (von Rad 1978, 178).

This universal perspective we find throughout God's story. His goal "is not to pick out an individual here and there for His kingdom, but to re-create for Himself that one family which He purposed in the first creation" (54wsot, 72-73). Salvation is the restoration of shalom in all the relationships in which every human being is placed: to God, to fellow humans, to creation and to the self. "It means the healing of that which is wounded, the mending of that which is broken, the setting free of that which is bound" (56ss, 14). When we look at the end of God's story with this world we see this state of wholeness in individual lives as well as in the life of humankind as a whole.

> What is promised as the goal of history, that which makes possible responsible action in history, is something which heals the dichotomy between the private and the public worlds which death creates. The Holy City as John portrays it in the final book of our Bible is in one sense the consummation of all public history. It represents the goal of the whole story of civilization, which is the creation of the true city. It is perfect in beauty and unity. And into it all the nations of the earth will bring their treasures. The great sculptured panels beside the long flight of steps leading up to the central throne at Persepolis portray all the nations bringing their distinctive gifts to the feet of the Emperor Darius. Perhaps some such picture inspired the writer of the apocalypse. The achievements of human civilization, art, technology, and culture are not obliterated. All that is unclean is excluded, but all that is worthy will find its place as an offering to the King of kings. That is the vision which these words suggest. But at the same time the Holy City is the place where the journey of each soul finds at last its goal. "The throne of the Lamb shall be in it, and his servants shall worship him; they shall see his face, and his name shall be on their foreheads" (Rev 22:3-4). (89gps, 115)

We currently live in between these two poles, creation and new creation. And the bible interprets the events of history as part of this story which God moves towards the end that he has envisioned, planned and will bring about. The driving force behind history is the will of a personal God, who is actively involved in planning, promising, and carrying out his promises. History is the interpretation of events in light of their significance for the whole story. This interpretation is only possible if the direction and the outcome of the story are known. The outcome of the story is made known to us in the promises of God.

> Our common experience of change is interpreted as history only when there is some belief in a promise; then change is experienced as movement towards the fulfilment of that promise. The promise means that we begin to look forward. The promise creates the dynamism of history. (68bima, 10)

For Newbigin the biblical view of the unity of humankind is, however, not identical with the meta-narrative of modernity, in which one part of the world dominates the others and imposes its own paradigm on the rest of the world. Newbigin clearly interprets the drawing of the nations into one common history in an eschatological perspective. The unity of humankind is something that God is bringing about. It is something that has begun with the realization of the necessity of the unity of nations, but it can only come about where the human family gathers around the person of Jesus Christ. "There is no place at which mankind can receive the gift of unity except at the mercy-seat which God has provided" (61icd, 9). The secularized attempts to bring about a perfected society – the idea of progress whether exemplified in Marxism or in capitalism – will not lead us there. "The promise is the same – a total renewal of all things. [But the] agent is no longer God" (68bima, 11). The Christological center is therefore indispensable for the universal unity of humankind.

> It was in the World Missionary Conference of 1910 that "Faith and Order" was conceived in the mind of Charles Brent, and the great text of the early protagonists of the movement was the prayer of Jesus "that they may all be one, that the world may believe." In this missionary sense the unity of mankind was the ultimate horizon of the quest for unity. It must therefore be said emphatically that the kind of concern for visible ecclesial union which sought unity as an end in itself, which was uninterested in the unity of mankind, was a departure from the original intention.
>
> But it would equally be a deviation if the unity of mankind were to be conceived otherwise than from a Christological centre. This is in fact what has often happened. (83ckac, 1)

The biblical vision of one universal story as God's story not only challenges the secularized attempts to bring about a just society. It also challenges the individualization and fragmentation of the story which is characteristic for postmodernity. Postmodern thinking with its emphasis on the local stories has led to a denial of a vision for the whole and a loss of the sense of the oneness of humankind. In this mood of fragmentation religions are seen as instruments of private salvation. Christians are not exempt from this tendency, and we have seen Newbigin's critique of the individualization of the Christian hope.

On the other hand we find attempts to instrumentalize religions for the sake of saving humankind from self-extinction. Philosophical and ethical constructs try to provide a framework, into which all religions can fit. These are attempts to regain a view for the whole amidst the fragmentation of postmodernity, attempts to find a paradigm for unity in light of the plurality of nations, cultures and religions (see e.g. Hick 2001; Knitter 1985; Küng 1990).

Newbigin shares their concern for the unity of humankind, a unity which allows for the plurality of nations and cultures. But he challenges these human constructs on the basis of the biblical story which has the person of Jesus Christ at its center. The fact that this center is refused or relativized or reinterpreted in the models of religious pluralism shows that they have a different basis and propose a different solution. Newbigin rather sees in the biblical story a meta-narrative that allows for both unity and plurality, centered around the person of Jesus Christ whom God has placed in the center of his story with this world.

2. Particular Salvation – Jesus Christ, the Son

God's story with this world has a center point which is at the same time its turning point. "[T]he centre point of the story is the birth, life, death, resurrection and ascension of Jesus and the coming of His Spirit to His disciples" (54wsot, 76). Everything in the biblical story either points in anticipation towards this center point of world history or expands what happened there, pointing from there towards the end of the world in anticipation of the fulfillment of the story. The center point of the story tells of the one decisive act in which God has acted in human history for the sake of all humanity and the cosmos.

> [E]verything will depend upon the faith that history has a centre from which it takes its meaning. The public history of mankind will be seen as a coherent reality which has a real centre and a real end. The centre (in the Christian understanding) is the life and death and resurrection of Jesus. The end is not, of course, the end-product of historical development as conceived in the eighteenth century doctrine of progress; to think that would be to deny the judgment upon history which is embodied in the cross. The end is the new creation of which the resurrection of Jesus is the first-fruit. But this new creation is the true consummation of the shared history of mankind and of nature. It is symbolized not in the idea of disembodied survival for the individual, but in the vision of a city which is at the same time the gift of God and the true goal of the story of civilization. The meaning of the story as a whole will have been grasped in the only way which is possible, not by induction from the generality of experience but by a revelation in the form of happenings which are grasped by faith as the selfcommunication of the one whose purpose the story embodies. The 'happenedness' of these events which form the clue to the whole will be essential to the faith. And the faith will be expressed in a life of discipleship in the shared life of humanity, seen not just as illustrations of the faith or as exercises in personal spiritual growth, but as participation in the story whose centre has been discerned in the events. (79cjh, 204-205)

For Newbigin the particularity of Christ may be a scandal, but it is not a problem. Far from it. "Universality and particularity do not contradict one another but require one another" (95os, 67). The underlying principle here is what Cullman calls the "principle of representation" (Cullmann 1962). Newbigin characterizes the progression of the story: "Although the perspective is cosmic and universal, at each stage the story proceeds by a process of narrowing. The broad picture is replaced at each stage by a close-up focused on one picture of the whole" (95os, 31). As such the story moves forward from God's dealing with humankind as a whole, towards his dealing with Abraham and Israel, gradually focusing in on the one true representative of humankind, the new Adam, Jesus Christ. The story moves from the many to the one. In him God has acted decisively once and for all. The death of Christ is the turning point of history in which the evil one and his powers have been defeated. In his resurrection and ascension Christ has been presented as victor and Lord.

From this event—the death and resurrection of Christ – mission receives its basic characteristic, namely, that it is the proclamation of Christ's kingship (see Michel 1941, 262). Now the story again moves forward by the principle of representation, this time from the one to the many. The underlying pattern in the movement of the story is God's election. "The key to the relation between the universal and the particular is God's way of election. The one (or the few) is chosen for the sake of the many; the particular is chosen for the sake of the universal" (95os, 68). The universal saving will of God, the universal character of his story, and the particularity of salvation in the person of Jesus Christ are brought together through election, a pattern that has been characteristic of God's story from the beginning.

What began as the decisive victory on the cross and has led to Christ's lordship in the present will end in the consummation of Christ's reign at the completion of history. Christ will bring the consummation of God's kingdom and establish a new creation, a new humankind in which justice and shalom shall reign. Any attempt to bring about human unity apart from Christ is doomed to fail. Newbigin captures the NT emphasis on the centrality of Christ and never wavers. In his essay "Religious pluralism and the uniqueness of Jesus Christ" he cautions:

> The World Council of Churches has been asked, at two general assemblies, to accept statements that seemed to call in question the uniqueness, decisiveness, and centrality of Jesus Christ. It has resisted. If, in the pull of the strong current, it should agree to go with the present tide, it would become an irrelevance in the spiritual struggles that lie ahead of us. I pray and believe that it will not. (89rpuj, 53)

Eugene Stockwell makes a similar point when he relates a conversation he had with Newbigin:

> The conversation was brief and he had but one message: keep Jesus Christ central in all that you do, and persist always in reminding the WCC of the centrality of Jesus Christ. Distilled in that counsel was the commitment of a lifetime of a man who had wrestled with countless ideas, who had been the architect of many ecclesiastical structures, who had moved easily from the poverty of Indian villages to the heady realms of theological scholarship, and through it all knew and grew in the conviction that all of it, as life itself, has only one center and reason for being, Jesus Christ the Lord of all. (Anastasios 1990, 95-96)

3. Witness to the World – God, the Holy Spirit

The role of the Holy Spirit with regard to the kingdom of God is twofold. He is (a) a down payment and a foretaste of the end, a guarantee of things to come; and he is (b) the one who leads the proclamation of Christ's lordship; he is in charge of God's mission.

"The Spirit brings the reality of the new world to come into the midst of the old world that is" (95os, 63). The Holy Spirit plays the important role in the eschatological tension between the presence and the future of Christ's reign. He is the one who brings the reality of salvation, that is yet invisible, into the presence of this world. This is not only true for the life of the individual believer and for the church, but also for the world as such. The Spirit brings the reality of salvation into this present world through the life of the disciples, the church. In that sense he is the foretaste of the end. "The Spirit is a foretaste of the messianic feast. The presence of the Spirit is a real presence of the love, joy, and peace that belong to God's perfect reign, but it is not yet the fullness of these things. It is the sign that the last things have begun" (95os, 62). The Spirit as sign and foretaste of God's reign is also the down payment which guarantees the final fulfillment. Newbigin refers to the NT word *arrabon*, a "cash deposit paid as a pledge of the full amount to be paid later ... the advance installment that will make [the disciples] the living evidences of the reality that is promised" (95os, 58). As such the Spirit is the guarantee for the eschatological verification of Christ's victory and lordship that the world is still awaiting.

The second emphasis regarding the Spirit's role in the context of the kingdom is his leadership in the proclamation of Christ's lordship. Newbigin stresses the fact that it is not the church which is in charge of mission, as if the Spirit were coming alongside the church to support it in its mission. Quite the contrary. It is the Spirit who is in charge of the ongoing proclamation of Christ's lordship. "It is the Holy Spirit who leads the way, opening a door here that the church must then obediently enter, kindling a flame there that the church must lovingly tend" (95os, 64). To follow the leadership of the Spirit is a journey full of surprises for the church.

> At this point the church has to keep silence. It is not in control of the mission. Another is in control, and his fresh works will repeatedly surprise the church, compelling it to stop talking and to listen. Because the Spirit himself is sovereign over the mission, the church can only be the attentive servant. In sober truth the Spirit is himself the witness who goes before the church in its missionary journey. The church's witness is secondary and derivative. The church is witness insofar as it follows obediently where the Spirit leads. (95os, 61)

Witness to Jesus Christ is the work of the Holy Spirit. The church participates in the task and proclaims the facts of God's acting to the world. It is therefore not a one-way-relationship from the church to people of other faiths, but rather a triangular relationship in which the Spirit speaks both to the church and to people of other faiths. In the process, the goal is not only for people of other faiths to switch allegiance to Jesus Christ. Part of the process is for the church to gain a deeper understanding of the gospel. It is in the missionary encounter that the church faces new theological questions and is led by the Spirit to a deeper understanding of the truth (John 16:12-15). In this twofold process the new community is extended.

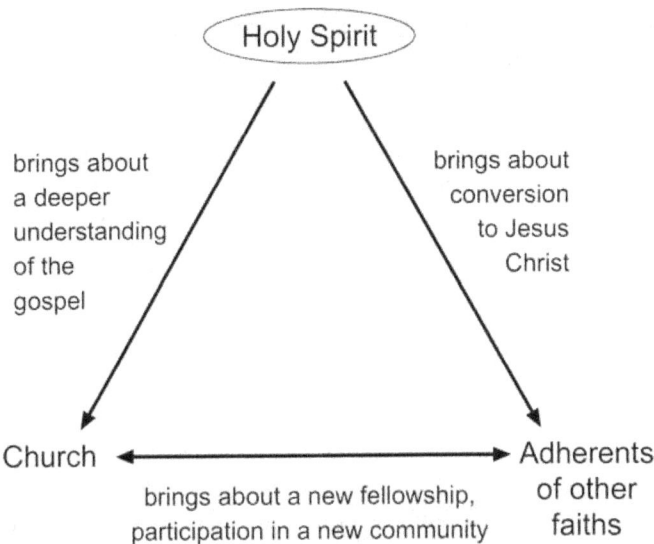

Figure 1: The work of the Holy Spirit in the missionary encounter

Only after we recognize this view of the Spirit in the context of Christ's lordship can we find the proper place for the church in mission.

4. Election for Responsibility – The Church as Bearer of the Witness

For Newbigin the doctrine of election is the key element that holds the universal saving will of God together with his particular saving act in the person of Jesus Christ. God does not reveal himself simultaneously or as equally available to all human beings through some kind of private religious experience.

> There is, of course, ... [this] objection. It was classically expressed in the saying attributed to Rousseau: "If God wanted to say something to Jean Jacques Rousseau, why did He have to go round by Moses to say it?" ... Should not "the transcendent" be equally and simultaneously available to every human being? Very clearly there lies behind the complaint that very ancient belief to which I have referred: the belief that in the last analysis I am a solitary soul with my own relationship with the Transcendent – whatever he, she, or it may be. And that belief is false. It rests upon an atomistic spirituality that contradicts what is most fundamental in human nature, namely that our life is only fully human as we are bound up with one another in mutual caring and responsibility. ... God's action for the salvation of the whole human family cannot be a series of private transactions within a multitude of individual souls; it is something wrought out in public history, and history is always concrete and specific. (89rpuj, 53)

Newbigin critiques the individualism that expresses itself in the demand that God must reveal himself to every individual soul irrespective of and apart from historical circumstances. This demand grows out of an understanding of the human being as an isolated individual and understands religion as a private, inner experience of the individual soul without any connections to or direct implications for other human beings. Any connection to others (e.g. in receiving religious teaching) is merely incidental. Newbigin argues against this focus on the fate of the individual soul with a reference to the social character of the human being. Humans are beings in community. "The human in the Bible exists only in relationship with other persons and only as part of the created world" (95os, 69). This is not by chance. It corresponds to the fellowship and communion that exits between the persons of the Trinity. Being created in the image of God includes that we are created to reflect in our community the fellowship of God, the Father, the Son and the Spirit.

> Interpersonal relatedness belongs to the very being of God. Therefore there can be no salvation for human beings except in relatedness. No one can be made whole except by being restored to the wholeness of that being-in-relatedness for which God made us and the world and which is the image of that being-in-relatedness which is the being of God himself. ... There is no salvation except in a mutual relatedness that reflects that eternal relatedness-in-love which is the being of the triune God. Therefore salvation can only be by way of election: one must be chosen and called and sent with the word of salvation to the other. (95os, 70-77)

In other words, God's choice of sending the elect in order to bring salvation from one to the other is not an arbitrary choice. It is intrinsically bound to the character of salvation. In the process of carrying the word of salvation from one to the other not only is a message communicated but also a new community is created. The Spirit not only restores the relationship between the (new) believer and God, but also creates a new communion between the one who brings the message and the one who accepts the message (see figure 1, p. 161). Thus the gospel not only moves across the human bridge but also at the same time creates the community which is the firstfruits of the new humankind. That new fellowship is at the heart of salvation. Therefore it is not only appropriate but also necessary that the gospel should move from one person to another via the human bridge in order to bring about the new community.

Election, in this understanding, is not viewed as a privileged status of a few, but as election for responsibility. "The one (or the few) is chosen for the sake of the many; the particular is chosen for the sake of the universal" (95os, 68). Hunsberger has summarized this central theme of Newbigin's theology in a very precise and comprehensive way:

> One is chosen by God to bear the blessing to another. The particularity of the choice reflects both the personal character of God (which implies the freedom to act and to choose the time and place of such action) and the social character of human life. It is congruent with the nature of salvation (it reconciles as it is received at the hand of an 'other') and the scope of it (it is intended for all). Far from creating or intensifying the 'problem' of particularity, election for witness is the pattern which makes the inevitable particularity of a personal God's his-

torical actions universal. The particular choice is designed to bear the blessing to all. (Hunsberger 1998a, 235)

This understanding points out the place of the church in the context of the kingdom of God. The church is not to be equated with the kingdom. The church carries forward the witness of Christ's lordship which is the witness of the Spirit. And as the Spirit moves and brings people into that fellowship of believers, he creates the new community which is the foretaste of what lies ahead. Newbigin has come to describe this relationship between church and kingdom with his famous triad: sign, instrument and foretaste of the kingdom.

> The church is only true to its calling when it is a sign, an instrument and a foretaste of the kingdom. But, on the other hand, talk about the kingdom is mere ideology if it is not tied to the name of Jesus in whom the kingdom is present and if it does not invite men and women to recognize that presence, to do the U-turn, to become part of that company that (sinful as it has always been) acknowledges Jesus as the one in whom God's kingdom is present and so seeks to honour him, to serve him, to follow him. (87mcw, 12-13)

The kingdom with its king is the overarching concept; the church is sign, instrument and foretaste.

5. The Kingdom of God – Christ's Lordship in Eschatological Perspective

In 1941 Newbigin expressed his understanding of the kingdom of God in contrast to three general ideas prevalent at the time of the late 1930s, early 1940s. One was the optimistic view of progress as human achievement with all its bright expectations for the future. The other was the dichotomy between a social understanding and an individualistic understanding of the Christian hope which was at the center of the social gospel versus fundamentalist debate of the 1920s. The third paradigm was Dodd's theology of "realized eschatology." In his Bangalore lectures Newbigin dealt with these three ideas and expressed his own view in distinction from them. His understanding of the eschatological tension has continued to provide the framework for his theological reflections. I will begin by sketching the future dimension of the kingdom first, and postpone the outline of the present dimension of the kingdom. I do so, because the mission of the church – to be the sign, instrument and foretaste of God's kingdom today – requires a clear vision of what will be, in order to be the foretaste of that which is to come.

5.1. The Future Kingdom – A New Creation

At the center of Newbigin's theology of the kingdom is the vision of a new creation. "In the center of the picture is the hope of a new world, a re-created universe in which the travail of history shall find its completion and its rest" (41kgip, 46). Newbigin speaks of "a cosmic renewal or restoration"

(41kgip, 28). It is the restoration of the whole of creation according to God's initial plan. As such, it is much wider than a view of heaven populated by a number of individual souls. Newbigin has a truly cosmic perspective.

This new creation is exclusively God's work. It is not reached by human efforts. "There is no straight line of development from here to the Kingdom" (41kgip, 47). Here Newbigin distinguishes his view from that of a secular view of progress that takes the biblical idea of a linear history and combines it with a rationalist and romanticized view of humanity leading to an optimistic trust in human possibilities to shape a better future. Newbigin also contrasts his understanding with a reductionist view that interprets the kingdom as "the progressive realization of good in the life of the world, [which] is simply a Christianized version of the secular idea of progress" (41kgip, 21). Rather the new creation will be exclusively God's own work. "That is to say, the Kingdom of Heaven is to *come* on earth in the sense that this existing age is to be terminated and the divine sovereignty which is now effective in heaven is to become effective on earth" (41kgip, 27).

This future state of the kingdom is a real future. Newbigin agrees with Dodd that the kingdom bears upon our present life. But he insists – in contrast to Dodd – that this can only be so because the eschaton is a real event in the future, not merely a symbolic expression for certain spiritual experiences of the Christian life. A mere symbolic understanding of the eschatological expressions in the NT turns into "the proverbial carrot dangled before the nose of the donkey – something which is always just ahead, but never reached" (54pccc, 122). Such a view finally loses its power to convict. It would mean "to write off hope … as a misunderstanding" (41kgip, 39).

The future establishment of God's kingdom will, however, also be a day of judgment (41kgip, 29). All human beings will be judged according to their deeds. It will be the day where the final decision will be made about the admission to or the exclusion from the kingdom. This day of judgment will mean the eradication of all evil and the final vindication of goodness. Without this outlook the "conflict between what is and what ought to be" would not be spiritually bearable (41kgip, 40). Newbigin sees in the history of this world not a simple growth of good winning over evil. Good and evil are growing together in this world. They are thus leading to the final conflict between Christ and Anti-Christ. In this development the final judgment by God will not be an arbitrary termination of history, arresting the growth of goodness; it will be the necessary and final eradication of all evil. "The whole present order, characterized by the triumph of evil forces, by corruption and death, is to be replaced by the heavenly order, characterized by the sovereignty of God and the abolition of corruption and death" (41kgip, 27). Since it is God's judgment we may not presume to know the outcome of God's final verdict. Therefore we must strictly withhold all final judgments. The final word is God's, not ours.

God's evaluation of every human's life's work will also extend to the lives of the believers. For them, too, there is no direct line into the kingdom. Life in the kingdom is not a mere extension of this present life. The entrance to the kingdom is through death and resurrection. The reality of death hovers not only over our personalities, but also over all our labors and achievements. "[A]ll is destined sometime to be swept away and forgotten. Everything in the end ... is destined to be buried in the dust of failure and death" (41kgip, 47). But as death includes all of our lives, so does resurrection. Not only our bodies but also every single deed which we have offered to Christ will be found again in the heavenly kingdom. "Every faithful act of service, every honest labor to make the world a better place, which seemed to have been forever lost and forgotten in the rubble of history, will be seen on that day to have contributed to the perfect fellowship of God's Kingdom" (41kgip, 47). This view strengthens not only the sense of responsibility we have before God concerning what we do with our lives. It also gives encouragement and hope to realize that any single deed has the potential to contribute to and be found again in God's kingdom.

The expectation of the future revelation of God's kingdom thus impacts our present lives. But it can do so only because of the reality of what is to come and the factuality of what has happened in the past, as the reign of God was not only announced but also embodied in the person and ministry of Jesus Christ.

> The mission of Jesus was to announce and embody the reign of God, a reign which claims jurisdiction over the whole created world and all that is in it. The conflict between that claim and the power that exercises usurped dominion in the world was fought and settled on the cross. The victory lies on the other side of death. Yet in the resurrection of Jesus and in the gift of the Spirit we have received now, in this age, a pledge and foretaste of that victory. The horizon of all our action in the world, therefore, is not an earthly utopia but the heavenly city which is God's new creation. The key to a right answering of our question lies in a true eschatology.
>
> The Bible closes with a vision of the holy city coming down from heaven to earth. It is the vision of a consummation which embraces both the public and the private life of men and women. There is no dichotomy between these two. Those who die before that day are laid to rest in a "dormitory" around the church where the living continue to worship. When the Day comes, all together will share the same end – judgment and, for the blessed, the heavenly city. (83os84, 34-35)

The present – hidden – reign of Christ and the future revelation of his reign cannot be separated. Therefore the church continues to await that final revelation and, by establishing signs of Christ's reign, strives for that day to come.

> Christians of all persuasions pray, "Your kingdom come." What are we, as Christians, asking for when we so pray? We already believe that God is the Supreme Ruler. If, nevertheless, we pray for Gods kingly rule to come, then we are asking for something different from the present state of affairs. We are, surely, rejecting and rebelling against the almighty power of analogy. We are looking for something new, radically new. If, however, there can never be within history something radically new, what is the point of this prayer? In truth, of course, we are emboldened to pray this prayer, to make this unreason-

able petition, because we believe that in Jesus this kingly rule has in fact broken into our history in an event which is without analogy except the analogy of creation and the analogy of the final consummation of all things. Apart from these unique events, for which there are no other analogies, the petition would surely be a mere aspiration without justification in the experience of human history. (95pc, 82)

The certainty of the future advent of God's reign is based on the factuality of its past advent, the hidden presence of his reign here and now. In this perspective every act of obedience in the present is a recognition of the lordship of Christ, both present and future. This not only makes Christian involvement in the world meaningful and gives it a perspective beyond death. It also turns every act of obedience into both a proleptic answer to the petition "Your kingdom come" and at the same time into a prayer for the full and final revelation of God's reign.

> It is advent rather than future. He is coming to meet us, and whatever we do – whether it is our most private prayers or our most public political action – is simply offered to him for whatever place it may have in his blessed kingdom. Here is the clue to meaningful action in a meaningful history: it is the translation into action of the prayer: "Your kingdom come, your will be done, as in heaven so on earth." (89gps, 102)

It has become clear in this discourse that for Newbigin both poles of the tension – the present and the future of God's reign – are interconnected and must not be separated. With regard to this tension he can therefore say:

> The tensions in the teaching of the New Testament about the kingdom are not, therefore, to be rationalised away. The kingdom is both present and future. It is present in that, through the total work of Jesus, we are given here and now the foretaste, the first-fruit, the arrabon of its grace and peace. It is future in that the story of which our lives are apart, the story of creation and of the human family, is not a meaningless and mindless pantomime but a movement directed towards a real goal, a real event in which it becomes clear that something has been accomplished which makes all the agony and conflict worthy of our participation as rational and moral beings. That goal, that accomplishment, which forms the proper horizon for purposeful action, is in one sense known and in another sense not known. It is known in that in Jesus we have seen the one in whom all human and cosmic history is in the end to find its coherence. Therefore where he is present, the end is at hand. Our true horizon beckons here and now. It is here, at the very door. But in another sense the goal is not known. It is, according to a saying which surely cannot have been invented by the Church, unknown even to Jesus. In all this tangled web of good and evil which makes up the human story, only the Father knows what possibilities for good remain, what further frontiers remain for the human family to cross, what further opportunities for new good remain. Only he knows when and how to bring the story of his creation to its completion.

> For the practical business of discipleship the implications of this knowing and not knowing are clear. We know the one who is to come, but we do not know

when and how he will come. Therefore 'you must be ready, for the Son of Man is coming at an hour you do not expect' (Luke 12.40). (93kogh, 12)

This brings us back to our present situation. What does it mean when we speak of the presence of the kingdom?

5.2. The Present Kingdom – The Prolepsis of the End

In his critique of Dodd Newbigin did agree with him that the eschatological kingdom does bear on the present. The kingdom is present and active in Christ. "The new age has come. The promise is fulfilled. The reign of God has broken into this world" (68bima, 14). Whoever meets Christ and receives him experiences the power of the kingdom, tastes the powers of the age to come.

> [T]he central proclamation of the New Testament is that in Christ the new age has already dawned. In the words of the very first proclamation of the gospel, "The Kingdom of God has come near." In Christ the powers of the new age are at work. The domain of Heaven has touched that of earth and God's rule is actually being exercised in the world through Jesus. Those who accept Him come within the sphere of operations of the powers of the Kingdom: they may in fact be said to have been translated out of the present age into the new age which is to come. The new age is no longer something in the distant future. It is already present proleptically. Christians have already, as it is said, tasted the powers of the age to come.
>
> Or, using the metaphor of space instead of that of time – they are said to be a colony of heaven, an outpost of the transcendent Kingdom of Heaven within the ordinary world of men. (41kgip, 27)

To talk about the kingdom is to talk about Christ, since the kingdom of God is present and active in and through him. Any talk of the kingdom without reference to Christ degrades the kingdom to an ideology. This is the key to answer those who see a discrepancy between the message of the gospels (with their focus on the kingdom) and the message of Paul's letters in the NT (with their focus on the centrality of Christ). The supposed discrepancy dissolves when we realize that the reign of God is present in the person of Jesus Christ. To talk about the kingdom is to talk about Jesus (87mcw, 6-7). And vice versa: The confession of the early church – "Jesus is Lord" – is a contextualized way of proclaiming the kingdom of God (i.e. the lordship of Christ) in the context of the Roman world. To proclaim the kingdom, is to proclaim the lordship of Jesus Christ.

While the kingdom is revealed in Christ, it is at the same time still hidden in his cross. It takes the Spirit to reveal the presence of the kingdom by granting faith to see and experience it (95os, 53). This hiddenness of the kingdom in the cross of Christ also extends to the mission of the church. The mission of the church is characterized by the sign of the cross (John 20, 19-23; see 87mcw, 23). Thus, the glory of the kingdom is hidden in the suffering of the church as it is hidden in the cross of Christ. Compassion and suffering become the signs of the church in its mission. "One might almost say that in the

New Testament suffering is the primary form of witness to Jesus Christ" (62bomm, 4). But in its weakness and suffering the church makes the hidden lordship of Christ visible to the world. "The presence of the Holy Spirit means that Jesus is known as Lord, and that the community which knows him as Lord becomes something like a fluorescent screen in which the hidden sovereignty of Jesus is made visible for others" (60whal, 18). The recognition of the 'hiddenness of the kingdom' has implications for the way the church carries out its mission.

> The church represents the presence of the reign of God in the life of the world, not in the triumphalist sense (as the "successful" cause) and not in the moralistic sense (as the "righteous" cause), but in the sense that it is the place where the mystery of the kingdom present in the dying and rising of Jesus is made present here and now so that all people, righteous and unrighteous, are enabled to taste and share the love of God before whom all are unrighteous and all are accepted as righteous. It is the place where the glory of God ("glory as of an only son") actually abides among us so that the love of God is available to sin-burdened men and women (John 17:22-23). It is the place where the power of God is manifested in a community of sinners. It is the place where the promise of Jesus is fulfilled: "I, when I am lifted up from the earth, will draw all men to myself" (John 12:32). It is the place where the reign of God is present as love shared among the unlovely. (95os, 54)

The church goes to its task with humility as God's servant to the world (see 63jsmc, 33). But humility pairs with hope where the church begins to tackle the challenges of the present, with an eye on the future consummation of the kingdom. Even though it knows it cannot build the kingdom of God (68bima, 24-25), it also knows that everything it does in Christ's name is not in vain. Christian action becomes "a prayer for the coming of the Kingdom."

> This faith enables us to be at the same time realistic and hopeful. We can be realistic, knowing that no human project can eliminate the powers of darkness as they operate in human life. This realism delivers us from the utopian fanaticisms which have condemned millions of people to misery and death in the cause of an imagined future. But at the same time we can be hopeful, acting hopefully in apparently hopeless situations, not dreaming of an absolute perfection on this side of death, but doing resolutely that relative good which is possible now, doing it as an offering to the Lord who is able to take it and keep it for the perfect kingdom which is promised. In this sense, to use a phrase of Schweitzer, our actions in the public life of the world are acted prayers for the kingdom. They do not themselves lead directly to the kingdom. They are acted prayers for its coming and as such they act as signs of its reality and so enable others to act in hope. (89gps, 114-115)

Even though the goal is not the establishment of a perfected society on earth, yet love, faith and hope do not allow the church to sit idle. They spur it on to get involved; they even result in the transformation of society (41kgip, 55; see page 61). As "those for whom the horizon is already bright with the dawn of a new day" we are called to be "signs and agents and witnesses to others of his promise ... messengers of God to the old world, which is his world and which he wills to renew in perfect reconciliation to himself" (68bima, 19-20). This Christian perspective – looking to a real future consummation of the kingdom that has already dawned in Christ combined with the understanding that every little action done in the name of Christ today is not in vain – provides true hope. And that hope, together with compassion, is most important for facing the needs of the world. The significance of the church's involvement in the world is not the scope of its programs. It is the sign-character of its witness (87mcw, 12). Thus the church takes its compassion and hope from its king and in bearing witness points the world towards its king.

6. A Comprehensive View of Christian Mission in Kingdom-Perspective

The central elements of Newbigin's view of the kingdom in the context of his theology of mission may be illustrated by the following model.

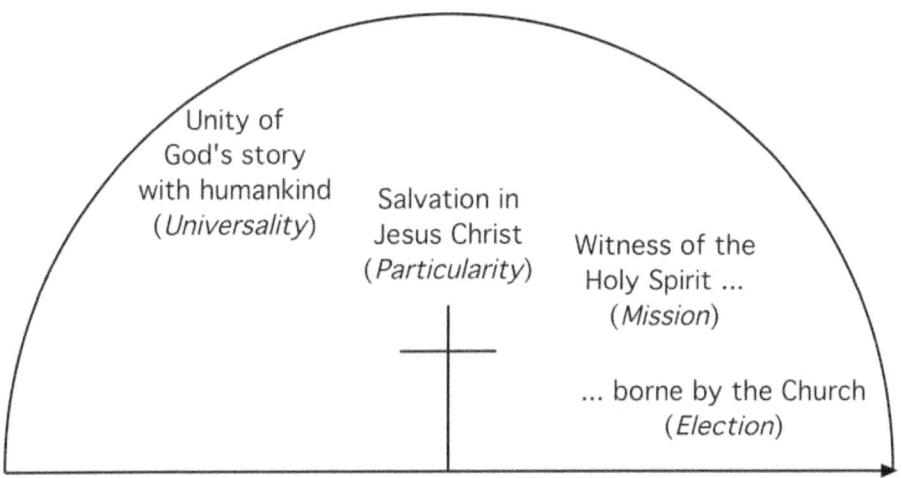

Figure 2: A comprehensive view of mission in kingdom-perspective

A model is not to be understood as a replication of truth but rather as a mental map for one's orientation. Any map is selective and reduces reality to a limited number of important markers. Its value depends on the selection of the markers (How relevant are they for the representation of the whole in light of the purpose of the map?) and the accuracy of the depiction of the selected markers (Does their place in the map correspond to reality?). In this sense this model is presented here, not as a comprehensive summary of Newbigin's theology of mission, but rather as a map that tries to capture the central themes of Newbigin's work.

The arch illustrates the unity and cohesiveness of God's story with humankind. The cross of Jesus Christ is both the center point and turning point of world history. On both sides of the cross God works by the principle of representation, first from the many to the one (from the time of Abraham to the person of Jesus), then from the one to the many (from the day of resurrection and Pentecost to the end of time). From the time of resurrection, ascension and Pentecost the Spirit takes the message of Christ's lordship and directs its proclamation to the world. The witness of the Spirit is borne by the church as the community of the elect. All of this happens in the context of the eschatological orientation of the story as a whole. God moves the story towards its goal, the full establishment of his kingship, the complete restoration of his shalom, God living with his creation in eternity.

This model picks up the Trinitarian emphasis of Newbigin's theology of mission, the centrality of the person of Christ, the key role that election plays in Newbigin's thinking, and the overall historical-eschatological framework, in which everything is embedded.

Chapter 5

Implications of Newbigin's Eschatological Framework for His Understanding of Mission

The task in this chapter will be to look at the implications which a right understanding of eschatology has for Newbigin's understanding of mission. I am concentrating here on five areas that have come to the fore in the course of this study. First, I will look at a holistic understanding of mission and how this develops out of a "right eschatology." Second, I will turn to the understanding of the gospel as "public truth," especially in light of the challenges of postmodernity which refuses to accept an overarching meta-narrative as foundation for hermeneutics. How can this claim of the gospel be upheld in this kind of a context? Third, I will look at the role of the church in a secular society with a focus on the eschatological and cultural tension. Fourth, I will examine Newbigin's view of religions and how he sees the witness of the gospel in a religiously pluralistic context embedded in the eschatological framework of God's story. Finally, I will consider Newbigin's epistemology which provides the basis for his understanding. I intend to show that in all of these areas the eschatological orientation of history is foundational for Newbigin's thinking. A "right eschatology" is essential for right understanding and right acting.

1. Holistic Understanding of Mission in Eschatological Tension

Since the end of the 19th century eschatology has again become a major theme in theological studies (see Wiedenmann 1965). Among scholars who hold to a historical understanding of eschatology there is today general agreement about the tension between the presence and the future of God's kingdom. Bosch can say: "As a matter of fact, one could make a case for the view that practically all contemporary schools of eschatology and missionary thinking, in one way or another, are offshoots of the salvation-history approach – even if some of them might prefer to deny this ancestry" (Bosch 1991, 503-504). We have seen this tension in Newbigin's writings as one of the foundational elements of his understanding of the kingdom, both in a number of references to NT passages (41kgip, 87mcw, 93kogh) as well as in his critique of realized eschatology (41kgip, 54pccc).

Even though there is general agreement on this tension in biblical eschatology and granted that this tension is not to be dissolved in either direction, the questions still remain (1) how this tension is to be understood, and (2) what the implications of this tension are for the mission of the church in the present.

1.1. Hidden, not Yet Manifest

In order to sharpen the exposition of Newbigin's understanding of this tension I would like to contrast his understanding with one that takes a slightly different approach. To do that I have chosen to refer to Karl Heim, an evangelical theologian in the first half of the 20th century at the theological faculty in Tübingen, Germany. I have chosen Heim because his influence has been strong in German evangelicalism. Karl Heim has published a series of books under the general theme "*Der evangelische Glaube und das Denken der Gegenwart.*" One of these books deals with the relationship between reconciliation and world-transformation (Heim 1975, originally published in 1952). In this book Heim deals with the relationship between the first and second coming of Christ which is part of the tension of the presence and the future of God's kingdom. He concentrates his presentation on two central questions that humankind has to deal with, namely the *Schuldfrage* and the *Machtfrage*, the question of guilt and the question of power respectively. The question of guilt deals with our sin and our relationship with God. The question of power includes the aspects of physical existence (*Körperlichkeit*), joy and vitality (*Freude und Lebenskraft*), the cognitive penetration of the world (*das forschende, denkende und verstehende Eindringen in die Welt*), and the aspect of beauty (*Schönheit*). Basically this includes everything that occupies us as human beings in our everyday life, whether it be wealth and poverty, recognition and insignificance in public life, life and death, happiness and pain, knowledge and ignorance, beauty and ugliness (Heim 1975, 30-31). First we have to note that Heim does not relegate the question of power out of the sphere of the gospel. This is an important correction of the 19th century's liberal interpretation of the kingdom as a merely inner experience with a purely moral emphasis (see Braaten 1983, 124; Goppelt 1978, 101-102). However Heim concedes that in the days of his earthly life Christ chose to deal only with the question of guilt, not with the question of power (Heim 1975, 47). Heim argues the reason for Christ's choice is that the question of guilt is the central question of human existence. The question of power will be answered only at the time of the consummation of the world (*Weltvollendung*). However Heim sees the consummation of the world beginning with the resurrection of Jesus Christ (Heim 1975, 54). The resurrection of Christ cannot be understood as an inner worldly event like other events of history. It is the breaking in of the new age into the present (Heim 1975, 162). This is a clear expression of the tension between the presence and the future of the kingdom. The end has already begun in the resurrection of Jesus Christ. However despite the fact that Heim explicitly refers to the resurrection of Christ as the beginning of the solution for the question of power, he remains stuck in the dichotomy between spirit and matter, expressed in the terms "question of guilt" and "question of power."

What we see in Heim's work is an overlapping of two different hermeneutical keys for understanding salvation. On the one hand Heim takes up the prevalent dichotomy between "spiritual" and "material." He does show that both aspects are part of the biblical understanding of salvation yet his thinking remains caught in the dichotomy. On the other hand Heim shows the eschatological tension of the NT that salvation has come and at the same time is yet to come. Heim is consistent in keeping the eschatological tension by pointing out that the consummation of the world and thereby the solution of the "question of power" has begun with Christ's resurrection and therefore is both present and future. However this is not true for the reception and continuation of his work. Current references to Heim's phrases "question of guilt" and "question of power" show that the Greek dualism rather than the eschatological tension have become the hermeneutical key for understanding salvation. For example Hille states:

> With the victory of Christ over Satan he [Satan] is once and for all deprived of his right [to accuse the believer]; the question of guilt is solved. However until the public appearance of Jesus at his second coming and the taking over of power by Christ which is associated with this event, the question of power remains unresolved. (Hille 1994, 1750)

Hille clearly associates the resolution of the question of guilt with Christ's death on the cross and the resolution of the question of power with his second coming. Using the Greek dichotomy of spirit versus matter as hermeneutical key in fact dissolves the eschatological tension of the "already now – not yet" into two distinct chronological steps where the first step deals exclusively with the inner world of the soul and the second step deals with the outer world of human existence. This is of course the crux of the debate that has occupied evangelical theology of mission in the 1980s, namely the question of the relationship between evangelism and social work in mission. We see here again what Newbigin has critiqued in a different context, namely that the Greek dichotomy of spirit versus matter de facto destroys the eschatological tension and dissolves it into a simple chronology (see p. 73).

To sharpen the understanding of the distinction between Heim's and Newbigin's interpretation I will use the following model[4].

---

[4] For the understanding and limitations of the use of models see p. 169.

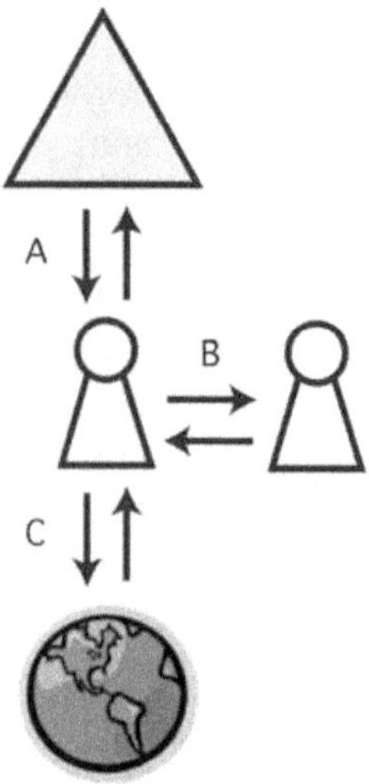

Chapter 5: Implications of Newbigin's Eschatological Framework

	Creation	Fall	Salvation
	Shalom as love, peace, faithfulness, wholeness	Culpable loss of shalom, disharmony, alienation	Restoration of shalom
A:	Image of God	Shame, estrangement	Reconciliation, children of God
B:	Man and woman, family and society	Alienation, accusation	New community of reconciliation
C:	Living by and caring for creation	Hardship, failure, pain	Work as service and ministry, sign of God's kingdom

Figure 3: Three central relationships of human existence

In the biblical story human beings are placed in three crucial relationships. Adam is placed (a) in a relationship with his creator, (b) in relationship with another human being, his companion Eve, and (c) in relationship with the rest of creation which in the Western tradition we summarize with the term "nature." The biblical narrative hints at an order of these relationships. The first statement we find is that man is created in the image and likeness of God; then we read that human beings are created as man and woman; and finally the two are given responsibility to care for the world (Gen 1:26-28). A similar order is found in Genesis 2. Man is created a living *nefesh*, a being that longs for his creator and is dependent upon him (see Wolff 1977, 25ff). He is given the task to care for God's creation, to live by it, and to name it. And he receives a companion from the hand of his creator. Here too the relationship with God is first. The story of the other two relationships is told in a different order. In the beginning all of these relationships were characterized by *shalom*, a relationship of wholeness, well-being, mutual love, and peace. Genesis 3 then tells the story how all three of these relationships were damaged. Again we find the same order as in Genesis 1. First the relationship with God is broken when Adam and Eve give in to the temptation to mistrust God and disobey him, resulting in shame and the loss of relationship. As an immediate result the *shalom* between man and woman is lost as well. They feel ashamed of themselves in the presence of each other. Adam accuses his wife. Alienation sets in. Finally their sin brings with it a curse that puts a strain on their relationship to the rest of creation (the problem of hardship, failure in work, and pain).

Von Rad points out that the Hebrew understanding of sin does not allow for a strict distinction between sin as act on the one hand and a related punishment or judgment on the other hand, as if the second step were something completely separate from the first. The Hebrew usage of the terms "*awon*" and "*chata*" rather includes both aspects, namely the actual deed and the fruit of this deed. It is an organic understanding in which the deed cannot be thought of apart from its fruit (von Rad 1978, 277-281). In this sense the culpable loss of shalom affects all three relationships. It would be a misunderstanding to reduce sin to the relationship with God and understand the loss of shalom in the social and cultural relationship as a separate event. The act of mistrusting and disobeying God and wanting to be like him and the fruits of this act – namely the loss of shalom in all three relationships – are inseparable in the biblical understanding.

The biblical view of salvation is seen in the same framework. It is nothing else but the restoration of the shalom in all of these relationships. Here now we come to the decisive difference between the popular perception of Heim's position (see Hille 1994) and Newbigin's position. Interpreting the popular perception of Heim's position in the framework of this model, Christ in his first coming dealt only with the first relationship of the three, namely the restoration of the fellowship with God ("question of guilt"). The solving of the "question of power" – dealing with the other two relationships – has been postponed until the end (see figure 4).

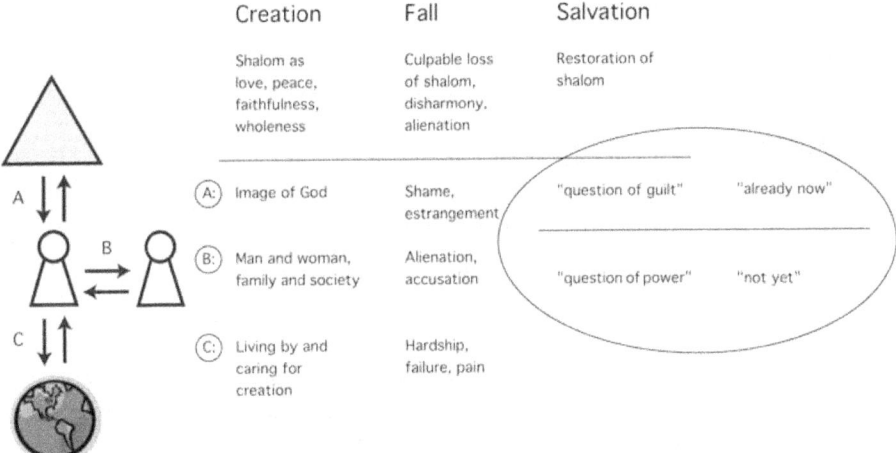

Figure 4: "Question of guilt" and "Question of power"

Interpreting Newbigin's position in the framework of this model shows a different picture. Here we find a true tension of the "already now" and "not yet" in all three relationships. Christ has died on the cross not only to restore our relationship with God, but also to bring reconciliation to our social relationships and to restore our relationship to the cosmos. The "already now" of Christ's reign extends to all three of these relationships. However at the same time we find that all three relationships are still characterized by the "not yet" of this present age. We are forgiven and reconciled to God, and yet we continue to struggle with sin (*simul justus et peccator*). We do live in renewed relationships in God's eschatological community, the church which is the firstfruits of the new humankind, and yet we continue to sin against each other. We live in a renewed relationship to creation (serving Christ with what we do), and yet even our best contributions in the service of Christ are still penetrated by false motivation and are still prone to failure. Thus in Christ all of our relationships are characterized by the presence of Christ's reign, yet we also still long for the future fulfillment of God's shalom (see figure 5).

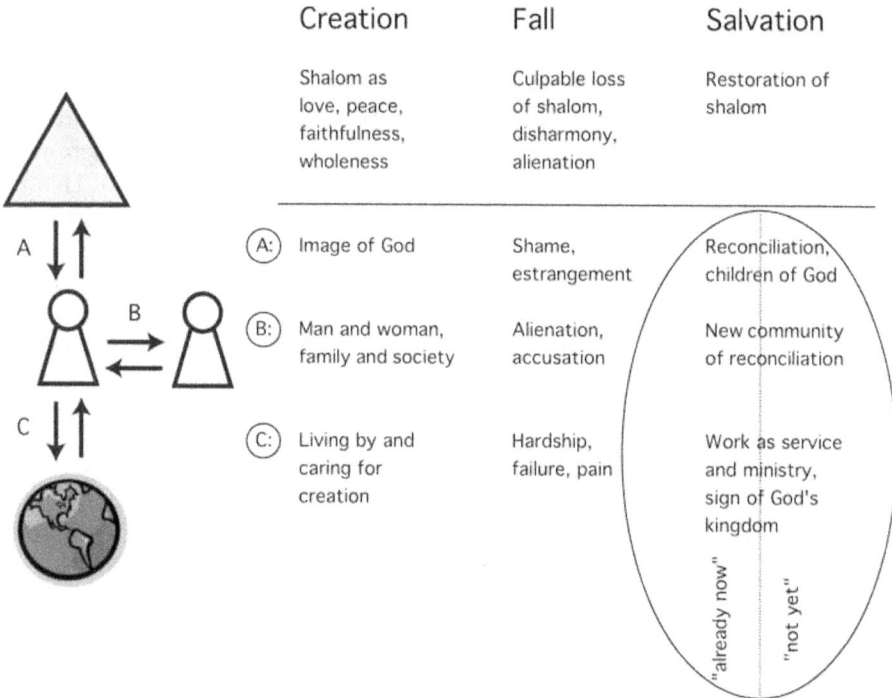

Figure 5: Salvation in eschatological tension

One more objection must be dealt with. One might argue that there is a factual difference between the spiritual and material dimensions of salvation, namely that the spiritual life that is bestowed upon us in Christ is lasting into eternity while our bodies are still part of this age and therefore are still subject to death. This perspective seems to support the Greek dichotomist view according to which the spiritual aspect of salvation has been brought about by Christ's first coming and the material aspect of salvation will be brought about by his second coming. However this view does not recognize that both dimensions are in fact characterized by the eschatological tension. Our relationship with God in the present is not only characterized by the tension of *simul justus et peccator*. It is also a relationship by faith and not yet by sight. This is part of the eschatological tension with regard to the so-called spiritual dimension. On the other hand, the so-called material dimension of salvation is not simply postponed until the end of time. The NT speaks highly even of the mortal human body as "temple of God" (1Cor 6:15-20). And Paul compares the decaying body to a seed out of which Christ will bring forth an eternal body which is no longer subject to transience. Against the prevalent Greek devaluation of the physical body the NT upholds that the human person in its completeness is included in the salvation that Christ has brought about through his death (see 1Thess 5:23).

The discussion shows that it is not enough to formally hold on to the eschatological tension. The question is, how do we interpret it. Newbigin's critique of the Greek dualism of matter versus spirit makes us aware of the pitfall that has been illustrated here by the exemplification of the position of Karl Heim and its – somewhat distorted – reception in evangelical theology, a pitfall which has influenced evangelical theology of mission for quite some time.

Newbigin has explicitly expressed himself on how that tension needs to be understood. The tension between the presence and the future of God's kingdom is the tension between "hidden" and "revealed," not a tension between "incomplete" and "complete" (see 89gps, 105). In the terms of the model above: the present kingdom includes all three relationships, not just the relationship to God. Christ's reign already extends over the cosmos. It is not incomplete. There are no areas that do not yet fall under his jurisdiction. All power and authority is given to him. But the reign of Christ is not yet revealed. And as long as the kingdom is hidden from the world, the powers of rebellion are still at work and we experience their influence in all of our relationships.

Newbigin's position thoroughly challenges the Greek dualism of matter versus spirit. And he challenges us to think clearly in order to remain true to the tension the NT sets before us. That has consequences for our missionary practice. At least two consequences of the observations made so far need to be noted here. We already have come across these in the study of Newbigin's writings. For one, remaining true to the tension of the presence and the future of the kingdom leads to a holistic understanding of mission as proclamation in word *and* deed. Second, remaining true to the tension of the presence and the future of the kingdom puts forward suffering as the true mark of Christian mission.

1.2. Mission in Word and Deed

When we refuse to reduce salvation in the present to the relationship between the believer and God and instead see the tension between the "already now" and the "not yet" in all three relationships of the believer, it follows necessarily that mission cannot concern itself only with the verbal proclamation of the gospel, addressing the "spiritual dimension" of people. Newbigin points out that even where mission organizations have explicitly tried to separate the spiritual from the social, missionaries were still drawn into social service simply because they could not neglect the immediate needs of the people around them (95os, 91-92). This shows that the discussion about the relationship between evangelism and social-political involvement is more a problem of mission theoreticians than of mission practitioners. However it underscores the need for clearer theological thinking since the dichotomy between theory and practice in itself needs to be challenged by a more holistic approach to learning and ministry.

We have seen that the biblical understanding of shalom is holistic and denotes well-being in all relationships. But it is centered around the restored relationship with God, the reconciliation of humankind with God that was brought about by Christ. The destruction of the shalom in all human relationships (spiritual, social, cultural, bio-physical, psychological) had its roots in the distrust of and rebellion against God. The loss of shalom is the terrible fruit of this.

What is true for the culpable loss of the shalom is also true for the merciful restoration of the shalom. It too is centered around the restoration of the human relationship with God, namely forgiveness and reconciliation. The restored relationship with God is the center of gravity around which shalom in its holistic meaning revolves. As Goppelt points out:

> God's kingdom also brings new conditions, a new society, but it does not come by changing the conditions but rather out of the center of the world-events: It comes when the relationship between God and man is healed [*heil wird*] in the sense of the Old Testament promise of the new covenant. Jesus does not think like Philo philosophically-spiritualistically; he rather thinks theocentrically. (Goppelt 1978, 120 – my translation)

While many proposals have been made to define the relationship between the spiritual aspect of mission and the socio-political aspect of it (see Stott 1996, 165-213; Nicholls 1985; Berneburg 1997) no true consensus has been reached with regard to defining the relationship in a single phrase. The question of "priority of evangelism" continued to be a controversial point in the discussion. Berneburg proposes to talk instead about the "centrality of evangelism" (Berneburg 1997, Berneburg 1998). This proposal essentially picks up the concern which Goppelt expresses, namely that salvation grows out of the restoration of the relationship between God and humankind. The discussion illustrates the difficulty to describe the relationship without becoming captive again to the Greek dichotomy of spirit versus matter. What we observe in the NT is a restoration of shalom that centers on the relationship with God but that also includes all other aspects of human existence. Newbigin refers to the character of the gospel itself and to the fact of the incarnation to point out that the dichotomy between word and deed is incompatible to the gospel. "[I]ndeed it is the very nature of the gospel itself which always defeats these attempts to separate the word from the deed, to give one primacy over the other, because the gospel is precisely good news of the Word made flesh" (86cwk, 99). Newbigin sees the Greek dichotomy creep in wherever we separate the kingdom from the name of Jesus.

> The preaching of Jesus without the preaching of the kingdom distorts salvation into a religious experience of personal salvation, that does not commit itself to

> getting involved with the power of evil in this world. It therefore is a "preaching of cheap grace." ...
>
> The preaching of the kingdom without the preaching of Jesus distorts salvation into an ideological crusade, not only betraying people with false expectations but "deliver[ing] people into the hands of demonic powers, for whenever a particular political or social programme is identified with the kingdom of God, those who follow become the victims of forces that they cannot control". (87mcw, 9)

The answer to overcome this dichotomy is to keep the NT message of the kingdom together with the message that Jesus Christ as personal savior is the Lord of this kingdom. Newbigin argues for a truly holistic view of proclamation by word and deed.

> Our preaching is mere empty words if it does not have behind it a costly engagement with the powers of evil, with all the powers that rob men and women of their humanity, and if it does not call men and women to share in the same costly engagement. But, equally, our programmes for teaching, healing, feeding the hungry, caring for the sick and action for justice and freedom are futile if they do not point beyond themselves to a reality greater than they – to the great healer, the great liberator, the one who is himself the living bread. In themselves, as a contribution to solving the problems of the nation and the world, our programmes are a mere drop in the ocean. Quantitatively they are insignificant. But as signs pointing beyond themselves they can be powerful indeed, leading men and women to him who is the power of God and the wisdom of God. (87mcw, 12)

Mission involvement in the immediate problems is significant in a twofold sense. The sign is real in the present. Yet at the same time it points beyond itself; it is a foretaste of the eternal; it signifies the future consummation of the shalom. What characterizes this kind of involvement is compassion, the suffering with Christ, with people, with creation (Rom 8:17,22-25). In this sense mission is more than verbal proclamation. It is the proleptic realization of Christ's reign. Yet, we are not establishing the kingdom. That is something only Christ himself can and will do.

Klaus Bockmühl carefully examined the different understandings of mission in the discussion that followed the development of the 1960s (Bockmühl 2000, originally published between 1960 and 1976). His sharp focus on the issues is exemplary of what is needed today. For instance, in referring to the Frankfurter Declaration of 1970 and its critique of the term "agenda of the world," Bockmühl observes with great subtlety, "The mistake of this formula ["the world sets the agenda"] is, that it throws together both, the needs of human beings as created beings – which full well *do* concern the Christian – and the ideological demands [of the world] – to which the Christian may not bow" (Bockmühl 2000, 135 – my translation). Bockmühl points out that diaconical service is not just a result of mission, but is an integral part of mission. He explicitly rejects a ranking of the two aspects. While the WCC sees "humanization" as the "intention" of God's work but apart from Christianization, the Frankfurt declaration sees humanization as a consequence ("a product", "an indirect result", Beyerhaus 1971, 114) of the Christian proclamation. Bockmühl contends that the biblical teaching criticizes and surpasses both of these viewpoints. "[Biblical teaching] often speaks of the 'humanization,' i.e. the new being and the new behavior of the human being as the *intention* of *Christianization*. It bases deeper ... than the Geneva concept and it aims further than the Frankfurt declaration" (Bockmühl 2000, 136 – my translation, emphasis in the original). Bockmühl regrets that the false ideological foundation (mission re-interpreted as humanization) in the end spoils and corrupts the appropriate concern for shalom and elicits an extreme counter response, which again ignores the legitimate concern. The result has been a polarization, and the legitimate concerns remain un-addressed.

Newbigin shares this regret. In a personal letter to Albrecht Hauser in December 1989 he states:

> I am very interested in your comments on Manila. How sad that we seem to be unnecessarily polarized. I have just come from a missionary conference where the dominant note was 'We must keep our mouth shut and listen to the poor' – the polar opposite of Manila. How I long for a great body of people who can say 'Yes, we must listen but we must also speak of what God has done in Jesus Christ.' (98plah)

David Bosch summarizes the importance of keeping in tension both aspects, the present and the future dimension of the kingdom. In light of Newbigin's work one can only underscore this summary.

> It has become clear, however, that neither the eschatologization nor the historicization of mission satisfies. In its fixation on the parousia, the first has neglected the problems of this world and thereby crippled Christian mission. In its preoccupation with this world to the exclusion of the transcendent dimension, the second has robbed people of ultimate meaning and of a teleological dimension without which nobody can survive (cf Moltmann 1975:20-24).
>
> We need a way beyond both. We need an eschatology for mission which is both future-directed and oriented to the here and now. It must be an eschatology that holds in creative and redemptive tension the already and the not yet; the world of sin and rebellion, and the world God loves; the new age that has already begun and the old that has not yet ended (Manson 1953:370f); justice as well as justification; the gospel of liberation and the gospel of salvation. (Bosch 1991, 508; see also Shenk 1996 and Berneburg 1998, 26)

I contend that Newbigin in his thorough commitment to remain true to the eschatological tension of the kingdom provides a guideline for mission theology neither to destroy the tension between the presence and the future by falling into the trap of Greek dualism of matter versus spirit, nor to destroy the tension between the presence and the future by attempting to establish the reign of God in our own strength in the present. It will not be enough to theoretically clarify the relationship between evangelism and social-political involvement. The tension has to be lived. Here is one key contribution of the eschatological orientation of God's story to mission theology in the present.

The editors of Glasser's work on the relationship between the kingdom and mission draw the same conclusion when they summarize the contribution of an understanding of mission that orientates itself on the centrality of the kingdom of God in the NT.

> Glasser's Kingdom of God paradigm has done at least four things for missiology.
>
> First, the Kingdom of God concept broadens missiological reflection beyond a predominantly individualized and vertical understanding of salvation to a holistic view of the interaction of church and world.
>
> Second, Glasser's Kingdom missiology breaks the impasse between evangelism and social action that has plagued Protestant evangelicals.
>
> Third, Kingdom of God missiology creates the possibility of new conversation among evangelicals, representatives of the conciliar movement, Roman Catholics, Orthodox, Pentecostals, and charismatics.
>
> Fourth, Glasser's own personal pilgrimage made him deeply aware of the social and political implications of the Kingdom of God that challenges all governments, all forms of racism, all social structures that would seek to deify themselves. (Glasser et al. 2003, 12)

This summary underscores what we have observed in Newbigin's work so far.

1.3. Suffering as the Primary Form of Witness to Jesus Christ

John Bright closes his study about the kingdom of God with a final chapter on the cross. He comments:

> We must stand before that Cross which is, and must remain, our redemption. In that Cross we shall find our true destiny as the servant people of God, and also our victory – for the Cross *is* the victory of the Kingdom of God in us, and only through a Church that has known it is the victorious proclamation of the Kingdom in the world possible. (Bright 1953, 270)

It is clear from the context of Bright's study that he does not mean for the church to know the cross in the sense of a rational and spiritual acknowledgement for its salvation, but rather that the whole existence of the church is to be characterized by the cross. Bright here speaks of knowing the cross by experience. It is this mark of the cross that we find in the life and ministry of Paul.

> But we have this treasure in jars of clay to show that this all-surpassing power is from God and not from us. We are hard pressed on every side, but not crushed; perplexed, but not in despair; persecuted, but not abandoned; struck down, but not destroyed. We always carry around in our body the death of Jesus, so that the life of Jesus may also be revealed in our body. For we who are alive are always being given over to death for Jesus' sake, so that his life may be revealed in our mortal body. (2Cor 4:7-11)

Newbigin comments on this passage by saying, "It ought to be seen as the classic definition of mission. Paul's apostolate ... is the carrying forward through the ongoing life of the world of the victorious passion of Jesus" (87mcw, 24).

The suffering of the church in the context of its mission is caused by the conflict with the powers and principalities which have usurped the place that rightly belongs to Christ. "To announce the imminence of the Kingdom, to announce that God's reign of justice is about to break into the world, is necessarily to be on a collision course with the presently reigning powers" (86cwk, 100). The church is called to expose and challenge the sinful structures and ideologies that hold people in bondage. But the church can only do so in the way of Christ, not by power or domination, but in the way of the cross.

Confronting the powers also means identification and compassion with those who suffer under those powers. It means to suffer with (com-passion) the world, the broken, the poor, the oppressed, the sick, those who yearn for the consummation of the kingdom to be revealed. It is a suffering towards life, identifying with the birth-pangs of God's new creation (Bosch 1991, 510). Mission requires this costly engagement. It can be costly both as verbal proclamation and as proclamation in deed. Both are under the sign of the cross.

> There are situations where the word is easy and the deed is costly; there are situations where the deed is easy and the word is costly. Whether in word or in deed, what is required in every situation is that we be faithful to him who said to his disciples: "As the father sent me, so I send you," and showed them his hands and his side. (87mcw, 14)

One of the central passages in which Newbigin sees the role of suffering in the sending of the church exemplified is John 20:19-21.

> On the evening of that first day of the week, when the disciples were together, with the doors locked for fear of the Jews, Jesus came and stood among them and said, "Peace be with you!" After he said this, he showed them his hands and side. The disciples were overjoyed when they saw the Lord. Again Jesus said, "Peace be with you! As the Father has sent me, I am sending you." (John 20:19-21)

Newbigin says:

> It was the scars of the passion in his risen body that assured the frightened disciples that it was really Jesus who stood among them. It will be those same scars in the corporate life of the church that will authenticate it as indeed the body of Christ, the bearer of his mission, the presence of the kingdom. It will not be enough for the church to place a cross on the top of its buildings or in the centre of its altars or on the robes of its clergy. The marks of the cross will have to be recognizable also in the lives of its members if the church is to be the authentic presence of the kingdom. (87mcw, 23)

The church will not succeed in its mission by demonstrating its strength before the world, but only by identifying in the name of Christ with those who are poor and poor in spirit.

In a time when the church is very much concerned with mission strategies, strategic planning, and developing programs that allow it to measure its success in its mission, it is in danger of becoming captive to a mechanistic paradigm that underlies the globalization tendencies of the present. In this context it is important to recognize the validity of Newbigin's reference to the suffering of the church. The significance of our involvement in mission has more to do with who we are than with what we do. Newbigin's reference to the suffering of the church grows out of an organic understanding of mission in which our identification with Christ is at the center of our mission. Looking at mission this way we realize that the church in the West must learn from the church in those parts of the world where the engagement with powers and principalities is really costly. One may think here only of the problem of persecution and the resistance Christians face in the Islamic world.

The church will not convince the world of the validity of its mission and its message from a position of power, but rather from a position in which it is willing to identify with the marginal, ready to suffer with them and bear the marks of the cross. This is the eschatological perspective of victory, which can see in the suffering and death of Christ the victory over the powers of rebellion.

> [T]his breaking in of God's reign does not take the form of a successful political movement to remove the reigning powers and replace them with rulers who will faithfully execute God's justice. It takes the form of a shameful and humiliating defeat, which, however, in the event of the resurrection is interpreted to chosen witnesses as the decisive victory of God's Kingdom. He reigns from the tree. (86cwk, 100)

Only with this eschatological perspective will the church be able to resist the dominant paradigm of the world and be a true witness to the victory and lordship of Christ.

2. The Gospel as Public Truth

The gospel tells the story of God's acting in this world. Newbigin's concern is to present the gospel to the world in a way that is true to its character. It must not be interpreted as a form of religious doctrine, as a way to personal salvation. If we believe this to be the character of the gospel, then we have no right to approach adherents of other faiths with a call to conversion (60mcan). On the other hand Newbigin also rejects the identification of the gospel with a political, ideological program like e.g. the theocratic understanding of Islam (69fc, 48-49). His eschatological view of history provides the framework to keep that tension between "not a private religion" on the one hand and "not a public ideological program" on the other hand. The gospel is public truth in the sense that it is the decisive encounter of God with particular human beings in the particularities of history which calls individuals with their life stories to become an active part of God's ongoing story and to let the overarching story of God be the frame of reference for everything they do (69fc, 49).

The question then arises: What does this characteristic of the gospel mean for its presentation to the world? How is the gospel to be presented to the world?

I will look at this question in three steps: First, how can the church present the gospel as truth in a postmodern, pluralist context that does not recognize a shared meta-narrative as unified interpretive framework? Second, how can it argue for a shared meta-narrative without falling into the modern trap? And third, what does it mean to bring all aspects of life under the rule of Christ in light of the eschatological tension?

2.1. Truth Claims in a Postmodern Context

There are only two options for approaching the challenge to proclaim the gospel as public truth in a context which does not share a meta-narrative as its foundation. One is the attempt to argue for a return to a positivist understanding of reality in which a unified meta-narrative is naturally accepted. The other is to find a way forward through an instrumentalist relativization of truth in order to arrive at firm ground on the other side of the postmodern 'swamp' (Hiebert 1999, 66). This approach understands postmodernity not as a state to be in but as a time of liminality, as a time of transition, "a movement away from something and toward something else not yet present or identifiable" (Hunsberger 2002, 96). I would like to illustrate these two fundamentally different approaches first by comparing two different proposals for the task of contextualization, namely the proposals of Peter Beyerhaus and Kevin Vanhoozer. I will then take a look at how Hunsberger characterizes the challenge which the postmodern transition presents to the church's presentation of the gospel and see how he builds on the foundation that Newbigin has helped to lay.

2.1.1. Beyerhaus and Vanhoozer

German missiologist Peter Beyerhaus provides an extensive discussion on the theological issues of contextual theologies (Beyerhaus 1996). He places the question in the wider historical context of mission (chapters 2-4) and hermeneutics (chapters 5-7). He shows how the dominance of the historical-critical method in theological research has undermined the biblical understanding of revelation (by differentiating between the witness of the biblical texts to the Christ event and revelation as such) and the authority of the biblical texts themselves (by the strict application of Troeltsch's criteria of critique, analogy, and correlation). The historical-critical method has led to the deconstruction of the unity of the biblical message (by emphasizing the theologies of different biblical authors) and to the deconstruction of the biblical canon itself (by interpreting the biblical texts as voices among others in the hermeneutical search for meaning). For Beyerhaus this deconstruction has prepared the way for what he calls "the contextual relativization of biblical authority" (Beyerhaus 1996, 197).

However Beyerhaus acknowledges the legitimate issues of contextual theology. He names as positive contributions of contextualization: the uncovering of hermeneutical biases, exegetical discoveries in community, the discovery of social dimensions of biblical texts, and the importance of correlative translation of the biblical message. But he strongly cautions the church and the mission movement against the dangers of contextual hermeneutics. He names explicitly the continuous erosion of the canon of the bible, the loss of a unified, normative dogmatics, and the anthropocentric seizure of the biblical revelation-documents. These developments result in the loss of the apostolic authority of the church, a change in the understanding of salvation in missions, the danger of the ideologization of mission, and the polarization of the mission movement as seen in the 1970s. He calls for a pneumatic, salvation-historic understanding of the Scriptures as foundation for mission (Beyerhaus 1996, 282-391). His call focuses (1) on recapturing the spiritual, sacramental character of the Scriptures as God's Word in human language. Because the Scriptures are inspired by God's Spirit they can only be understood under the guidance of the Spirit. His call focuses (2) on the hermeneutical key that lets us rediscover the unity of the biblical testimony as a whole. Beyerhaus sees this key in God's salvation-plan (*Heilsplan Gottes*) as it is revealed in the Scriptures (Beyerhaus 1996, 282).

Beyerhaus' work is very thorough and he states his case clearly. In order to fend off a pluralism of contextual theologies he bases the authority of the church on the faithful transmission of both the message (*kerygma*) and the proper exposition of that message (*didache*) as the church has received it (Beyerhaus 1996, 265). Beyerhaus sees this dual focus on scripture and tradition at work even in the Protestant Churches despite their formal principle of *sola scriptura*. Over the centuries they have striven faithfully to guard the identity of the gospel message and its proper exposition. Beyerhaus sees the church breaking away from this tradition when it begins to focus on the challenges and needs the various contexts present, thus relativizing the authoritative nature of the biblical text. "The Christian mission breaks away from this hitherto valid formal principle when it introduces in its place a principle of contextual hermeneutics" (Beyerhaus 1996, 266 – my translation). For Beyerhaus the authority of the church in mission and the authenticity of its message thus depend on the faithful transmission of both, *kerygma* and *didache*. With his hermeneutical proposal he aims to safeguard the authoritative character of the biblical texts as well as the unity of the global church and a global theology. The basis for his proposal is – if I understand him correctly – a positivist hermeneutics which sees the historical creeds of the church as binding for the church in any context. The Protestant distinction between the Scriptures as "*norma normans*" and the historical creeds as "*norma normata*" (Joest 1989, 84) is blurred in this hermeneutical approach.

Vanhoozer suggests to move in a different direction to overcome the postmodern pluralist relativism. He recognizes that in today's pluralistic epistemology a positivist claim for truth simply will not be acknowledged as such. It will necessarily be relativized by the hearer in light of his or her own instrumentalist view. That leaves the person with an absolute truth-claim in the dilemma that his or her truth claim will not be recognized as what it was intended to be. How then can we communicate revelation in a pluralist context?

Vanhoozer points out how Christ not only staked a claim for truth ("I am the way, the truth, the life"), but that he also staked his life on that claim. He calls this an "epistemology of the cross."

> In a postmodern setting it is no longer enough to justify truth claims propositionally. An epistemology of the cross will not be merely evidentialist. It is not enough to state a proposition; one must stake a claim, and ultimately oneself, and this for two reasons. First, the truth of the claim is not a matter of propositional content only. What is at stake is the very notion of truth as a way of life, and thus the notion that truth matters (individually and socially). What is needed in an apathetic age and situation of ironic indifference is a truth for which one can live and die (Kierkegaard). ...
>
> The vocation of the Christian theologian is to be an interpreter-martyr: a truth-teller, a truth-doer, a truth-sufferer. Truth requires evangelical passion, not postmodern passivity; person appropriation, not calculation. The theologian is to embody in his or her person the core of Christian culture, in order to provide a focus for Christian wisdom. ...
>
> There is a tie between defending the truth and living faithfully. The challenge of Christian mission today, the challenge of staking a theological truth claim, is nothing less than displaying in one's life the way of Jesus Christ: not Heidegger's (nor Socrates') "being-toward-death" but a distinctively Christian *being-toward-resurrection*. This is not a matter of epistemological foundationalism so much as it is a demonstration of the integrity and uniqueness of Christian wisdom. (Vanhoozer 1999, 139-156)

Vanhoozer does not suggest to return to a pre-instrumentalist understanding of truth. His approach "to stake a claim for truth" allows the evangelical Christian to establish a place for – what Newbigin calls – "public truth" in the midst of an instrumentalist, pluralistic environment. The argument that supports this claim of truth is not so much propositional. It is rather appropriational. The person who stakes a claim for God's truth testifies with his or her life – and possibly even death – that this stake for truth is in fact true. For the post-modernist this might initially seem no different than his own epistemology. Only after a person commits herself to Christ's claim of truth, does the person realize, that Christ's claim of truth and his "staking his life on his truth-claim" is not instrumentalist but did in fact change reality, create new reality. It is historical truth.

The focus on an integration of propositional truth and appropriated truth is at the core of Vanhoozer's emphasis on wisdom over knowledge.

> [T]heology in a postmodern context must reorient itself to wisdom rather than to knowledge. Wisdom, I believe, is the means of integrating what modernity and postmodernity alike have torn asunder: metaphysics and morals, theory and practice, fact and value. Wisdom is a matter of knowing certain things but also of making one's knowledge fruitful. It is a matter of being able appropriately to apply truth to the matter at hand. Wisdom provides an effective means for integrating seeing and doing, judging and acting. (Vanhoozer 1999, 132)

This focus on wisdom includes a recovery of imagination and epistemological virtues. "The imagination, the faculty of perceiving the whole, is an integral ingredient in wisdom. The wise person relates to God, the world, and others in a way that is fitting, and hence in a manner that leads to human flourishing (and to the glory of God): 'In all that he (she) does, he (she) prospers' (Ps 1:3)" (Vanhoozer 1999, 133). Wisdom cannot be gained apart from epistemic virtues. "[V]irtue epistemology highlights one especially noteworthy idea, namely, that epistemology is an affair of the heart. Everything begins with a desire for truth" (Vanhoozer 1999, 136).

Vanhoozer in his essay makes a strong case for a truly holistic view of "knowing" and "being" by focusing on wisdom. He is thus able to reintroduce into the discussion a thoroughly biblical concept that is in many ways more true to human life than the rationalistic emphasis on knowledge. And with his focus on claiming a stake and staking one's life on that claim of truth he is able to move beyond the dilemma of relativism.

In this sense Vanhoozer calls for an appropriational approach to hermeneutics that goes beyond the propositional. It requires the witness to first appropriate Christ's truth claim for him- or herself. Then it calls the witness to stake a claim for truth (Christ's truth) in his or her own context, and to stake his or her life on that very claim of truth. Not that the martyrdom of the witness makes the truth-claim come true. But by the martyrdom others may be convinced, so that they too stake out this very truth claim of Christ.

The comparison between Beyerhaus and Vanhoozer shows the two options for the proclamation of truth in a pluralistic environment. Both agree that we need to move away from pluralistic relativism. The question is: do we need to go back to positivism? And, can we ever do that? Vanhoozer presents a different way beyond both a positivist rationalism and a postmodern relativism by reclaiming an understanding of truth as wisdom. By doing so he shows a way how the church can present the truth claim of the gospel to the world in a post-modern context. This is congruent with Newbigin's call for presenting the gospel as public truth, as a look at Hunsberger's position will show.

2.1.2. Hunsberger

Hunsberger builds on Newbigin's understanding of the gospel as public truth as he attempts to outline the challenge of presenting the gospel in the postmodern transition. The basis for his approach is found in the fundamental tension with regard to the gospel-culture relationship at any given place and time.

> Thus the gospel approaches every culture with affirmation and reception (so that there is no place given to culture-rejection or culture-bashing), yet with the element of critique and discontinuity (calling the people of every culture into new community). For the churches of the West, this means maintaining the readiness to recognize unwarranted accommodations to their culture in order to disentangle themselves, while discovering the Spirit's creative work to make the church a faithfully Western incarnation of the gospel. (Hunsberger 1998a, 278-279)

What are the elements that make the church in a postmodern Western society a "faithful incarnation of the gospel"?

Hunsberger begins by pointing out that the generation in the postmodern tradition not only hungers for connecting relationships but is also searching for meaning. The test that is applied to any claim for truth and meaning is the test of authenticity. What is needed is therefore not primarily a convincing verbal proclamation of truth but an embodiment of truth, in Newbigin's words: an indwelling of the story. This corresponds to the character of the Christian understanding of truth as historical truth which combines the elements of the factual (the rootedness in historical events) with the personal (understanding oneself as part of the ongoing story). Hunsberger qualifies this understanding of truth as personal, perspectival, and practiced truth.

Christian truth is personal because it is embodied in the person of Jesus of Nazareth. It is revealed in his person and it is communicated in the relationship of one person to another. Jesus himself points out this personal character of knowing God when he says, "No one knows the Father except the Son and those to whom the Son chooses to reveal him" (Matt 11:27). Here for Newbigin Polanyi's reference about knowing as 'personal knowing' and the emphasis of his theological teacher John Oman on the personhood of God come together. "Truth ... is known in the relationship of persons" (Hunsberger 2002, 101). It is known in the story which reveals the character, the actions and the purposes of God. It is "not some static, objective thing existing independently somewhere, but it is wrapped up in a willing, acting divine person" (Hunsberger 2002, 102).

Speaking of truth as embodied truth brings with it necessarily the element of cultural and historical particularity. In Newbigin's words:

> Neither at the beginning, nor at any subsequent time, is there or can there be a gospel that is not embodied in a culturally conditioned form of words. The idea that one can or could at any time separate out by some process of distillation a pure gospel unadulterated by any cultural accretions is an illusion. (86fg, 4)

This is what Hunsberger calls the perspectival character of truth. Truth can only be perceived from a person's own particular cultural-linguistic perspective. And it is embedded in the particularities of life. From this it does not necessarily follow that truth is really unknowable, which is the conclusion of the relativist. However this understanding of truth does require a communal approach to the seeking of truth, an approach that Newbigin – following Polanyi – has consistently argued for.

Finally truth is known by receiving it as it comes to us through a web of relationships which themselves are characterized by the truth which is communicated. It is thus received in the form of an embodiment, by a community which indwells the story. There is therefore no reason to lament the loss of objective truth. The church is rather called to rediscover the unity of believing and obeying.

> Only a practiced truth bears the stamp of authenticity and livability. In the postmodern transition, people do not look for better (objective!) arguments

about God's presence or purposes, but they look for demonstrations of it being lived in terms of contemporary life. (Hunsberger 2002, 103)

Here we find the same emphasis that we saw in Vanhoozer's approach, a holistic understanding of cognitive appropriation and life appropriation. In Newbigin's terms, since there is no acultural or supracultural version of the gospel, it is the calling of the church to be the "living hermeneutic of the message" for the world (80ykc, 43). It is impossible to communicate the gospel only verbally. The characteristic of truth as personal, perspectival and practiced truth requires that it be embodied in a community and thus be presented to the world.

Speaking of the church as "hermeneutic of the gospel" for the world is another way of speaking of it as the firstfruits of the new creation. As sign, instrument, and foretaste of God's kingdom the church embodies the truth of the gospel. And it is here that the world may know the truth, personified in Jesus Christ. Here we see how the eschatological understanding of the church as firstfruits of the kingdom merges with a comprehensive understanding of truth as wisdom rather than mere knowledge. In this sense the postmodern critique of positivism challenges the church to gain a deeper understanding of the character of truth as such.

2.2. Presenting the Gospel as Meta-Narrative to the World

So far we have been looking at the question of how the church is to present the truth of the gospel to the world in a postmodern, pluralistic context. The next question is: How can the church lead people who live with a plurality of stories to the recapturing of a universal meta-narrative without falling into the modern trap? What distinguishes the biblical meta-narrative from the meta-narrative of modernity?

Taber in his essay "The gospel as authentic meta-narrative" (Taber 2002) makes an important contribution to that question. There is an inherent tension which is felt in today's globalization processes. It is the tension between the global pressure to conformity on the one hand and the local freedom to be different on the other. However this is not a balanced tension. What has been true for the colonial period repeats itself again in today's global economic world. A major aspect of globalization is "the global extension of ... domination, exploitation, and pauperization of the world's powerless populations by the affluent minority" (Taber 2002, 183). Only this time the major players are transnational economic conglomerations rather than nation states. The church too has not been guiltless in these processes. There has been "an unrecognized tension between the modern agenda and the gospel agenda" (Taber 2002, 186). The church therefore is called today not only to challenge this global, modern paradigm, but to develop a global view that is distinct from it. The modern paradigm has a view of the fundamental unity of humankind; but it tends to overcome the tensions by imposing homogenization. It is precisely this aspect of coercion and homogenization that causes the postmodern reaction with its emphasis on differences and its rejection of an over-arching meta-narrative.

> Milbank argues persuasively that postmodernists, whatever their differences, share in common three dominant concepts: "a historicist 'genealogy', ... an 'ontology of difference' ... and 'ethical nihilism.'" What he means is that the postmodernists deny that anything might be permanent or universal in human experience, that the differences between persons and groups override commonalities, and that there is no foundation for any substantive ethics beyond the will-to-power. (Taber 2002, 188)

Taber values the critique of the modern paradigm. But instead of letting the world slide into a turmoil of conflicting particularities he sees in the gospel a different paradigm, a global meta-narrative that is not characterized by coercion and homogenization. He finds the model for this gospel way in two incidents in the NT, namely, the cross of Christ and the events of Pentecost.

> I suggest, in fact, that the gospel of the kingdom of God is the only valid universal meta-narrative, the only one which is not ruthlessly homogenizing and totalitarian, because it is the only one based on self-sacrificing love instead of worldly power, the only one offered by a king on a cross, the only one offered by a conquering lion who turns out to be a slaughtered lamb (Rev 5:1-10). This is the guarantee that it is not totalitarian. Pentecost, if correctly understood, is the guarantee that it is not homogenizing. (Taber 2002, 189)

Taber expands on the NT references to a "breathtakingly universal, global perspective and ambition" of the early apostles (Taber 2002, 189). It is this global dimension that Newbigin has in mind when he says: "The fellowship created by the Holy Spirit is both local and universal. ... But God's love embraces the whole world, and that fact must find expression in the form of the Christian fellowship" (58obog, 23). Taber's references to the cross and to the events of Pentecost point out the important differences between the biblical global vision and the modern paradigm that continues to shape today's globalization tendencies. The cross is not the imposing of a new paradigm. It is rather the offer of a new relationship. The unity of the global fellowship of the church is not imposed from above. It is received as a gift at the foot of the cross of Christ (see 61icd, 9). The symbol of the cross and the suffering person of Christ are the answer to the postmodern critique that truth claims are concealed assertions of power. Weston points out

> that part of Newbigin's response to the postmodern challenge about "power" is to insist that the biblical story itself revolves around a suffering and dying savior. This enables him to hold together a commitment to the gospel story as "metanarrative" as well as an emphasis upon "publishing" it evangelistically, in the knowledge that the claims of the story itself undercut the postmodern challenge about "power." (Weston 2004, 244)

Taber rightly sets the events of Pentecost in relationship to the story of the tower of Babel (Genesis 11). The result of the human attempt to unify the family of nations has ended in the confusion of languages and the disability to understand each other. In this context it is interesting to note that the multiplicity of languages does appear not only in Genesis 11 (Gen 11:7-9) as part of God's judgment but also in Genesis 10 (Gen 10:5, 20, 31), which tells the story of God's blessing on humankind. The fact that the multiplicity of languages appears in both lines of thought – judgment and blessing – at least leaves us with a certain ambiguity. That the plurality of languages is not the central issue in Genesis 11 is underscored by the fact that Pentecost – which is the reversal of the tower of Babel – does not reverse the fact of the multiplicity of languages. It rather leads to a new understanding across the language barriers. The plurality of languages continues, but it becomes reconciled plurality, centered around the person of Jesus Christ and given as a gift by the Spirit.

These characteristics of the biblical meta-narrative have not always been recognized and taken into account in the history of the church and its expansion into the world. The modern tendency of homogenization exemplifies itself in the fact that e.g. the mastery of the English language and the access to modern means of travel and communication have become prerequisites for the participation in the global dimension of the community of the church. The export of theological curricula across the globe and the emphasis on uniformity in language, liturgy and doctrine in the history of the church are examples of how the church has bought into the modern paradigm rather than developing its patterns from a biblical view of reconciled diversity which centers around Christ.

Taber picks up Newbigin's concern for unity which is distinct from uniformity. "Properly speaking, the Church is just the people of God, just humanity remade in Christ. It should therefore have as much variety as the human race itself" (61ftow, 82). Newbigin therefore usually speaks of "one human family" or the "family of nations" (e.g. 48dacp, 30; 89gps, 68). So the event of the cross of Christ as the gift of unity to the family of nations and the event of Pentecost as unity in reconciled diversity, given by the Spirit and centered around the risen Christ, underscore the postmodern critique of the modern paradigm and at the same time lead beyond its fragmentation to a true unity, "the only valid universal meta-narrative" (Taber 2002, 189).

2.3. Bringing All Aspects of Life Under the Lordship of Christ

It has been Newbigin's concern from the very beginning to bring all of life's aspects under the rule of Christ. This not only includes the issues of personal life but also the issues of communal and national life. In the words of Wainwright: "The Christian faith might be about more than this world, but it was not about less" (Wainwright 2000, 238). This holistic view of the Christian life includes economic and political engagement and the debate about the issues involved. As early as in his Bangalore lectures in 1941 Newbigin points out that the political sphere cannot be excluded from Christian involvement in the world, especially since the complexities of modern life (political, social, economic) extend so much influence on individual lives that the individual as such does not have any control over vast areas of his life (41kgip, 53; see page 60). To exclude the political, social, and economic spheres of life from the sphere of Christian influence and engagement would mean the surrender of these areas to powers in contradiction to Christ. It would – in reverse – mean the exclusion of vast areas of life from the dominion of Christ's reign.

The engagement of social and political issues is required by the fact that there is no neutral territory. One cannot exclude parts of human life from the lordship of Christ and assume that these aspects are then neutral and we remain free to make our own decisions. "The decision for Christians is not whether or not to become involved as Christians in public affairs. It is whether our responsibilities in the public sphere are to be discharged under the kingship of Christ or under the dominion of the evil one" (83os84, 41).

As we have seen, Newbigin traces the split between the public and the private sphere to the Enlightenment which was a reaction against the Constantinian alliance between Church and state. The challenge for today is therefore to bring both spheres together under the lordship of Christ without "falling into the 'Constantinian trap'" (83os84, 36).

The framework for Newbigin to think about this challenge is the eschatological tension of the presence and the future of God's kingdom. In this tension he holds that humanization and salvation belong together but must not be simply identified. This was Newbigin's concern in his critique of the developments in Uppsala in 1968, and he debated the issue with M.M.Thomas (71rsh, 72bck). There can never be an "absolute identification of any human cause with the reign of God" (86cwk, 105). The cross of Christ is the mark which does not allow such an identification because it is both, the sign of God's identification with the world and at the same time the sign of his judgment over the world. We all stand condemned at the foot of the cross.

The decisive issue for Newbigin is that the church is in fact called to get involved in the political, social, and economic issues of the world, but it can only make a meaningful contribution when its hope is rooted beyond history. The "true otherworldliness of the gospel" must be "held together with its true this-worldliness" (86cwk, 104).

> Unless the radical otherworldliness of the gospel message is acknowledged, the real role of the church in politics will be hopelessly compromised. ...
>
> This otherworldly reference of the church is essential to its this-worldly mission ...
>
> The church exists as sign and foretaste of the gift that is promised; in all its members it is called to act now in the light of the promised future: that is its proper this-worldliness. But the church maintains at its heart, through the word and sacraments of the gospel, its witness to a reality which is not of this world. ... The church has a real purchase in the world's life only insofar as it finds a point of reference beyond the life of this world. Only the hope which enters

into the inner shrine behind the curtain provides us with an anchor which cannot be moved by any storm or tide. (86cwk, 101, 104, 106-107)

Newbigin acknowledges that it is difficult to express this concern without making false compromises on one side or the other (86cwk, 104). This dialectic of the church's proper this-worldliness and its proper other-worldliness relates directly to the understanding of salvation in the framework of the eschatological tension of Christ's reign.

What then are the specific contributions the church can make to the economic and political issues which are at stake in a given context?

2.3.1. Unmasking the Powers

For one, it is the task of the church to unmask the claims of the powers, the ideologies, social, political, and economic systems for what they truly are (see 86cwk, 100; 92eh; 98fp, 144).

There is some debate today about the interpretation of the group of words that is generally summarized under the term "principalities and powers." The main question is whether these "principalities and powers" are to be understood as personal spiritual beings or as impersonal structures. Some promote the understanding of structures out of a concern to demythologize the Pauline use of these terms (see O'Brien's reference to Käsemann; O'Brien 1981, 1). Critics of this interpretation rightly point out that here a Western materialistic worldview is serving as hermeneutical key to guide the interpretation (Wendland and Hachibamba 2000, 342).

A thorough exegetical study needs to distinguish between "elements" and "principles" on the one hand and "principalities" and "powers" on the other. *Stoicheia* (elements, principles) is used by Paul in Galatians 4 to denote the Jewish law and in Colossians 2 to refer to religion before and outside of Christ (Eßer 1977, 532). Even though there is some debate, these seem to be references to impersonal structures. The group of words for "principalities and powers" (*archon, exousiai, dynamis, kosmokrator* ...) is used by Paul summarily without clear distinction mostly for "powers and rulers in the heavenly realms" (which supports the view of personal spiritual beings) and in a few places for governmental authorities and structures (Romans 13; Tit 3:1). Wherever Paul refers to the powers in the heavenly realms he is not interested in details of hierarchy in the spiritual world, in contrast to Jewish apocalyptic. His emphasis is solely on proclaiming the lordship of Christ over all powers there are, earthly and heavenly (see Col 2:10, 15). Lightfoot suggests that while the primary reference is to spiritual powers, the terms also refer to earthly dignitaries and earthly powers and need to be understood comprehensively. However it seems to me that he proposes a personal understanding of the powers, both spiritual and human, not a structural one (Lightfoot 1955, 152-153; see also Berkhof 1977; Betz a.o. 1977; Noll 1998; O'Brien 1992; Piggin 2001; Stott 1979; Wendland 1999; Wink 1995).

An exegetical analysis is beyond the scope of this paper. But apart from the exegetical work an anthropological and sociological observation supports the notion that the powers as personal beings cannot be thought of apart from the idea of structures. Human beings cannot live without forming some kind of structures, sociological, political, economical, cultural and religious structures. An understanding of the world, human language and interaction would be impossible without such structures. From a Christian perspective one must recognize that none of these structures can simply be classified as positive, negative, or neutral (Lingenfelter 1992, 18). The fact that human beings construct their world and act in it as sinners necessarily brings with it that the structures which humans create are themselves tainted by human sinfulness. Even those structures which might be assessed as "neutral" are subject to abuse by individual human beings.

From the fact that human structures (political, economic, social, cultural, religious) are thus contaminated by human sinfulness it follows that the gospel cannot simply work through and with these structures. It rather confronts them and challenges these human systems (see Lingenfelter 1992, 19). In light of this foundational insight from anthropology and sociology one has to agree with Newbigin's emphasis on unmasking the sinful character of human structures, apart from the exegetical concerns one might have on the above mentioned debate.

We have already seen Newbigin's critique of both Marxism and capitalism (e.g. 83os84, 43). After the collapse of the communist bloc Newbigin sees the two global challenges for the church in the unrestrained principle of a free-market economy with its globalizing tendencies and the claim of Islam (92eh). Forrester summarizes Newbigin's concern: The church "must ... seek to unmask and confront the false economic, social, and political ideologies of the age as well as the simplistic pragmatism so characteristic of the Anglo-Saxon mindset" (Forrester 2002, 5). Newbigin has tried to do just that.

2.3.2. Contributing a Biblical View of Humanity

In his 1984 lecture "The welfare state: A Christian perspective" Newbigin sees the problems of the modern welfare state rooted in the fact that it "is an attempt to found a social order based on the satisfaction of needs upon an economic order based on the satisfaction of wants" (85wscp, 10). In order to reach a just perspective on human needs and wants it is important to have a clear vision of the purpose of human existence.

> [I|f there is no publicly accepted truth about the end for which human beings exist, but only a multitude of private opinions on the matter; then it follows – firstly – that there is no way of adjudicating between wants and needs, and – secondly – that there is no way of logically grounding rights either in needs or in wants. (85wscp, 10)

So apart from unmasking the prevailing ideologies and political and social systems for what they really are, it is the church's task to contribute the perspective of a biblical anthropology to the public worldview in order to clarify the purpose of human existence. Newbigin summarizes:

> It is entrusted to the Church, not as one among a variety of options for the private cultivation of the religious life, but as publicly revealed truth for which Je-

> sus Christ bore witness before Pontius Pilate, public truth, truth for all, the reality against which all other claims of truth have to be tested. It is that human beings are created for fellowship with one another in a mutual love which is the free gift of God whose inner life is the perfect mutuality of love – Father Son and Spirit; that happiness consists in participation in this love which is the being of God; and that participation in it is made possible and is offered as a gift to sinful men and women by the justifying work of Christ and the sanctifying work of the Holy Spirit. In the light of this given reality, all projects for the pursuit of happiness as the separate right of each individual human being are exposed as self-destructive folly, and all definitions whether of want or of need are to be tested in the light of this – the one thing needful, which is to be along with one's brothers and sisters on the way which does actually lead to the end for which all things were created and in which all human beings can find their blessedness. (85wscp, 10-11)

Newbigin places the life of the individual into God's overarching story and argues that only in this context real needs can be understood and individual wants can be evaluated for what they truly are.

2.3.3. Exemplifying the Biblical Perspective of Human Existence in a Local Community

Besides unmasking prevailing ideologies and pointing out a biblical anthropology it is the task of the church to exemplify this biblical perspective of human existence in a local community. The experience of evangelism in the Indian villages serves as an example of what Newbigin means.

> During my visits to the hundreds of small villages in my old diocese in South India, I was often asked to speak to the non-Christians of the village just before going into the village church to conduct a service with the Christian congregation. I have often stood at the door of a little church, with the Christian congregation seated on the ground in the middle of a great circle of Hindus and Muslims standing around. As I have opened the Scriptures and tried to preach the Word of God to them, I have always known that my words would only carry weight, would only be believed, if those standing around could recognize in those seated in the middle that the promises of God were being fulfilled; if they could see that this new community in the village represented a new kind of body in which the old divisions of caste and education and temperament were being transcended in a new form of brotherhood. If they could not see anything of the kind, they would not be likely to believe. (61icd, 24; see also Niles 1962, 197)

The challenge for the church is to present in its life the love of God, to not only speak of it but to demonstrate before the world what community according to the will of God looks like (66hrsm, 108). "[T]he most important contribution which the Church can make to a new social order is to be itself a new social order" (91tt, 85).

The result for the community as a whole can be twofold. For one, the church can bring hope into situations where there is no expectation at all for the betterment of the current situation. For Newbigin it was a striking realization when he came back to England and saw the situation in the inner cities that, "[t]he commodity in shortest supply is hope" (87po, 356; see also 83os84, 1). Christian hope which is anchored beyond history can contribute a new perspective to situations which are lacking hope. This is one of the fundamental insights for the work among the poor and the marginal in today's societies. What Christian hope can contribute is a sense that people are not simply at the mercy of their circumstances but can regain a sense of dignity and a sense of power, which enables them to engage in community building.

> Community is about people; people living within a specific area, sharing common ties and interacting with one another. Community is built when the conditions are right for creative interaction around issues of common concern by people who share a sense of connectedness and belonging. It is people working together to create the kind of environment they want to live in. This is taken for granted in communities of wealth and privilege, but not so in communities of the poor.
>
> Building community, therefore, is essentially the task and prerogative of the people whose lives are invested in that community's future. This is an important point because too often, development work among the poor has been little more than outsider agencies doing things for people. ... But whenever people are unable to participate in the important decisions affecting their lives and community, they are rendered powerless. And it is powerlessness that ultimately destroys people and communities.
>
> Empowerment happens when people who are without power begin to speak, decide and act for themselves, when those without power insist in power sharing with the powerful, when people recover the God-given dignity of being human. (Luscombe 1995, 56-57)

Empowerment goes hand in hand with recovering the God-given dignity of being human, of being created in the image of God.

> While the main work in Smokey Mountain centers on material help, the most important goal is to evoke a sense of dignity and worth in each resident. Only by helping each individual feel loved and worthy is it possible to create a community. Once the community is formed, however, it is from within this community that faith is lived, deepened and celebrated in love. Only the poor have the power to truly help themselves and shape their own destiny. To encourage growth and development, this aspect of their faith must not be taken away. Instead, we should encourage the poor to develop this power. (Beltran 1995, 55)

Here we come full circle to Newbigin again when he identifies the contribution of the church as the exemplification of biblical anthropology. It is the vocation of the human being to live in fellowship with God and – out of this relationship – to live in the renewal of all other relationships which are part of human existence. Newbigin refers to the experience of a project undertaken by the churches in Madras.

> The Churches in Madras undertook to equip 48 of the worst slums in the City with modern sanitation units, as a pilot project for the whole city. While the work was in progress, one of the slum residents challenged one of the Church workers: 'What are you doing this for? Have you come to convert us?' (76bsr8)

Newbigin comments:

> The true meaning of these activities is that they are – or may be – signs of the reign of God, and the word 'sign' has to be given the full meaning that is has in the Gospels. They are, or may be, signs in the sense that the works of Jesus were signs, signs which can be understood and so lead to faith, hope and love, or can be stumbling blocks which lead to unbelief (Luke 7:18-23). (76bsr8)

In this sense they also aim for conversion. Signs of the kingdom want to bring about change. "The answer which was in fact given to the question in the Madras slum was 'Yes, of course we want to convert you; you don't think we want to leave you as you are – do you?'" (76bsr8). In the same way as the social and political contribution of the church is seen in a holistic manner, so also conversion here is seen in a holistic way, not merely as change of one's religious affiliation but as a change of allegiance that encompasses all aspects of human existence. The church's contribution of hope to a community will necessarily include the reference to the source of hope and to a way of life that is characterized by this hope.

A second possible outcome of the exemplification of the purpose of human existence in the life of a renewed community is that it may become the model for social involvement on a bigger scale. As an example one may think of the social changes that grew out of the evangelical revivals in England (see Stott 1999, 17-21) and Germany (see Bockmühl 1985, 42-51) in the 18th and 19th century. Forrester quotes Hauerwas as a summary of Newbigin's intentions:

> The task of the church [is] to pioneer those institutions and practices that the wider society has not learned as forms of justice. ... The church, therefore, must act as a *paradigmatic community* in the hope of providing some indication of what the world can be but is not. ... *The church does not have, but rather is a social ethic.* That is, she is a social ethic inasmuch as she functions as a *criteriological institution* – that is, an institution that has learned to embody the form of truth that is charity as revealed in the person and work of Christ. (Forrester 2002, 11 – emphasis added by Forrester; originally Hauerwas 1977, 142-143)

Forrester critiques that Newbigin does not provide concrete suggestions for social application. But the strength in Newbigin's contribution is certainly his focus on the theological foundation. At its center is the challenge to the church not to give in to the split of a public and private sphere of life but to continue the struggle to bring all aspects of life under the lordship of Christ. This cannot be done by coercion. That would be a lapse back into the Constantinian age. It would at the same time be an attempt to dissolve the eschatological tension, trying to establish the reign of God in the here and now.

The eschatological tension does not allow that. But by the same token the eschatological tension also refuses any individualization of the Christian faith. That would be nothing else but the dissolving of the eschatological tension into the future, leaving the present situation of the world outside of the sphere of Christ's reign. The eschatological tension of salvation requires the church to live in the redemptive tension of a proper this-worldliness and a proper other-worldliness and in this tension to proclaim the gospel as public truth, not as religious teaching.

3. The Church in Eschatological Tension

It is not necessary here to repeat all that has been said about Newbigin's understanding of the church in the eschatological context, an understanding which is summarized in the triad: the church as sign, instrument and foretaste (or firstfruits) of God's kingdom. Newbigin summarizes:

> Each of these words is important. They [the Christians in a given place] are to be a *sign*, pointing men to something that is beyond their present horizon but can give guidance and hope now; an *instrument* (not the only one) that God can use for his work of healing, liberating, and blessing; and a *firstfruit* – a place where men and women can have a real taste now of the joy and freedom God intends for us all. (94awis, 33; emphasis in the original)

The task in this section will be to examine some of the tensions this eschatological understanding brings with it for an understanding of the church in its relation to the world.

3.1. A Christian Vision for Society – Avoiding the Fall into the Constantinian Trap

There appears to be a tension in Newbigin's writings between his emphasis on the gospel as public truth on the one hand with the challenge for the church to bring all aspects of life – public and private – under the lordship of Christ, and his recognition of the end of the Christendom era on the other. This tension appears in Newbigin's writings as early as 1983 (83os84; 86fg; 89gps) and is explicitly addressed in his latest publications (98fp; 98cmsc), in which Newbigin deals with the challenges that the secularization of Western society has brought. The relegation of purpose and value into the private sphere of life and the concentration on value-free, objective facts in public life leads to the erosion of a common basis for living together as a community. This undermining of the foundation of shared values in Europe today is challenged by a vigorous appearance of Islam in general and religious fundamentalism in particular. Islam with its theocratic view of society is not uncertain about the direction of human history. Religious fundamentalism argues that it has the foundations which have been given up in the process of secularization. The current situation in Europe proves Weber's prophecy of the marginalization of religion wrong. In this situation it is again the task of the church to critically engage both religious and secular ideologies and to point out the distinctiveness of the gospel in contrast to them.

Newbigin argues that "in the last analysis it is only the gospel that can provide the basis for a society which is free, but in which freedom does not lead into disintegration and destruction" (98fp, 22). He explains:

> The reason for this lies in the unique character of the gospel itself. It is in the fact that God's decisive revelation of his wisdom and power was made in the crucifixion of the beloved Son, that in his resurrection from the dead we have the assurance that, in spite of all appearances, God does reign, that in the commission to the Church we have responsibility to bear witness throughout history to its end that God does reign, and that until the end God has provided a space and a time in which the reconciliation of our sinful race is possible, not by coercion but by freely given faith, love and obedience. (98fp, 22)

That is the theological foundation for Newbigin's argument which we have seen all along. Biblical anthropology recognizes that human beings can only truly live and be human when they are in relationship with God. But from the beginning this relationship has not been a forced one. It is offered as a gift with the real possibility of rejecting this gift and as a result living with the consequences of that decision. Whatever the choice is going to be, it brings with it a specific view of human existence and of the foundations of society. The present secular model suggests a secularized view of the world as foundation for society, and a view of privatized religion, in which each individual is free to choose for himself. This may sound appropriate in the present pluralist situation. But what is often overlooked is that secularism is not a neutral model. It is in itself a distinct view of the world. The problem with the secular unrestrained embrace of pluralism is that it ultimately destroys any possibility for a shared foundation upon which to build society. Instead of a shared foundation we find a pluralism of individualized values. Instead of finding orientation we are all forced to become "heretics" (Berger 1979), making our own choices about what we regard to be true. The challenge for the church is how to counter this state of disorientation with the gospel, how to influence society – without resorting to a Constantinian model.

It is in this context that Newbigin calls for a "Christian society." Of course this immediately raises the idea of a return to Christendom. This is, however, not what Newbigin proposes. How then is Newbigin's proposal of a "Christian society" different from the Constantinian paradigm? We have to go back a bit to understand Newbigin's train of thought.

Newbigin's thorough critique of the Enlightenment does not mean that he rejects all that the Enlightenment has brought us. Quite the contrary. The rejection of the territorial principle after the religious wars in the 16th and 17th century allowed people for the first time to practice religious freedom. And it furthered the recognition that religion is a matter of personal commitment (98fp, 138-139; 98cmsc, 101). Newbigin recognizes these as achievements on which there can be no turning back. But, he argues, "it is also certain that we cannot stand still" (98fp, 135).

The problem of liberalism is that if God is taken out of the sphere of public truth, then we are left with the rule of the collective. And that means we have no guard against any form of ideology that may take over.

> As long as the claim for the rights of every human person is grounded in the gift of the divine Creator, they have a firm basis in reality. But if belief in the existence of God ceases to be part of public truth, if nothing exists except the totality of what is accessible to observation and reason, there would seem to be no grounds for affirming the rights of an individual against the collective, or of a minority against the majority. In the end, the collective must prevail over the individual units. Without any basis in a supernatural reality, the liberal state slides inevitably towards the rule of the collective, mobilized, as it can so easily be, by some ideology or some charismatic leader. ...
>
> It is not without reason that the ancient writers regarded democracy as the last station on the line to anarchy and tyranny. (98fp, 140, 145)

The whole concept of human rights only makes sense when these rights are understood as something given by the creator. This then implies that there are human responsibilities towards that creator (98fp, 141). The elimination of the creator leads to the elimination of human responsibility to the creator. And this takes away the counterbalance to the privilege of human rights. We are left with rights, but without responsibility. It also means the giving up of a shared vision of the creator's purposes for this world.

> If the truth about the meaning and purpose of human life is something in principle unknowable, then there are no grounds for defending the liberal doctrine of human nature and destiny. The helplessness of liberal societies in the face of militant religious fundamentalism amply illustrates this point. If the truth about these ultimate matters is unknowable, then there are no arguments except those of the gun and the bomb. (98fp, 142)

If the purpose of the world is ultimately unknowable, then any value judgment is really arbitrary. All doors are open for moral anarchy to creep in. "Conduct becomes a matter of purely personal choice based on personally preferred 'values.' There are no barriers to halt the gradual slide into moral anarchy which liberal societies are witnessing at the present time" (98fp, 143).

Newbigin proposes that the solution to this dilemma lies in the recapturing of a public eschatology.

> [T]he eschatology of the Bible is a public eschatology. Its focus is not the destiny of the individual but the triumph of Christ in the fulfillment of the purpose of the entire creation. New heavens, a new earth and a holy city are the symbols by which it is described. Certainly, of course, there is an inescapable individual element here. One may, through cowardice and unbelief, miss the way and be lost. But the goal is public, not private. A privatized eschatology fails to send Christians into the public realm; fails to challenge them to see the care and nurture and guidance of the public life of community and nation as an integral part of their responsibility to God; fails therefore to act in the public square in ways which correspond to the reality of what God intends and has

Chapter 5: Implications of Newbigin's Eschatological Framework

promised; fails to unmask effectively the follies which dominate the public square with promises of what cannot be. (98fp, 144)

A biblical eschatological vision relativizes the human use of power by reminding it of its accountability towards God. The tension between Romans 13 which portrays the political order as "a ministry ordained by God" and Revelation 13 "where the same power is depicted as a manifestation of Satan" is consistent throughout the bible (98fp, 146). Any use of human power is therefore ambivalent and must be reminded of its accountability before God.

The eschatological vision on the other hand determines how the church approaches the world with its witness. The truth of the gospel can only be offered by the church as an invitation. And that includes the tolerance to accept its rejection.

> What is unique about the Christian gospel is that those who are called to be its witnesses are committed to the public affirmation that it is true – true for all peoples at all times – and are at the same time forbidden to use coercion to enforce it. They are therefore required to be tolerant of denial, not in the agnostic sense in which the word 'toleration' is often used; not in the sense that we must tolerate all beliefs because truth is unknowable and all have equal rights. The toleration which a Christian is required to exercise is not something which he must exercise *in spite of* his or her belief that the gospel is true, but precisely *because of* this belief. (98fp, 148-149)

Newbigin points out that the church has to question the assumption that a secular state is neutral. Relegating all religions into the private sphere does not mean religious neutrality in the public sphere. The secular paradigm entails a specific view of the world which embodies truth claims of its own which must be challenged by the gospel (98fp, 152). Newbigin responds with his conviction that only a Christian foundation can form the basis of a "secular society" in the sense of a tolerating society which he distinguishes from a society based on the ideology of secularism.

> I have already drawn attention to the fact that the phrase 'a secular society' can be understood in two radically different ways. It may on the one hand refer to a society or an educational system in which different religious beliefs are given equal opportunity to flourish, but may on the other hand refer to a society or an educational system which is dominated by the ideology of secularism, by the belief that all things can be satisfactorily explained without any reference to divine revelation or to any supra-natural realities. I am affirming that in the last analysis it is only the Christian gospel which can sustain a secular society or a secular educational system in the former and proper sense. (98fp, 160)

Newbigin argues for a society which is tolerant in the sense that it allows its members to dissent. However his argument is that this can only become reality if the foundation of this society is not secular (i.e. based on secularism) but is decidedly Christian (based on a biblical view of the world). That is why Newbigin calls for a Christian society, "one in which Christians form[..] a sufficiently large proportion of the total population to exert a preponderant influence on public life" (98fp, 153). It is the vision of a society in which those whose thought and practice set the tone and direction of the different sectors of public life include a large number of Christian men and women who have thought through the implications of the Christian faith for those areas of the life of society. (94awis, 173)

Newbigin suggests a number of issues the church has to keep in mind to accomplish the task. The church must remember the ambiguity of all use of power and must remind those in power of their accountability before God. The church is called to act in eschatological expectation on the conviction that the biblical view of the world is part of public truth, namely that all aspects of life are ultimately to be brought under the lordship of Christ. This commitment requires a true view of the priesthood of all believers, each one serving the Lord Jesus Christ in her specific calling and area of expertise, whether it be business, labor, politics or culture (98fp, 157-158). Newbigin thus tries to characterize and distinguish what he calls a "Christian society" – in the sense of a tolerant society built on a Christian worldview – in contrast to the Constantinian paradigm (98fp, 162, 163). The question is: Is this vision of a tolerant Christian society a helpful model for the church in the present?

The reservation that is usually expressed is: How do those members of society who do not share the Christian commitment view the wielding of influence of Christians on the foundations of social life? Will and must it not be seen as a hegemonic rule of one religious group over and against other interests – religious, moral, or social? These are serious questions to consider. At the same time we have to ask ourselves: What are the alternatives to the involvement of the church in public life?

I agree with Newbigin that in the end only the gospel can provide the foundation for a society which is – in the true sense of the word – tolerant of other beliefs which it considers to be false (98fp, 142). This must be maintained despite the assumed superiority of a secular foundation of society with its alleged neutrality. A secular society will have to declare secularism the specific shared worldview as its foundation, which means that it commits to a specific view of the world and can tolerate religious pluralism only as long as religion remains part of the private sphere of the individual members of society. It has no other option than to make the rule of the collective the basis for society, which may push minorities to the margins and makes the society vulnerable to be overtaken by some ideology.

In contrast the biblical meta-narrative carries the claim to be public truth, but does so in a way that does not allow coercion and instead requires toleration of dissent. This is exemplified in the cross of Christ. It is this characteristic that qualifies the Christian worldview as a foundation for a truly tolerant society. Here again we see how the eschatological dynamic shapes the Christian view of the world. The toleration of dissent is part of the tension between the present hiddenness and the future revelation of Christ's rule. The church strives for the day when the lordship of Christ will be revealed to and recognized by all. And yet it cannot bring about that day but only witness to it by establishing signs of Christ's reign.

Chapter 5: Implications of Newbigin's Eschatological Framework 203

In practice, wherever the Christian population forms a large part in society, Christians in fact need to attempt to live the way that Newbigin proposes. Any refusal to do so would mean to surrender the gospel to the private sphere and take it out of the public sphere of life, leaving the public sphere to other interest groups. As Newbigin says the question of power cannot be evaded.

> How is this world of assumptions formed? Obviously through all the means of education and communication existing in society. Who controls these means? The question of power is inescapable. Whatever their pretensions, schools teach children to believe something and not something else. There is no 'secular' neutrality. Christians cannot evade the responsibility which a democratic society gives to every citizen to seek access to the levers of power. (89gps, 224)

This is where Newbigin places his emphasis. The danger of Christians in the West today is to accept uncritically the relegation of religion to the private sphere of life and thus to neglect their responsibility for the public life of society of which they are a part.

Wherever the Christian population forms a significant part of society and does not shy away from exercising influence on public life, the "Constantinian trap" remains a dangerous reality. To be more specific, the danger is to regard the tasks of church and state to be almost identical, to view the church as partner of the state which champions the state's interest, and to regard the enemies of church and state as identical. These are the very characteristics with which Bosch depicts the Constantinian model (Bosch 1993, 90). What is called for is a self-critical dissociation of church and state on the one hand (see 86fg, 130-131; 89gps, 222-224), and yet an active engagement of Christians in the public sphere on the other.

Goheen makes us aware how Newbigin's proposal differs from the Constantinian model (Goheen 2002b). First, Newbigin – following Polanyi – takes as a starting point a model of "committed pluralism" in which the freedom to differ is respected but there is shared commitment to seek the truth together. This model combines the emphasis of a shared public truth and the recognition that there is no easy positivist grasp of it. Second, Newbigin sees the problem of the Christendom era in the fact that the church exercised power, not that Christians exercised power.

> Newbigin advocates the neo-Calvinist notion of sphere sovereignty, the doctrine that God has given in the creation order a measure of autonomy to each of the various areas of human life such as art, science, politics, and so on. The institutionalized church has no direct authority over these spheres; rather it is shaped by God's law order discerned and implemented by those within that sphere. ... So while the church as an organized body has no right to exercise power over these spheres, Christians with insight into these areas may exercise power. (Goheen 2002b, 47-48; see also Goheen 1999a)

Newbigin further qualifies the use of power as power "in the way of the cross." It is not coercive power but power that leaves room for dissent. These are clear and important distinctions which set Newbigin's proposal apart from the Constantinian model. However Goheen recognizes:

> We come here to a dilemma that, as far as I know, Newbigin never resolved. If a Christian exercises political authority, where does s/he allow room for freedom and dissent and where is there a required submission to the law that has been fashioned in light of the gospel? (Goheen 2002b, 48-49)

At the core of this question is the important distinction between a community approach to the understanding of truth, which Newbigin acknowledges, and the rule of the collective, which he criticizes. A community approach to the understanding of truth means a shared commitment to seek the truth together, essentially a critical realist paradigm which recognizes a dimension of truth apart from the knowing subject. This allows for the recognition of Christ's lordship, even though we do not yet know in detail how the lordship of Christ is to work itself out in all spheres of human life. The rule of the collective on the other hand functions according to an instrumentalist paradigm by making the common denominator of its members' individual contributions the foundation of community life. This by default excludes the recognition of the lordship of Christ. Newbigin's call to the church is therefore essentially a call to engage not only in the discussion on specific values and aspects of a society's foundation – that too is required – but also in the discussion on the epistemological question that underlies this foundation. Newbigin's proposal must therefore not be understood from a positivist perspective ("the Constantinian trap"), nor from an instrumentalist perspective (a Christian majority as rule of the collective), but from a critical-realist perspective. It is a call for the members of the church to engage in the public debate on both, the epistemological questions as well as the values and foundations of social life. The goal is to foster the acknowledgement of Christ's lordship also in the public sphere, without being coercive and still allowing for dissent. It is the challenge to draw out the public implications of the gospel's claim (see Hunsberger 2006).

The question that Goheen raises (Goheen 2002b, 48-49; see above) would be easily answered in both, a society based on the Constantinian model and in a society based on the rule of the collective. The fact that Newbigin leaves the question unanswered underscores that his proposal is different from both alternatives.

The central difference lies in the eschatological dimension of Newbigin's proposal, which grows out of the awareness of the eschatological character of God's story. The proposed "Christian society" is not the realization of the kingdom. Newbigin keeps the other-worldliness of the gospel in mind. The kingdom is not to be established by the use of that power whose exercise Newbigin calls for. The exercise of power – i.e. the wielding of influence by Christians in their respective spheres of life in order to establish signs of Christ's rule – is to be used to witness to the kingdom, not to establish it. "The church may function as salt in society, but the fullness of God's kingdom is at the end" (Goheen 2002b, 49).

Newbigin distinguishes his proposal from the Constantinian model and he does so by referring to the eschatological, provisional character of the church's involvement in the world.

> Christian discipleship is a following of Jesus in the power of his risen life on the way which he went. That way is neither the way of purely interior spiritual

pilgrimage, nor is it the way of realpolitik for the creation of a new social order. It goes the way that Jesus went, right into the heart of the world's business and politics, with a claim which is both uncompromising and vulnerable. It looks for a world of justice and peace, not as the product of its own action but as the gift of God who raises the dead and "calls into existence the things that do not exist" (Rom 4:17). It looks for the holy city not as the product of its policies but as the gift of God. Yet it knows that to seek escape from politics into a private spirituality would be to turn one's back on the true city. It looks for the city "whose builder and maker is God", but it knows that the road to the city goes down out of sight, the way Jesus went, into that dark valley where both our selves and all our works must disappear and be buried under the rubble of history. It therefore does not invest in any political programme (whether conceived in the style of a restored "Christendom" or in the style of a classless society where all coercive government will have withered away) the hopes and expectations which belong properly only to the city which God has promised. There can be no repetitions of Constantine, either on the left or on the right. What is required is a faithful discipleship, following Jesus on the road he went, and living by the hope of which his resurrection is the outward pledge and the gift of the Spirit the inward foretaste. Such discipleship will be concerned equally in the private and in the public spheres to make visible that understanding and ordering of life which takes as its "fiduciary framework" the revelation of himself which God has given in Jesus. It will provide occasions for the creation of visible signs of the invisible kingship of God. (83os84, 37)

It is interesting to compare Newbigin's proposal with Bosch's. Bosch, like Newbigin, argues for a "world-formative" understanding of the church. But in his position we find a stronger distinction between the roles of church and state. His analysis begins where Newbigin does, with a look at the necessary foundations for a society to exist. Bosch suggests that the church "contribute" to a shared moral vision of a society (Bosch 1993, 95). Newbigin suggests that the church "exert a preponderant influence on public life" (98fp, 153). Both Newbigin and Bosch agree that it is important for the church to challenge the fundamental split between public truth and private truth and to contribute to the foundation of society. However the way Bosch phrases the contribution of the church is less prone to be misunderstood than Newbigin's "Christian society." And it is stated in broader terms and not limited to a situation in which the Christian community forms a significant part of the population as a whole (see 98fp, 153). Bosch thus avoids the controversy which Newbigin invites with his choice of words.

> Finally, in our mission to Caesar we should remember that, in the long run, a society, any society, can only survive if it can rely on the assumed virtue of its citizens. It can only succeed if certain controls and morals have been implanted into its citizens. This means that even a pluralist or secularist society will *remain* dependent upon the witness and existence of believers, that is, of persons whose integrity and good conduct can be relied upon. It is only a shared moral vision that can hold society together. ... If we can continue to contribute to this vision, our mission will be a blessing to all. Since we know of the reality of sin in individual

and corporate life, we will remain anti-utopian, sober, and watchful, not fooling ourselves into believing that we shall build the ideal society here on earth or losing hope when there are setbacks and when the social and political fabric remains fragile and under pressure. In this way we will be doing our utmost for the peace of the city, calling people to true conversion – a conversion that includes social responsibility and a moral vision for society. (Bosch 1993, 95)

While I concede to Newbigin's critics that the choice of terminology invites false associations with the Christendom model, I still agree with the thrust of Newbigin's argument. The fundamental difference between the Christendom model and Newbigin's proposal is Newbigin's awareness of the eschatological, provisional character of the Christian involvement in the public sphere. That does, however, not devalue this involvement. It rather puts it into the right perspective.

3.2. Ministers in the Secular World – The Tension between an Anabaptist Model and a Reformed Model of the Church

The question of Christian involvement in the public life of society involves the tension between the Anabaptist model and the Reformed model of the church. Goheen refers to Bosch's differentiation between different models of the Christian church (Bosch 1993) and shows how Newbigin's ecclesiology can contribute to a synopsis of elements of both the Anabaptist and the Reformed model.

The Anabaptist model views the church as an alternative community in tension with the world and its culture. The Reformed model on the other hand sees the church more as an integral part of the society and culture in which it is placed. In its extreme form this can lead to the identification of the church with the dominant culture. The background for these two models is found in the two major phases of early church history.

> During the early years of its life, the church understood her identity as resident aliens. There was a redemptive tension between the church and her culture. The church understood itself to be an alternative community that was nourished by an alternative story. This contrast community was not one that ignored the public life of society by being reshaped into a private institution that provided an otherworldly and spiritual salvation for its members. Rather it was publicly subversive by a life of radical discipleship that existed as a kind of antibody in society. However, with the Constantinian shift the story that governed the church's life and the story that governed cultural development were merged. The redemptive tension was lost as the church became part of the constellation of powers within the empire. Her identity was shaped by her place in culture rather than by the story of the kingdom of God. The end result was cultural captivity. (Goheen 2002b, 39)

The disestablishment of the church in the Western world today reverses this development. It is another major shift in the history of the church and can be viewed as a positive change since it allows the church to focus anew on its original story and has the potential to free it again from its cultural captivity.

Newbigin's ecclesiological contribution is often seen as a contribution to the alternative community model. According to Goheen, Bevans associates Newbigin with the "countercultural model" of contextualization. The same is true for Griffioen (Goheen 2002b, 39-40). Goheen agrees with the central accents of the alternative community model but sees the need to balance it with aspects which arise out of Newbigin's Reformed understanding of the church.

Goheen points out three essential theological convictions of Newbigin (Goheen 2002b, 41-43) which we have already seen in the course of this study: the eschatological understanding of the church as "provisional incorporation of mankind into Jesus Christ" (94awis, 53); the comprehensive scope and restorative nature of salvation; and the conviction that Christ's lordship extends over all. "Christ is not just the Lord of Christians; he is Lord of all, absolutely and without qualification" (93ua, 203). Newbigin's understanding of mission is based on these fundamental convictions.

The mission of the church has a threefold thrust. For one, the church is a model of the life of the kingdom. This is the emphasis we have seen above that "the most important contribution which the Church can make to a new social order is to be itself a new social order" (91tt, 85). Second, the corporate witness of the church to the world encompasses both service and evangelism. It is an holistic and a communal outreach. And finally Newbigin emphasizes the importance of the witness of the individual members of the community in their daily lives (Goheen 2002b, 44).

Goheen argues that in today's attempts by the GOCN to build on Newbigin's missiological approach the role of the witness of laypeople in their social surroundings needs to get more attention. This important aspect of Newbigin's missional understanding is needed in order to balance the alternative community model and keep it from turning into a parallel community model (Goheen 2002b, 54). What are the characteristics of Newbigin's emphasis on the missionary calling of laypeople?

Newbigin sees the witness of laypeople in their social surroundings of neighborhood and work as the primary witness of the church, "the Church's front-line troops in her engagement with the world" (51ott, 6). Here he picks up the concern for the laity that was raised in the ecumenical movement in the 1940s and 1950s (Congar 1957; Kraemer 1958). But this is also the most neglected area of the witness of the church. It is an area which is left to the individual believers. However it is here where they need the most support of the church, because they may be called to make decisions which cause them and their families to suffer for their convictions. And the issues are complex. The challenge comes on different levels:

> Look at a few examples illustrating different levels of the problem.
>
> (a) A man in a big store is expected to persuade customers to buy a product which he knows to be worthless. Does he obey the orders of his employer or does he challenge the firm and risk starvation for himself and his dependents?

(b) On a second level, a professional man becomes aware that the standard of professional ethics in his profession is basically wrong. How far ought he to go in defying the professional standard and risking the loss of status and livelihood for himself and his dependents?

(c) Another level of the problem: a business man finds himself in such a fiercely competitive market that apart from any question of business ethics, his success inevitably means loss and perhaps disaster for others. His business ethics may be irreproachable but how does he read the Sermon on the Mount? (60bsft, 110)

Newbigin sees the challenges and the costly character of the choices that Christians face as individuals in these situations. He challenges the church to truly support the individual witnesses in their situations.

> Are we taking seriously our duty to support them in their warfare? Do we seriously regard them as the front-line troops? ... What about the scores of Christians working in offices and shops in that part of the city? Have we ever done anything seriously to strengthen their Christian witness, to help them in facing the very difficult ethical problems which they have to meet every day, to give them the assurance that the whole fellowship is behind them in their daily spiritual warfare? (51ott, 6; quoted in Goheen 2002b, 50)

The support needs to include the strengthening of faith through prayer, word and sacrament. There needs to be emotional support and sharing in the struggles so that people don't face these challenges – which also affect the well-being of their families – alone.

> [T]hey are not decisions which ought to be taken in solitude. We ought not to ask each Christian in solitude to bear the burden of the real front line warfare of the Kingdom of God. There must be opportunities for those who are in the same kind of situation to think together about what are the next critical points at which change is possible, and the Church as whole must find ways of expressing its solidarity with those who stand in these frontier situations, who have to make decisions that may cost not only their own livelihood but also that of their families. (60bsft, 111)

The support must focus on equipping people by providing them the opportunities for discussing the challenges they face among themselves so that they may find ways to implement possible changes in their spheres of life, changes which correspond to the character of Christ (see 80ykc, 62). Traditional forms of church life may not be adequate for this kind of support. Newbigin sees the need for smaller groups which are not organized according to the territorial principle, but which rather bring people from the same walk of life together to provide the network for support needed. Here Newbigin's critique of the denominational principle also takes effect. The support for laypeople in their ministry calls for structures that extend beyond denominational lines and that are small and flexible enough to meet the specific needs. "There is a need for 'frontier groups,' groups of Christians working in the same sectors of public life, meeting to thrash out the controversial issues of the business or profession in the light of their faith" (89gps, 230-231).

This situation also calls for a different emphasis in pastoral ministry where the role of the pastor is understood not only as bringing people together and leading them in worship as a congregation but also as equipping people for their specific sending into the world, for their "spiritual act of worship," to use Paul's terminology from Rom 12:1 (see 89gps, 231).

> At the most sophisticated level we have to think of our task in a city like Madras to train our lay members who are playing key roles in the life of government, business and the professions to become ministers of Christ in these secular situations. All of this is involved in our calling and ordination. It is for this purpose that we have set up such institutions as the Community Service Centre, in order that there may be opportunities for Christians in various secular callings to learn how they can become effective ministers of Christ in their daily work. ...
>
> The ordained pastor is called to train all the members committed to his care for *their* ministry in the world, even though some of them have not yet woken up to the fact that there is a ministry to which they are called. ...
>
> We ought not to be content until we can honestly say that we are helping every member of the Church to fulfill his ministry in the secular world. (77gs, 76-77)

This focus on the missionary witness of laypeople in their respective professions and the support they need from the church for their ministry is something that is easily neglected where churches focus on structures and programs that concentrate on themselves as organizations and/or on their corporate outreach into the community (Weston 1998, 54-57). Newbigin saw the need for greater flexibility of organizational structures in order to strengthen laypeople in their witness to the world.

Goheen summarizes how the alternative community model of the church needs to be complemented by this focus on the missionary witness in the professional world.

> One of the enduring tensions is how to be in the world yet not of it. The new stress of the alternative community model drawing on the rich Anabaptist tradition of not being of the world is an important corrective for the Western church who lives in a state of cultural captivity or "an advanced case of syncretism," as Newbigin has said – thanks in large part to her Constantinian tradition. The further emphasis of the communal dimension is also important. However, this stress on the church as alternative community has led to a neglect of the fact that the primary place where a missionary encounter takes place is in the world, in the Monday to Saturday lives of believers. The result is that little has been done to challenge the local congregation in the way of structures and leadership to equip believers for their callings. Indeed, a stress on the calling of believers would not diminish the importance of the institutional church but would highlight the need for structures that equip the various members for mission. (Goheen 2002b, 54)

3.3. The Church as Provisional Body in Eschatological and Cultural Tension

The fact that the church is placed in this world but takes its essential character from the eschatological goal has consequences for the relationship of church and culture (Hunsberger 1998a; see p. 34). For Newbigin the organizational form of the church is always secondary. Form and structure must in some way correspond to the surrounding culture and to the challenges at hand in order to be relevant. But they are ultimately subject to the theological essence and calling of the church. As an organism the church needs an organization which supports it in its central tasks. The organic paradigm is the prevalent one. The proper concern for appropriate cultural forms and structures must not compromise the essence of the church, its calling for mission in unity. Therefore cultural factors of territoriality or denomination must not be allowed to hinder the witness of the church to the world, neither in its corporal form nor in the ministry of the individual believers. They have to be secondary, for the church does not exist for its own sake but it is the representation of Christ for and in a specific place and time.

> [T]he church is the "provisional incorporation of humankind into Jesus Christ." All humankind is incorporated in Adam. We are all part of this natural human world. Jesus Christ is the last Adam, and the Church is the provisional incorporation of humankind into Christ. It is provisional in two senses: in the sense that not all humankind is so incorporated, and in the sense that those who are so incorporated are not yet fully conformed to the image of Christ. So the Church is a provisional body; it looks forward. It is its very nature to look forward, but it looks forward in two ways – and both must be equally stressed – one, to the full formation of Christ in all its members, to the growth of its members in holiness to the stature of Jesus Christ; and two, to the incorporation of all of humanity.
>
> But in talking about the world you have to talk about that segment of the world in which you are placed, and the Church has to be recognizable as *for* that place. ... [I]t is of the very essence of the Church that it is *for* that place, for that section of the world for which it has been made responsible. And the *for* has to be defined christologically. In other words, the Church is *for* that place in a sense that is determined by the sense in which Christ is *for* the world. ... [T]he Church is for the world against the world. The Church is against the world for the world. The Church is for the human community in that place, that village, that city, that nation, in the sense that Christ is for the world. And that must be the determining criterion at every point. (94awis, 53-54)

There is no other possibility than to describe the character of the church in this kind of a dialectic. Newbigin mentions both the eschatological and the cultural tension. The eschatological tension is described as a two-fold one: (1) The eschatological "not yet" is related to the Christ-like character of the church and its members. The church is called to be a foretaste of the eschatological kingdom despite all its imperfection and shortcomings. (2) In another sense the eschatological tension involves the incorporation of humankind into the person of Jesus Christ. The church as the community of the elect is in the present the representative community, but it is so for the sake of humankind as a whole. The eschatological goal remains the incorporation of all of humanity into Jesus Christ.

Newbigin also mentions the cultural tension. The church is *for* the world not in the sense of a complete identification with it, but rather in the way that Christ was for the world. It has to be recognizable as for a specific place or community or culture, which places the emphasis on the continuity with culture. But it also has to be recognizable as Christ-like. That will include the challenge to be against the world, to challenge its plausibility structure and values with a different plausibility structure and different values. Newbigin has expressed this in the dialectic of being for the world by being against the world. This puts the emphasis on the side of discontinuity with culture. Both continuity and discontinuity with the surrounding culture present an ongoing challenge for the church (see 95os, 145-146). It is this cultural tension which has been expressed by Walls as the tension between the "indigenizing principle" – identification with a specific culture – and the "pilgrim principle" – dissociation from a given culture and challenging it with the gospel (Walls 1996, 3-15).

3.4. The Church Called to Mission in Unity

The eschatological orientation of the kingdom is essential for a true understanding of the essence of the church as well as its mission. It denotes the church as the "provisional incorporation of humankind into Jesus Christ" in the twofold sense that we have just seen. It provides a framework for understanding the cultural tension in which the church is placed, the tension of being in the world but not of the world, of being for the world by being against the world, of being culturally relevant but not becoming captive to culture. It prevents the misunderstanding of mission as church-centered mission and instead keeps the focus on the calling of the church, its participation in the *missio dei* – in unity. Both its sending into the world and its unity are essential to the true character of the church. Both are given to it by the Spirit as a gift and at the same time as a task to fulfill. The striving for and strengthening of the unity of the church and the theological debate about the true understanding of the gospel are an integral part of the church's calling. It is definitely part of this process to celebrate the plurality of expressions of faith in the one Lord Jesus Christ. However it will not be enough for the church to do just that. It also has to search and dialogue – under the guidance of the Spirit – to gain an understanding of the gospel that is true to its character and essence (see e.g. Acts 15).

The recent focus in the missiological debate on the church as community of reconciliation (see Bevans and Schroeder 2004; Schreiter 2005; Matthey 2005) underscores the importance of the question of the unity of the church in and for its mission. Ahrens says self-critically:

> Churches are unreliable [*unglaubwürdige*] witnesses of a reliable [*glaubwürdigen*] word. At the same time churches are places in which the irreplaceable *word of reconciliation* in its unwieldiness and danger for the churches them-

selves is preserved, sounded out, celebrated, and passed on. (Ahrens 2005, 171 – my translation).

The tension of *simul justus et peccator* does not relieve the church of its responsibility with regard to the word of reconciliation; it rather underscores the need for the preservation, for the thorough study, for the celebration, and for the proclamation of the word of reconciliation. The word of reconciliation presents a constant challenge for the church herself to be a reliable, credible witness of this reliable, credible word.

Both parts of this calling – to mission and unity – are placed in the context of the eschatological dynamic of history. The mission of the church will not end until the final day appears. In the same way the challenge to strive for unity in love and truth will not end until the Lord arrives. The value of various organizations which aim to help the church in the accomplishment of these tasks (e.g. WCC, LCWE, WEA) may be determined by the question, in which way these institutions help to achieve growth in both of these areas, the church's mission to the world and a striving towards greater unity in both truth and love. Newbigin's legacy in this context is that the two aspects – mission and unity – must not and cannot be separated from each other. Both will come to completion at Christ's return.

4. Bearing the Witness of the Spirit in a Pluralist Context

The church's calling is to bear the witness of the Spirit to the world. The world today is also in the West recognized as a religiously diverse world. Religious pluralism, however, is not a new phenomenon. But the fact that the diversity of religions is now experienced in its own cities forces the church in the West to reflect on the challenge which this situation presents for its witness. Newbigin who after more than 30 years abroad returned to Europe, so to speak with an outsider's view for the European challenge, can give us some guidance in this matter. The study will show that the question of witness in a pluralist context in Newbigin's thinking also is embedded in the eschatological tension of God's story with this world. I will begin by looking at Newbigin's characterization of religious pluralism.

4.1. Religious Pluralism

Religious pluralism as a fact needs to be distinguished from religious pluralism as an ideology (89gps, 14). It is religious pluralism as an ideology that presents the fundamental challenge for a proper understanding and proclamation of the gospel. Newbigin defines religious pluralism:

> Religious pluralism ... is the belief that the differences between the religions are not a matter of truth and falsehood, but of different perceptions of the one truth; that to speak of religious beliefs as true or false is inadmissible. Religious belief is a private matter. (89gps, 14)

This religious pluralism takes different forms.

4.1.1. Religious Pluralism in Hinduism

In Hinduism religious pluralism is based on the understanding that the

> reality behind all the manifold appearance and all the ceaseless change which our five senses report to us is one undifferentiated and unchanging spirit and that that spirit is identical with our own spirit. That spirit is defined as 'pure awareness distinct from bodily states and mental happenings' ...
>
> This pure awareness, however, this naked condition of pure selfhood, is normally beyond our power to realize. In proportion as we depart from it, the world takes on an appearance of multiplicity and diversity. (61ftow, 36)

This apparent multiplicity and diversity is what we perceive in the phenomenal world. But it is illusory, not in the sense that the phenomenal world as such is an illusion but "that the appearance of multiplicity and change is illusory" (61ftow, 36). In light of this it is obvious that the incarnation of Jesus Christ, even though it may be perceived as one appearance of the undifferentiated *Brahman* in the diverse world of phenomenological appearance, cannot be understood as a once and for all revelation of the ultimate spirit. The emphasis of Hinduism is not on knowing the supreme spirit, but on realizing one's own union with the supreme spirit. Knowing implies distinction between the person who knows and a person or object which is known. It is therefore still part of the phenomenal world with its illusionary character of plurality and diversity. The experience of mystical union with the supreme spirit is beyond knowing and is therefore in no way contingent on the particularities of the phenomenal world and human history.

> Within such a view of reality, there is room for almost infinite tolerance. Human nature varies, and each man is free to join the stream of living religion at the place to which his nature and environment lead him. There is no place for mutual criticism or hostility. Each man must be encouraged to be faithful to the religious path of his choice but, at the same time, to penetrate behind the forms of religion, its alleged revelations, its creeds and dogmas and rituals, to find through them (and it does not matter what they are) the one truth, which is not a dogmatic statement or a personal meeting but an experience of identity with the Supreme Being. (61ftow, 38)

Newbigin points out that this view of the world – impressive as it might seem – is itself placed upon a faith commitment. It is neither inevitable nor is it necessarily superior.

> [T]he Hindu mystic begins by abstracting himself from all apprehensions of phenomena. ... He has what he set out to seek. From the standpoint he has taken, all multiplicity has ceased to exist, because he has deliberately shut it out of his attention. But to conclude that this experience is the clue to ultimate reality is not a logical deduction, but a leap of faith; for the whole question is: What is the relation of that ultimate reality to the multiplicity of phenomena? (61ftow, 39)

It is this question of the relationship between the ultimate and the specific, between the universal and the particular that is at the heart of the issue of religious pluralism. The answer that is given to this question determines the understanding of reality and of salvation.

> We face here, surely, an ultimate decision, which is, in the last resort, a decision of faith: ... whether salvation is by absorption into the Supreme Being, conceived as undifferentiated and unchanging spirit abstracted from all contact with phenomena, or whether it is by reconciliation to the Supreme Being, conceived as personal will active in and through phenomena. Here is the dividing line between all religions. (61ftow, 39)

4.1.2. Religious Pluralism in the West

Religious pluralism in the West, on the other hand, has arisen out of the humanist tradition which encompasses both a "rationalist tradition ... which affirms human reason as the organ through which alone truth may be known," and a

> spiritualist tradition ... which affirms the capacity of the human spirit to make direct contact through mystical experience with the ultimate source of being and truth. What these have in common is the conviction, one might say rather the unquestioned assumption, that historical events are not a source of ultimate truth. (89gps, 2)

This double strand of rationalism and spiritual experience has fostered the split that characterizes Western societies of the present, the split between facts as "public truth" and values as "private truth." Science provides us with hard facts which are and must be acknowledged by everybody. There is no ideological pluralism in the sphere of facts as public truth. Differences, if they arise, need to be debated and explored until this exploration leads to a better, unified understanding of reality. Religion on the other hand is not seen as based on facts but on personal experience. Religions are therefore not part of the debate about public truth. They are part of the private sphere of values. The question of truth in the realm of the religions has in fact been abandoned. Religions have become not a matter of truth but a matter of taste.

Christian theological reflection on religious pluralism needs to relate this plurality of religions and human experiences to the particularity of the event of Christ's death and resurrection which stands at the center of the biblical understanding of salvation. The central question for a Christian theology of religions is: How do the universal saving will of God and the particularity of the Christ event relate to each other? Before we can address this question, we have to look at Newbigin's understanding of "religion."

4.2. Religion

Newbigin uses the term religion with a certain ambiguity that reflects the general shift in the understanding of religion in modern Western societies. Generally speaking,

Chapter 5: Implications of Newbigin's Eschatological Framework

> [t]he different religions are the social embodiments of different ways of apprehending the ultimate reality, the source and goal of our being – whether or not the word "God" is used to designate that reality. ... the religions make truth-claims about what that reality is. (88cfwr, 317)

However in the West the understanding of religion has changed.

> I am thinking rather of the way in which that attitude to religion which is characteristic of India has (with obvious modifications) become widespread among Western Christians. It is an attitude that no longer sees religions as providing the intellectual framework within which public life is understood, but rather sees "religions" as alternative paths to personal salvation, offering a range of options within which each person is free to choose and between which one does not argue about conflicting truth-claims. (88cfwr, 312)

Newbigin is aware of different usages of the term religion, but he does not attempt to distinguish carefully between them. "Religion is from one point of view an aspect of culture, but this is not the whole of religion" (89gps, 14). Newbigin tends to use the term in a more fundamental way, understanding it as the underlying worldview of a given culture.

> [T]he word "religion" is intended to denote all those commitments that, in the intention of their adherents, have an overriding authority over all other commitments and provide the framework within which all experience is grasped and all ideas are judged. In this sense the word will include an ideology such as Marxism, which functions, both for the committed individual and for societies under Marxist control, as such an ultimate commitment.

> ... I am using it [the word "religion"] to refer to that which has final authority for a believer or a society, both in the sense that it determines one's scale of values and in the sense that it provides the models, the basic patterns through which the believer grasps and organizes his or her experience. (95os, 160-161)

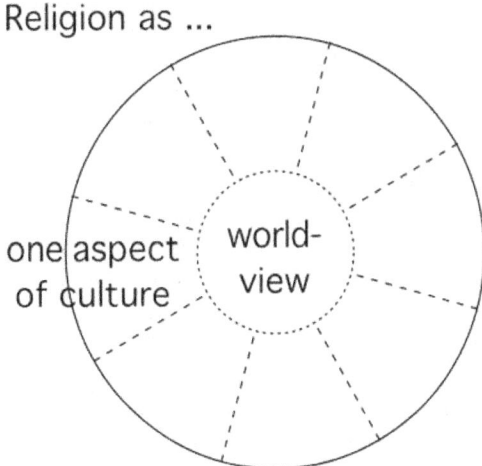

Figure 6: Different understandings of "religion"

This distinction between religion as one aspect of culture on the one hand and religion as comprehensive worldview on the other is an important one (see figure 6). Religion as one aspect of culture looks at the phenomenology of religions, i.e. their rituals, traditions, and religious practices. These are expressions of deeper convictions which are found in their myths, oral traditions, and sacred writings. These again are related to the underlying worldview which gives meaning to the whole of human life.

Newbigin's usage of the term religion in the sense of comprehensive worldview is related to his distinction between cultural pluralism and religious pluralism (89gps, 14). For Newbigin the two are not on the same plane. Cultural pluralism is an attitude which – generally speaking – the church embraces, since the whole diversity of humankind is meant to be part of the church as the new humankind (61icd, 12; 89gps, 14). Newbigin argues for a plurality of cultural expressions which are based on a shared view of the world. If religion were to be understood as merely one aspect of culture, religious pluralism would have to be embraced as well. We would have no right to challenge another person's faith and religious practice. Newbigin's rejection of religious pluralism as an ideology is a rejection of a pluralism of worldviews (63rtdt, 17).

In this sense Newbigin's understanding of religion as framework for understanding the world and evaluating ideas also includes ideologies. It is quite possible for a person to profess to a certain religion (e.g. Christianity), while in reality his or her commitment lies with a different ideology (e.g. capitalist secularism). In this case, the ideology would be the real religion, namely the framework through which the person interprets reality and defines his or her values and behavior, while the religion which a person nominally confesses to would be religion in the sense of one aspect of his or her culture. The tendency in the West to relegate religion to the private sphere of life must be seen in the context of this model. Religion is reduced to one aspect of culture. The foundational worldview can be something quite different.

While religion (in the sense of underlying worldview) is central in the life of any person for the understanding of reality and for determining values and behavior, Newbigin calls into question the opinion that religion (as one aspect of culture, as religious practice) is the primary sphere for a person's encounter with God. God does not necessarily and primarily meet people in their religious practices. This is not so say that religious experiences of people of other faiths are invalid or do not entail any encounter with the living God at all. Newbigin refrains from judgment here. Christ is in fact "the true light that gives light to every man" (John 1:9). But, Newbigin emphasizes, there is no indication that this "giving of light" refers to the religious experience of man. John in his gospel points out that "the light shines *in the darkness*" (John 1:5, emphasis added). And in fact as the gospel of John continues, the reader finds out that the darkness is strongest among those who are strongly religious. It is the Pharisees who reject Jesus and have him crucified, not the tax collectors and sinners. The paradox here is that the obstacle to receiving the revelation of God in Christ is precisely the sense of one's own religious achievements. This is true also for missionary encounters in the present. The strongest resistance to the gospel often comes from the sincerely religious. That is an important aspect for the question of the continuity between the religions and the gospel.

4.3. Continuity and Discontinuity

How then does Newbigin view religious experiences of people of other faiths? On the one hand he characterizes religions as human attempts to build on the witness to God that humans have in their heart. Yet he also recognizes that no human attempt can ever lead to the goal strived for.

> Man, estranged from God, has yet the witness to God in his heart. He seeks to build upon that witness the edifice of his religions and his morals. St. Paul has shown us once for all how, in the sphere of morals, this effort to obey God's law leads not to union with God but to estrangement. The farther the effort is pressed, the greater the estrangement. (61ftow, 73)

That which is required – namely love for God – "can never be achieved – it can only be received, and then given back" (61ftow, 73). This radical critique of human religious efforts does, however, not entail a judgment on the person and his or her religious experience.

> His religion is certainly not one of mere falsehood or mere illusion. It is the response – in many cases a response which has a nobility and seriousness that puts us to shame – to the real witness that God has placed in the heart of every man. We have no vantage point from which we have any right to judge that response. But the coming of the gospel means quite simply and seriously the end of it. That which all religions seek, namely a true vision of God and a true union with him, can only be the gift of God; and that gift is given in Jesus Christ. Christ is the end of religion in the same sense that he is the end of the law. (61ftow, 74)

Newbigin here as well as in his later writings strictly refrains from passing judgment on another person and his or her religious practice. He is strictly concerned with the theological question of how to view the religions from a biblical perspective. While he recognizes an element of continuity (the witness of God in the human heart) he points out the element of discontinuity, namely the need for repentance and the fact that the point of contact for the gospel is not – as is usually assumed – the religious effort of a person. The point of contact for the gospel is rather the other person's humanity, the

> simple facts of human experience which are – so to say – pre-religious. I mean those elementary matters in which man's consciousness of absolute obligation expresses itself, in the human relationships of home and street and market place. It is an illusion to suppose that it is men's religion which will best enable them to understand the gospel; indeed, if my argument is true, men's religion may be the point at which they are farthest away from any possibility of understanding it. (61ftow, 74)

In "The Finality of Christ" Newbigin summarizes his point of view in three statements:

> What does this proclamation and summons mean for the interpretation of human experience, and especially of human religious experience, apart from and before the acceptance of the Gospel?
>
> (i) It does not mean that the reality of religious experience outside of faith in Jesus Christ is denied. ...
>
> (ii) Nevertheless, having said this, it must also be said that acceptance of Jesus Christ as Lord means radical repentance and conversion from all pre-Christian experience. ... The total fact of the Cross, which is the focus of the Gospel, makes it impossible to describe the relationship between faith in Christ and other forms of religious commitment in terms simply of continuity and fulfillment. There is a radical discontinuity.
>
> (iii) And yet it is not a total discontinuity. ... This element of continuity is confirmed in the experience of many who have become converts to Christianity from other religions. Even though this conversion involves a radical discontinuity, yet there is very often the strong conviction afterwards that it was the living and true God who was dealing with them in the days of their pre-Christian wrestlings.
>
> One may sum up the three points which I have tried to make in some such way as the following: the Gospel has a double relationship to man's experience, and to the wisdom founded upon it, apart from the knowledge of God in Jesus Christ. It is a relationship both of continuity and of discontinuity. The Gospel demands and effects a radical break with, and conversion from, the wisdom that is based upon other experience; yet mature reflection by those who have experienced this break suggests that it is the same God who has been dealing with them all along. He has never been without witness even when they did not know him as he has revealed himself in Jesus. (69fc, 59-60)

This summarizes well the dialectical tension that Newbigin perceives in understanding religions, as well as the emphasis he places. Continuity is found in the fact that people of all faiths are part of God's story and that it is the very God which the gospel reveals who is dealing with them, even in the time when they do not know him in the person of Jesus Christ. But there remains a mystery about this relationship. We do not know what to make of the religious experiences of people who live outside of faith in Jesus Christ. However, and this is Newbigin's emphasis, once the gospel is proclaimed everything changes. The cross of Christ is the judgment on all aspects of our lives, including our religious achievements. This is the element of discontinuity. There can be no direct line from our religious efforts to the achievement of salvation. All are called to repentance and can only receive salvation as a gift at the foot of Christ's cross. Thus the gospel cannot be simply understood as the fulfillment of the religions. The tension between continuity and discontinuity remains: "radical, but not total discontinuity."

4.4. Critical Engagement of Proposed Solutions

In light of this position Newbigin evaluates various answers given to the question about the relationship between the religions and the gospel. Following Newbigin's structure and adding his critique of Hick, I summarize seven positions.

1. "Other religions and ideologies are wholly false and the Christian has nothing to learn from them" (95os, 169). Newbigin rejects this view of total discontinuity. He points to the history of bible translation where indigenous terms must be used for the translation of the biblical term *theos*. Without this continuity, communication of the gospel would be in fact impossible.

> The name of the God revealed in Jesus Christ can only be known by using those names for God that have been developed within the non-Christian systems of belief and worship. It is therefore impossible to claim that there is a total discontinuity between the two. (95os, 169-170)

2. "The non-Christian religions are the work of devils and their similarities to Christianity are the results of demonic cunning" (95os, 170). Newbigin recognizes an element of truth in this, even though he does not identify with this position. Since "religion is the sphere in which one surrenders oneself to something greater than oneself," "the sphere of religions is the battlefield *par excellence* of the demonic" (95os, 170). He refers to the fact stated above that it is often the noblest religious people who "most emphatically reject the gospel" (95os, 170).

3. "Other religions are a preparation for Christ: the gospel fulfills them" (95os, 170). This view was strong at the 1910 Edinburgh Conference. Newbigin argues that a close look at the different religions reveals that they ask different questions and cannot be easily understood on one continuum. He quotes Rudolf Otto: "The different religions turn on different axes." Each religion must therefore "be understood on its own terms and along the line of its own central axis" (95os, 171).

4. Another view "seeks 'values' in the religions and claims that while many values are indeed to be found in them, it is only in Christianity that all values are found in their proper balance and relationship" (95os, 171). This was the prominent view at the 1928 conference in Jerusalem. Against this view Newbigin emphasizes the importance of repentance. "Christ is not merely the continuation of human traditions: coming to him involves the surrender of the most precious traditions. The 'values' of the religions do not together add up to him who alone is the truth" (95os, 171).

5. The Roman Catholic position in the *Ecclesiam Suam* (1964) depicts "the world religions ... as concentric circles, having the Roman Catholic church at the center and other Christians, Jews, Muslims, other theists, other religionists, and atheists at progressively greater distances" (95os, 171-172). Newbigin's critique is again that religions cannot be evaluated by their distance from Christianity but must rather be understood on their own terms.

6. Newbigin then mentions the Roman Catholic position "that the non-Christian religions are the means through which God's saving will reaches

those who have not yet been reached by the gospel" (95os, 172). Newbigin refutes the uncritical assumption that "it is religion among all the activities of the human spirit that is the sphere of God's saving action" (95os, 172). But most of all, Newbigin criticizes the presumptuous attitude "that our position as Christians entitles us to know and declare what is God's final judgment upon other people" (95os, 173). From this we have to refrain.

7. Finally Newbigin engages in greater length the position which presents a philosophical or ethical framework into which all religions are to be included in a kaleidoscope of cultural and religious diversity. Newbigin engages representatives of this theological debate, whether it be Toynbee and Hocking (61ftow), or Hick, Smith, Knitter and others (89rmcu, 90rm, 95os). Among them he deals in detail with John Hick. Hick has proposed a "Copernican revolution" by which he means "a shift from the dogma that Christianity is at the center to the realization that it is God who is at the center, and that all the religions of mankind, including our own, serve and revolve round him" (Hick quoted in 95os, 163). Newbigin's critique of this statement calls attention to the fact that "God and the religions are not objects of the same class" (95os, 163) as are the earth and the planets. The analogy is flawed since what can be compared is not God and the religions, but a personal perception of God and other religions' perceptions of God.

> The two realities that are accessible and comparable are God as I conceive him and God as the world religions conceive him. What claims to be a model of the unity of religions turns out in fact to be the claim that one theologian's conception of God is the reality that is the central essence of all religions. This is the trap into which every program of the unity of the religions is bound to fall. (95os, 163)

Newbigin refutes the idea that a viewpoint can be achieved from which all religions can be judged objectively, namely from the outside, without requiring the person who does the evaluation to take a specific point of view. There is no knowledge without the personal commitment to a – provisional – set of assumptions. His critique of Hick focuses on uncovering these hidden assumptions and bringing them into the open. This he does also in his critique of the famous story of the blind men and the elephant.

> [T]he real point of the story is constantly overlooked. The story is told from the point of view of the king and his courtiers, who are not blind but can see that the blind men are unable to grasp the full reality of the elephant and are only able to get hold of part of the truth. The story is constantly told in order to neutralize the affirmation of the great religions, to suggest that they learn humility and recognize that none of them can have more than one aspect of the truth. But, of course, the real point of the story is exactly the opposite. If the king were also blind there would be no story. The story is told by the king, and it is the immensely arrogant claim of one who sees the full truth which all the world's religions are only groping after. It embodies the claim to know the full reality which relativizes all the claims of the religions and philosophies. (89gps, 9-10)

A second critique of Hick focuses on his call to "move emphatically from the confessional to the truth-seeking stance in dialogue" (Hick quoted in 95os, 165). Newbigin points out the implicit inference: "The implication is that those who take the confessional stance are not seekers after truth. This is surely a very serious matter. One cannot enter into real dialogue if one begins by denying the intellectual integrity of one's partner" (95os, 166). For Newbigin the confessional stance and the truth-seeking stance are not mutually exclusive. The hidden assumption in Hick's proposal in fact elevates his own position from being one partner in the dialogue to a position where he in effect claims he has an overarching view of the whole. "There is therefore no dialogue, no encounter. There is only the monologue of the one who is awake addressed to those who are presumed to be asleep, or who have not yet wholly roused themselves from their 'dogmatic slumbers'" (95os, 167). Newbigin for his part makes his commitment clear.

> My point is that I know of no basis, no axiom, no necessity of thought that requires me to believe that a historic person and a series of historic events provide a less reliable starting point for the adventure of knowing than does the highly sophisticated mental construct of a philosopher. (95os, 166)

He summarizes his critique of Hick:

> I must repeat the simple truth that no standpoint is available to anyone except the point where they stand; that there is no platform from which one can claim to have an "objective" view that supersedes all the "subjective" faith-commitments of the world's faiths; that everyone must take their stand on the floor of the arena, on the same level with every other, and there engage in the real encounter of ultimate commitment with those who have also staked their lives on their vision of the truth. (95os, 168)

Here Newbigin's eschatological framework comes to bear on his understanding of the religions and the fact of religious pluralism. While we are still in the middle of the story there simply is no possibility for us to assume an outside viewpoint from which we could evaluate the religions or see the outcome of the story. We must all make a choice about our own position from which to interpret the story, and then enter into the conversation with those who have chosen a different position. Here we see the eschatological character of Newbigin's epistemology to which I will turn in the next section.

4.5. Summary: The Gospel and the Religions

The key elements of Newbigin's view on the gospel and the religions may be summarized in five points.

4.5.1. The Universal and the Particular – The Doctrine of Election

We have seen that the question about the relationship between the universal saving will of God and the particularity of the Christ event as salvific event with universal significance is at the center of a biblical theology of religions. Newbigin sees the connecting link in the doctrine of election. The doctrine of election is not to be misunderstood as privilege of the few but rather as responsibility of the few for the sake of the many. From the beginning God's plan of salvation is directed towards all of humankind. The relational character of God and of human beings as well as the character of salvation as restoration of community in fact require that the invitation to salvation be extended to people of all nations and cultures and times via the bridge of human contact. What is passed on is not religious teaching but the gift of participation in the new humankind, the foretaste and firstfruits of the new creation.

4.5.2. Public Truth and Private Truth – The Character of the Gospel

God as personal God is involved in history, leading the history of this cosmos to the goal that he has established. The gospel tells this story of God with his world. It is therefore not to be relegated into the sphere of private values as if it were a religious teaching on reaching salvation for individual souls. The gospel draws people with their particular life stories into the one story of the world, of which Christ's death and resurrection form the center point. In this sense the gospel is public truth. Newbigin initially phrased the title of his engagement with other religions "Christianity among the religions" (69fc), but later changed it to "The Gospel among the religions" (95os). This reflects the specific character of the gospel as public truth in contrast to other religious teachings.

> It [the gospel] is not the teaching of a new way of personal salvation after the manner of the Buddha. Nor is it the announcement of a theocratic kingdom in the manner of Islam. ... It is the announcement of an event which concerns the whole human situation and not merely one aspect of it – the religious aspect, for example. It is the announcement of the reign of God present and active. ... It is neither simply the announcement of a new religious doctrine, nor the launching of a new secular programme. ... It is the announcement of the decisive encounter of God with men ... with mankind as a whole, with human history as a whole, indeed with the whole creation. It concerns the consummation of all things. Its character as 'final' lies in this fact. (69fc, 48-49)

In this comparison between different religious understandings we observe again an eschatological dimension. Religion which aims for personal salvation like Buddhism is essentially ahistorical. Religion which understands itself as the establishment of a theocratic rule like Islam is characterized by an immanent eschatology. The rule of God is established here and now. Newbigin sets the gospel in contrast to both of these. He neither allows the gospel to be reduced to an ahistorical individual religious way of salvation; nor does he allow for a world-immanent establishment of the rule of God as if the church could be identified with the kingdom (see 95os, 139). The gospel is public truth because God has acted and is still acting today in history and thus meets human beings in the particularity of their life stories and draws them into his story with its eschatological orientation and goal, the final revelation of the lordship of Christ. This character of the gospel as public truth must be emphasized in the encounter with other religious traditions as well as in the encounter with the humanist Western worldview.

4.5.3. Neither Individualism nor Universalism – The Cosmic Character of Salvation

Newbigin's critique of the reduction of salvation to individual salvation has consequences for the often asked question: Can a Hindu – or any member of another non-Christian religion for that matter – be saved? Newbigin points out that the question as such springs from the same individualistic thinking which understands religion as a way to private salvation. Newbigin consequently and consistently rejects the question. He shifts the focus away from the individual person and tries to get the whole of God's story in focus, centering on God and his glory.

> If we refuse ... these forms of reductionism, then the question we have to ask is not, "What will happen to this person's soul after death?" but "What is the end which gives meaning to this person's story as part of God's whole story?" ...
>
> The whole discussion of the role of the world religions and secular ideologies from the point of view of the Christian faith is skewed if it begins with the question, Who is going to be saved at the end? That is a question which God alone will answer, and it is arrogant presumption on the part of theologians to suppose that it is their business to answer it. We have to begin with the mighty work of grace in Jesus Christ and ask, How is he to be honored and glorified? The goal of missions is the glory of God. (89gps, 178-180)

For Newbigin the problem lies already in the way the question is formulated. Whenever the destiny of any individual soul is considered apart from its place in God's story then history is robbed of its meaning. Earth is reduced to the training place for individual souls in their preparation for a heavenly world. For Newbigin the individual life story of a person and the global history of the world belong intrinsically together. The two cannot and must not be separated. However here we face a question which we cannot answer. In which way God integrates the life-story of a person who did not or could not get to know him through the gospel into his story with humankind as a whole remains a mystery to us.

Instead of trying to answer this question, Newbigin consistently leads his readers to the point of the clear responsibility to which the gospel calls those who hear it. The gospel presents itself always as a challenge to those it addresses and calls for repentance and commitment here and now, a commitment to participate as representative elect in the sending of the church as a witness to the world. We are neither entitled to satisfy our curiosity about the fate of those who have not heard the gospel, nor are we to extend judgment on them.

> We must not presume to prejudge the last judgment. We know a few things, but they are not enough: that the call of God is to all men; that those whom He chooses to convert are few; and that those few are chosen not for themselves but for the sake of all. If they forget that, they will be rejected. (66c, 42)

Because we are not entitled to pronounce judgment on others, Newbigin also rejects the conclusion of a universal salvation. He points out that there is a real possibility of rejecting the gospel.

> There can be no doubt that just as the perspective of the Bible is the whole history of humanity and of the cosmos, so also it is full of what one may call universalist overtones. ... On the other hand there are equally clear and much more numerous passages, especially in the New Testament, that speak of a coming judgment and of the possibility of being rejected. ... We would part company with the New Testament altogether if we ignored it. (95os, 78-79)

Newbigin holds on to the tension between the universal character of salvation on one hand and the necessity of a personal answer on the other hand. And this includes the real possibility of not being a part of that salvation.

4.5.4. No Neutral Standpoint – Witness and Dialogue

Christian witness is neither the advocating of a religious philosophy nor the assertion of a claim for Christianity as religion. It is the announcement of a historic event. God has acted in Jesus Christ at a specific place and a specific time in human history. Christ is the representative elect in whom all of humankind is represented. His death and resurrection are the true center of history, the center point that changes the course of history and anticipates the outcome of the story. Jesus Christ is Lord.

The mission of the church is to witness to this fact. Witness to people of other faiths always begins by using language and frameworks that are foreign to the gospel but familiar to the hearers. The concepts are gradually changed and filled with biblical meanings as the story is told and the new community of believers struggles with understanding both the gospel and its own culture. If communication is to happen at all, it can only happen within frameworks that are familiar to the people who listen.

Witness therefore is always in context, answering to new questions along the way. In this sense it cannot be separated from dialogue. Newbigin prefers "conversation" to "dialogue" because the term "dialogue" is often associated with an anti-confessional, anti-witness emphasis. Newbigin rejects this dichotomy. He sees witnessing as one central element of dialogue.

> "[W]itness" is the proper word because the function of a witness is not to develop conclusions out of already known data, but simply to point to, report, affirm that which cannot come into the argument at all except simply as a new datum, a reality which is attested by a witness. (82lhc, 14)

The main contribution of the church to the dialogue with people of other faiths is therefore the telling of the overarching story of God with humankind which gives meaning to both the individual life stories as well as human history in general.

> [T]he essential contribution of the Christian to the dialogue will simply be the telling of the story, the story of Jesus, the story of the Bible. The story is itself, as Paul says, the power of God for salvation. The Christian must tell it, not because

she lacks respect for the many excellencies of her companions – many of whom may be better, more godly, more worthy of respect than she is. She tells it simply as one who has been chosen and called by God to be part of the company which is entrusted with the story. It is not her business to convert the others. She will indeed – out of love for them – long that they may come to share the joy that she knows and pray that they may indeed do so. But it is only the Holy Spirit of God who can so touch the hearts and consciences of the others that they are brought to accept the story as true and to put their trust in Jesus. (89gps, 182)

Since no neutral standpoint is available to anyone it is important to be clear about one's own commitment and to enter into the conversation with people of others faiths on the basis of that commitment. From this perspective Newbigin encourages the church to participate in dialogue with people of other faiths on the basis of our shared human nature, having been created in the image of God; to find signs of the kindness and justice of God everywhere; to work with people of all faiths for the good of the community; and to expect that "the Holy Spirit can and will use this dialogue to do his own sovereign work, to glorify Jesus by converting to him both the partners in the dialogue" (77bpmi, 268).

4.5.5. Meeting People of Other Faiths At the Foot of the Cross

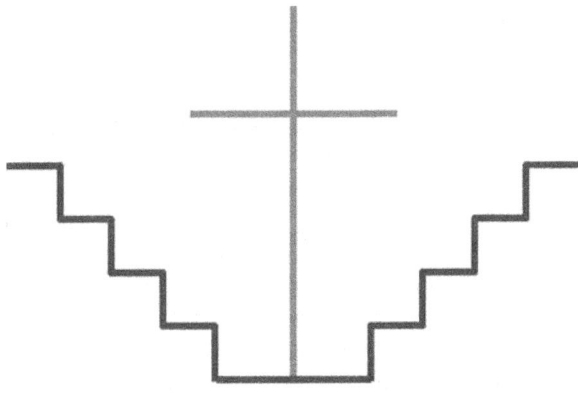

Figure 7:
Meeting people of other faiths at the foot of the cross (Source: 95os, 181)

Using a simple drawing from Walter Freytag, Newbigin characterizes the encounter with people of other faiths as a meeting at the "bottom of our [religious] stairways," "at the foot of the cross" (95os, 180-181). The cross of Christ is God's judgment on all of human wisdom, including religious wisdom and achievements. This judgment encompasses both the Christian and people of other faiths. The fact of the cross does not allow the Christian to approach people of other faiths with a preconceived judgment on the other person's state of salvation. Salvation is an act of God's grace, not depending on a person's achievements. As Newbigin has pointed out, more often than not it is precisely the religious achievements that prevent acceptance of God's revelation and salvation. While the cross is the sign of God's judgment on all, calling people of all faiths to come down from their staircases of religious achievements, it is at the same time the sign of God's grace for all, the invitation to meet him at the cross.

> The staircases represent the many ways by which humans learn to rise toward the fulfillment of God's purpose. They include all the ethical and religious achievements that so richly adorn the cultures of humankind. But in the middle of them is placed a symbol that represents something of a different kind – a historic deed in which God exposed himself in a total vulnerability to all our purposes and in that meeting exposed us as the beloved of God who are, even in our highest religion, the enemies of God. The picture expresses the central paradox of the human situation, that God comes to meet us at the bottom of our stairways, not at the top; that our real ascent towards God's will for us takes us further away from the place where he actually meets us. "I came to call not the righteous, but sinners." Our meeting, therefore, with those of other faiths takes place at the bottom of the stairway, not at the top. "Christianity" as it develops in history takes on the form of one of those stairways. Christians also have to come down to the bottom of their stairway to meet the adherents of another faith. There has to be a kenosis, a "self-emptying." Christians do not meet their partners in dialogue as those who possess the truth and the holiness of God but as those who bear witness to a truth and holiness that are God's judgment on them and who are ready to hear the judgment spoken through the lips and life of their partner of another faith. (95os, 181-182)

Newbigin here not only upholds a thoroughly Christological center in his theology. His model also characterizes the witness of the church as "speaking from the bottom of its own staircase." The witness of the church cannot be other than being a humble witness, not calling people to change their religious staircase and try to improve their religious achievements on another religious avenue. It is rather a call to join with those who have recognized that salvation cannot be reached by one's own efforts but can only be received as a gift at the foot of the cross (see Matt 5:3). Newbigin's model exemplifies both the boldness of the church's claim – Christ is Lord – and the humility of its witness, not from a position of power. It is – in Bosch's words – witness in "bold humility" (Bosch 1991, 489).

4.5.6. The Eschatological Character of Newbigin's Theology of Religions

Newbigin's theology of religions is an integral part of his theology of mission. Both are characterized by their embeddedness in God's story with humankind as a whole, and both have a clear eschatological focus, looking forward to the day of the final revelation of Christ's lordship. The importance of the doctrine of election for the synopsis of the universal scope of God's salvific will and the particularity of his salvific act in the person of Jesus, the characteristic of the gospel as public truth as the story of God's involvement with his world, the refusal to foresee the final judgment, the insistence on the fact that there is no external objective viewpoint outside of the ongoing story available to any participant in the interreligious dialogue, and the emphasis that there can be no participation in God's salvation without a humble recognition of the cross of Christ as both, God's judgment on all human efforts and the place of his salvation – all of these elements are derived from the eschatological character of God's story and are clearly embedded in it.

From this foundation Newbigin challenges the ideology of religious pluralism. His epistemology is also embedded in this eschatological understanding.

5. Epistemology in the Eschatological Context

At one point Newbigin engaged in a brief argument with Netland regarding the role of reason for the evaluation of conflicting truth claims. Both Newbigin and Netland contributed an article to the book "Faith and Modernity" (Netland 1994, 94tam). The question in their debate is about the role reason plays in the proclamation of the truth of the gospel. Netland argues for a "positive or offensive apologetics" which goes beyond a "negative or defensive apologetics." While a defensive apologetics tries to establish the reasons for the Christian believer that he is justified to accept the truth claims of the Christian faith, positive apologetics

> is concerned to show that non-Christians too *ought* to accept the truth claims of Christianity. Thus the apologist here is very much on the offensive, trying to demonstrate that there is an important sense in which unbelievers too are epistemically obligated to accept Christian faith, or that it is unreasonable or irrational for them not to do so. (Netland 1994, 101)

Netland argues for criteria that are context-independent and cannot only appeal to human reason regardless of time and space, but provide rational reasons for the truthfulness of the claim of the gospel. He names the following examples: the logical principles of identity and non-contradiction, the general principles of adequacy, simplicity, coherence, and consistency (Netland 1994, 109). Netland claims that these principles are universally valid and do not depend on a specific culture. He goes into more detail in his book "Dissonant Voices" where he names two definitions and ten principles by which any religion can be tested for its inner coherence and consistency (Netland 1991, 180-195). Netland's conclusion is: "Although it cannot be argued here, I should state that the reason I believe one is justified in accepting the Christian faith as true is because it is the only worldview that satisfies the requirements of all the above criteria" (Netland 1991, 193).

Newbigin critiques Netland's attempt to search for context-independent criteria and "self-evident truths."

> We have to reject the idea, so widely accepted, that rational thought can provide us with a kind of reliable knowledge which is neutral in respect of religious commitment and therefore capable of providing a secure foundation for a knowledge of God which does not depend on his own acts of revelation and redemption in history. This supposed neutrality is no neutrality at all, because all

systematic human thought about the totality of our experience has to start from some belief about what is ultimate and fundamental – matter, spirit, life, reason or whatever. There is no neutral standpoint. (94tam, 68)

Newbigin critiques that Netland remains in the modernist dichotomy of objective criteria versus subjective criteria in the sense that these stand for demonstrable versus non-demonstrable criteria. Based on Polanyi's work Newbigin holds that there is no possibility to know anything apart from initially believing something. Critical doubt is only the second step in the process of knowing. Critical doubt requires the initial acceptance of something to be true. And this initial acceptance is always subjective. It requires a commitment of the knowing subject. Therefore there is no objective knowledge. Every process of knowing consists of a subjective dimension on the part of the knowing subject and of an objective dimension in so far as the knowing subject is trying to understand an object that is distinct from the knowing subject. The critique of Descartes' search for totally objective knowledge also calls Netland's proposal into question. Newbigin writes:

> This attempt to find 'context-independent' grounds for Christian faith is profoundly wrong. To be 'context-independent' one would have to be outside of history. One would in fact have to be God. This is exactly the temptation of modernism: 'You shall be as Gods', for only God is 'context-independent'. (94tam, 86-87)

Newbigin also challenges Netland's position with theological reasons. The fact that Christ did choose the disciples and that they did not choose him is in agreement with other biblical references to the work of the Spirit who is the central agent in bringing people to know Christ. The certainty of this knowledge rests neither in the human decision nor in human reason but in the trustworthy character of the one who calls us and leads us into a fuller understanding of the truth.

> We are invited to make a personal commitment to a personal Lord and to entrust our lives to his service. We are promised that as we so commit ourselves we shall be led step-by-step into a fuller understanding of the truth. ...
>
> If we are to use the word "certainty" here, then it is not the certainty of Descartes. It is the kind of certainty expressed in such words as those of the Scriptures: "I know whom I have believed, and I am sure that he is able to guard until that day what has been entrusted to me" (2Tim 1:12). ... [T]he locus of confidence (if one may put it so) is not in the competence of our own knowing, but in the faithfulness and reliability of the one who is known. The weight of confidence rests there and not here with us. (95pc, 66-67)

This kind of certainty, which rests in the faithfulness of God, stands in stark contrast to the certainty that Descartes envisioned, resting in the knowing subject.

> [This position] asks for a kind of knowledge which does not depend on the grace of God. It falls into the Cartesian trap – a kind of certainty which rests upon the knowing subject, and not upon the faithfulness of the One whom we

are enabled by grace to know. Paul says: I know whom I have believed (2Timothy 1:12), not 'I know the one whose existence I have demonstrated.' There is all the difference in the world between a certainty which rests wholly on the faithfulness of God, and a certainty which rests on a chain of human reasoning. (94tam, 87)

Newbigin also refers to the reference of Jesus that only the knowledge of truth can lead us into freedom (John 8:31).

> Here we seem to have a direct reversal of one of the axioms of modernity, namely, that freedom of inquiry, freedom to think and speak and publish, is the way – the only way – to the truth. Jesus appears to reverse this. Truth is not a fruit of freedom; it is the precondition for freedom. (95pc, 68)

Netland on the other hand argues that without any context-independent criteria there is no barrier against a total relativism (Netland 1994, 104). He critiques Newbigin for developing his argument in the plausibility structure of the (postmodern) West which has given up any claim for context-independent knowledge. For Netland it is important to hold on to the possibility of stating truth claims which are independent of particular contexts. "Are our views *merely* the products of our environment, or are we able to transcend to some extent the cumulative influences of history, culture, society, etc., so as to apprehend truths which are themselves distinct from particular contexts?" (Netland 1994, 104-105).

Newbigin shares Netland's concern about a total relativism. Newbigin too argues for the possibility to know truth. However he is approaching the problem from a different angle. While Netland seeks a rational basis that is independent from any context from which he would like to argue for the truth claim of the Christian faith, Newbigin sees this as an impossibility. All truth claims are part of a particular cultural and historical setting. However that does not necessarily entail the conclusion that none of them can be an expression of truth.

> There are no timeless truths; ... [I]t is obviously true that all our eternal truths and all our metanarratives are products of particular human histories. They are all socially and historically embodied. They do not exist in a suprahistorical, supracultural stratosphere. They are embodied in a particular language, using concepts, symbols, and models which have been developed in particular human communities. They are part of human culture, of particular human cultures. There is no reason to deny this.
>
> ... The (true) assertion that all truth claims are culturally and historically embodied does not entail the (false) assertion that none of them makes contact with a reality beyond the human mind. (95pc, 74)

Newbigin takes the postmodern critique of context-independent knowledge seriously. Yet at the same time he unmasks the postmodern claim – that consequently all truth claims can be nothing but mere human constructs – as a false, non-conclusive argument and refutes it.

Newbigin argues that there is no kind of knowledge that cannot be doubted. Every attempt to know requires an initial act of commitment, an act of believing before one can know. Here Newbigin follows Polanyi and MacIntyre and their reference to Augustine: *Credo ut intelligam*, "I believe in order that I may know." Newbigin is convinced of the necessity to first commit oneself to a specific tradition and to accept this tradition and its presuppositions at least preliminarily in order to enter into the process of knowing. This is a fundamental critique of Descartes' idea of objective knowledge. There is no human access to an objective, outside standpoint from which to understand reality with indubitable certainty.

This would seem to lead directly to an unimpeded pluralism, precisely the result Netland is concerned about. However Newbigin does not end up a pluralist. The key for his epistemology is God's story. "Newbigin asserted that the Christian story is 'objective' truth, as it comes from *outside* this world, but it will not be *proved* to be so until God gives his verdict at the end" (Foust 2002, 160). Newbigin insistently points out "that history derives its meaning not from forces within it, but from the goal which has been promised by God and has as its central clue the crucified and resurrected Christ" (Foust 2002, 156). In Newbigin's own words:

> If the place where we look for ultimate truth is in a story and if (as is the case) we are still in the middle of the story, then it follows that we walk by faith and not by sight. If ultimate truth is sought in an idea, a formula, or a set of timeless laws or principles, then we do not have to recognize the possibility that something totally unexpected may happen. Insofar as our knowledge is accurate, we shall be able to predict the future. Future and past are governed by the same laws, the same principles, and the same realities. But if we find ultimate truth in a story that has not yet been finished, we do not have that kind of certainty. The certainty we have rests on the faithfulness of the one whose story it is. We walk by faith. …
>
> [I]f the biblical story is true, the kind of certainty proper to a human being will be one which rests on the fidelity of God, not upon the competence of the human knower. It will be a kind of certainty which is inseparable from gratitude and trust. (95pc, 14, 28)

The fact that we are still in the middle of the story and that its outcome is still ahead of us entails that we can only respond in belief or in unbelief to the claims the bible makes about the interpretation of that story. "There can be no indubitable proofs" (95pc, 55).

Here the eschatological orientation of history based on the will of a personal God shows itself as the key for Newbigin's epistemology. We are part of an ongoing story. Therefore we don't have access to an outside view yet. We are given God's word regarding the outcome of the story. But there is no way to verify it objectively. We need to commit ourselves in faith to this view of the world. Therefore Newbigin can only point to the end of history for the final verification of the Christian truth claim.

> There is no external criterion above us both to which I and my opposite number can appeal for a decision. The immediate outcome is a matter of the comparative

vigor and integrity of the two traditions; the ultimate outcome is at the end when the one who alone is judge sums up and gives the verdict. (89gps, 65)

Two things need to be noted here. The final verification of the truth claim of the Christian faith will only be given at the end of history, when Christ is revealed as the true Lord and judge of all. This is Newbigin's "eschatological epistemology" (Foust 2002, 162). As long as we are on the way "we live by faith, not by sight" (2Cor 5:7). That is a central statement in Newbigin's epistemology.

> However, the test of adequacy does not claim to offer the kind of indubitable certainty which the Cartesian programme claimed. Final certainty belongs to the day of judgment. Until that day, the Christian is called to walk by faith, which is the gift of him who has reconciled us to himself through the cross. The idea that there is available to human beings a kind of indubitable certainty which is independent of divine grace is an illusion. (94tam, 81)

Yet this is not the end of the discussion. In both quotations Newbigin points to a preliminary qualification that underscores the truth claim of the Christian plausibility structure in the present. "The immediate outcome [in contrast to the ultimate outcome] is a matter of the comparative vigor and integrity of the two traditions" (89gps, 65). He speaks of the "test of adequacy" (94tam, 81), which means, there also is in the present an engagement of the different traditions, or to use Berger's term, of the different plausibility structures. The Christian who is in this world but not of this world is part of two plausibility structures and is thus engaged in both an internal and an external dialogue between the two.

> There is thus an internal dialogue in which the question at stake is: "Which is more adequate for grasping and coping with reality with which all human beings are faced?" This is a dialogue about truth. In this dialogue the two traditions of rationality are compared with one another in respect of their adequacy to the realities with which all human beings have to deal. And, obviously, this internal dialogue is the necessary precondition for the external dialogue which is at the center of a missionary's proper concern. Although the two ways of reasoning are not mutually translatable except to a limited degree, that does not mean that they cannot be compared in respect of their adequacy to enable human beings to know and cope with reality. (89gps, 56)

For Newbigin the recognition of the absence of context-independent criteria does not mean the end of the conversation. Even though the final answer will be given only at the end of history, there is the possibility to mutually engage the different plausibility structures and to reach a tentative conclusion about their adequacy to explain and make sense of human reality.

> The obvious implication of this argument, therefore, is that the proper form of apologetics is the preaching of the gospel itself and the demonstration – which is not merely or primarily a matter of words – that it does provide the *best foundation* for a way of grasping and dealing with the mystery of our existence in this universe. Needless to say, this demonstration can never be more than *partial and*

tentative. It is, according to the gospel, only on the day of judgment that the demonstration will be complete and decisive. Until then, my commitment to the truth of the gospel is a commitment of faith. (95pc, 94; emphasis added)

Even though the test of adequacy does not provide indubitable certainty, it nevertheless allows the Christian to invite people of other persuasions to engage in an exploration of the adequacy of the Christian plausibility structure (see also Hempelmann 2004). However it is essential for Newbigin that the Christian in this conversation does not take the starting point from the contemporary plausibility structure but rather from the gospel itself and its inherent plausibility structure.

> There is a long tradition of Christian theology that goes under the name "apologetics" and that seeks to respond to this question and to demonstrate the "reasonableness of Christianity". The assumption often underlying titles of this kind is that the gospel can be made acceptable by showing that it does not contravene the requirements of reason as we understand them within the contemporary plausibility structure. The heart of my argument is that this is a mistaken policy. The story the church is commissioned to tell, if it is true, is bound to call into question any plausibility structure which is founded on other assumptions. The affirmation that the One by whom and through whom and for whom all creation exists is to be identified with a man who was crucified and rose bodily from the dead cannot possibly be accommodated within any plausibility structure except one of which it is the cornerstone. In any other place in the structure it can only be a stone of stumbling. The reasonableness of Christianity will be demonstrated (insofar as it can be) not by adjusting its claims to the requirements of a preexisting structure of thought but by showing how it can provide an alternative foundation for a different structure. (95pc, 93-94)

By emphasizing the distinction between two different plausibility structures Newbigin steers away from the danger to let the gospel become captive to any specific worldview. The gospel rather comes with its own authority and challenges the plausibility structure of any given culture. Whenever a person becomes convinced of the truth of the gospel this is the result of the work of the Spirit, not a consequence of some context-independent argument. The result is a certainty that does not rest on human reason but on the faithful character of God. It also is the beginning of a new way in which a new understanding of the world is sought, where the gospel is allowed to examine and challenge the contemporary plausibility structure rather than be confined by it.

Excursus: Karl Barth's Critique of Rationalism

Karl Barth in his critique of rationalism has made an important point that contributes to the issue debated here. Barth develops his thought from a critique of the theological developments of the 18th and 19th century. Scholastic theology in its attempt to form a Grand Unifying Theory of reality followed the idea of the *logos spermatikos* from the church fathers, but the emphasis shifted away from "seeds of truth" planted into philosophy towards the faculty of human reason and the human capacity to know these truths. With the introduction of the term "nature" into the discussion about religions, a major shift occurred. For the church fathers the subject was the *logos*, the divine, but scholastic theology started to focus on the natural faculties of the human being. Natural rationalism (*natura rationalis*) started to become the keyword (Galling 2000, 27672; Printed ed. Vol.5, 978).

Barth's critique of natural theology begins with the rationalistic tendencies of Neo-Protestantism. Neo-Protestant theologians (Joh. Franz Buddeus 1667-1729, Salomon van Til 1643-1713) used the concept of "natural religion" to argue that Christianity was the true religion, the superior religion. Barth points out that their approach – supporting the Christian religion by rational arguments and presenting it as the superior religion – has in fact prepared the way for the relativization of revelation. It is based on the premise, that revelation can be not only understood but adequately justified on the basis of human reason. This tendency is reinforced through rising rationalism. Natural religion was seen not simply as human possibility to understand divine revelation, but as premise to understand the fullness of divine revelation. Barth shows in detail how this rationalistic approach to revelation has turned theocentric theology – with the authority of divine revelation at its center – into anthropocentric theology – with the authority of human reason at its center; in other words, it has turned theology into philosophy. In essence it is nothing less than the sell-out of true theology.

> [A]t the end of the Foreword to vol. I of his dogmatics (1925) R. Seeberg calmly remarks that it might have been better to write a 'philosophy of religion' instead of a dogmatics; but interested philosophers and historians would, of course, take it in that way without sharing his particular theological presuppositions. Weighing all the circumstances, we must regard an utterance of this kind as a more significant and serious symptom than the very worst pages in the books of a Strauss or a Feuerbach. It shows that at the end of the period which started with Buddeus theology had lost any serious intention of taking itself seriously as theology. (Barth 1956, 291)

So while in the beginning the idea of natural theology was used to argue for the truth and superiority of the Christian religion, it ultimately confirmed the assumption that revelation would necessarily conform to human reason. In this process theology allowed human reason to become the ultimate source of the evaluation of truth. That is the reason why Barth argues so strongly against natural theology. Newbigin argues in a similar way:

> In trying to counter skepticism by calling in the help of philosophy to prove the existence of God, rather than by inviting people to believe in God's own revelation of himself in Jesus Christ, the Church abandoned its own proper ground and provided ... the tools for modern atheism. (91tt, 3)

Against this backdrop of 200 years of rationalistic influence on Christian theology Barth raises his voice for the supremacy of divine revelation over and against all human reason. It is a call for a new theocentric focus of theology, a call for a "theology from above," versus a "theology from below" which takes the human quest for salvation as its starting point.

While Barth was concerned with the relationship between revelation and religion, which is not at the center of this discussion, his argument about the consequences of the rationalist support of revelation must not be overlooked. The search for context-independent criteria which support and underscore the truth claim of the gospel in order to convince people that they "too *ought* to accept the truth claims of Christianity" (Netland 2004, 101) is in danger of following the same road that Barth has outlined in his critique. This excursus underlines Newbigin's critique of Netland's search for context-independent criteria. Apart from the fact that no such objective viewpoint is available for us as human beings, even if it were, the attempt to justify and support the claim of divine revelation with human reason would lead us down a dangerous road as Barth has shown. Human reason must not be allowed to take the position of judging the truth claim of divine revelation – even if it is initially done in order to support that very claim. This can only lead to the destruction of the authority of revelation as such. Newbigin in return insists that

> [A]uthority resides in Him who is the Author of all being. And since personal being can only be known in so far as the person chooses to reveal himself, and cannot be known by the methods which are appropriate to the investigation of impersonal matters and processes, authority must rest on divine revelation. (94tam, 60)

The witness of the church requires dialogue with the plausibility structure of the world. And in this conversation the vigor and integrity of the Christian worldview plays a role in underscoring the witness. But to convince a person of the truth of the Christian revelation can only be the work of the Spirit, not the work of the witness and his or her arguments.

> [O]ne must distinguish between the ways by which people are drawn to faith (which are as various as are the varieties of human nature and experience) and the foundation on which faith rests. This foundation cannot be anything provided by the philosopher. It can only be the action of God himself. The only ultimate authority in the new creation is its Author. (94tam, 70)

Here Newbigin explicitly points out the external authority that keeps the world from sliding into a pluralist relativism. He accepts the arguments of the sociologists of human knowledge which point out the impossibility of context-independent reasoning. Newbigin too is left with the necessity to make an initial faith commitment to a specific plausibility structure. And he can argue only from his own perspective. The reasons which support his plausibility structure are merely providing a provisional certainty by affirming the adequacy of the biblical plausibility structures for dealing with human reality. The final judgment on the truth of the different plausibility structures, however, will be given at the end of history. With this understanding Newbigin stays in the eschatological tension and remains true to the indispensability of divine revelation for human knowledge. And yet he recognizes the need and the possibility to engage in dialogue with people who hold to other plausibility structures and present the witness of the Spirit to them, a witness which the Spirit may use to lead them to this very same certainty of faith.

> If I am committed to seeking to understand what happened from within this Christian tradition, that is a decision for which I am responsible. But this decision and commitment is delivered from mere subjectivity by being made – as Polanyi would say – with universal intent. In other words, I cannot treat it as simply a personal decision; I am bound to publish it, to commend it to others, and to seek to show in the practice of life today that it is the rational tradition which is capable of giving greater coherence and intelligibility to all experience than any other tradition. (89gps, 77)

Commending the plausibility structure of the gospel to others may sound very much like Netland's positive apologetics. And like Newbigin Netland too acknowledges "that the very act of knowing anything at all is dependent on the sustaining and enabling grace of God" (Netland 1994, 107). However where Netland and Newbigin seem to part ways is in their understanding of the role that reason plays for the certainty of knowledge. While Netland is arguing for context-independent criteria for supporting the truth claims of the gospel, Newbigin is convinced that this kind of certainty can only be given at the culmination of history. In the present we have no choice but to commit ourselves to a specific view of the world. Reason does play a role, tentatively demonstrating the adequacy of the biblical worldview. But reason can never and – as Barth has shown – must never become the support structure to underscore the truth claim of the gospel. The personal commitment to the truth claim of the gospel in its own authority is always the first step. We believe in order to understand. And this commitment entails a challenge to our whole lives. "I can only affirm the objectivity of a truth claim which I make by committing myself to live and act in accordance with this claim" (95pc, 75; see also Vanhoozer 1999). Our certainty is given to us by the Spirit. It will be revealed for all only at the consummation of history.

Chapter 6

Conclusion

It has been the purpose of this study to show how the eschatological orientation of the biblical story and the eschatological tension between the present fulfillment and the future revelation of Christ's reign are of fundamental importance for Newbigin's theology of mission.

1. Retrospect

It is quite interesting to return at the conclusion of this study to the beginnings of Newbigin's theological formation at Westminster College which he describes in the fourth chapter of his autobiography (85ua, 30-38). There we find early expressions of his strong conviction about the centrality and objectivity of "the finished work of Christ" (85ua, 30). We find Newbigin leading a study on "The Kingdom of God and History" (85ua, 31). During these years Newbigin felt the disappointment about the rift between the evangelical CICCU and the supposedly liberal SCM. On the other hand, these were years which brought him in contact with a great number of influential ecumenical leaders, most prominent among them J. H. Oldham and W. Temple. Newbigin especially mentions that Oldham's ideas on church, community and state had a great influence on him. In the course of his involvement in the SCM he, together with A. Nash, drafted a statement that saw the church as "a foretaste of the new world for which we look," emphasizing the unity of the church not as unity built on "similarity of opinion, of programme or of temperament: it is the unity born of God's act of love in Christ received and answered in its members" (85ua, 34). During these years Newbigin took part in the first Swanwick camp which combined both practical work for the community and evangelistic campaigns. It was a step towards overcoming the tension between the advocates of direct evangelism and the promoters of the concern for social justice. In retrospect Newbigin observes: "[S]ceptics and critics had become friends and we ourselves had learned a lot both about the world and about the Gospel" (85ua, 35). Also his awareness of the "endemic injustice of the capitalist system" (85ua, 36) goes back to the early days of his theological studies.

A reading of Newbigin's reflections on that time in Cambridge reveals that all of the thematic aspects of this study have their roots in the time of his early theological formation, that they have continued to occupy him throughout his ministry and have found expression in his publications as he engaged the issues which the church faced in its participation in God's mission to the world. This underscores the sense of continuity in Newbigin's thinking which we have seen in the course of this study.

2. Summary

I have shown how the eschatological orientation and the eschatological tension are fundamental for Newbigin's understanding of history: God is leading the history of the cosmos to the day of consummation when the lordship of Christ will be revealed to all and the new creation will be established.

The eschatological orientation and the eschatological tension are fundamental for Newbigin's understanding of the character of the gospel as public truth. The gospel is neither religious teaching for private salvation, nor is it the launching of a program of humanization for the here and now. The character of the gospel as public truth demands that all spheres of life be brought under the lordship of Christ. But the establishment of the kingdom is a gift of God. It cannot be brought about by human efforts.

The eschatological orientation and the eschatological tension are fundamental for Newbigin's understanding of the church: It is sign, instrument, and foretaste of God's kingdom, the provisional incorporation of humankind into Christ, looking forward to the day when all its members will be fully conformed to the image of Christ and when all of humanity will be incorporated into Christ. Until that day it lives in the tension of a proper other-worldliness and a proper this-worldliness, in the tension of identification with the world and its cultures and dissociation from the world and its cultures, understanding its character in light of both a counter-cultural model and a model which emphasizes the identification of the church with a given culture. In light of the characterization of the church as the provisional incorporation of humankind into Christ, the church understands the importance of its unity for its mission to the world, and – despite all the shortcomings and setbacks of the "not yet" – continues to strive for a true unification of the one body of Christ.

The eschatological orientation and the eschatological tension are fundamental for Newbigin's understanding of mission. The understanding of mission refuses to be drawn into the Greek dichotomy of spirit versus matter and enables the church to keep a truly integrated view of mission in both word and deed, without dissolving the tension to either a purely other-worldliness nor distorting its sending into a program of humanization. This tension makes the mark of Christ's cross the mark of authenticity of the church's mission. Christ's death on the cross is seen in light of the eschatological outcome of history as the decisive victory over all powers and principalities. In the spirit of "bold humility" the church continues Christ's mission and proclaims the lordship of Christ, unmasking the powers as usurpers, thus pointing people of all times and places to the one who is the true Lord of all.

The eschatological orientation and the eschatological tension are fundamental for Newbigin's understanding of the church's witness in the context of religious pluralism. The church refuses to judge the religious experiences of people of other faiths apart from their encounter with Jesus Christ. This judgment belongs to Christ at the end of time. The gospel instead emphasizes the responsibility of those who have received the gospel and are now called to respond. Wherever the gospel is made known it calls people regardless of their religious affiliation to the foot of the cross to receive there God's judgment on their achievements – including their religious achievements – and the restoration of shalom for all their relationships as a gift from God.

Lastly, the eschatological orientation and the eschatological tension are fundamental for Newbigin's epistemology. To know the orientation and the outcome of the story while we are still in the middle of it we depend on God's self-revelation. The truth of it will only be revealed at the consummation of the story. In the present we have no other option than to make a choice about our commitment and to present our understanding of truth to the world. Rational arguments with regard to the coherence and adequacy of the biblical view of the world may give a tentative certainty. But our certainty finally rests on the faithfulness of a personal God, not on the competence of the human knower. We walk by faith until the revelation of Christ as Lord will finally reveal the truth to all.

3. Outlook

The question now remains: What does this mean for us at the beginning of a new century? Even a brief review of the events of the last few years, beginning with the turn of the millenium, shows how fast and drastically political changes can effect developments in mission. Pocock, van Rheenen, and McConnell address the question of "the changing face of world missions" on a broader basis and try to provide some orientation (Pocock et al. 2005). In light of global changes the church is constantly challenged to rethink its missionary task.

That is, however, not a new development. It is precisely what Newbigin has been doing during his lifetime. The argument of this dissertation is that a view for the eschatological direction of God's story with his world provides an important point of reference for the church to guide it in this process of reflection. It is the mission of the church which gives meaning to the interim time between the past and future revelation of Christ's reign. In reverse terms: The eschatological tension between the death and resurrection of Christ as the inauguration of his reign and his future return as its consummation provides the framework from which the church draws an adequate understanding of its participation in God's mission to the world. Therefore the church must always get its bearings for its mission-theology and its mission-practice from the eschatological orientation of God's story.

In what ways does the eschatological orientation of God's story bear upon the understanding and practice of mission? I will point out a few of the implications this might have for current missiological challenges.

3.1. The Story Character of the Gospel

The debate on contextualization, beginning in the early 1970s, has made us aware of the pitfalls of a positivist understanding of theology with its emphasis on one universal dogmatics applicable regardless of temporal, cultural, and socio-political circumstances. The dominance of Western theology in association with Western philosophy has rightly been challenged and questioned by churches in the Two-thirds World. Questioning the validity of a universal systematic theology, however, raises the question of the unity of theology as such. Do we have to give up the search for unity in theology in general, or are there other ways to pursue that sense of unity? Here biblical theology with its focus on the story character of the gospel provides an answer. The gospel is not only intended for all. It also encompasses human beings of all times and places. It gives people a place in God's story. The gospel presents us with a view of understanding our own life story as part of God's overarching story, integrated with the life stories of other people into the story of one community which centers around the person of Jesus Christ. This is what gives meaning and dignity to each individual story.

This story character of the gospel is – in my view – essential for thinking through the challenges which current globalization trends present to the church, whether we look at world migration or at the expansion of the free-market economic system.

> The God who scattered the nations at the tower of Babel is in these days bringing the nations back together through the millions of immigrants who are filling our cities. It is only the power of the gospel lived out in the community of believers that can make such diversity into a new humanity. (John Leonard, quoted in Pocock 2005, 40)

The impact of migration on the societies in Europe for example is a far greater challenge than the governments had originally perceived. The reactions in the Netherlands after the murder of film director Theo van Gogh in November 2004 or the responses to the republication of the Muhammad caricatures of a Danish caricaturist in a French newspaper in January 2006 illustrate how grave the challenges are. According to a recent article in "Die Welt," around the year 2010 more than 50% of all city dwellers in Germany under the age of 40 will have migration backgrounds (Lutz 2006). It is important that the church in Europe recognizes the implications of these developments for its mission. But it is also important that the church does not remain captive to a monocultural view, attempting to bring people into the church, and yet not recognizing that the church itself needs to change in this process in order that it may become the place where people of all nations can truly find their home as God's family. The paradigm of the expansion of the free-market economic system does not provide a model for the church and its mission (see Taber 2002). The dangers of new kinds of colonialism are all too real. The church needs to understand itself as the provisional incorporation of humankind into Jesus Christ. A growing awareness that the center of global Christianity has shifted away from the North and the West may help the Western church to free itself from a monocultural captivity. It needs to look at the question how both global and local dimensions can be incorporated in its ministry. The church in its global dimension needs to understand itself as a hermeneutical community focusing on one Lord and deriving its self understanding and its mission from one gospel. The theological focus on the story character of the gospel as God's story with humankind as a whole is an essential point of reference for this reflection.

3.2. The Gospel as Public Truth

In chapter five I have dealt extensively with this subject, which is one of the major emphases in Newbigin's work. Here I only want to underscore the relevance of this theme in light of current developments in Europe. The fact that the number of Muslim believers in European countries is on the rise is well known. The fact that the Muslim understanding of religion is very different from the common Western understanding of religion is, however, not often reflected in public discourse. The Western relegation of religion into the private sphere of life appears to be a paradigm that can easily accommodate religious pluralism. Whether one prays to Jesus Christ or to Allah doesn't seem to make a big difference. Muslims, of course, would never conceive it that way. Islam cannot be reduced to a private religion without concern for the public sphere. Its goal is expansion of the *ummah* and the establishment of Allah's law, the *shariah*, in all spheres of private and public life. The contribution which Newbigin brings to this debate is that the gospel is distinct from both the prevalent Western (and Eastern) view of religion as path to private salvation and the Islamic understanding of religion as the establishment of a theocracy.

And here is the challenge for the church. It needs to communicate to people immersed in the Western culture that the gospel is not just one more way to private salvation. It is part of the church's calling to make clear the implications of the gospel's claim for the public sphere – for the good of society as a whole. On the other hand, the church needs to distinguish the gospel message carefully from the Islamic paradigm of a world immanent theocracy. The key here is to keep the eschatological reservation in focus. The reign of Christ in the present is hidden, not yet revealed. The church is not able to establish that reign. It can only establish signs of that reign which point people to the person of Jesus Christ.

The growth of Islamic influence on European societies comes at a time when the secularized West has little to say to counter that claim. If the church does not break free from the Western relegation of religion into the private sphere, it must ultimately leave public discourse to the growing influence of Islam and to the rule of the majority.

In light of these developments the strengthening of Christian believers for their respective ministries in their spheres of influence in public life becomes ever more important. This is even more so as the social contexts today change ever more rapidly. I don't need to repeat that we are not talking about a return to the Constantinian age. But the church must reflect on the question of its structures in light of the missionary challenges its members face, not in light of the historical development of these structures nor in light of their functions for the church as an organization. Goheen has made an important contribution to that debate with his call for a synopsis of an Anabaptist model and a Reformed model of the church.

3.3. Mission in Tension

One of the prominent missiological questions of the recent past has been the question about the relationship between the verbal proclamation of the gospel and the socio-political involvement of the church as part of its mission. Using the term "holistic mission" will not ultimately answer the question. This kind of ministry has to be lived in order to be true. I have shown in chapter five how a true focus on the eschatological tension of the presence and the future of Christ's reign may help the church to overcome the Greek dichotomy of matter vs. spirit so that it is neither caught up in concerning itself only with people's souls nor ends up reducing mission to a program of world-immanent humanization.

The tension between the presence and future of Christ's reign reveals itself in other areas as well. There is the tension between an eager expectation of the saving intervention by Christ in a specific situation of need on the one hand and the fact that his answer to our petitions may turn out quite different from what we expected and had hoped for on the other. One prominent biblical example is the experience of John the Baptist (Matt 11:1-6). John could not only wish for his liberation from prison. The OT promises about the coming of the Messiah clearly confirmed that the liberation of prisoners would be part of the Messiah's ministry (Isa 35:5-6; 61:1). And yet, while Jesus confirmed that the OT promises were being fulfilled in him (Matt 11:4-5), he challenged John not to doubt him when his own situation seemed to contradict this claim (Matt 11:6).

The church and its individual members do encounter similar situations. We too are challenged not to let the apparent failure of Christ's salvific intervention to materialize become a stumbling block for our faith. It is not as if Christ would fail to "intervene" (see 63rtdt, 27). The challenge is to trust him that he is yet acting as sovereign Lord. The cross of Christ and his resurrection give a whole new perspective to these experiences of suffering that require perseverance in light of an apparent lack of victory. As Newbigin has pointed out victory is hidden in the suffering, and the mark of the cross is an integral part of the church's mission.

Wherever the church faces suffering in its mission it needs to get its bearings from the eschatological tension of Christ's reign. We may not be able to solve a whole lot of problems in the world. We will often have no answer to the problem of suffering, individual and corporate. We may at times feel overwhelmed by the experience of slow growth in mission or no growth at all. The sheer immensity of problems like e.g. the HIV-pandemic in many countries of Africa may seem to beat us. It is in situations like these that the eschatological dialectic of the presence and the future of Christ's reign can give us a perspective that is both realistic and hopeful at the same time. The true contribution of the church is not that it can provide answers in times of suffering. The true contribution is that it comes alongside those who suffer and shares with them the story of the one who came to take up our infirmities and carry our sorrows (Isa 53:4), who established the victory over the powers of evil on the cross once and for all, and in whose name we too can regain hope and stand up to challenge the powers with an eye on the future consummation of Christ's reign. This understanding of mission requires commitment and a long term perspective. Answers might be quickly delivered. But identification requires the building of trust and the sharing of one's life with others. This is the way that hope is truly communicated.

3.4. Proclaiming Truth as Wisdom

Whoever takes a closer look at the challenges for mission cannot overlook the developments in the sphere of religions. Here we no longer talk only about the encounter of the gospel with world religions. The trend towards multiple spiritualities (Pocock et al. 2005, 79-104) incorporates elements of both world religions and folk religious practices. The global actuality of religious pluralism has reached the West again, not only as a present reality but increasingly as a paradigm to embrace. Where unity is sought at all, the philosophical construct of an "ultimate real" behind the various religious expressions and the relegation of religious experience into the private sphere of life are rapidly gaining support in Western society.

The church has to face both the epistemological challenge of knowing truth and the missiological challenge of proclaiming truth in a pluralist context. This is at the core of Newbigin's concern. In a personal letter to Albrecht Hauser he writes in December 1988:

> I fear we are witnessing something akin to what happened to Greek civilization in the end, namely an abandonment of the faith that ultimate truth is knowable. The writings we criticize [The Myth of Christian Uniqueness, ed by P. Knitter and J. Hick] are evidence of a profound failure of nerve and an abandonment of the greatest thing that human beings can aim for, namely to grasp and to be grasped by truth. (98plah)

Again, I don't want to repeat here what I have said earlier. Suffice it to say that we need to think of truth as "a way of life," as "wisdom rather than [...] knowledge" (Vanhoozer 1999, 132 and 139). Speaking about truth in a pluralist context requires our integrity as witnesses, that we live by the very truth which we proclaim. Nothing else will convince the world of the truthfulness of the gospel. And our own conviction of the truthful character of the gospel rests on the truthful character of a personal God who has factually acted in history and has thus revealed himself. The eschatological verification we are still awaiting. In the meantime it is our calling to be the "hermeneutic of the gospel" for the world (80ykc, 63).

4. Final Word

The eschatological character of the church's mission is beautifully expressed by Newbigin in an experience which he tells from his time in India. It illustrates the sign-character of the church's mission, namely to reflect the glory of Christ, which is in the process of coming into this world and brings the light of the future (in the sense of *advent*) into the present.

> I think that a very good and valid symbol of our mission is to be found in an experience with which those of us who have lived in India are familiar. When we have to go to a distant village in our pastoral duty we try to start very early in the morning, so that we do not have to walk in the heat of the day. And it sometimes happens that we have to set off in total darkness; perhaps we are going towards the west so that there is no light in the sky and everything is dark. But as we go, a party of people travelling the opposite way comes to meet us. There will be at least a faint light on their faces. If we stop and ask them: "Where does the light come from?", they will simply ask us to turn round (do the U-turn) and look towards the east. A new day is dawning, and the light we saw was just its faint reflection in the faces of those going that way. They did not possess the light; it was a light given to them. The church is that company which, going the opposite way to the majority, facing not from life towards death, but from death towards life, is given already the first glow of the light of a new day. It is that light that is the witness. (87mcw, 21)

Reference List

Primary Literature

37cfmw
> 1937. *Christian freedom in the modern world.* London: Student Christian Movement Press.

38cibc
> 1938. Can I be a Christian? – VIII. *The Spectator* 1938 (May 6): 800.

41kgip
> 2003. The Kingdom of God and the idea of progress. In *Signs amid the rubble: The purposes of God in human history*, ed. G. Wainwright, 1-55. Grand Rapids, Mich.: W.B. Eerdmans Pub.

42wig
> 1942. *What is the gospel? SCM Study Series No.6.* Madras: Christian Literature Society.

45ofmi
> 1945. The ordained foreign missionary in the Indian church. *International Review of Missions* 34: 86-94.

48csu
> 1948. The Ceylon scheme of union: A South Indian view. *South India Churchman* (June): 162-163.

48dacp
> 1948. The duty and authority of the church to preach the gospel. In *The Church's Witness to God's Design, Amsterdam Assembly Series, Vol.2*, ed. H. Kraemer and L. Newbigin, 19-35. New York: Harper Brothers.

48rc
> 1948. *The reunion of the church: A defence of the South India scheme.* London: SCM Press.

50eea
> 1950. The evangelization of Eastern Asia. *International Review of Mission* 39 (1950): 137-145. Original Publication: The Evangelization of Eastern Asia. In: The Christian Prospect in Eastern Asia: Papers and Minutes of the Eastern Asia Christian Conference, Bangkok, December 3-11, 1949, 77-87. New York: Friendship.

51ott
> 1951. *Our task today.* A charge given to the fourth meeting of the diocesan council, Tirumangalam, December 18-20, 1951. Unpublished paper.

Reference List 245

51sid
1951. *A South India diary.* London: SCM Press. 1952 American edition. *That all may be one. A South India diary – the story of an experiment in Christian unity.* New York: Association Press. New prologue by E.H. Johnson. 1961 Revised edition. London: SCM. New foreword and epilogue.

51wich
1951. What is the Christian hope? *Listener* (20 September) 1951: 464-465.

52clwc
1952. The Christian layman in the world and in the church. *National Christian Council Review* 72: 185-189.

52nch
1952. The nature of the Christian hope. *Ecumenical Review* 4: 282-284.

53ccgc
1953. Can the churches give a common message to the world. *Theology Today* 9: 512-518.

53ch
1953. The Christian hope. In *Missions under the cross*, ed. N. Goodall, 107-116. New York: Friendship Press, distributed for the International Missionary Council. Address given in 1952 at the enlarged meeting of the IMC at Willingen.

53hg
1953. *The household of God: Lectures on the nature of the church.* London: SCM Press. Kerr Lectures given at Trinity College, Glasgow, November 1952. 1954 American edition. New York: Friendship Press. Section headings added. 1964 Revised edition. London: SCM. 1998 Reprinted. Carlisle: Paternoster Press.

53mc
1953. *The ministry of the Church, ordained, paid and unpaid.* London: Edinburgh House Press. Reprinted as The Ministry of the Church. *National Christian Council Review* 73: 351-355.

54rgo
1954. *Review of God's order: The Ephesian letter and this present time*, by John A. MacKay. *Theology Today* 10: 543-547.

54lwlc
1954. The life and witness of the local church. In *The Church in a changing world: Addresses and reports of the National Christian Council of India, Guntur, November 5-10*, 1953, 7-16. Mysore: Wesley Press.

54pccc
1954. The present Christ and the coming Christ. *Ecumenical Review* 6, no. 2: 118-123.

54wsot
: 1954. Why study the Old Testament? *National Christian Council Review* 74: 71-76.

55qutr
: 1955. The quest for unity through religion. *Journal of Religion* 35: 17-33. Thomas Memorial Lecture given at the University of Chicago, 1954. 1955 Reprinted in *Indian Journal of Theology* 4, no. 2: 1-17.

56ss
: 1956. *Sin and salvation*. London: SCM Press. Republished in 1957 Philadelphia: Westminster Press; 1968 Madras: Christian Literature Society.

56wgc
: 1956. The wretchedness and greatness of the church. *National Christian Council Review* 76: 472-477. Sermon preached at the united service during the triennial meeting of the National Christian Council of India, Allahabad.

56wjc
: 1956. Witnessing to Jesus Christ. In *Presenting Christ to India today, three addresses and a sermon delivered to the Synod of the Church of South India, Tiruchirappalli, January 1956,* ed. P. D. Devanandan, A. E. Inbanathan, A. J. Appasamy and L. Newbigin, 57-62. Madras: Christian Literature Society.

57nuws
: 1957. The nature of the unity we seek: From the Church of South India. *Religion in Life* 26, no. 2: 181-190.

58lmc
: 1958. The life and mission of the church. In *The Life and Mission of the Church*, ed. C. I. Itty. Bangalore, India: Student Christian Movement of India, 4-9. Reprinted 1959 in *Chaplain* 16, no. 2: 37-43.

58obog
: 1958. *One body, one gospel, one world. The Christian mission today.* New York: Friendship Press.

59guhc
: 1959. The gathering up of history into Christ. In *The Missionary Church in East and West*, ed. C. C. West and D. Paton, 81-90. London: SCM. Address given in 1957 at the Ecumenical Institute in Bossey.

59scmt
: 1959. The summons to Christian mission today. *International Review of Mission* 48: 177-189. Address given at the Annual Dinner of the North American Advisory Committee of the IMC, New York, November 1958.

59wgdu
: 1959. Will God dwell upon earth? *National Christian Council Review* 79: 99-102. Text of a sermon preached at the dedication of a chapel in a Christian college.

60bicu
: 1960. Basic issues in church union. In *We were brought together*, ed. D. M. Taylor, 155-169. Sydney: Australian Council for the WCC. Address given at the National Conference of Australian Churches, Melbourne, February 1960.

60bsft
: 1960. Bible studies: Four talks on 1 Peter. In *We were brought together*, ed. D. M. Taylor, 93-123. Sydney: Australian Council for the WCC. Addresses given at the National Conference of Australian Churches, Melbourne, February 1960.

60lmc
: 1960. The life and mission of the church. In *We were brought together*, ed. D. M. Taylor, 59-69. Sydney: Australian Council for the WCC. Keynote address given at the National Conference of Australian Churches, Melbourne, February 1960.

60mcan
: 1960. *Mission of the church to all the nations.* Address given at the NCC [CUSA] General Assembly, San Francisco, December 5.

60muc
: 1960. *The mission and unity of the church.* Grahamstown, South Africa: Rhodes University. Peter Ainslie memorial lecture 11, 17 October 1960. Republished in 1963: Is there still a missionary job today? In *563 St.Columba: Fourteenth Centenary, 1963.* Glasgow: Iona Community.

60pop
: 1960. The pattern of partnership. In *A decisive hour for the Christian mission*, ed. L. Newbigin, W. A. Visser't Hooft, and D. T. Niles, 34-45. London: SCM Press.

60rc
: 1960. *The reunion of the church: A defence of the South India scheme.* Rev. 2d ed. London: SCM Press.

60whal
: 1960. The work of the Holy Spirit in the life of the Asian churches. In *A decisive hour for the Christian mission*, ed. L. Newbigin, W. A. Visser't Hooft, and D. T. Niles, 18-33. London: SCM Press.

61ftow
> 1961. *A faith for this one world? Religious Book Club 145.* London: SCM Press. The William Belden Noble Lectures given at Harvard, November 1958.

61icd
> 1961. *Is Christ divided? A plea for Christian unity in a revolutionary age.* Grand Rapids: Eerdmans.

61uam
> 1961. Unity and mission. *Covenant Quarterly* 19 (November): 3-6.

62bomm
> 1962. Bringing our missionary methods under the word of God. *Occasional Bulletin from the Missionary Research Library* 13, no. 11: 1-9. Address at a mission consultation of the Presbyterian Church, U.S.

62clu
> 1962. The church – local and universal. In *The Church – local and universal: Things we face together*, ed. L. T. Lyall and L. Newbigin, 20-28. London: World Dominion Press.

62f/mm
> 1962. Foreword. In *Missionary methods: St. Paul's or ours?* ed. R. Allen, i-iii. Grand Rapids: Eerdmans.

62mdem
> 1962. The missionary dimension of the ecumenical movement. *Ecumenical Review* 14 (Ja 1962): 207-215. Reprinted in *International Review of Mission* 70 (October 1981): 240-246. Newbigin's address at the integration of the International Missionary Council and the World Council of Churches at the opening session of the Third Assembly of the World Council of Churches held in New Delhi, November 19, 1961.

63curm
> 1963. *The church's unity in relation to its missionary task.* Atlanta, Ga. Issued by Board of Women's Work Presbyterian Church U.S. A message given at a Pre-Assembly Conference on World Missions and Evangelism, sponsored by the Board of World Missions and the Division of Evangelism of the Board of Church Extension, Presbyterian Church, U.S.

63jsmc
> 1963. Jesus the servant and man's community. In *Christ's call to service now*, ed. A. Reeves, 23-33. London: SCM Press. Address given at the Student Christian Congress, Bristol, January 1-6, 1963.

63rtdt
> 1963. *The relevance of Trinitarian doctrine for today's mission, CWME Study Pamphlet No.2.* London: Edinburgh House Press. 1964 American

edition: *Trinitarian faith and today's mission*. Richmond: John Knox Press. 1998 *Reissued as Trinitarian doctrine for today's mission*. Carlisle: Paternoster Press.

64ccre
1964. The church: Catholic, Reformed, and Evangelical. *Episcopalian* 129: 12-15, 48.

66c
1966. Conversion. *Religion and Society (Bangalore)* 13, no. 4: 30-42. Notes of an address given at the Nasrapur Consultation, March 1966. Originally published as: Conversion. *National Christian Council Review* 86: 309-323. Also published in *Renewal for mission*, ed. David Lyon and Albert Manuel, 33-46. Madras: CLS (1967).

66hrsm
1966. *Honest religion for secular man*. Philadelphia: Westminster Press. Original edition, *Honest religion for secular man* . London: SCM. The Firth Lectures, University of Nottingham, November 1964. Republished in 1967 by Lucknow Publishing House.

68bima
1968. *Behold, I make all things new*. Madras: Christian Literature Society. Talks given at a youth conference in Kerala, May 1968.

69fc
1969. *The finality of Christ*. London/Richmond: SCM/John Knox Press. The Lyman Beecher Lectures, Yale Divinity School, April 1966. Also given as the James Reid Lectures at Cambridge University.

70bsl
1970. Bible study lectures. Cross and resurrection. *Mid-Stream* 9 (Fall): 193-231. Also published in 1970 as: The Bible Study Lectures. In: *Digest of the Proceedings of the Ninth Meeting of the Consultation on Christian Union*, ed. Paul A.Crow, 193-231. Princeton: Consultation on Church Union. Lectures given in St. Louis, Missouri on March 9-13, 1970.

70cu
1970. Co-operation and unity. *International Review of Mission* 59: 67-74.

70msc
1970. Mission to six continents. In *A history of the ecumenical movement. Vol. 2, 1948-1968*, ed. H. E. Fey, 171-197. London/Philadelphia: SPCK/Westminster.

71csc
1971. The church as a servant community. *National Christian Council Review* 91: 256-264.

71rsh
: 1971. Review of *Salvation and humanisation*, by M M Thomas, 1971. *Religion and Society (Bangalore)* 18 (March): 71-80.

72bck
: 1972. Baptism, the church and koinonia. Three letters and a comment. *Religion and Society (Bangalore)* 19 (March): 69-90.

72hsc
: 1972. *The Holy Spirit and the church*. Madras: Christian Literature Society. Address originally given at a convention in Madras, April 1972.

73fsvu
: 1973. *The form and structure of the visible unity of the Church*. In *So sende ich euch: Festschrift für D.Dr.Martin Pörksen zum 70. Geburtstag*; ed. by Otto Wack et al., 124-141. Korntal bei Stuttgart: Evang. Missionsverlag. Also published in two parts as: *The form and structure of the visible unity of the Church*. *National Christian Council Review* 92 (1972): 444-451 and 93 (1973): 4-18. Republished in *One in Christ* 13 (1977): 107-126.

73snhc
: 1973. Salvation, the new humanity and cultural-communal solidarity. *Bangalore Theological Forum* 5, no. 2: 1-11.

74sh
: 1974. Salvation and humanization. A discussion, co-authored with M. M. Thomas. In *Crucial issues in mission today*, ed. G. H. Anderson and T. F. Stransky, 217-229. New York/Grand Rapids: Paulist Press/Eerdmans.

75bwku
: 1975. 'But what kind of unity?' *National Christian Council Review* 95: 487-491.

76aopa
: 1976. All in one place or all of one sort. In *Creation, Christ and culture*, ed. R. W. A. McKinney, 288-306. Edinburgh: T & T Clark. Response to *Christian unity and Christian diversity*, by John Macquarrie. London: SCM. Reprinted in *Mid-Stream*, 15: 323-341.

76bsr8
: 1976. *Bible study on Romans 8*. Bible study given at the conference on "Church in the inner city" in Birmingham, Sep 1976. Unpublished paper. See www.newbigin.net for 76bsr8.pdf.

77bpmi
: 1977. The basis, purpose and manner of inter-faith dialogue. *Scottish Journal of Theology* 30, no. 3: 253-270. German translations: Christen im Dialog mit Nichtchristen. *Theologie der Gegenwart* 20, no. 3: 159-166.

Also: Dialog zwischen verschiedenen Glauben. *Zeitschrift für Mission* 3, no. 2: 83-98.

77gs

1977. *'The Good Shepherd'. Meditations on Christian ministry in today's world*. Rev. 1st American ed. Grand Rapids, Mich.: Eerdmans. Original edition, 1974 Madras: Christian Literature Society.

77trsp

1977. Teaching religion in a secular plural society. *Learning for Living* 17, no. 2: 82-88. Address given at the annual general meeting of the Christian Education Movement. 1978 reprinted in: *Christianity in the classroom*, ed Christian Education Movement, 1-11. London. 1982 reprinted in *New directions in religious education*, ed. John Hull, 97-108. London: Falmer Press.

77wilc

1977. What is a local church truly united? *Ecumenical Review* 29 (April): 115-128.

78ctc

1978. Christ and the cultures. *Scottish Journal of Theology* 31, no. 1: 1-22. A paper read to the 1977 Conference of the Society for the Study of Theology. Adapted as part of chapter nine of *The open secret*, see 78os.

78os

1978. *The open secret: Sketches for a missionary theology*. London: SPCK. 1978 American edition. Grand Rapids: Eerdmans. 1995 Revised edition. New subtitle: *An introduction to the theology of mission*. Grand Rapids: Eerdmans.

79cjh

1979. The centrality of Jesus for history. In *Incarnation and myth: The debate continued*, ed. M. Goulder, 197-210. Grand Rapids: Eerdmans. Followed by a comment on Lesslie Newbigin's Essay, by Maurice Wiles, 211-213.

80cwu

1980. Common witness and unity. *International Review of Mission* 69 (April): 158-160. Written for the Joint Working Group Study on Common Witness of the Roman Catholic Church and the World Council of Churches, Venice, 29 May-2 June, 1979.

80htsh

1980. He that sitteth in the heavens shall laugh. In *Imagination and the future*, ed. J. A. Henley, 3-7. Melbourne: Hawthorne Press.

80ykc

1980. *Your kingdom come: Reflections on the theme of the Melbourne*

Conference on World Mission and Evangelism 1980. Leeds: John Paul The Preacher's Press. Written in preparation for the Melbourne 1980 conference of the Commission on World Mission and Evangelism, WCC, and presented as the Waldstrom Lectures at the Theological Seminary of the Swedish Covenant Church, Lidingo, September 1979. 1980: American edition. *Sign of the Kingdom*. Grand Rapids: Eerdmans.

81pc

1981. Politics and the covenant. *Theology* 84: 356-363.

82buc

1982. Bishops in a united church. In *Bishops but what kind*, ed. P. Moore, 149-161. London: SPCK.

82ccee

1982. Cross-currents in ecumenical and evangelical understandings of mission. *International Bulletin of Missionary Research* 6, no. 4: 146-151. Responses by Paul Schrotenboer and C. Peter Wagner, pp.152-154. Reply by Lesslie Newbigin pp.154-155.

82lhc

1982. *The light has come: An exposition of the Fourth Gospel*. Edinburgh/Grand Rapids, Mich.: Handsel Press/W.B. Eerdmans.

83ckac

1983. *Christ, kingdom and church: A reflection on the papers of George Yule and Andrew Kirk*. Unpublished paper, located in Selly Oak archives. (Approximate date).

83cwr

1983. Christ and the world of religions. *Churchman* 97, no. 1: 16-30. Written for a collection of reflections on the theme of the Vancouver 1983 WCC Assembly, "Jesus Christ, the Life of the World." 1984 reprinted in *Reformed Review* 37 (Spring): 202-213.

83os84

1983. *The other side of 1984: Questions for the churches*. Geneva: World Council of Churches.

85cfsw

1985. *Christian faith in a secularized world*. Unpublished paper. See www.newbigin.net for 85cfsw.pdf.

85cwbc

1987. Can the West be converted? *International Bulletin of Missionary Research* 11: 2-7. See also: *Princeton Seminary Bulletin* 6, no. 1: 25-37 (1985).

85fc
1985. A fellowship of churches. *Ecumenical Review* 37: 175-181.

85ua
1985. *Unfinished agenda: An autobiography.* Grand Rapids: W.B. Eerdmans.

85wscp
1985. *The welfare state. A Christian perspective.* Oxford: Oxford Institute for Church and Society. The Gore Memorial Lecture given at Westminster Abbey in November 1984. Republished in Theology 88: 173-182.

86bep
1986. A British and European perspective. In *Entering the Kingdom: A fresh look at conversion*, ed. M. Hill, 57-68. Middlesex, UK: British Church Growth Association/MARC Europe.

86bvdw
1986. The biblical vision: Deed and word inseparable. *Concern* 28, no. 8: 1-3, 36.

86cwk
2003. Church, world, kingdom. In *Signs amid the rubble: The purposes of God in human history*, ed. G. Wainwright, 95-109. Grand Rapids: W.B. Eerdmans. The third of the Henry Martyn lectures, delivered at the university of Cambridge in 1986.

86fg
1986. *Foolishness to the Greeks: The Gospel and Western culture.* London/Geneva/Grand Rapids: SPCK/WCC/W.B. Eerdmans. The Benjamin B. Warfield Lectures given at Princeton Theological Seminary, March 1984.

87mcw
1987. *Mission in Christ's way: Bible studies.* Geneva: World Council of Churches.

87po
1987. The pastor's opportunities. VI. Evangelism in the city. *Expository Times* 98: 355-358. Reprinted as: Evangelism in the City. *Reformed Review* 41 (Autumn 1987): 3-8.

88bcw
1988. On being the church for the world. In *The Parish church*, ed. G. Ecclestone, 25-42. Oxford: A .R. Mowbray.

88cfwr
1988. The Christian faith and the world religions. In *Keeping the faith: Essays to mark the centenary of Lux Mundi*, ed. G. Wainwright, 310-340. London/Philadelphia: SPCK/Fortress Press.

88rsts
: 1988. Religion, science and truth in the school curriculum. *Theology* 91: 186-193.

88spts
: 1988. A sermon preached at the thanksgiving service for the 50th anniversary of the Tambaram Conference of the International Missionary Council. *International Review of Mission* 77: 325-331.

88st
: 1988. The significance of Tambaram – fifty years later. *Missionalia* 16, no. 2: 79-85.

89gps
: 1989. *The Gospel in a pluralist society*. Geneva/Grand Rapids: WCC/Eerdmans.

89m90
: 1989. Mission in the 1990s: Two views. *International Bulletin of Missionary Research* 13, no. 3: 98-102.

89rmcu
: 1989. Review of *The Myth of Christian Uniqueness*, ed. John Hick and Paul Knitter. *Ecumenical Review* 41, no. 3: 468-469.

89rpuj
: 1989. Religious pluralism and the uniqueness of Jesus Christ. *International Bulletin of Missionary Research* 13, no. 2: 50-54.

90bgso
: 1990. The Bible: God's story and ours. *Reform* (January): 7. Part of a series of eleven articles published in the magazine of the United Reformed Church.

90chs
: 1990. *Come Holy Spirit: Renew the whole creation*. Birmingham, Eng.: Selly Oak Colleges. Address given to the Ecumenical Summer School at St. Andrew's Hall, Selly Oak Colleges.

90ea
: 1990. Episcopacy and authority. *Churchman* 104, no. 4: 335-339. 1991 reprinted in *Liberate oversight: Episcopal ministry today*, ed. G. Ogilvie, 17-21. Bramcote, Notts: Grove Books.

90goc
: 1990. *The gospel and our culture*. London: Catholic Missionary Education Centre. Mission Today Pamphlet no. 47.

90mmwc
1990. A mission to modern Western culture. In *The San Antonio report. Your will be done: Mission in Christ's way*, ed. F. R. Wilson, 162-166. Geneva: WCC Publications.

90qast
1990. A question to ask. A story to tell. *Reform* (November): 11. Part of a series of eleven articles published in the magazine of the United Reformed Church.

90rm
1990. Religion for the marketplace. In *Christian uniqueness reconsidered: The myth of a pluralistic theology of religions*, ed. G. D'Costa, 135-148. Maryknoll: Orbis Books.

90ttph
1990. This is the turning point of history. *Reform* (April): 4. Part of a series of eleven articles published in the magazine of the United Reformed Church. Newbigin gave the title: "The turning point of history."

90witc
1990. *What is the culture?* Unpublished paper. Address at the first regional conference jointly sponsored by the Gospel and Our Culture and the British and Foreign Bible Society, on the theme "Mission to Our Culture in the Light of Scripture and the Christian Tradition," held at Hoddesdon, Hertfordshire, on Oct 15-17, 1990. See www.newbigin.net for 90witc.pdf.

91bifr
1991. The bible and inter-faith relations. Coauthored with H. Dan Beeby. In *Using the bible today: Contemporary interpretations of Scripture*, ed. D. Cohn-Sherbok, 180-187. London: Bellew Publishing.

91tt
1991. *Truth to tell: The gospel as public truth.* London/Grand Rapids: SPCK/W. B. Eerdmans. Oosterhaven Lecture series at Western Theological Seminary, Holland, Michigan.

91uo
1991. Union, organic. In *Dictionary of the ecumenical movement*, ed. N. Lossky, J. M. Bonino, J. S. Pobee, T. F. Stransky, G. Wainwright, and P. Webb, 1028-1030. Geneva/Grand Rapids: WCC/Eerdmans.

91uoa
1991. Unity of 'all in each place'. In *Dictionary of the ecumenical movement*, ed. N. Lossky, J. M. Bonino, J. S. Pobee, T. F. Stransky, G. Wainwright, and P. Webb, 1043-1046. Geneva/Grand Rapids: WCC/Eerdmans.

92eh
: 1992. The end of history. *The Gospel and Our Culture (U.K.)* 13: 1-2.

92lwav
: 1992. The legacy of W. A. Visser't Hooft. *International Bulletin of Missionary Research* 16, no. 2: 78-82.

92rpuj
: 1992. Religious pluralism and the uniqueness of Jesus Christ. In *Many other ways? Questions of religious pluralism*, ed. M. Bage, R. E. Hedlund, and P. B. Thomas, 69-80. Madras: ISPCK, for the Church Growth Research Centre McGavran Institute.

92wj
: 1992. Whose justice? *Ecumenical Review* 44, no. 3: 308-311.

93cfwk
: 1993. Certain faith. What kind of certainty? *Tyndale Bulletin* 44, no. 2: 339-350.

93kogh
: 1993. The kingdom of God and our hopes for the future. In *The Kingdom of God and human society*, ed. R. Barbour, 1-12. Edinburgh: T & T Clark.

93reit
: 1994. Ecumenical Amnesia. Review of *Ecumenism in transition: A paradigm shift in the ecumenical movement?* by Konrad Raiser. *International Bulletin of Missionary Research* 18, no. 1: 2-5. Originally published in 1993 in: *One in Christ* 29, no. 3: 269-275.

93rpma
: 1993. Religious pluralism: A missiological approach. *Studia Missionalia* 42: 227-244.

93ua
: 1993. *Unfinished agenda: An updated autobiography*. Edinburgh/London/Geneva: Saint Andrew Press/SPCK/WCC.

94awis
: 1994. *A word in season: Perspectives on Christian world missions*. Edinburgh/Grand Rapids, Mich.: Saint Andrews Press/W.B. Eerdmans. Collection of works, most of them previously unpublished or published only in languages other than English.

94cc
: 1994. Confessing Christ in a Multi-Religion society. *Scottish Bulletin of Evangelical Theology* 12 (Autumn): 125-136.

94rtkr
> 1994. Reply to Konrad Raiser. *International Bulletin of Missionary Research* 18, no. 2: 51-52. See also 93reit and Raiser 1994.

94tam
> 1994. Truth and authority in modernity. In *Faith and Modernity*, ed. P. Sampson, V. Samuel, and C. Sugden, 60-88. Oxford, U.K.: Regnum Books. Paper read at the Conference of the Lausanne Committee on World Evangelisation in Modern Western Culture held in Uppsala, Sweden, in 1993.

95nblh
> 1995. *New birth into a living hope.* Unpublished paper. Keynote address on 1 Peter 1:3 given on August 28, 1995 at the European Area Council of the World Alliance of Reformed Churches in Edinburgh. See www.newbigin.net for 95nblh.pdf.

95os
> 1995. *The open secret: An introduction to the theology of mission.* Rev. ed. Grand Rapids: Eerdmans.

95pc
> 1995. *Proper confidence: Faith, doubt, and certainty in Christian discipleship.* Grand Rapids: Eerdmans.

96ac
> 2003. "... and culture." In *Signs amid the rubble: The purposes of God in human history*, ed. G. Wainwright, 116-121. Grand Rapids: W.B. Eerdmans. Address delivered to the World Conference on Mission and Evangelism in Salvador de Bahia, Brazil, Dec. 1996.

96lpe
> 1996. Lay presidency at the eucharist. *Mid-Stream* 35 (April): 177-182. Reprinted in *Theology* 99: 366-370.

96mic
> 1996. Modernity in context. In *Modern, postmodern and Christian*, ed. J. J. Reid, L. Newbigin, and D. J. Pullinger, 1-12. Carberry, Scotland: Handsel Press.

96tam
> 1996. *Truth and authority in modernity.* Christian Mission and Modern Culture Series, ed. A. Neely, H. W. Pipkin, and W. R. Shenk. Valley Forge, Pa.: Trinity Press International.

96tg
> 2003. "The gospel ..." In *Signs amid the rubble: The purposes of God in human history*, ed. G. Wainwright, 113-115. Grand Rapids: W.B. Eerd-

mans. Address delivered to the World Conference on Mission and Evangelism in Salvador de Bahia, Brazil, Dec. 1996.

97dgc
1997. The dialogue of gospel and culture. Reflections on the Conference on World Mission and Evangelism, Salvador, Bahia, Brazil. *International Bulletin of Missionary Research* 21, no. 2: 50-52.

97tapt
1997. The Trinity as public truth. In *The Trinity in a pluralistic age*, ed. K. J. Vanhoozer, 1-8. Grand Rapids/Cambridge, U.K.: Eerdmans. Presented at the Fifth Edinburgh Dogmatics Conference on "The Trinity in a Pluralistic Age" held at Edinburgh, August 31 to September 3, 1993.

98agt
1998. Announcing God's tangible and universal kingdom. *Auburn Report* 10, no. 5: 8-10. The second in a two-part series.

98cmsc
1998. Can a modern society be Christian? In *Christian witness in society. A tribute to M. M. Thomas*, ed. K. C. Abraham, 95-108. Bangalore: Board of Theological Education, Senate of Serampore College.

98ewm
1998. Evangelism and the whole mission of the church. *Auburn Report* 10, no. 4: 7-9. The first in a two-part series.

98fp
1998. *Faith and power: Christianity and Islam in 'secular' Britain*. London: SPCK. Coauthored with Jenny Taylor and Lamin Sanneh. Newbigin coauthored the preface and "The secular myth" (pp. 3-24), and authored "A light to the nations: Theology in politics" (pp. 135-165).

98hg
1998. *The household of God: Lectures on the nature of the church*. Carlisle: Paternoster Press. Original edition, *The household of God: Lectures on the nature of the church*. London: SCM, 1953 (53hg).

98plah
1998. *Personal letters to Albrecht Hauser*. Unpublished excerpts of personal correspondence with Kirchenrat der Evangelischen Landeskirche Württemberg und Fachreferent für Mission, Albrecht Hauser, Stuttgart, compiled by Hauser on Jan 31, 1998.

99wtb
1999. *A walk through the Bible*. Louisville, Ky.: Westminster John Knox Press.

Secondary Literature

Advisory Commission. 1954. Report of the advisory commission on the main theme of the second assembly. Christ – the hope of the world. In *The Christian hope and the task of the church: six ecumenical surveys and the report of the Assembly*, ed. World Council of Churches: Part VI, i-51. New York: Harper.

Advisory Commission, Lesslie Newbigin, and W. A. Visser't Hooft. 1951. The first report of the advisory commission on the theme of the Second Assembly of the World Council of Churches. *Ecumenical Review* 4, no. 1: 71-79.

Ahrens, Theodor. 2005. Versöhnung in der ökumenischen Diskussion. *Zeitschrift für Mission* 31, no. 3: 162-173.

Aleaz, K. P. 2002. The globalization of poverty and the exploitation of the gospel. In *A scandalous prophet: The way of mission after Newbigin*, ed. Thomas F. Foust, George R. Hunsberger, Andrew J. Kirk, and Werner Ustorf, 165-173. Grand Rapids: Eerdmans.

Anastasios (Yannoulatos). 1990. In tribute to Bishop Lesslie Newbigin. *International Review of Mission* 79: 86-101.

Anderson, Gerald H. 1971. Theology of mission. In *Concise dictionary of the christian world mission*, ed. Stephen C. Neill, Gerald H. Anderson, and John Goodwin, 594-595. Nashville and New York: Abingdon Press.

Arias, Mortimer. 1976. That the world may believe. *International Review of Mission* 65: 13-46.

_____. 1984. *Announcing the reign of God: Evangelization and the subversive memory of Jesus*. Philadelphia: Fortress.

Aydin, Mahmut. 2002. Globalization and the gospel: A Muslim view. In *A scandalous prophet: The way of mission after Newbigin*, ed. Thomas F. Foust, George R. Hunsberger, Andrew J. Kirk, and Werner Ustorf, 174-181. Grand Rapids: Eerdmans.

Bailyes, Alan J. 1996. Evangelical and Ecumenical Understandings of Mission. *International Review of Mission* 85: 485-503.

Barth, Karl. 1956. *Church dogmatics. Vol. 1/2*. Edinburgh: T.& T. Clark.

Bauckham, Richard. 2003. *Bible and Mission: Christian witness in a postmodern world*. Carlisle/Grand Rapids: Paternoster/Baker Academic.

Beltran, Benigno. 1995. Tomorrow is our permanent address: Toward a trinitarian theology for the city. In *Signs of hope in the city*, ed. Robert C. Linthicum, 17-21. Monrovia, Calif.: Marc.

Berger, Peter L. 1979. *The heretical imperative: Contemporary possibilities of religious affirmation*. Garden City, N.Y.: Anchor Press.

Berkhof, Hendrikus. 1964. The summing up of all things. In *Key words of the Gospel: Bible studies delivered at the Mexico meeting of the World Council of Churches Commission on World Mission and Evangelism, 1963*, ed. Hendrikus Berkhof and Philip Potter, 107-115. London: SCM Press.

——————. 1977. *Christ and the powers*. Scottdale, Pa.: Herald Press.

——————. 1979. *Christ the meaning of history*. Grand Rapids: Baker.

Berneburg, Erhard. 1997. *Das Verhältnis von Verkündigung und sozialer Aktion in der evangelikalen Missionstheorie: Unter besonderer Berücksichtigung der Lausanner Bewegung für Weltevangelisation (1974-1989)*. Reihe Systematisch-theologische Monographien. Wuppertal: R. Brockhaus Verlag.

——————. 1998. Auf dem Wege zu einem "integrierten Missionsverständnis": Weiterführendes zu einer 25-jährigen Debatte. *Ichthys* 14, no. 26: 35-40.

Betz, Otto, Christian Blendinger, and Lothar Coenen. 1977. Macht. In *Theologisches Begriffslexikon zum Neuen Testament*, ed. Lothar Coenen, Erich Beyreuther, and Hans Bietenhard, 922-935. 4th ed. Wuppertal: R. Brockhaus

Bevans, Stephen B., and Roger Schroeder. 2004. *Constants in context: A theology of mission for today*. American Society of Missiology Series. Maryknoll: Orbis.

Beyerhaus, Peter. 1969. The ministry of crossing frontiers. In *The Church crossing frontiers: Essays on the nature of mission; In honor of Bengt Sundkler*, ed. Peter Beyerhaus, 36-54. Lund: Gleerup.

——————. 1971. *Missions – which way? Humanization of redemption*. Grand Rapids: Zondervan.

——————. 1974. Mission and humanization. In *Crucial issues in mission today*, ed. Gerald H. Anderson and Thomas F. Stransky, 231-245. New York/Grand Rapids: Paulist Press/Eerdmans.

——————. 1992. *God's kingdom and the utopian error: Discerning the biblical kingdom of God from its political counterfeits*. Wheaton, Ill.: Crossways Books.

——————————. 1996. *Er sandte sein Wort: Theologie der christlichen Mission*. Bad Liebenzell/Wuppertal: R. Brockhaus/VLM.

——————————. 1999. Lesslie Newbigin – missionarischer Apologet. *Diakrisis* 20, no. 2: 98-103.

Beyerhaus, Peter, and World Council of Churches. 1973. *Bangkok '73. Anfang oder Ende der Weltmission? Ein gruppendynamisches Experiment*. Neuhausen-Stuttgart: Hänssler-Verlag.

Blocher, Henri. 1992. The Kingdom of God and evil. *Evangelical Review of Theology* 16: 435-444.

Bockmühl, Klaus. 1983. *Verkündigung und soziale Verantwortung*. Gießen/Basel: Brunnen Verlag. Original edition, *Evangelism and Social Responsibility*. Exeter: Paternoster.

——————————. 1985. *Die Aktualität des Pietismus*. Theologie und Dienst 45. Gießen: Brunnen.

——————————. 2000. *Was heißt heute Mission? Entscheidungsfragen der neueren Missionstheologie*. Gießen: Brunnen Verlag.

Bosch, David J. 1967. Heilsgeschichte und Mission. In *Oikonomia: Heilgeschichte als Thema der Theologie*, ed. Felix Christ, 386-394. Hamburg-Bergstedt: Reich.

——————————. 1976. Crosscurrents in modern mission. *Missionalia* 4: 56-84.

——————————. 1980. The Melbourne Conference between guilt and hope. *International Review of Mission* 69: 512-518.

——————————. 1991. *Transforming mission: Paradigm shifts in theology of mission*. Maryknoll: Orbis Books.

——————————. 1993. God's reign and the rulers of this world: Missiological reflections on church-state relationships. In *The good news of the Kingdom: Mission theology for the third millenium*, ed. Charles Van Engen, Dean S. Gilliland, and Paul Pierson, 89-95. Maryknoll: Orbis.

Bosch, David Jacobus, W. A. Saayman, and J. J. Kritzinger, eds. 1996. *Mission in bold humility: David Bosch's work considered*. Maryknoll: Orbis Books.

Braaten, Carl E. 1983. *Principles of Lutheran theology*. Philadelphia: Fortress Press.

Bright, John. 1953. *The kingdom of God: The biblical concept and its meaning for the church*. Nashville: Abingdon.

Butin, Philip W. 1999. Is Jesus still lord? Lesslie Newbigin on the place of Christ in trinitarian ecclesiology. In *Ecumenical theology in worship, doctrine, and life*, ed. David S. Cunningham, Ralph Del Colle, and Lucas Lamadrid, 196-206. Oxford: Oxford Univ. Press.

Carson, D. A. 1996. *The gagging of God: Christianity confronts pluralism*. Grand Rapids: Zondervan.

Castro, Emilio. 1980. Your Kingdom come. *International Review of Mission* 69: 255-264.

──────────. 1981. Mission today and tomorrow: A conversation with Emilio Castro. *International Bulletin of Missionary Research* 5: 108-111.

Congar, Yves. 1985. *Lay people in the church: A study for a theology of laity*. London/Westminster: G. Chapman/Christian Classics. Original edition, 1957 (engl.).

Conway, Martin. 1980. A step further. *International Review of Mission* 69: 546-555.

──────────. 1994. Lesslie Newbigin's faith pilgrimage. *Mission Studies* 11, no. 2: 191-202.

Costas, Orlando E. 1980. Impressions on Melbourne. *International Review of Mission* 69: 529-531.

──────────. 1987. Evangelical theology in the Two Thirds world. *Evangelical Review of Theology* 11: 65-77.

Cray, Graham. 1988. A theology of the kingdom. *Transformation* 5, no. 4: 24-31.

Cullmann, Oscar. 1961. Eschatology and missions in the New Testament. In *The theology of the Christian mission*, ed. Gerald H. Anderson, 42-54. Nashville/New York: Abingdon Press.

──────────. 1962. *Christ and time: The primitive Christian conception of time and history*. London: SCM Press. Original edition, Christus und die Zeit (1946).

──────────. 1967. *Salvation in history*. New York: Harper & Row.

Elwell, Walter A., ed. 1996. *Evangelical dictionary of biblical theology*. Grand Rapids: Baker.

Eßer, Hans-Helmut. 1977. Gesetz. In *Theologisches Begriffslexikon zum Neuen Testament*, ed. Lothar Coenen, Erich Beyreuther, and Hans Bietenhard, 520-534. 4th ed. Wuppertal: R. Brockhaus

Falconer, Alan D. 1987. Significant events in the ecumenical movement. *Ecumenical Review* 39: 376-387.

Fee, Gordon D. 1991. The kingdom of God and the church's global mission. In *Called and empowered: Global mission in Pentecostal perspective*, ed. Murray A. Dempster, Byron D. Klaus, and Douglas Petersen, 7-21. Peabody: Hendrickson.

Fey, Harold Edward, ed. 1970. *The ecumenical advance: A history of the ecumenical movement*, Volume 2: 1948-1968. Philadelphia: Westminster Press.

Forrester, Duncan B. 2002. Lesslie Newbigin as public theologian. In *A scandalous prophet: The way of mission after Newbigin*, ed. Thomas F. Foust, George R. Hunsberger, Andrew J. Kirk, and Werner Ustorf, 3-12. Grand Rapids: Eerdmans.

Foust, Thomas F. 2002. Lesslie Newbigin's epistemology: A dual discourse? In *A scandalous prophet: The way of mission after Newbigin*, ed. Thomas F. Foust, George R. Hunsberger, Andrew J. Kirk, and Werner Ustorf, 153-162. Grand Rapids: Eerdmans.

Foust, Thomas F., George R. Hunsberger, Andrew J. Kirk, and Werner Ustorf, eds. 2002. *A scandalous prophet: The way of mission after Newbigin*. Grand Rapids: Eerdmans.

Fuellenbach, John. 1995. *The kingdom of God: The message of Jesus today*. Maryknoll, N.Y.: Orbis Books.

Fueter, Paul D. 1980. Melbourne: Mission for the eighties. *International Review of Mission* 69: 539-542.

Galling, Kurt, ed. 2000. *Die Religion in Geschichte und Gegenwart: Handwörterbuch für Theologie und Religionswissenschaft*. 3.Aufl. (1956-1965), CD-ROM edition. Berlin: Directmedia.

Garrett, Susan R. 2003. Christ and the present evil age. *Interpretation* 57: 370-384.

Glasser, Arthur. 1973. Salvation – yesterday, tommorow, and today. In *The evangelical response to Bangkok*, ed. Ralph D. Winter, 103-108. South Pasadena, Calif.: William Carey Library.

_____. 1976. *Crucial dimensions in world evangelization*. South Pasadena, Calif.: William Carey Library.

_____. 1979. Reconciliation between ecumenical and evangelical theologies and theologians of mission. *Missionalia* 7, no. 3: 99-114.

_____. 1985. Vatican II and mission, 1965-1985. *Missiology* 13, no. 4: 487-499.

_____. 1986a. The conciliar debate. In *Entering the Kingdom: A fresh look at conversion*, ed. Monica Hill, 84-97. Middlesex, UK: British Church Growth Association/MARC Europe.

_____. 1986b. An international perspective. In *Entering the Kingdom: A fresh look at conversion*, ed. Monica Hill, 22-38. Middlesex, UK: British Church Growth Association/MARC Europe.

_____. 1987. The evolution of evangelical mission theology since World War II. *Evangelical Review of Theology* 11: 53-64.

Glasser, Arthur F., Charles E. van Engen, Dean S. Gilliland, and Shawn B. Redford, eds. 2003. *Announcing the kingdom: The story of God's mission in the Bible*. Grand Rapids: Baker Academic.

Glasser, Arthur, and Donald Anderson McGavran. 1983. *Contemporary theologies of mission*. Grand Rapids, Mich.: Baker Book House.

Goheen, Michael W. 1999a. Mission and the public life of Western culture: The Kuyperian tradition. *The Gospel and Our Culture (U.K.)* no. 26: 6-8.

_____. 1999b. Toward a missiology of Western culture. *European Journal of Theology* 8, no. 2: 155-168.

_____. 2000. *"As the Father has sent Me, I am sending you"*: J.E. Lesslie Newbigin's missionary ecclesiology. Zoetermeer (Netherlands): Boekencentrum.

_____. 2002a. Is Lesslie Newbigin's model of contextualization anticultural? *Mission Studies* 19, no. 2-38: 136-158.

_____. 2002b. The missional calling of believers in the world: Lesslie Newbigin's contribution. In *A scandalous prophet: The way of mission after Newbigin*, ed. Thomas F. Foust, George R. Hunsberger, Andrew J. Kirk, and Werner Ustorf, 37-54. Grand Rapids: Eerdmans.

_____. 2004. The future of mission in the World Council of Churches. *Mission Studies* 21: 97-111.

Goodall, Norman. 1953. *Missions under the Cross: Addresses delivered at the enlarged meeting of the Committee of the International Missionary Council at Willingen, in Germany, 1952; with statements issued by the meeting*. London: Edinburgh House Press; distributed in the U.S.A. by Friendship Press New York.

Goppelt, Leonhard. 1978. *Theologie des Neuen Testaments*. Göttingen: UTB Vandenhoeck.

Gort, Jerald O. 1980. Melbourne 1980: A missiological interpretation. *International Review of Mission* 69: 557-574.

Hathaway, Brian. 1990. The kingdom manifesto. *Transformation* 7, no. 3: 6-10.

Hauerwas, Stanley. 1977. *Truthfulness and tragedy.* Notre Dame: University Press.

Haymes, Brian. 2000. Radical discipleship: the Anabaptist tradition. *The Gospel and Our Culture (U.K.)* no. 27: 6-7.

Heim, Karl. 1975. *Jesus der Weltvollender. Der Glaube an die Versöhung und Weltverwandlung.* Der evangelische Glaube und das Denken der Gegenwart, ed. Karl Heim. Wuppertal: Aussaat.

Helfenstein, Pius Franz. 1998. *Grundlagen des interreligiösen Dialogs: Theologische Rechtfertigungsversuche in der ökumenischen Bewegung und die Verbindung des trinitarischen Denkens mit dem pluralistischen Ansatz.* Frankfurt a.M.: Otto Lembeck.

Hempelmann, Heinzpeter. 1984. Heilsgeschichte am Ende? In *Epochen der Heilsgeschichte: Beiträge zur Förderung heilsgeschichtlicher Theologie,* ed. Helge Stadelmann, 39-54. Wuppertal: R. Brockhaus.

_____. 2004. *Wie lassen sich christliche Werte in einer säkularen Gesellschaft plausibilisieren?* Published on Feb 5, 2004. Electronic resource, see: http://www.liebenzeller-mission.de/hph/dat/werte.pdf.

Henry, Carl F. H. 1961a. Missions at Delhi. *Christianity Today* 5 (April 24): 24-26.

_____. 1961b. A new crisis in foreign missions. *Christianity Today* 5 (April 24): 3-14.

_____. 1961c. Report on New Delhi. *Christianity Today* 6 (December 22): 3-7.

Hick, John. 2001. *Gott und seine vielen Namen.* Frankfurt a.M.: Verlag Otto Lembeck. Original edition, *God has many names* 1982.

Hiebert, Paul G. 1993. Evangelism, church, and kingdom. In *The good news of the kingdom: Mission theology for the third millenium; Essays in honor of Arthur F. Glasser,* ed. Charles Edward Van Engen, Dean S. Gilliland, and Paul Pierson, 153-161. Maryknoll: Orbis.

_____. 1994. *Anthropological reflections on missiological issues.* Grand Rapids, Mich.: Baker Books.

_____. 1999. *The missiological implications of epistemological shifts: Affirming truth in a modern/postmodern world.* Christian Mission and Modern Culture. Harrisburg, Pa.: Trinity Press International.

Hille, Rolf. 1994. Satan, Dämon, Besessenheit. In *Evangelisches Lexikon für Theologie und Gemeinde,* ed. Helmut Burkhardt, Uwe Swarat, Otto Betz,

Michael Herbst, Gerhard Ruhbach, and Theo Sorg, 3: 1748-1751. Wuppertal/Zürich: R. Brockhaus.

————————. 2002. Transition from modernity to post-modernity: A theological evaluation. *European Journal of Theology* 11, no. 2: 87-107.

Hocking, W. E., ed. 1933. *Rethinking missions: A laymen's inquiry after one hundred years.* New York.

————————. 1956. The coming world civilization. New York: Harper.

Hoedemaker, Bert. 1995. The Legacy of J. C. Hoekendijk. *International Bulletin of Missionary Research* 19: 166-170.

————————. 1998. The unity of humankind. Problems and promises of an indispensable ecumenical theme. *Ecumenical Review* 50: 307-314.

Hoekendijk, J. C. 1952. The church in missionary thinking. *International Review of Mission* 41: 324-336.

Horton, Walter Marshall, Paul David Devanandan, Clarence Tucker Craig, Pierre Maury, Karl Hartenstein, and Basil Ioannidis. 1952. Comments on the first report of the advisory commission on the theme of the Second Assembly. *Ecumenical Review* 4, no. 2: 161-173.

Hunsberger, George R. 1991a. The changing face of ministry: Christian leadership for the twenty-first century. *Reformed Review* 44, no. 3: 223-245.

————————. 1991b. The Newbigin gauntlet: Developing a domestic missiology for North America. *Missiology* 19, no. 3: 391-408.

————————. 1995. Cutting the Christendom knot. In *Christian ethics in ecumenical context: theology, culture, and politics in dialogue*, ed. Shin Chiba, George R. Hunsberger, Lester Edwin J. Ruiz, and Charles C. West, 53-71. Grand Rapids, Mich.: W.B. Eerdmans Pub. Co.

————————. 1998a. *Bearing the witness of the Spirit: Lesslie Newbigin's theology of cultural plurality.* Grand Rapids: Eerdmans.

————————. 1998b. Conversion and community: Revisiting the Lesslie Newbigin – M. M. Thomas debate. *International Bulletin of Missionary Research* 22, no. 3: 112-117.

————————. 1998c. Cultivating ways of Christ for people in the postmodern transition. Resources in the vision of Lesslie Newbigin. *Journal for Preachers* 22, no. 1: 12-18.

————————. 1999. Biography as missiology: The case of Lesslie Newbigin. *Missiology* 27, no. 4: 523-531.

———————. 2002. The church in the postmodern transition. In *A scandalous prophet: The way of mission after Newbigin*, ed. Thomas F. Foust, George R. Hunsberger, Andrew J. Kirk, and Werner Ustorf, 95-106. Grand Rapids: Eerdmans.

———————. 2006. The missional voice and posture of public theologizing. *Missiology* 34 (1): 15-28.

Joest, Wilfried. 1989. *Dogmatik Bd. 1: Die Wirklichkeit Gottes*. Göttingen: Vandenhoeck & Ruprecht.

Kennard, Douglas Welker. 1999. A Thiselton-Ricoeur hermeneutic. In *The relationship between epistemology, hermeneutics, biblical theology and contextualization: Understanding truth*, ed. Douglas Welker Kennard, 117-151. Lewiston: Edwin Mellen.

Kettle, David. 2001. Lesslie Newbigin, Christendom and the public truth of the Gospel. *Anvil* 18, no.2: 107-115.

Kinnamon, Michael, and Brian E. Cope, eds. 1997. *The ecumenical movement: An anthology of key texts and voices*. Geneva/Grand Rapids, Mich.: WCC Publications/Eerdmans.

Kirk, J. Andrew. 1999. Understanding the epistemological predicament of the contemporary West. In *To stake a claim: Mission and the Western crisis of knowledge*, ed. J. Andrew Kirk and Kevin J. Vanhoozer, 3-52. Maryknoll: Orbis Books.

Kirk, J. Andrew, and Kevin J. Vanhoozer, eds. 1999. *To stake a claim: Mission and the Western crisis of knowledge*. Maryknoll: Orbis Books.

Knitter, Paul F. 1985. *No other name? A critical survey of Christian attitudes toward the world religions*. Maryknoll: Orbis Books.

Kraemer, Hendrik. 1956. *The Christian message in a non-Christian world*. Grand Rapids, MI: Kregel Publications.

———————. 1958. *A theology of the laity*. Philadelphia: Westminster Press.

Kramm, Thomas. 1979. *Analyse und Bewährung theologischer Modelle zur Begründung der Mission: Entscheidungskriterien in der aktuellen Auseinandersetzung zwischen einem heilsgeschichtlichekklesiologischen und einem geschichtlicheschatologischen Missionsverständnis*. Aachen: Missio Aktuell Verlag.

Kraus, C. Norman. 1958. *Dispensationalism in America: Its rise and development*. Richmond: John Knox Press.

Kümmel, Werner Georg. 1974. Heilsgeschichte im Neuen Testament? In *Neues Testament und Kirche: Für Rudolf Schnackenburg z. 60. Geburtstag am 5. Jan. 1974 von Freunden u. Kollegen gewidmet*, ed. Rudolf Schnackenburg and Joachim Gnilka, 434-457. Freiburg (im Breisgau)/Basel/Wien: Herder.

Küng, Hans. 1990. *Projekt Weltethos*. München: Piper.

Künneth, Walter. 1984. Mitte und Struktur biblischer Heilsgeschichte. In *Epochen der Heilsgeschichte: Beiträge zur Förderung heilsgeschichtlicher Theologie*, ed. Helge Stadelmann, 30-38. Wuppertal: R. Brockhaus.

Ladd, George Eldon. 1952. *Crucial questions about the kingdom of God: The sixth annual mid-year lectures of 1952 delivered at Western Conservative Baptist Theological Seminary of Portland*, Oregon. Grand Rapids: Eerdmans.

──────────────. 1974a. *The presence of the future: The eschatology of biblical realism*. Grand Rapids, Mich.: Eerdmans.

──────────────. 1974b. *A Theology of the New Testament*. Grand Rapids: W.B. Eerdmans.

Lessing, Eckhard. 1984. Die Bedeutung der Heilsgeschichte in der ökumenischen Diskussion. *Evangelische Theologie* 44, no. 3: 227-240.

Lightfoot, Joseph Barber. 1955. *Saint Paul's epistles to the Colossians and to Philemon*. Grand Rapids: Zondervan. Original edition 1879.

Lingenfelter, Sherwood G. 1992. *Transforming culture: A challenge for Christian mission*. Grand Rapids: Baker.

Linthicum, Robert C. 1995. *Signs of hope in the city*. Monrovia, Calif.: Marc.

Luscombe, Kenneth L. 1995. Organizing for community. In *Signs of hope in the city*, ed. Robert C. Linthicum, 56-63. Monrovia, Calif.: Marc.

Lutz, Martin. 2006. Bald mehr Migranten als Deutsche. *Die Welt*, 15. März 2006.

Margull, Hans Jochen, and World Council of Churches. 1968. *Mission als Strukturprinzip: Ein Arbeitsbuch zur Frage missionarischer Gemeinden*. Genf: Oekumenischer Rat der Kirchen.

Matthey, Jacques. 2005. Versöhnung im ökumenischen missionstheologischen Diskurs. *Zeitschrift für Mission* 31, no. 3: 174-191.

McGavran, Donald Anderson. 1977. *The Conciliar-evangelical debate: The crucial documents, 1964-1976: Expanded edition of Eye of the storm, The Great debate in mission, including documents on Bangkok and Nairobi*. South Pasadena, Calif.: William Carey Library.

Metzger, Wolfgang. 1953. *Karl Hartenstein: Ein Leben für Kirche und Mission*. Stuttgart: Evangelischer Missionsverlag.

Michel, Otto. 1941. Menschensohn und Völkerwelt. *Evangelische Missions-Zeitschrift* 2, no. 1: 257-267.

Moltmann, Jürgen. 1984. Verschränkte Zeiten der Geschichte. *Evangelische Theologie* 44, no. 3: 213-227.

──────────────. 1996. *The coming of God: Christian eschatology*. Minneapolis: Fortress Press.

Moltmann, Jürgen, Miroslav Volf, Carmen Krieg, and Thomas Kucharz. 1996. *The future of theology: Essays in honor of Jürgen Moltmann*. Grand Rapids: Eerdmans.

Moreau, A. Scott, Harold A. Netland, and Charles Van Engen. 2000. *Evangelical dictionary of world missions*. Grand Rapids: Baker Book House.

Mutiso-Mbinda, John, and World Council of Churches. 1993. *Concepts of mission in the World Council of Churches, 1961 to 1991: A study of the historical developments in the understanding of Christian mission in the documents of the World Council of Churches from New Delhi to Canberra*. Rome: N. Domenici-Pécheux.

Müller-Fahrenholz, Geiko. 1974. *Heilsgeschichte zwischen Ideologie und Prophetie: Profile und Kritik heilsgeschichtlicher Theorien in der ökumenischen Bewegung zwischen 1948 und 1968*. Freiburg: Herder.

Neill, Stephen, Gerald H. Anderson, and John Goodwin. 1971. *Concise dictionary of the Christian world mission*. Nashville: Abingdon.

Netland, Harold A. 1991. *Dissonant voices: Religious pluralism and the question of truth*. Vancouver: Regent College Publishing.

──────────────. 1994. Truth, authority and modernity: Shopping for truth in a supermarket of worldviews. In *Faith and modernity*, ed. Philip Sampson, Vinay Samuel, and Chris Sugden, 89-115. Oxford, England: Irvine Calif.

Neuer, Werner. 1999. Interreligiöser Dialog als Notwendigkeit, Chance und Gefahr. *In Kein anderer Name: Die Einzigartigkeit Jesu Christi und das Gespräch mit nichtchristlichen Religionen; Festschrift zum 70.Geburtstag von Peter Beyerhaus*, ed. Thomas Schirrmacher, 188-214. Nürnberg: VTR Publications.

Neve, Herbert T. 1968. *Quellen der Erneuerung: Auf der Suche nach beweglichen Strukturen für die Kirche*. Genf: Ökumenischer Rat der Kirchen.

Nicholls, Bruce, Lausanne Committee for World Evangelization, and World Evangelical Fellowship. 1986. *In word and deed: Evangelism and social responsibility*. Grand Rapids: W.B. Eerdmans.

Niles, Daniel Thambyrajah. 1962. *Upon the earth: The mission of God and the missionary enterprise of the churches*. New York: McGraw-Hill.

Noll, Stephen F. 1998. *Angels of light, powers of darkness*. Downers Grove: InterVarsity Press.

O'Brien, Peter T. 1981. Principalities and powers and their relationship to structures. *Reformed Theological Review* 40, no. 1: 1-10.

_____. 1992. Principalities and powers: Opponents of the church. *Evangelical Review of Theology* 16 (October): 353-384.

Oman, John. 1942. *Honest religion*. Cambridge: The University Press.

_____. 1960. *Grace and personality*. Collins: Fontana Library. Original edition, Oman, John Wood: 1917. *Grace and Personality*, Cambridge: University Press.

Ott, Bernhard. 1996. *Schalom – Das Projekt Gottes*. Weisenheim am Berg: Agape.

Perrin, Norman. 1966. *The Kingdom of God in the teaching of Jesus*. London: S.C.M. Press.

Piggin, F.S. 2001. Principalities and powers. In *Evangelical dictionary of theology*, ed. Walter A. Elwell, 956-957. Grand Rapids: Baker Academic.

Pocock, Michael, Gailyn van Rheenen, and Douglas McConnell, eds. 2005. *The changing face of world missions: Engaging contemporary issues and trends*. Grand Rapids: Baker.

Polanyi, Michael. 1964. *Personal knowledge: Towards a post-critical philosophy*. New York/Evanston: Harper & Row.

Raiser, Konrad. 1991. *Ecumenism in transition: A paradigm shift in the ecumenical movement?* Geneva: WCC Publications.

_____. 1994. Is ecumenical apologetics sufficient? A response to Lesslie Newbigin's "Ecumenical Amnesia" – Comment/reply. *International Bulletin of Missionary Research* 18, no. 2: 50-51.

_____. 1997. *To be the church: Challenges and hopes for a new millennium*. Geneva: WCC Publications.

Reppenhagen, Martin. 1997. Mission aus Bindung an Christus: Lesslie Newbigins missionstheologischer Ansatz. *Theologische Beiträge* 28, no. 2: 79-94.

Ricoeur, Paul and John B. Thompson. 1981. *Paul Ricoeur: Hermeneutics and the human sciences; Essays on language, action and interpretation*. Cambridge: Cambridge University Press.

Ridderbos, Herman. 1979. *Church, world, kingdom*. Wetenskaplike bydraes van die pu vir cho. Pochefstroom, South Africa: Instituut vir die Bevordering van Calvinisme.

Samartha, Stanley J. 1980. The Kingdom of God in a religiously plural world. *Ecumenical Review* 32: 152-165.

Sampson, Philip, Vinay Samuel, and Chris Sugden, eds. 1994. *Faith and modernity*. Oxford, England: Irvine Calif.

Samuel, Vinay. 1999. A Jubilee Call: A letter to the World Council of Churches by evangelical participants at Harare. *Anvil: An Anglican Evangelical Journal for Theology and Mission* 16, no. 1: 13-18.

Samuel, Vinay, and Albrecht Hauser, eds. 1989. *Proclaiming Christ in Christ's way: Studies in integral evangelism; Essays presented to Walter Arnold on the occasion of his 60th birthday*. Oxford, U.K.: Regnum Books.

Samuel, Vinay, and Chris Sugden. 1999. *Mission as transformation: A theology of the whole gospel*. Oxford/Irvine: Regnum Books International.

Sautter, Gerhard. 1985. *Heilsgeschichte und Mission: Zum Verständnis der Heilsgeschichte in der Missionstheologie; Am Beispiel der Weltmissionskonferenzen und der ökumenischen Weltkirchenkonferenzen bis 1975 und der evangelikalen Erklärungen von Wheaton, Frankfurt, Berlin und Lausanne: Mit einer biblischen Grundlegung heilsgeschichtlichen Denkens*. Gießen: Brunnen.

Scherer, James A., and Stephen B. Bevans, eds. 1992. *New directions in mission and evangelization 1: Basic statements* 1974-1991. Maryknoll: Orbis.

Schlunk, Martin. 1939. *Das Wunder der Kirche unter den Völkern der Erde: Bericht über die Weltmissions-Konferenz in Tambaram (Südindien) 1938*. Stuttgart/Basel: Evang. Missionsverlag.

Schmidt-Leukel, Perry. 2002. Mission and trinitarian theology. In *A scandalous prophet: The way of mission after Newbigin*, ed. Thomas F. Foust, George R. Hunsberger, Andrew J. Kirk, and Werner Ustorf, 57-64. Grand Rapids: Eerdmans.

Schnabel, Eckhard J. 1993. *Das Reich Gottes als Wirklichkeit und Hoffnung: Neuere Entwicklungen in der evangelikalen Theologie*. TVG-Orientierung. Wuppertal: R. Brockhaus.

Schreiter, Robert J. 2005. *Reconciliation as a new paradigm of mission.* http://www.oikoumene.org/PLEN_14_May_Reconciliatio.1004+B6Jkw9 MA_.0.html. Accessed Sep. 20, 2005.

Schwarz, Gerold. 1980. *Mission, Gemeinde und Ökumene in der Theologie Karl Hartensteins.* Stuttgart: Calwer Verlag.

──────────────. 1994. Karl Hartenstein 1894-1952. Missions with a focus on "the end." In *Mission legacies: Biographical studies of leaders of the modern missionary movement,* ed. Gerald H. Anderson, Robert T. Coote, Norman A. Horner, and James M. Phillips, 591-601. Maryknoll: Orbis.

Schwarz, Hans. 2000. *Eschatology.* Grand Rapids: Eerdmans.

Scott, Drusilla. 1995. *Everyman revived: The common sense of Michael Polanyi.* Grand Rapids: William B. Eerdmans.

Scott, Waldron. 1981. The significance of Pattaya. *Missiology* 9, no. 1: 57-76.

Sharpe, Eric J. 1974. New directions in the theology of mission. *Evangelical Quarterly* 46: 8-24.

Shenk, Wilbert R. 1996. The mission dynamic. In *Mission in bold humility: David Bosch's work considered,* ed. David Jacobus Bosch, W. A. Saayman, and J. J. Kritzinger, 83-93. Maryknoll: Orbis Books.

──────────────. 1999. *Changing frontiers of mission.* Maryknoll: Orbis.

Sittler, Joseph A. 1962. Called to unity. *Ecumenical Review* 14: 177-187.

Smith, Fred. 1999. An evangelical evaluation of key elements in Lesslie Newbigin's apologetics. Ph.D. diss., Southwestern Baptist Theological Seminary.

Snyder, Howard A. 1991. *Models of the kingdom.* Nashville: Abingdon.

Stackhouse, John Gordon, ed. 2000. *Evangelical futures: A conversation on theological method.* Grand Rapids: Baker Book House.

Stadelmann, Helge. 1986. *Glaube und Geschichte: Heilsgeschichte als Thema der Theologie.* Gießen/Basel; Wuppertal: Brunnen; R. Brockhaus.

Stockwell, Eugene L. 1981. A conciliar reaction. *Missiology* 9, no. 1: 53-56.

Stott, John R. W. 1979. *God's new society.* The Bible speaks Today, ed. John R. W. Stott. Leicester: Inter-Varsity Press.

──────────────. ed. 1996. *Making Christ known: Historic mission documents from the Lausanne movement, 1974-1989.* Grand Rapids: Eerdmans.

──────────────. 1999. *Human rights and human wrongs: Major issues for a new century.* Grand Rapids: Baker Books.

Stowe, David M. 1981. What did Melbourne say? *Missiology* 9, no. 1: 23-35.

Stransky, Thomas F. 1981. A Roman Catholic reflection. *Missiology* 9, no. 1: 41-51.

Taber, Charles R. 1981. Some evangelical questions. *Missiology* 9, no. 1: 87-91.

——————. 2002. The gospel as authentic meta-narrative. In *A scandalous prophet: The way of mission after Newbigin*, ed. Thomas F. Foust, George R. Hunsberger, Andrew J. Kirk, and Werner Ustorf, 182-194. Grand Rapids: Eerdmans.

Thiselton, Anthony C. 1992. *New horizons in hermeneutics: The theory and practice of transforming biblical reading*. Grand Rapids: Zondervan.

——————. 1995. *Interpreting God and the postmodern self: On meaning, manipulation, and promise*. Grand Rapids: Eerdmans.

Thomas, V. Matthew. 1997. *The centrality of Christ and inter-religious dialogue in the theology of Lesslie Newbigin*. Ottawa: National Library of Canada/Bibliothèque nationale du Canada.

Van Engen, Charles. 1996. *Mission on the way: Issues in mission theology*. Grand Rapids: Baker Book House.

——————. 2000. Theology of mission. In *Evangelical Dictionary of World Missions*, ed. A. Scott Moreau, Harold A. Netland, and Charles Van Engen, 949-951. Grand Rapids: Baker.

Van Engen, Charles, Dean S. Gilliland, and Paul Pierson, eds. 1993. *The good news of the Kingdom: Mission theology for the third millenium*. Maryknoll: Orbis.

Vanhoozer, Kevin J. 1998. *Is there a meaning in this text? The Bible, the reader, and the morality of literary knowledge*. Grand Rapids: Zondervan.

——————. 1999. The trials of truth. In *To stake a claim: Mission and the Western crisis of knowledge*, ed. J. Andrew Kirk and Kevin J. Vanhoozer, 120-156. Maryknoll: Orbis.

von Rad, Gerhard. 1978. *Theologie des Alten Testaments Bd.1*. München: Chr. Kaiser.

Wainwright, Geoffrey. 1988. The last things. In *Keeping the faith: Essays to mark the centenary of Lux Mundi*, ed. Geoffrey Wainwright, 341-370. Philadelphia/Allison Park, Pa.: Fortress Press/Pickwick Publications.

——————. 2000. *Lesslie Newbigin: A theological life*. Oxford: Oxford University Press.

―――――――――. ed. 2003. *Signs amid the rubble: The purposes of God in human history*. Grand Rapids, Mich.: W.B. Eerdmans.

Walker, Andrew. 1988. Interview with bishop Lesslie Newbigin. In *Different gospels: Christian Orthodoxy*, ed. Andrew Walker, 30-41. London: Hodder and Stoughton.

Walls, Andrew F. 1996. *The missionary movement in Christian history: Studies in the transmission of faith*. Maryknoll: Orbis Books.

Wendland, Ernst R. 1999. Contextualising the potentates, principalities and powers in the epistle to the Ephesians. *Neotestamentica* 33, no. 1: 199-223.

Wendland, Ernst R. and Salimo Hachibamba. 2000. A central African perspective on contextualizing the Ephesian potentates, principalities, and powers. *Missiology* 28, no. 3: 341-363.

West, Charles C. 1998. Newbigin, James Edward Lesslie. In *Biographical Dictionary of Christian Missions*, ed. Gerald H. Anderson, 491. New York: Simon and Schuster Macmillan.

Weston, Paul. 1996. Evangelism: Some biblical and contemporary perspectives. *Evangelical Review of Theology* 20 (July): 248-258.

―――――――――. 1998. Pathways to faith: Reflections on congregational evangelism. *Scottish Bulletin of Evangelical Theology* 16 (Spring): 45-57.

―――――――――. 1999. Gospel, mission and culture: The contribution of Lesslie Newbigin. In *Witness to the world: Papers from the second Oak Hill College Annual School of Theology*, ed. David Peterson, 32-62. Carlisle Eng.: Paternoster Press.

―――――――――. 1999. Truth, subjectivism and the art of apologetics. *Anvil* 16, no. 3: 173-185.

―――――――――. 2004. Lesslie Newbigin: A postmodern missiologist? *Mission Studies* 21, no. 2: 229-248.

White, Hugh C. 1988. Introduction: Speech Act Theory and Literary Criticism. *Semeia*, 41: 1-24.

Wiedenmann, Ludwig. 1965. *Mission und Eschatologie: Eine Analyse der neueren deutschen evangelischen Missionstheologie*. Konfessionskundliche und kontroverstheologische Studien, Bd. 15. Paderborn: Verl. Bonifacius-Druckerei.

Wilson, Frederick R. ed. 1990. *The San Antonio report: Your will be done – mission in Christ's way*. Geneva: WCC Publications.

Wink, Walter. 1986. *Unmasking the powers: The invisible forces that determine human existence*. Philadelphia: Fortress Press.

_____.1995. Principalities and powers: A different worldview. *Church and Society* 85: 18-28.

Wolff, Hans-Walter. 1977. *Anthropologie des Alten Testaments.* München: Chr. Kaiser.

World Council of Churches. 1955. *The Evanston report: The Second Assembly of the World Council of Churches, 1954.* New York: Harper.

_____. 1980. *Your kingdom come: Mission perspectives; Report on the World Conference on Mission and Evangelism, Melbourne, Australia, 12-25 May, 1980.* Geneva: Commission on World Mission and Evangelism WCC.

Yates, Timothy. 1994. *Christian mission in the twentieth century.* Cambridge: Cambridge University Press.

Young, Frances. 2002. The uncontainable God: Pre-Christendom doctrine of Trinity. In *A scandalous prophet: The way of mission after Newbigin*, ed. Thomas F. Foust, George R. Hunsberger, Andrew J. Kirk, and Werner Ustorf, 84-91. Grand Rapids: Eerdmans.

www.ingramcontent.com/pod-product-compliance
Lightning Source LLC
Chambersburg PA
CBHW070243230426
43664CB00014B/2394